Kenneth L. Brown

People of Salé

Tradition and change in a Moroccan city 1830–1930

Harvard University Press
Cambridge, Massachusetts
1976

Library of Congress Catalog Card Number 76-474
ISBN 0-674-66155-9

Printed in Great Britain

Contents

List of illustrations *page* vi
List of tables viii
Preface ix
Acknowledgements xiii
Transliteration xv
Abbreviations xvii
Chronology xviii
Introduction 1

Part I

Market and town

I Along the crossroads 15
II Within the walls 27

Part II

The fabric of society

III Categories and relationships 52
IV Saints and scholars 66
V Religious practice and belief 85
VI Cultural tenacity 100

Part III

The disruption of economic life

VII Free trade and imperialism 119
VIII The impoverishment of the many 129
IX The enrichment of the few 155

Part IV

Reflections of and reactions to change

X A community in crisis 176
XI Reassertion of an identity 193
Conclusions 207

Notes and references 225
Bibliography 251
Index 261

List of illustrations

Figures

1 From Richard Simson's map of Morocco, 1637 *page* 14
2 Morocco: general 16
3 The region and tribal groups surrounding Salé 18
4 The estuary of the Bou Regreg and the cities of the two banks, Rabat and Salé 24
5 The Madina of Salé: its cemeteries, gardens, orchards and vineyards 28
6 Salé: main gates and arteries of circulation 30
7 The commercial area from the Ceuta Gate 32
8 Entering the market place from the Fez Gate 34
9 The residential quarter of the Great Mosque 36
10 The Jewish quarter and the new quarter of Sidi Turki 38
11 House layout 40
12 K. al-ithāf al-wajīz bi-akhbār al-ʿudwatayh li-mawlay ʿAbd al-Azīz 189
13 'Concerning the distinctive characteristics and tendencies of the people of Salé' 249
14 Dahir of honour and respect 250

Plates

1 *a* Ḥājj ʿAlī ʿAwwād, qadi (Si Ahmed el Haouari, *Guide de pèlerinage aux lieux saints de l'Islam et de tourisme en Orient*, Rabat, 1935, p. 113)
b Muḥammad aṣ-Ṣubīhī, governor (*ibid.*, p. 286)
c Rabbi Raphaël Ankaoua (*Revue des études islamiques*, 1930, pp. 314–15)
d Slawis in a welcoming party for the visit of Kaiser Wilhelm II, Tangier, 1905 (Ibn Zīdān, *Itḥaf aʿlām al-nās*, Rabat, 1929)
facing page 44
2 *a* Gate of the Small Port (bāb al-muraysa) (Office National Marocain de Tourisme)
b Aerial view of Salé, *c.* 1950 (Office National Marocain de Tourisme) 45

3 *a* Sanctuary of Sīdī ʿAbd Allah b. Ḥassûn, *c.* 1920 (Schmitt)
b The city and its terraces, *c.* 1920 (Schmitt)
c A city and a people dressed in white (Office National Marocain de Tourisme) 76
4 *a* Street in residential area leading to the Great Mosque (Office National Marocain de Tourisme)
b Entrance to the Great Mosque; to the left, the Merinid Madrasa (Office National Marocain de Tourisme)
c The Great Market Place, *c.* 1920 (Office National Marocain de Tourisme) 77

List of tables

1	Population figures	*page* 47
2	Urban growth	48
3	Manufacturing industries of Rabat and Salé, 1865	133
4	The value attached to various occupations	140
5	Occupations by ethnic category	152

Preface

This book is about the people who lived in the Moroccan city of Salé during the century between 1830 and 1930. I have tried to describe and interpret life in this urban community during a period of social and economic change and to relate this description and interpretation to more general problems of urban social history. I chose to study Salé out of an interest in Muslim cities engendered as a student of Islamic history. I wanted to discover and understand how townsmen in the Muslim world had managed their lives. It would be less than honest if I disavowed the naivety and romanticism that fed my initial intellectual curiosity and led me to my subject, and to Morocco—the Far West of Islam. I decided on Salé because I felt that it was a forbidding and fascinating city. I also believed—to caricature my attitude—that it had remained somehow sealed in 'traditionalism' and only awaited my intrepid visit to achieve its immortality. Actually my ambition was more limited: I simply wanted to study and immortalise the inhabitants of one quarter within the town. But such a subject seemed too artificial and scanty, and I received encouragement to take on the past of the whole city. I took that advice and received more than I bargained for. That was almost ten years ago, and I have been involved with Salé, in one way or another, ever since then.

In some ways the initial intention of this study has maintained itself, viz., to understand Salé as a living urban community, and to communicate my belief that its past was real. At the same time, the central focus of my work has shifted. Thus the facts are not always made to speak for themselves; they are often marshalled to explain the structure of social life and the process of historical change. Furthermore I have not only tried to describe the Slawis (the townsmen of Salé) but attempted to define the ideology of Slawiness. Finally, the whole study depends on the particular historical context in which it has been placed—that of European colonialism. I have chronicled and interpreted the effects in Salé of growing European interventionism, both during the pre-colonial (1830–1912) and during the early colonial period.

In the Introduction I have drawn the reader's attention to the general problems touched upon in this study: characteristics of pre-industrial, Muslim cities and ways in which Third World urban communities have responded to colonialism. The main body of the book divides into four parts: (1) the ecology of the town, its surroundings and internal distribution of space; (2) the social structure and cultural values of the community; (3) the changing patterns of economic life; (4) the responses of townsmen to externally imposed crises. In the Conclusions I return to comparative issues and suggest explanations for the apparent paradox between conservatism and adaptiveness in the city's social history during this period.

There remains something to be said concerning conditions and methods of research. I began my preparations while a student at the University of California, Los Angeles. Shortly before I left for France and Morocco in 1965 I received a copy of a study of Salé by M. Naciri, Professor of Geography at Université Mohammed V in Rabat.[1] This study provided an invaluable point of departure and has guided my research and thinking about Salé at almost every step of the way. In Morocco I had the good fortune of being introduced by Professor Naciri to his native city of Salé; for his guidance and friendship and for much of what I learned about the city I am deeply grateful to him.

Before proceeding to Morocco I spent six months in Paris consulting all the available source material concerning Salé in the archives and libraries. Printed and manuscript accounts by travellers, reports by consular officials, military observers, officers of Les Affaires Indigènes and Contrôleurs Civils, and teachers in the Alliance Israélite school provided invaluable background material for research in Morocco. Particularly useful were materials in the archives of the Centre de Hautes Études Administratives sur l'Afrique et l'Asie Modernes (CHEAM), the Alliance Israélite Universelle, and La Section Historique du Maroc, formerly housed in the Moroccan Consulate in Paris.

For twenty-one months, between December 1965 and September 1967, I lived and worked in Morocco, generally in Salé itself. During this period I consulted all of the relevant Arabic materials that I was able to locate. The most useful of these were the local histories of Salé: the printed edition of Nāṣirī's compendium and two manuscripts by Dukkālī.[2] I also made use of land records in the Rabat office of the Conservation Foncière, and books, articles, newspapers and scattered documents in the National Library and Archives (Bibliothèque Générale de Rabat) and the Palace Library, and made a brief and partially successful foray into the disordered archives of the Ministère des Affaires Administratives. Several collections of family papers in Salé also proved valuable, particularly those of the Ṣubīḥīs and Bin Saʿīds. Although I do not believe that I exploited most of the personal documents that may be found in Salé, insistent enquiries about private papers during the

[1] 'Salé. Étude de géographie urbaine', *Revue de Géographie du Maroc*, Nos. 3–4, 1963, pp. 11–82.

[2] *Cf.* appendix I, 'A note on Salé's historians', in K. Brown, 'An urban view of Moroccan history: Salé, 1000–1800', *Hespéris-Tamuda*, XII, 1971.

second year of my stay did yield many important local sources. There is an incalculable amount of historical documentation in private possession in Morocco, which, hopefully, will become accessible for research purposes in the coming years.

The archival material made it possible to reconstitute the surface structure of Salé's social history. Field research was necessary to get at the deep structure of actual social relationships and processes of thought. When I arrived in Morocco I began to study the Arabic dialect spoken in Salé and continued to do so throughout my stay. After the first few months I was able to carry out interviews, but during the second year increased fluency and ease in the language allowed me to collect a large amount of information in this manner. Accounts and explanations of events, personalities, relationships, institutions, beliefs, values, etc., provided by old people proved invaluable for understanding and reconstructing the tenor of life in the city, especially during the first decades of this century. I interviewed approximately fifty men and several women between the ages of fifty-five and eighty-five. In a few cases these interviews were tape-recorded, otherwise I took notes during or after each meeting. All the material that I gathered, whether from written or oral sources, was whenever possible cross-checked, and both sorts of documentation were critically evaluated for biases.

The difficulties involved in working with both written and oral sources should be kept in mind. In both cases, but particularly in written documents, there was a strong tendency not to take the names of the dead in vain. In interviews one could overcome this inhibition through discreet questioning. An additional problem, and one which has not been successfully resolved to my satisfaction, stems from the scantiness of information concerning women and poor people, and the sub-culture of poverty. The written sources reveal precious little about the lives of women and common people, and in interviews I was not sufficiently aware of this lacuna until I had left the field and begun to write.

In preparing this book I have become increasingly aware of the sociological interest that is implicit in the material. The first draft was written while I was a Carnegie Fellow of the Committee for the Comparative Study of New Nations at the University of Chicago and was submitted in 1969 as a PhD dissertation at UCLA. Revised versions were drafted while I was a Research Associate in the Center for Middle Eastern Studies and the Department of History at Chicago, and a Simon Fellow at the University of Manchester. At each step of the way I have tried to sharpen the focus of my approach so as to suggest comparisons between the city's social history and other urban communities, and the processses of social change that they experienced. At the same time I hope that I have not lost sight of my original object—to bring to life the past of these people of Salé.

K. L. B.

Acknowledgements

So many teachers, colleagues and friends have guided and encouraged me in the research for and the preparation of this book that I can only attempt to begin to thank them. To the late Professor G. E. von Grunebaum I owe my interest in Muslim cities, and a deep debt of gratitude for his supervision and steady support during the writing of an earlier work submitted as a PhD dissertation at the University of California, Los Angeles. I am also grateful to my teachers, to Jacques Berque for having introduced me to North African studies and for his comments on the dissertation, and to Nikki Keddie, Abdallah Laroui, and George Sabagh for their guidance and advice.

At various times and places along the way I have benefited immeasurably from discussions with and suggestions from Joseph Bell, Edmund Burke, the late Lloyd Fallers, Clifford and Hildred Geertz, Ernest Gellner, Mohamed Guessous, David Hart, Doyle Hatt, Lawrence Rosen and Robert McAdams. I also want to thank those past or present colleagues at Manchester—Edmund Bosworth, John Comaroff, Kingsley Garbett, Michael Gilsenan, Keith Hart, Derek Latham and Brian Roberts, who have read, commented upon, and jogged me through parts of the revised manuscript.

In Morocco I was educated and befriended by so many people that it has become impossible to mention but all too few of them. I owe a special debt of gratitude to ʿAbd as-Salam Bin Suda for his guidance through the archives, and for his contagious fascination with his country—its history and its society. And to Mohamed Naciri, Zubayr and Zineb Naciri, and Mahammed Qandil, I want to express my deep appreciation for having immersed me in the life of Salé.

For the use of library and archival facilities in Paris I thank the staffs of the Centre des Hautes Études Asiatiques et Musulmanes, the Alliance Israélite, and the Section Historique du Maroc and its former director, Mlle C. de la Varonne. I owe an equal debt of thanks in Morocco to Messieurs Abdullah Regragui and Ibrahim al-Kittani of the Bibliothèque Générale, Rabat, to Muhammad al-Mnuni of the Palace Archives, and to His Excellency Mahammad Bahnini for access to the Archives of Administrative Affairs.

The research upon which this study is based was made possible by a Fulbright–Hayes Fellowship from the US Department of Education. During the various stages of writing I received support from the Near Eastern Center, University of California at Los Angeles, the Committee for the Comparative Study of New Nations and the Center for Middle Eastern Studies, University of Chicago, and from a Simon Fellowship at the University of Manchester. To all of these groups and institutions I am most grateful. Like the individuals mentioned above, they are quite absolved from any responsibility for what I have written, but I am pleased to acknowledge that their assistance to me was invaluable in the completion of this book. Thanks are due, as well, to a devoted pool of typists—E. Gillett, Joan Gibson and Julie Owen. The maps were drawn by Keith Hood of Manchester University. Finally I am grateful to the staff of the University Press for their help in preparing the manuscript for publication.

Transliteration

Consonants

ء	ʾ	ز	z	ق	q
ب	b	س	s	ك	k
ت	t	ش	sh	ل	l
ث	th	ص	ṣ	م	m
ج	j	ض	ḍ	ن	n
ح	ḥ	ط	ṭ	ه	h
خ	kh	ظ	ẓ	و	w
د	d	ع	ʿ	ى	y
ذ	dh	غ	gh	ة	-a (in construct state: -at)
ر	r	ف	f		

Vowels

Short:	ـَ	a	Long: ا or ى	ā	Doubled	ـيّ	-iyy-
	ـُ	u	و	ū	Diphthongs	وْ	aw
	ـِ	i	ى	ī		ىْ	ay

Arabic words, names of places and Moroccan dynasties, have been rendered according to their customary spelling in English in so far as they are found in standard dictionaries. Place names, where no English form exists, have been rendered according to Standard French usage.

The pronunciation of colloquial Moroccan Arabic often differs greatly from that of classical Arabic or from what one might imagine from French practices of transliteration. In those cases where it seemed important to give the colloquial form I have done so, using the same system of transcription for consonants noted above, and rendering vowels in a simplified way so that pronunciation might be most easily represented to speakers of English. For a more precise treatment of phonology the reader may refer to R. S. Harrell, *A Short Grammar of Moroccan Arabic*, Washington, D.C., 1962. I have called attention to colloquial usages by the abbreviation *coll.*, sometimes adding in parentheses the classical equivalent, abbreviated *cl.* In the index, classical forms will be noted following the transliteration adopted in the text.

This method presents difficulties, especially in regard to individual and place names. I have tried to explain some of these problems and the intricacies of colloquial Moroccan pronunciation and its various transliteration schemes within the body of the text. Nonetheless the attempt at consistency had to be compromised at times for the sake of accepted usage: thus, for example, the French-inspired Salé has been retained as the name of the city under study rather than the archaic English Sallee (or Salee), classical Arabic Salā, or colloquial Slā. On the other hand, the inhabitants of the city are called Slawis from the colloquial, rather than the French Salétins, or the classical Arabic Salāwī-s.

Abbreviations

KI	Aḥmad b. Khālid an-Nāṣirī as-Salāwī, *Kitāb al-istiqṣā li-akhbār duwal al-Maghrib al-Aqṣā* (four vols. in two), Cairo, 1894.
IA	Ibn ʿAlī ad-Dukkālī, *Itḥāf ashrāf al-malā bi-baʿḍ akhbār ar-Ribāṭ wa-Salā*, Salé, n.d., MS No. D 11, AGR.
IW	Ibn ʿAlī ad-Dukkālī, *Kitāb al-Itḥāf al-wajīz bi-akhbār al-ʿudwatayn li-Mawlāy ʿAbd al-Azīz*, Salé, 1912, MS No. D 1320, AGR.
PA	*Palace Archives*, Rabat.
AGR	*Archives Générales de Rabat* (Bibliothèque Générale).
AAI	*Archives de l'Alliance Israélite*, Paris.
SI	H. de Castries, *Les sources inédites de l'histoire du Maroc*, twenty-four vols., 1905– .
VT	Mission scientifique du Maroc, *Villes et tribus du Maroc. Rabat et sa région*, vols. I–IV, Paris, 1919.
Hesp.	*Hespéris*, I (1921)–XLII (1955); continuation as *Hespéris-Tamuda*, I (1956).
RMM	*Revue du monde musulman*, I (1907)–LXVI (1926).
AM	*Archives marocaines*, I (1904)–XXXIII (1934).
GAL	C. Brockelmann, *Geschichte der arabischen Literatur*, vols. I–II, Leiden, 1945–49, supplement, vols. I–III, Leiden, 1937–42.
EI	*Encyclopedia of Islam*.
EI²	*Encyclopedia of Islam*, second edition.

Chronology

Sultans

ʿAbd ar-Raḥmān	1822–59
Muḥammad IV	1859–73
Ḥasan I	1873–94
ʿAbd al-ʿAzīz	1894–1908
ʿAbd al-Ḥāfiẓ	1908–13
Yūsuf	1913–27
Muḥammad V	1927–61
Ḥasan II	1961

Principal events

French conquest and beginning of the occupation of Algeria	1830
Moroccan army defeated by the French at battle of Isly	1844
French bombardment of Salé	1851
Anglo-Moroccan commercial treaty	1856
Spanish-Moroccan war and occupation of Tetuan	1859–60
Spanish-Moroccan commercial treaty	1861
French occupation of Touat	1899–1900
Rebellion of Bū Ḥmara	1903–08
Act of Algeciras	1906
French occupation of Oujda, Casablanca and the Chaouia plain	1907–10
Spanish occupation of Nador and Salwan	1909
French occupation of Rabat and Meknes	1911
Establishment of the French and Spanish protectorates	1912
Abdication of ʿAbd al-Ḥāfiẓ	1913
Rif war	1921–26
Berber Dahir	1930

In a word, a historical phenomenon can never be understood apart from its moment in time. This is true of every evolutionary stage, our own and others. As the old Arab proverb has it, 'Men resemble their times more than they do their fathers.'* Disregard of this Oriental wisdom has sometimes brought discredit to the study of the past.

Marc Bloch, *The Historian's Craft*

* *an-nāsu ashbahu bi-zamānihim minhum bi-ābā'ihim.*

Introduction

. . . the 'Sallee Rovers' bulked more largely in history and romance, and were the cause of more diplomatic missions, correspondence and expense, than it seems possible to believe so despicable a band of ruffians could ever become to maritime powers owning guns enough to pound this den of thieves into its native dust.

R. Brown, 1890[1]

The inhabitants of Slā—called Slāwis—were always proud and independent and are still considered aristocrats.

Budgett Meakin, 1901[2]

At the turn of this century the small white city along Morocco's Atlantic coast and on the northern bank of the Bou Regreg river enjoyed an unusual reputation because of its venerability. Called Salā in classical Arabic, Slā in the local dialect and Salé or Sallee on the tongues and maps of Europeans, its fame was closely associated with history and religion.[3] The name of the city had descended from that of an ancient (perhaps seventh century B.C.) Phoenician settlement situated upstream and on the opposite bank of the river, a settlement which later became the Roman metropolis of Salā Colonia. When the religion of Islam spread into Morocco, during the period between the eighth and the eleventh centuries, these two banks of the Bou Regreg were on the frontier where Muslim armies fought against Christians and heretics. From these wars there emerged in 1030 the Muslim city of Salé on the northern bank of the river.

In this study of Salé's social history between 1830 and 1930, we shall be concerned with a place and a population that had an urban tradition of some two and a half millennia and a recorded history of nine hundred years. The three generations of Slawis who lived in the city during the century between 1830 and 1930 placed a high value on their historical and religious heritage. They were tied to the past and to their beliefs, and were basically conservative and traditionalist in their outlook. At the same time they had to—and successfully did—adapt themselves to a period af accelerated social change. This apparent paradox between conservatism and adaptiveness poses a fundamental and fascinating problem, and it is the elaboration and the analysis of that problem that guides the ordering of the material which follows.

Shortly after the French established a protectorate over Morocco in 1912

Salé was described in detail by an indigenous historian. He portrayed the city as a centre of civilisation and commerce, a port of embarkation to wage war against non-Muslims, a place of saints and a refuge for ascetics and scholars.[4] The Slawis maintained a local and a national reputation for civilisation—that 'civilised culture' (*al-ḥaḍāra*) ascribed to only four cities in Morocco: Fez, Tetuan, Rabat and Salé. They had a style of life which was defined in the Moroccan context as the ideal of sophisticated urbanity, and they excelled at those occupations associated with cities, viz., learning, commerce and craftsmanship. Scholars, merchants and craftsmen held in common their identity as civilised and cultured townsmen. A generation later, in 1930, the reputation of the city and its inhabitants remained much the same and still assumed great importance in their self-image. The population had been greatly increased by migration from the countryside and become more heterogeneous; the economic and social structure had undergone considerable changes; but the ideology of a socially and culturally cohesive community had not appreciably weakened or altered.

A similar process may be seen in regard to the city's renown for war and piracy against non-Muslims, immortalised in the English imagination by Defoe's description of the Salee Rovers. The last expedition of privateers from Salé took place in 1827, when several Austrian ships were forced into the Bou Regreg river. Two years later Austria responded by laying siege to the port of Larache, and the sultan then decided to renounce all further maritime expeditions. Yet in 1851 Salé's cannons responded to the bombardment of the city by a French squadron of warships, and the people rejoiced over their latest defence of Islam in its war against unbelievers. In the coming generation the Slawis did not take up arms to fight for the preservation of their religion, city or country, but they did resist with intransigence the political and cultural domination of European colonialism. This resistance, not unexpectedly, reinforced Salé's image among foreigners as Morocco's most fanatical city. However, as this study should make clear, the Slawis' commitment to religion, at times enthusiastic and zealous, should not be regarded as unreasonable or fanatical. As I shall show, religion in Salé provided people with the means to assert their cultural identity, and eventually became a crucial factor in the nationalist struggle.

The religious inclinations of the Slawis were also connected with the city's fame as a centre of saints, sufis and scholars. The tombs of the pious dotted the townscape and provided justifications and places for festivals, pilgrimages, sanctuaries, religious orders, mosques and schoolrooms. The most important tombs belonged to a fourteenth-century mystic from Islamic Spain (Sīdī Aḥmad b. ʿĀshir), a sixteenth-century scholar from a village north of Fez (Sīdī ʿAbd Allah b. Ḥassūn), and a seventeenth-century local merchant turned warrior (Sīdī Aḥmad Ḥajjī).[5] All these men were considered saints, i.e. 'friends of God' (*walī*, pl. *awliyā'*) who could perform miracles, and the Slawis venerated their memory and visited their tombs.

The descendants of these saints, sufis and scholars, as well as the numerous descendants of the Prophet who lived in the city, enjoyed a degree of respect from their neighbours, but they did not inherit important socio-economic, political or religious roles. There were no powerful holy families in Salé such as those found dominating communities elsewhere in Morocco or in other areas of the Muslim world. Salé's saints, their tombs and the activities associated with them provided their descendants and custodians with a small amount of income, a little prestige and no power. There were, however, townsmen who achieved eminence because of their religious expertise. In the lodges of the religious orders, in the mosques and in the law courts sufi leaders, scholars and judges achieved positions of importance because of their intellectual qualities and spiritual or educational 'diplomas'. Their behaviour and teachings set the intellectual and moral tone of the city and reflected the ideals exemplified in the lives of its previous religious and intellectual elites. These men of piety or learning were men of their times who achieved their renown before they were fitted to the stereotypes of saint, sufi or scholar. Even the young men with a modern education, who achieved prominence in the late 1920s and played significant roles in the beginnings of nationalism, took on some of the characteristics of these stereotyped religious leaders.

In a rather summary fashion I have indicated the significance accorded to history and religion in accounting for the reputation enjoyed by the community of Salé during the period 1830–1930. It was a reputation consciously invoked and perpetuated by the people of the city in order to ensure that they were judged by others according to the images that they presented of themselves. Much of this study will attempt to reconstruct the diverse and complex lives of real people in actual situations. Nonetheless it is important to keep in mind this sketch of Homo Slawicus because of the insistence by Slawis on the historical continuity and the common social identity of their town and its inhabitants. In their view the ideal Slawi was cultivated, refined, astute, self-controlled and intransigent in his beliefs. He combined the best qualities found among other Moroccans: the learning and civilised behaviour of the Fasis (the people of Fez) and the shrewd discernment, discipline and resolve of the Berbers. (And he lacked stereotyped characteristics of these others: the softness and self-indulgence of the Fasis and the ignorance and crudeness of the Berbers.) This common identity was unique, shaped by the particular history of the city and anchored by the religion of Islam, as it was understood, experienced and lived in the city.

The Slawis identified themselves as a community. They had what we may call a 'conscious model' of community and expressed it through the concept of *ahl Salā* (coll. *hel Slā*)—'the people (or family) of Salé'. This concept contained within it a theory and an ideology: 'the people of Salé' lived and belonged together, resembled one another, were interrelated and interconnected to each other, and they shared common interests, beliefs, values, customs and characteristics of behaviour. The metaphor used to describe the community was the bucket (*qadūs*) of the waterwheel or noria, a device for irrigating gardens. It raised subterranean water and distributed it into irrigation ditches, drew from and replenished the same piece of land. The *qādūs* symbolised the community—people linked together by ties of agnation, affinity, loyalty and friendship and united by the ideas and practices of a commonly shared religion and style of life. It also symbolised the perpetuity of the community over time.

To describe Salé as a community and to emphasise the conscious model of its inhabitants does not imply a real separateness. The Slawis were very much a part of wider social, cultural, economic and political orders. Moreover I do not mean that the criteria used to define Slawiness were actually common to all Slawis or really differentiated them from all their neighbours. The community of Salé, in fact, was a cultural concept and a spiritual reality and not an inclusive, territorially defined set of social relationships. Individuals pursued their personal interests wherever they might lead them. Some had ties of interdependence with people in the countryside; others had connections with the *makhzan* in Fez or Marrakesh, or interactions with other townsmen and trade relations with Europeans. These social relationships which were external to the city directly and significantly affected the lives of Slawis. Thus the social structure and indeed the cultural characteristics of the people of the city were a good deal more fluid and less rigid than their concept of community suggests.

Between 1830 and 1930 the society and culture of Salé changed to a much greater extent than the people themselves generally cared to admit. By focusing on the concept of the city as a stable and integrated whole, on the one hand, and as a changing aggregation of people influenced by a wider spatial and temporal context on the other, I attempt to resolve the apparent contradiction between conservatism and adaptiveness. The self-conscious identity of the Slawis as a community which was socially and culturally cohesive reflected their basic conservatism. It postulated a group of people defined by inclusiveness and solidarity and by consensus and conformity to particular values and beliefs. Whatever their relationships with people outside of the city, and however much these affected the structure of society, the Slawis maintained that image of themselves as an integrated, moral community. They were greatly influenced by changes, but did not relinquish the notion of consistency and constancy in their way of life. They cloaked their adaptiveness to change with a conservatism expressed in the concept 'the people of Salé'.

This book, hopefully, will contribute to urban studies, and in particular to discussions about Muslim, pre-industrial and Third World cities. Morocco has an old urban tradition. The Romans built towns there, but the tradition derives from the cities constructed by the Muslims, such as Moulay Idris, Tetuan, Fez, Salé, Marrakesh, Rabat and Meknes. Amongst these, Fez, Tetuan, Rabat and Salé achieved reputations for the brilliance of their urban civilisation, such that they were considered the aristocracy of the cities of the Maghrib.[6] Little research has been carried out on the effects of the pre-colonial and colonial period on these cities, with the exception of M. Naciri's extremely important essay on the modern aspects of urban change in Salé. R. Le Tourneau's *magnum opus* on Fez concentrates on the pre-protectorate period, but gives scant attention to social change. J. Caillé's volume on Rabat and G. Deverdun's on Marrakesh also stop at 1912 and limit themselves mostly to archaeology and political history. The only work specifically concerned with urban social history is A. Adam's thesis on Casablanca, and as he admits in his introduction it was a city without tradition, a bourgeoisie or, at the beginning of this century, a citizenry.

Salé resembled other famous old urban centres of the Third World that underwent a relative economic decline during the modern colonial period. But it also underwent transformations and thereby retained some of its earlier importance. It had never been and did not become in the process of urban growth during the first two decades of colonial rule the kind of city described by Wirth. It fits Wirth's sociological definition of a city: a relatively large, dense and permanent settlement of heterogeneous individuals. But it lacked what Wirth considered the major identifying characteristics of the urban way of life: social relations dominated by a cash nexus and labour market; impersonal, superficial, transitory and segmental contacts amongst people; a high degree of variability in personal behaviour; an emphasis on formal procedures of social control and on the development of associations.[7] People living in Salé, like the urban dwellers of many Third World cities, were involved in complex networks, a structure of social relations.[8] What seems distinctive about Salé, during this period of change between 1830 and 1930, is the strong sense of identity as a social and cultural community common to its inhabitants. The city acted as a focal point of integration. Even when ethnic identities began to assume some importance with the increased immigration that followed the establishment of the protectorate, social fragmentation and conflict remained minimal.

Salé also contrasts in some important respects with other types of city, and for much the same reasons.[9] Thus, for example, in its spatial organisation the townscape of Salé resembled the typical Muslim city.[10] It was divided into general areas of residence and commerce, and tended to separate the living quarters of the highly urbanised townsmen from those of the marginal or peasant-like inhabitants. These characteristics, supposedly common to Muslim or pre-industrial towns (although they also exist in many Western, industrialised cities), have to be sociologically explained in regard to the particular context of Salé in order to assign any meaning to them. Salé's centres of activity—the market places, bazaar, court and Friday mosque—drew people together from wherever they lived or worked; it was a small city in both area and population, a place in which a man walked easily from home to shop, to buy, sell, pray, meet his friends or settle his affairs: a place where he could expect most faces to be familiar ones.

The heterogeneous composition of the community consisted of Muslims and Jews, speakers of Arabic and Berber, notables and masses, educated and illiterate, people of differing degrees of wealth or poverty, and men of various occupations and origins. These were cultural categories, not concrete, isolated social aggregations or classes. Social relationships within the community were generally loose and malleable, and characterised by a pattern of shifting coalitions, of networks of patrons and clients. Interest or interests held in common drew individuals into coalitions which were sometimes strengthened (but not determined) by descent, marriage or friendship. People in the city forged ties among themselves and with outsiders in relative freedom and ease and in order to satisfy or serve specific or general needs.[11] Contingencies and strategies played the greatest part in creating and destroying alliances. The structural factors of social life, such as territoriality, descent, occupation, etc., to which such importance is usually attributed in the models of Muslim or pre-industrial cities, simply do not apply in an analysis of Salé's society. To emphasise them would do violence to the subtle reality of social relationships.

Lapidus has noted that 'Muslim cities are never regarded as communities but as collections of isolated internal groups unable to co-operate in any endeavour of the whole. . . . Rarely have they been understood as living and vital organisms.'[12] In the Aleppo and Damascus of the Mamluk empire (1250–1517) he identifies the social relationships that made order and community possible: the affiliations of all classes and groups to the ulama, sheikhs and sufis diffused throughout the society, and other ties of solidarity that cut across class lines such as patronage, family, residence in a common quarter, and ethnic or religious community. It was a loose-knit, basically disaggregative society that tended to be relatively undifferentiated and whose fluid system of politics was defined by networks of overlapping and criss-crossing relationships. Government by the alien caste of Mamluk soldiers depended on their control of patronage, and this they accomplished through ties extended to every class in the cities.[13]

This description and analysis of Aleppo and Damascus under the Mamluks poses new questions about the social order of other Muslim cities and emphasises the importance of identifying the process and structure of urban life. These late medieval Muslim cities of the Arab East both resemble and differ from nineteenth-century Salé. The contrasts and comparisons can be briefly summarised. Salé was a living and vital community and similarly loose-knit and relatively undifferentiated. Where it substantially differed from medieval Aleppo and Damascus was in its basic aggregativeness. The Slawis had a highly developed sense of solidarity and municipal pride. Solidarity and pride and the existence of order rested on cross-cutting ties and shared values and on networks of personal relations and coalition groups of patrons and clients. Government lay in the hands of the central administration of the Moroccan sultanate, the *makhzan*; it delegated authority to officials who belonged to and lived in the city—the governor, judge, market inspector, administrator of pious endowments, customs officers and others. Each of these officials had direct links with the *makhzan* and the support of his own group of clients, and these in turn acted as patrons for their own clientèle groups. Although most of the city's inhabitants participated in coalition groups, no evidence suggests that all coalitions interlocked. Yet few people in the city appear to have been inaccessible to the rule of local government, and this was so not because of coercion or consent but by means of networks of personal relations and commonly held cultural values.

There was an 'Islamic' quality to life in Salé. It found expression not in the city's spatial organisation, social structure or political system but in the inhabitants' identification with a cultural ideal and a civilisation. A local historian articulated this sense of identification clearly and forcefully: 'When Islam arrived [in Salé], it brought with it the ideas of civilisation and culture, the knowledge of things. . . . It built up centres of learning, craftsmanship, and industry. . . . It solidified urban civilisation in Salé and uprooted its former culture.'[14] The cultural role of Salé was the most important factor in defining it as a Muslim city. That role consisted of carrying forward, developing and elaborating the established culture and civilisation of Islam. This type of city has been characterised by R. Redfield and M. Singer as 'orthogenetic', in contrast to the 'heterogenetic' city which creates original modes of thought whose authority goes beyond or conflicts with old cultures or civilisations.[15] Herein lay the basis of the Slawis self-view and their conservatism.

A part of this study is concerned with explaining how and why the Slawis so tenaciously sustained and vigorously asserted their cultural and religious tradition and identity over a period of three generations. The socialisation of children within the family, the education of males in schools, lodges and mosques, and the regular observance of religious practices all served to maintain continuities and to perpetuate those symbols and meanings that define a culture. But the vitality of self-assertion also was a reaction to the onslaught of colonialism—an assault at once economic, political and cultural. To understand the tenacity of culture in Salé also implies a consideration of social change.

I have chosen to concentrate on the period between 1830 and 1930 in order to trace in some detail the effects that the expansion of colonialism had on the lives of the Slawis. In choosing this dimension of time I am suggesting that the movement of a society from a 'traditional' to a 'modern' era proceeds over a number of generations and that it should not be situated in respect to historical turning points or views of 'before' and 'after' change. In terms of the periodisation of Moroccan history, I isolate the century between two watersheds—the beginning of French imperialism in North

Africa (the conquest of Algiers) and the emergence of modern Moroccan nationalism (the campaign against France's Berber policy).

Recent studies have shown that it is unjustifiable to consider the loss of Moroccan independence, i.e. the establishment of the protectorates in 1912, as the starting point of the country's modern history.[16] The French conquest of Algiers in 1830, the defeat of the sultan's army at Isly in 1844, and especially the 1859–60 Spanish-Moroccan war which led to the occupation of Tetuan and the subsequent payment of an enormous indemnity, effectively destroyed the basis of the empire. Moreover, as Miège has convincingly demonstrated, the economic domination of Morocco by Europeans began soon after the occupation of Algeria.[17]

The process of social change in Salé which concerns us unfolds in response to the continuous expansion of post-industrial colonialism. It begins in the era of informal imperialism by means of free trade and continues in the era of formal imperialism under the protectorate regimes.[18] Long before the world depression in 1930, most aspects of economic life in Salé had become inextricably tied to the conditions of the international market and finance system. Modern nationalism, which became manifest as a potent force in Salé during the summer of 1930, was a response to a particular economic crisis, as well as a rejection of political subjugation and cultural domination by France. It also marked the culmination of a period of social change. Between 1830 and 1930 the city had been transformed from a relatively homogeneous and integrated community with a largely self-sufficient and locally based economy into a diversified population largely dependent on extraneous economic factors.

Although the focus of my study is on a particular city, it does touch upon general problems concerning the effects of colonialism on the social and economic structures of Third World societies. A social history must consider social groupings, especially socio-economic classes, and try to understand the vicissitudes and the conflicts among those classes.[19] From one perspective the Slawis comprised a community of individuals tied together through networks of relationships and a common culture, internally divided by shifting alliances and coalition groups. We may also consider these townsmen from another perspective, that of social classes. The first mode of analysis interprets behaviour according to social and cultural links among individuals; the second interprets that same behaviour according to socio-economic categories of stratification.

Salé's social 'classes' do not fit the pattern associated with that structure of society which emerged from the industrial revolution in Europe. Yet the notion of class, stripped for the moment of its connotations of conflict or consciousness, draws attention to an inequality in the distribution of wealth, prestige and power. This inequality existed in the city, and it increased significantly as a result of the expansion of post-industrial colonialism.

A hierarchical pyramid of classes demonstrates this inequality more clearly than other conceptual models. At the top of the pyramid were the notables or elite. The rest of the population, the common people, were composed of undifferentiated townsmen who formed a middle rung, and the 'riff-raff' or marginal outsiders who made up a lower rung. The terms I have used were indigenous ones: notables (*aʿyān*) or elite (*al-khāṣṣa*), commoners or masses (*al-ʿāmma*), townsmen (*ahl al-bilād*), riff-raff (*as-sifla*) or outsiders (*al-barrāniyīn*). These were upper, middle and lower classes, or—in terms of income and life style—bourgeoisie, petty bourgeoisie and proletariat. These classes changed in composition and size and were permeable to upward and downward mobility, particularly during the last half of the nineteenth century.

The elite possessed wealth, prestige and power. They maintained a relatively high standard of living, a sophisticated style of life and a large measure of personal authority. They were government officials, leading scholars, prestigious holy men, wealthy farmers, tanners, craftsmen or merchants. The undifferentiated townsmen lacked the means to have luxury goods, worked as petty officials, shopkeepers, farmers, and mostly as craftsmen. The riff-raff or outsiders lacked an urban style and tended to be fishermen, hired workers, farm labourers, peddlers, domestics and slaves. The differences between these classes increased substantially during the period under study.

From the 1830s until the 1860s there was relative economic stability in Salé. Most people in the city drew their incomes from the growth, manufacture or sale of cotton or its products, and a variety of local crafts flourished. A large proportion of the population owned their own land, shops or homes. Differences in wealth were mitigated by its redistribution through ceremonies, gifts, loans and favours. Individuals accumulated and sometimes dissipated wealth by their achievements and failures, and similarly gained or lost prestige and power. Neither inheritance nor ascription determined a man's economic, social or political status.

During the next generation the conditions of economic life in the city changed. Imported goods from Europe, particularly cotton fabrics which were cheaper and superior to those of Salé, eliminated local cotton farming and the manufacture of cloth, and led to the decay of many of the craft industries. The export of raw materials from the countryside to Europe rather than to Morocco's cities paralleled the loss of markets for locally manufactured products. The commercial activities of the European nations and their mounting economic interests in Morocco, rampant inflation, recurrent crop failures and famines, combined in their effects to create a situation of almost constant crisis. In Salé the middle and lower classes became the principal victims of these crises, and many people were forced to abandon their occupation and sell their property in order to survive. The upper class, however, generally benefited from these conditions and prospered. The educated among them entered the expanding government bureaucracy, while others succeeded in involving themselves in the trade of European goods. In the last decades of the nineteenth century the elite, because of their governmental and commercial activities, were able to take advantage of the impoverishment of the masses and gain control over most of the city's property and its people.

It would be misleading to interpret this new wealth and power of the elite in terms of 'the rise of a capitalist class'. Yet in some ways a new bourgeoisie had emerged in the city, quite different from the earlier elite among the townsmen. In the first place, the economic changes caused by European expansion greatly enlarged the inequalities that had existed between the elite and the masses. Secondly, there was much less opportunity for upward social mobility and much less redistribution of wealth between the classes than there had been during the previous generation. The new bourgeoisie had lost its relative independence *vis-à-vis* the central government, and now depended almost entirely on official posts and on international trade. At the same time its interests and obligations within the local population had lessened in scope. This development was accompanied by small-scale trade in European manufactured goods by a kind of emergent petty bourgeoisie. For most people the decadence of the traditional crafts had led to widespread pauperisation without possibilities of redress.

By the early years of this century Salé, like most of Morocco's coastal cities, was breathing to the rhythm of international trade. Its elite lived by trade and government service. The *makhzan* had become a regime of wealth and learning, and some of the Slawis were a part of that regime. Their vested interests lay in maintaining the *status quo*—European economic involvement in Morocco without loss of its political independence. These interests, however, proved to be incompatible, and by 1912 Morocco had been divided into French and Spanish protectorates. During the next generation most of the elite retained some of their wealth, prestige and power, and the protectorate regime sought to consolidate their position for them by indirect rule. However, effective power in the city, as well as in the central government, was in the hands of French administrators, not Moroccans. Likewise, European settlers to a greater extent than natives capitalised on the opportunities for amassing wealth that had been created by the protectorate. The colonialists had not destroyed the new bourgeoisie, they had simply superseded it.

The French established a new Moroccan capital in Rabat, the neighbouring city across the river from Salé. The proximity of the new capital allowed some of the Slawis to work in the administration or to find profitable livelihoods in the building trades. At the same time, improved conditions of security and the development of communication facilities, such as roads and modern transport, made it possible for more people to work outside the city and for larger numbers of peasants to buy and sell in its market place and bazaar. Economic opportunities for the masses increased, and despite continual inflation during the early decades of colonial rule the level of living of some of the lower classes improved. Nonetheless there was a growing malaise in Salé and a deepening resentment of colonial domination among all classes during this early period of the protectorate.

When the world depression of 1930 struck, the economic situation in Salé worsened appreciably. The explanation for the events that took place in the city during that summer must take account of the economic factors involved. But the events also reveal many aspects of the process of social change in Salé and the importance of cultural and religious values and symbols in coping with change. The young men, many of them the sons of the bourgeoisie and recipients of a modern education in French or Arabic, successfully stirred up the population of the city in a campaign of protest against the French. Gradually, religion, the basis of the Slawis' cultural identity, became the rallying cry for political self-assertion.

I hope to demonstrate in the chapters that follow how the common social identity of Salé between 1830 and 1930 was maintained through a series of adjustments to rapidly changing conditions. My interpretation will emphasise the receptiveness of people in the city to religious symbols, and suggest why and how this made change tolerable. Yet these symbols also expressed a protest at once social and potentially political.

Another specific objective of this book is to show that the economic effects of colonialism had altered elements of the city's social structure without producing irreversible changes in the pattern of social relationships. Incipient social classes had emerged, but class consciousness or conflict remained minimal or non-existent. The Slawis continued to see themselves and sometimes acted as a community which was socially and culturally bound together.

Finally I hope to make the history of Salé seem alive by describing concrete persons and specific events. These descriptions seek to reveal and explain the states of mind of people in the city in regard to different circumstances or issues. During the decades before 1912 the solidarity and cohesiveness of the community weakened, and latent tensions on occasion became actual ones. But the establishment of the French protectorate and the resultant division of Morocco into two societies, foreign and indigenous, reinforced the tendencies within the city towards unity. Colonialism, identified in cultural as well as political terms, engendered a renewed sense of common identity and pride. Being a Slawi, however, in 1930 no longer meant simply identifying oneself in contrast to other Moroccans; it had become a means of confronting the colonialists as part of a national movement.

Part I Market and town

In the following two chapters I am concerned with the importance of Salé as a market (*sūq*) for a wide area extending far beyond its walls, and as an urban settlement (*madīna*) within an enclosed space. The relations of the city with its surrounding countryside were marked by several features: symbiosis in economic exchanges, a varying degree of social, cultural and political interaction, mutually antipathetic stereotypes. Salé's immediate environment was characterised by the nearness of the ocean, the maritime port, and the city of Rabat across the river. This environment, together with the natural resources and fertile land that were nearby, had an important influence on the way of life of the townsmen. It allowed most people to earn their livelihood from trade, crafts or farming.

Within the city the needs of living and working space were satisfied in particular ways, and these are described in some detail. Basically the pattern of the townscape was simple: a division between commercial and residential sectors, and a further division of the latter into a Jewish quarter, a predominantly bourgeois area, and an area largely populated by people considered to be only partially urbanised. The main lines of this plan did not alter during the period under study, but land use in some parts of the city changed completely in response to economic factors and population pressures.

Demographic growth in Salé during the period 1830–1930 is placed within the context of the general pattern of urbanisation in Morocco, in so far as it is known. Although the increase in population (from about 14,000 to 26,000) was less dramatic than in other cities, Salé remained one of the ten largest and most important urban centres of the country.

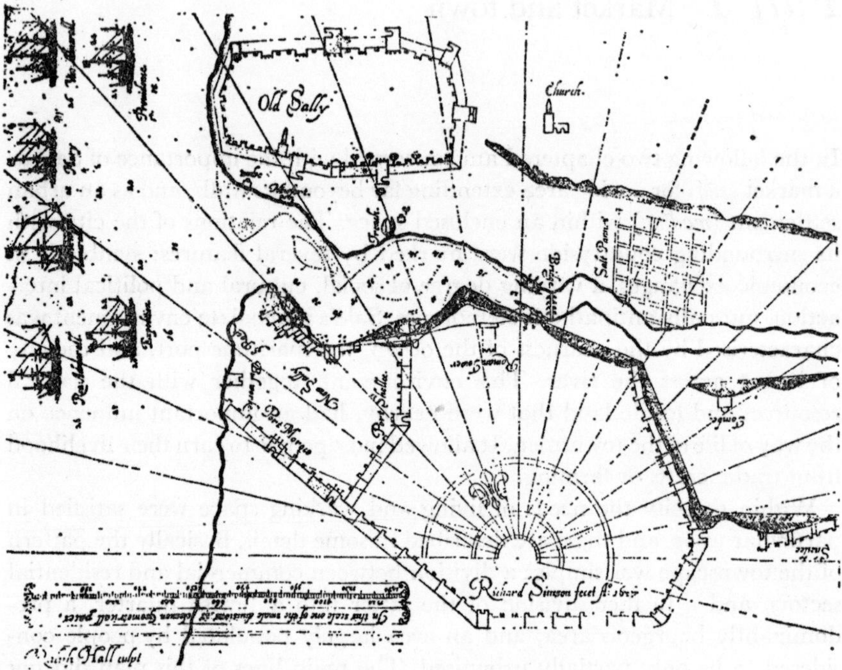

Fig. 1 From Richard Simson's map of Morocco, 1637

I Along the crossroads

. . . as long as this area was not conquered, kingship might at any time cease to exist and the Prince would be like a weaver without his loom.

Mouette, 1683[1]

Introduction

Throughout much of Morocco's history the only secure route between the northern and southern capitals of Fez and Marrakesh lay along the Atlantic coast. The unity and well-being of the kingdom depended upon control of the corridor from Fez to the ocean and the port of the Bou Regreg river. 'The Two Banks' (*al-ʿudwatayn* in the Arabic expression) of Salé and Rabat were considered the bloodline of the empire. Rabat was, in the phrase of Marshal Lyautey, 'the starting point of seven big natural routes which open out like a fan in every direction'. To control these routes, and to escape the geographical isolation of an inland capital, the French in 1913 transferred the capital from Fez to Rabat.[2]

The geographical situation of the two banks had long been important for economic, as well as strategic and political, reasons. They commanded the route that connected the two principal and complementary agricultural regions of the country—the Haouz, in the south, and the Gharb, to the north-east of Salé. The exchange of agricultural products and urban manufactured goods along this route had traditionally sustained and enriched the great trading centres of Marrakesh, Rabat, Salé, Meknes and Fez.

Before colonial rule travellers and traders in Morocco had to manage without wheeled vehicles or paved roads, and on routes that were often circuitous and unsafe. People and goods circulated regularly, however, regardless of the slowness, precariousness or cost. Thus, during much of the nineteenth century, travel between Salé and Fez passed north beyond the Sebou river before turning east, in order to skirt the sometimes turbulent area controlled by the Berber-speaking and pastoralist tribes of the Zemmour. When a direct route of some 125 miles was opened in 1890, the caravan trip from Salé to Fez still took four or five days.[3] Similarly the caravan route to Marrakesh entailed a trip of at least five days.

The political and economic importance of the Fez–Marrakesh road by way of the coast enhanced the influence and authority of Salé's leaders. The governor of the city often acted as an intermediary between the government and the leaders of the countryside, and negotiated matters of taxation and free passage for the sultan's ambulant court and army.[4] The influence the governor wielded at court and in the countryside stemmed from and

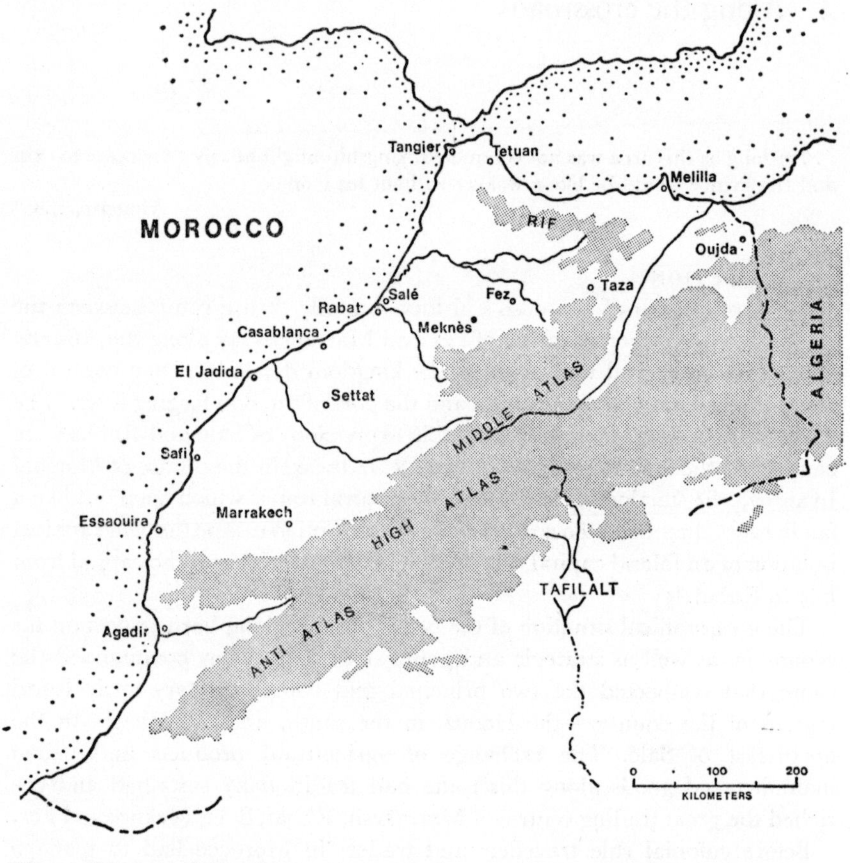

Fig. 2 Morocco: general

depended on his ability to maintain solid personal relations both within government circles and with rural leaders. Although the interests of city, central government and countryside differed in some respects, all had a need for the free movement of men and the flow and exchange of produce and goods. The city, and especially its leaders, played a pivotal role in establishing the understandings and relationships that were necessary to urban–rural coexistence and interdependence.

RURAL–URBAN RELATIONS

The immediate hinterland of Salé, an area of some 65,000 hectares,[5] had been inhabited since at least the middle of the nineteenth century by three Arabic-speaking tribal groups: to the north and along the coast for some ten miles, the ʿĀmir; to the south-east, the Ḥusayn; to the south, and on both banks of the Bou Regreg, the Sahūl. Almost half the area was covered by forests, and from them came the charcoal and wood that the city needed. On ʿĀmir soil were ʿUyūn Baraka—'Sources of Blessing'—the thirteen springs that provided the city with a good part of its water supply.

These three tribes had a little over 16,000 hectares of land under rotation in 1918, the earliest year for which there are records.[6] They cultivated wheat, millet, barley, beans, corn and chick-peas, and the Sahūl, especially, produced a significant surplus of wheat which was sold in Salé. They also practised stock farming and satisfied some of the city's needs for beef and mutton, and for skins and wool. Their combined population in 1916 was somewhat less than 9,000, not a very large number of buyers for the city's manufactured products but enough to fill its weekly Thursday markets.

These peasants on the outskirts of the city separated it from large, unstable and frequently troublesome confederations of tribal groupings: the Banū Ḥasan, to the north; the Zemmour, to the east; and the Zaʿir and ʿArab Ḥawziyya, to the south. The image of a buffer zone made up of small, unaffiliated tribes placed between the city and the large confederations beyond suggests itself. Yet, in effect, the ʿĀmir considered themselves to be an isolated fraction of the Banū Ḥasan, and at time so did the Sahūl. Thus when the Banū Ḥasan and Zemmour fought pitched battles in 1843, 1853, 1858 and 1910 the ʿĀmir and Sahūl sided with the Banū Ḥasan. As a result, some of these battles took place just beyond the walls of Salé. The pattern of relations between city and countryside, although disrupted by these upheavals, remained fundamentally the same. Economic exchanges and interdependencies were not limited by tribal boundaries or urban ramparts. Upheavals in the countryside endangered the city and isolated it, but they were temporary and when they ceased economic and political ties once again took their normal course.

Salé depended on agricultural products from the countryside, but it also needed to sell its manufactured or imported goods in the rural markets. In the city there were a large number of itinerant traders (*suwwāqa*). Many of them specialised in the sale of cloth and garments in the main markets of the Banū Ḥasan, where they enjoyed something of a monopoly in these goods. The only other traders in cloth in these markets were Jews from Ouezzan and Ksar el-Kabir, but they apparently sold different kinds of cloth and bought sewn garments from the Slawis to sell in their own cities. Other itinerant traders from Salé worked these markets as well, selling shoes, tea, coffee, sugar and candles. Jewish traders from the city also earned their livelihood in the countryside; they did not cross the Sebou river, but had a virtual monopoly in the markets of the Zemmour and Sahūl.

Most traders had guarantees of safe passage (*mizrag*) from important rural personalities living in the territories through which they passed. Usually someone identified with a local leader would accompany the Slawi traders through an area; when they moved on to an area under the control of another group they changed protectors. The guarantees given by rural leaders to the traders were considered a sacred trust, and in general they were effective. Brigandage was not widespread, and seldom went unpunished. For

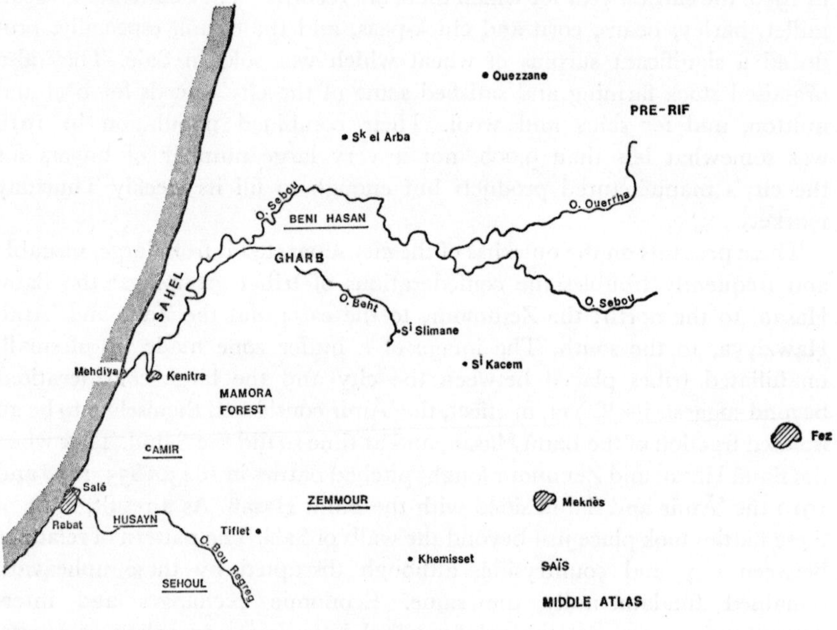

Fig. 3 The region and tribal groups surrounding Salé

the most part Slawi itinerant traders moved about the countryside with relative freedom and security, though not without hazard. On at least one occasion the protection and guarantees failed to work. In documents signed by the head rabbis of Rabat and Salé in 1891 the Alliance Israelite in Paris is requested to intercede with the sultan because three traders (one from Salé and two from Marrakesh) had been robbed and murdered while on their way to the markets of the Gharb to bring additional goods to a Jewish trader from Salé.[7] In normal conditions, however, the rural leaders protected traders and guaranteed their lives and property. During the two generations that preceded the establishment of the French protectorate hundreds of itinerant traders from Salé constantly peddled their goods in the countryside, and part of the economy of the city was geared to these rural markets.

It is important to emphasise the interdependence between the city and its countryside. Earlier studies mistakenly characterised urban–rural relations in terms of a permanent dichotomy and enmity. Thus Gautier described Salé as a city which 'begins abruptly, without transition, at the wall' and he explains this on the basis of a juxtaposition of two enemy peoples—townsmen and peasants. In his view the area beyond the walls 'was a veritable frontier, worse than that, a "no man's land"'.[8] Other studies stress the anarchy of the countryside, but see a dynamic process whereby upheavals periodically arise and subside, sometimes spreading to the area just outside the city. Thus Michaux-Bellaize writes that the Land of Dissidence (*bled s-sība*) came 'to the very doors' of Salé and Rabat before 1912.[9]

The discussion of *sība* as anarchy and dissidence in the French literature of the colonial period need not detain us here.[10] The Slawis used the term in their colloquial speech to express the notion of upheaval in the countryside, for example when a sultan died, or crops had failed or disease had become widespread. Thus during a cholera epidemic in 1854 some 6,000 people died in Rabat and Salé, and the ʿĀmir attacked the town, robbing travellers, pillaging gardens and destroying shops. The gates of the city were closed for several months. Similar circumstances arose in 1865 when a false rumour spread that Sultan ʿAbd ar-Raḥmān had died; robberies took place along the roads, the ʿĀmir surrounded the town, ravaged its gardens and prevented anyone from leaving or entering; once again the city's gates closed for several months.[11] These were times of *sība*, when the normal course of everyday life no longer held. A further example can be found in the famine conditions at the turn of this century, when large numbers of hungry people streamed into the city; these immigrants, as well as many of the townsmen, had to subsist on oats normally sold as fodder. During these periods of upheaval the normal relations between the people of the city and those of the countryside tended to break down. Fighting in the countryside, famines and epidemics—especially cholera—were recurrent, but not continual.[12] According to my very rough estimate, Salé was affected, on average, perhaps as often as once in four years between 1830 and 1910. Yet despite the recurrence of these upheavals city and hinterland usually maintained their exchanges, and indeed depended upon one another for their economic well-being.

A regional market place

Just as the traders of Salé maintained steady contact with the rural hinterland, so did the people of the countryside regularly stream into the city's weekly Thursday Market (*sūq al-khamīs*). Until early in this century Thursday's buying and selling took place within the city in an area called the Great

Market Place (*sūq al-kabīr*). With the establishment of the protectorate, the market increased its activity and, to accommodate the growing number of buyers and sellers, was moved outside Fez Gate, the main entrance to the city. The construction of rural market towns in the Gharb and a revolution in the means of transport greatly affected the movement of men and goods between town and countryside. More rural people now came to the market in Salé, and fewer Slawis left the city to work as itinerant traders. The townsmen no longer had to reach into the countryside to gain a living.

For the most part Salé was fed by its hinterland. Local products such as fruits, vegetables, fish and salt only supplemented the main staples grown by rural peasants. Wheat came to the city from Zemmour, Sahūl and to some extent from as far away as Dukkāla, the hinterland of El-Jadida; clarified butter, an important part of the Moroccan diet, was provided by the inhabitants of the Gharb. These products were bought by local wholesalers who, in turn, sold them in large quantities to retailers or wealthy inhabitants of the city. Most people tried to purchase non-perishable commodities only once or twice a year and stored them in their homes, and some had regular purchasing arrangements direct with farmers. In a few cases, particularly during the later years of the nineteenth century, when bad crop years had succeeded one another, Slawi wholesalers or simply rich men advanced money or seed to farmers before crops were planted. Unfortunately information on such relationships remains scanty, but from the available material there are no indications of rural agriculture having been generally under the control of urban landowners or moneylenders.

Personal contacts between the people of Salé and those of the surrounding tribes played a role in all exchanges. A curious example was a famous woman from the tribe of Zemmour called Q̣āna, who would often visit the qadi of Salé, ʿAli ʿAwwād, and arrange with him for the passage of Slawis among the Zemmour. The qadi himself sometimes hunted with a party of Slawis in the areas controlled by the Zemmour and enjoyed the hospitality of his friends among them. Other Zemmouris who frequented the market of Salé had social relations and friendships amongst the urban population, although some preferred to pitch their tents outside the walls of the city when they had to spend the night, out of some kind of vague fear of the former corsairs of Salé.[13]

The countryside within the ci

Peasants and townsmen were linked by religious beliefs and practices as well as by economic exchanges and political alliances. Some of the town's religious orders drew most of their followers from the rural population.[14] Thus, for example, the religious order founded in Salé in the seventeenth century by Sīdī Aḥmad Ḥajjī had a large following among the Zemmour. They contributed gifts to the descendants of the saint for the maintenance of the Ḥajjī lodge (*zāwiya*), and they came to pray in the lodge and, if necessary, to seek refuge in it. The lodge was an inviolable sanctuary (*ḥurma*) in which men might escape, at least temporarily, from a wide variety of exactions. Another religious order, the Kattāniyya, also had a large number of Zemmour followers, and, as a consequence, at the turn of the century Salé had become the second largest centre of the order. Disciples from the countryside also frequented other urban Sufi orders such as the Qādiriyya, Tuhāmiyya and Tijāniyya.

Both religion and economics drew large numbers of the surrounding rural population to the city during the three annual pilgrimage fairs (coll. *mūsim*) at the tombs of Salé's saints. At the *mūsim* of Sīdī Mūsā, a twelfth-century mystic, over a hundred tents were set up, most of them belonging to people from the Banū Ḥasan and the Sahūl. At the fair goods and animals were bought and sold, and sheep were slaughtered in sacrifice and distributed to the poor. At the same time the rural-based religious orders, such as the Aisāwa, Ḥamādsha and Bū ʿAzzāwiyya, gathered and prayed and danced during the two days and nights of the *mūsim*.[15]

Ties between townsmen and tribesmen sometimes became close-knit. A few of the ʿAlawīs in the city, descendants of the prophet and kinsmen of the sultan, had been given rural farms by the palace, and they employed sharecroppers from among the peasantry. Although these land holdings were not at all extensive, they did bind some of the peasants to urban landlords. A branch of the Nāṣiri family had alliances with people from the countryside and would go to them regularly to receive gifts, supplies of wheat, animals, etc. These alliances were strengthened by affinity. Thus one of the leaders of the ʿĀmir, Zirdānī, had married a daughter of Ibn al-Kabīr an-Nāṣirī, an important personage in Salé, while the latter's son and a *muftī* in the city had further increased the ties between the two families by marrying one of the rural qa'id's daughters. Because of the rules of Islamic inheritance law some of the Zirdānīs came to own property in Salé and a number of Nāṣirīs inherited property in the countryside.

The leaders from the countryside gave themselves a stake in Salé, usually by the purchase of a house.[16] Sometimes they lived in these houses themselves, but more often they were used by their sons who were studying in the city. A few of these men became permanent urban residents, while continuing to own property and to direct the affairs of their tribes. Thus the Gaddāra, the most important family of the Banū Ḥasan during the nineteenth century, owned a number of houses in Salé. Maḥammad al-Gaddārī, a qa'id of the Banū Ḥasan during the reign of Mawlāy Ḥasan, retired to Salé in 1894 when his tribe revolted against him because of the heavy taxes he had exacted. When he tried to have himself named governor of Salé the Slawis protested angrily. The matter was referred to Sultan ʿAbd al-ʿAzīz, who appointed Gaddārī governor of Ksar el-Kebir and later of Larache.

The tribes in the immediate vicinity of Salé—ʿĀmir, Ḥuṣayn, and Sahūl—

were under the administrative authority of the governor of the city. From the judiciary point of view they depended on the qadi, who appointed special assistants to deal with their affairs. The learned of the city, judges and notaries, jealously guarded their legal ascendancy over the countryside. When in 1914 the French disregarded this traditional relationship of urban domination and appointed ʿAllāl at-Taghrāwī of the Banū Ḥasan (at that time a respected savant and teacher in Salé) as qadi the Slawis vehemently protested against the appointment of an outsider, and moreover one of rural origin.

Rural people could integrate themselves into even the most prestigious circles of the city, but it usually took them several generations to do so. An example is aṭ-Ṭayyib b. Shlīḥ of the Banū Ḥasan, who made his way among the ulama of Salé. His uncle, an extremely rich and powerful man in the Gharb, had married a woman from an important urban family. (The fact that she had been divorced by one of the most influential men in Salé during the middle of the last century may have facilitated this match.) A daughter from the marriage was later given to her maternal cousin, a man who succeeded his father as governor of Salé. Meanwhile her paternal cousin, aṭ-Ṭayyib b. Shlīḥ, had become an intimate of her husband's family, received an advanced education, married into the Slawi community and then became a leading member of the ulama. Such ties and marriage alliances cemented the interdependence of the city and its hinterland in some cases, while in others they led simply to the absorption of rural immigrants into the urban social fabric.

The assimilation of rural elements into the urban population of Salé had a long historical precedent. The above-mentioned powerful urban family, to take but one of many possible examples, had originally come to Salé from the Gharb. A saintly lineage of the Banū Ḥasan had settled in Salé generations before when their ancestor Sīdī 'Bu Gettāya' had been buried there; so had the Ḥallāwiyyīn, Idrīsī *shurafā'* of the ʿĀmir, who nonetheless retained lands worked as tenant farms near Kenitra. Indeed, most of the population whose origins I was able to trace had migrated to the city from the countryside.

There was some movement in the opposite direction as well. Families of rural origin who had settled in the city in the past sometimes returned to the countryside. Thus some houses in Salé, owned by established urban families from the middle of the nineteenth century on, had previously been the property of people from the surrounding tribes whose descendants had migrated back to the villages. To further complicate the picture, we find some families who had been established in Salé for centuries—owning property, working at supposedly urban crafts, and even serving as respected secretaries and ulama—and who were, nonetheless, considered tribesmen rather than townsmen. Indeed, whole quarters of Salé were populated by people who were looked upon as rural peasants. The Friday mosque of Sīdī Aḥmad Ḥajjī in the centre of these quarters, near the Great Market place, used to overflow with the faithful during the noon prayer, and at times all the doors of the mosque had to be closed to keep out additional people. In the eyes of many townsmen that congregation was an extension of the countryside, a foreign body in the city proper. The stereotypes of urban and rural populations will be discussed below. What I have tried to show here is that Salé's ties extended into the countryside, and that the countryside had a place within the city itself; that these were not two separate worlds, but mobile individuals and groups whose mutual interests often brought and bound them together.[17]

The immediate environment

We have viewed at our leisure the city of Salee and Rabat, and their environs. It is a strange place and country. The land is a series of long, gentle, bare sweeping drives, at the edge cut out into cliffs and cones as if with a pastry cutter. About three miles north of Salee we descried through the mists of spray, a magnificent palace. It changed to a gaunt ruin. A little further on there is a kubbe, or saint's tomb, surmounted by a dome like the tombs of Judea and India. Next comes the point of Salee and over it flutters the red flag of the 'Rovers' [*sic*]. Gardens surround the town, and a few palm trees are seen among them. Between Salee and Rabat the river enters the sea over the bar.

(Urquhart, 1848)[18]

Salé and Rabat have been both separated and joined by the Bou Regreg river (Wādī Abū Raqrāq).[19] Although the river originates in the High Atlas mountains and tends to become torrential during the rainy season, the tide of the Atlantic Ocean is so powerful that it reverses the flow of the river for some nine miles inland. It is there that the delicious, deep-bodied herring known as shad (coll. *shebel*) spawn and grow.[20] Along the banks of the river salt marshes form; these are divided so that those on the right bank belong to Salé and those on the left bank belong to Rabat.

The mouth of the river, called *ri'a*—'simulation' of the ocean—formed the maritime port of the two cities. In the past it had extended inland for several miles and covered most of the area of sand that now lies between the southern wall of Salé and the river. But the course of the estuary had steadily altered, such that during the early years of this century old sailors remembered a larger and more easily accessible harbour within their lifetime.[21]

The sand bar at the entrance to the port had proved a definite advantage to the small, local pirate ships of the seventeenth and eighteenth centuries. But, as the sand bar increased, maritime commerce became progressively more difficult. An officers' manual written in 1844 reports that although the port is sufficiently large, fairly heavy ships cannot get past the banks of sand obstructing the entrance, the depth of water at high tide being only twelve feet, and at low tide merely six feet.[22] By 1912 the bar of the Bou Regreg was considered impassable for shipping during fifty-two days of the year. Ships of modest size continued to call at the port for trade, but, along with Mogador and Tetuan, Rabat and Salé had lost the pre-eminence in maritime commerce that had been theirs at the middle of the nineteenth century.[23]

The docks, customs house and all the main wholesale firms of the port had been situated in Rabat. This had led some scholars to ascribe to Rabat all the commercial activity of the port and to describe Salé as an isolated as

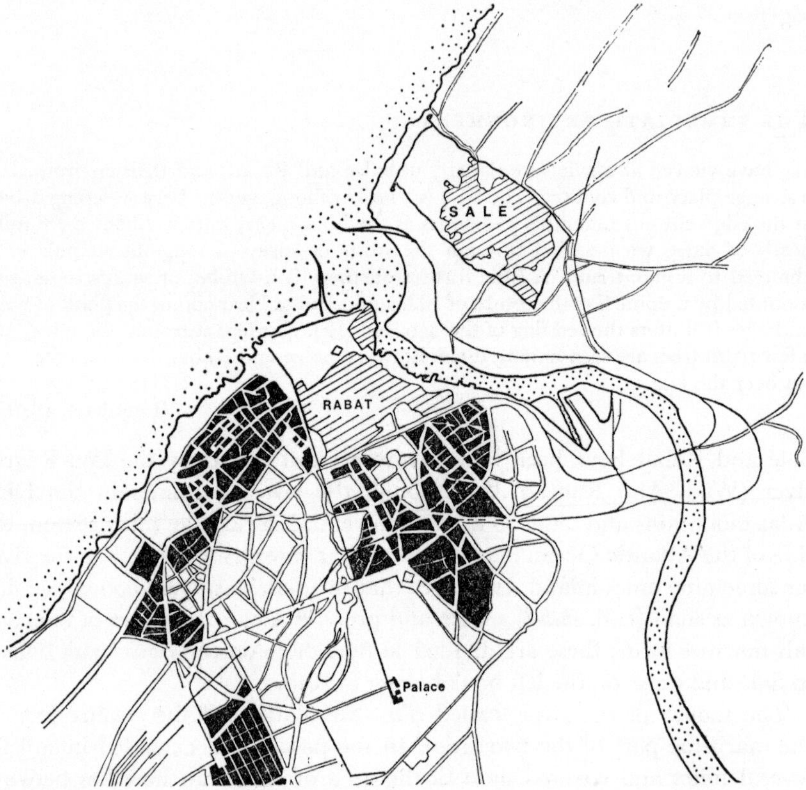

Fig. 4 The estuary of the Bou Regreg and the cities of the two banks, Rabat and Salé

well as fanatical community.[24] In fact Slawis had long served as administrators of customs at Rabat, and many of the Muslim and Jewish wholesale merchants along the main street of commerce, the Rue des Consuls, were from Salé, e.g. Ḥayōt, ʿAmmār, al-Qā'im, Ṣabūnjī, al-Ḥarsh and others. Mouette had pointed out as early as the seventeenth century that the richest Jewish and Muslim merchants of Rabat lived in Salé, and this situation continued, at least in part, to be the case during the nineteenth century.[25]

Nonetheless Salé was, as an old informant put it, a kind of poor relative of Rabat. He complained that Salé's carpets and *ḥanbals* (intricately woven thin woollen rugs) were transported and sold in Rabat and erroneously called 'Rabati', and that a Slawi had to cross the river to purchase a product manufactured in his own city, or even to buy home-grown vegetables. In effect the people of Salé had to and did cross the river to participate fully in the commercial importance of the port and the activity of Rabat. As an experienced French intelligence officer at the end of the last century noted, it was impossible from the point of view of commerce to distinguish between Rabat and Salé.[26] Economic relations joined the otherwise jealously separated cities. Thus combined, they followed Fez and Marrakesh in size and in importance as a market and centre of redistribution.[27]

The estuary of the Bou Regreg and the twin cities of Rabat and Salé are situated in a region of the sub-Atlantic plains known by geographers as the Moroccan Meseta.[28] The natural region of Salé, formed by the erosion of a carboniferous mountain range, lies between the depressions of the Sebou and Bou Regreg rivers. In the past the area up to the Sebou had been used for pasturage by herdsmen from Salé.[29] However, by the nineteenth century a narrow alluvial plain, bordered by the western advance of sand dunes and a region of quarries, extending from the Bou Regreg to a little beyond Bouknadel (16 km north of Salé), marked the limit of the city's agriculture and grazing lands.

The Slawis owned fertile agricultural land in this alluvial plain, and were able to grow cereals, vegetables and fruits. Within the walls of the city there were also excellent gardens, and the slopes and valleys bordering the rivers provided good pasturage for livestock kept by people living within the city. A travel account published in 1820 described the area in and around Salé as 'wonderously abundant in all the finest grain, leguminous plants, fruits, vegetables and cattle'.[30] Much of this was due to the availability of water. The average annual rainfall was around twenty-one inches, most of it between October and May, and the area abounded in water sources easily tapped to irrigate most cultivated land.

Until the end of the 1860s cotton, for which the climate was ideally suited, provided the most important crop of Salé, and when it proved no longer profitable the farms were converted into vineyards. Another agricultural conversion took place near the turn of this century when vineyards were transformed into crop-rotated vegetable gardens. Methods of irrigation changed with crops: cotton and grapes demanded little artificial irrigation, while vegetable gardens depended on irrigation even during the rainy season. The changes presented little difficulty, since water sources were plentiful and knowledge of irrigation practices was widespread.

Around the edges and within the walls of Salé were numerous irrigated private gardens (coll. *sāniya*, pl. *swānī*, literally 'water scoops'). In them the people of the city grew oranges, pomegranates, pears, apricots and lemons. Within a mile of the city, on the hill area called Biṭṭāna, spread a large number of extensive unirrigated gardens (coll. *jnān*, pl. *jnānāt* or *jnā'in*). When vineyards replaced cotton in these gardens Salé became known for a stimulating grape conserve (coll. *samit*), eaten on bread or mixed with water. It was among these gardens that the wealthy constructed summer homes or elaborate picnic facilities (coll. *menzeh*) and maintained their image as gentlemen farmers.

In the gardens and in the city life out of doors was pleasant. The average annual temperature approximated around 67°F (45°F in January, 83°F in August), although relative humidity averaged a less comfortable 75–84 per cent. Winds blowing off the Atlantic Ocean at times suddenly caused the weather to change or created storms much like the squalls of the Gulf Stream. Occasionally in the spring a hot, dry wind from the Sahara—the infamous 'Shergi'—whipped its way through the area and destroyed crops in its wake. But on the whole the climate was salubrious and favourable to agriculture and animal husbandry. Nature also provided an abundance of resources that could be used for construction: durable and easily hewn sandstone, quarry marble, clay for bricks and pottery, and unlimited sand of various types. Some seventeen miles east of the city was the Mamora Forest, the most important natural forest in Morocco. From its over five hundred square miles of cedar and cork oak trees came wood for buildings, ships and charcoal.

Within this natural environment and from these resources the people of Salé had constructed, shaped and maintained their city. They depended on their relations with the people of the countryside and drew their livelihood from trade, manufacturing and farming. The unique quality of their lives was in part due to their interactions with the wider environment. It also stemmed from the particular way of life inside the city itself.

II Within the walls

The walls around Salé marked off the physical space of the *madīna*, that is, of the city proper. Within those walls were urban landmarks and a landscape, and these lent form, as well as aesthetic order, to the pursuits and pleasures of the townspeople. In order to explain the spatial organisation of the city and its influence on the way and tenor of life I shall sketch in some detail the main areas, places and arteries of communication. This entails a description of centres of economic life, residential quarters, public buildings and reserves, and a discussion of the pattern of urban growth during the period under study.[1]

Areas of commerce

Throughout the nineteenth century Salé's Thursday Market (*sūq al-khamīs*) was held in an area today called the Great Market Place (*sūq al-kabīr*). From the Gate of Fez (*bāb fās*, sometimes called Thursday Gate—*bāb al-khamīs*) a long narrow street led to the Market Place, which stood approximately in the geographical centre of the city. Along this street were most of the twenty *funduqs*, the hotel-warehouses where country people coming to market spent the night, stored and, sometimes, sold their goods. In the Market Place, called until the late nineteenth century The Square for Wheat (*raḥbat az-zraʿ*), grain was sold throughout the week. In surrounding shops people could buy skins, wool, cereals, dry beans, garbanza beans, sorghum, corn and millet—the products brought to Salé by the surrounding tribes. On Thursday the rural people came to market to buy and sell animals and to provide themselves with the goods of the city. Rough statistics for these transactions during the early days of the protectorate tell us that each month some 1,200 bovines, 500–1,500 sheep, 400–500 goats, 100 horses, 120 mules and 300 donkeys changed hands, and that in 1916 some 800 loaded animals entered or left the city gates.[2]

In the afternoons the square became the Flea Market (*jōṭiyya*), and all sorts of used objects and goods could be bought at auctions or by haggling with local and rural peddlers. Most of the merchants in the shops around the square came from old-established urban families. In addition to those

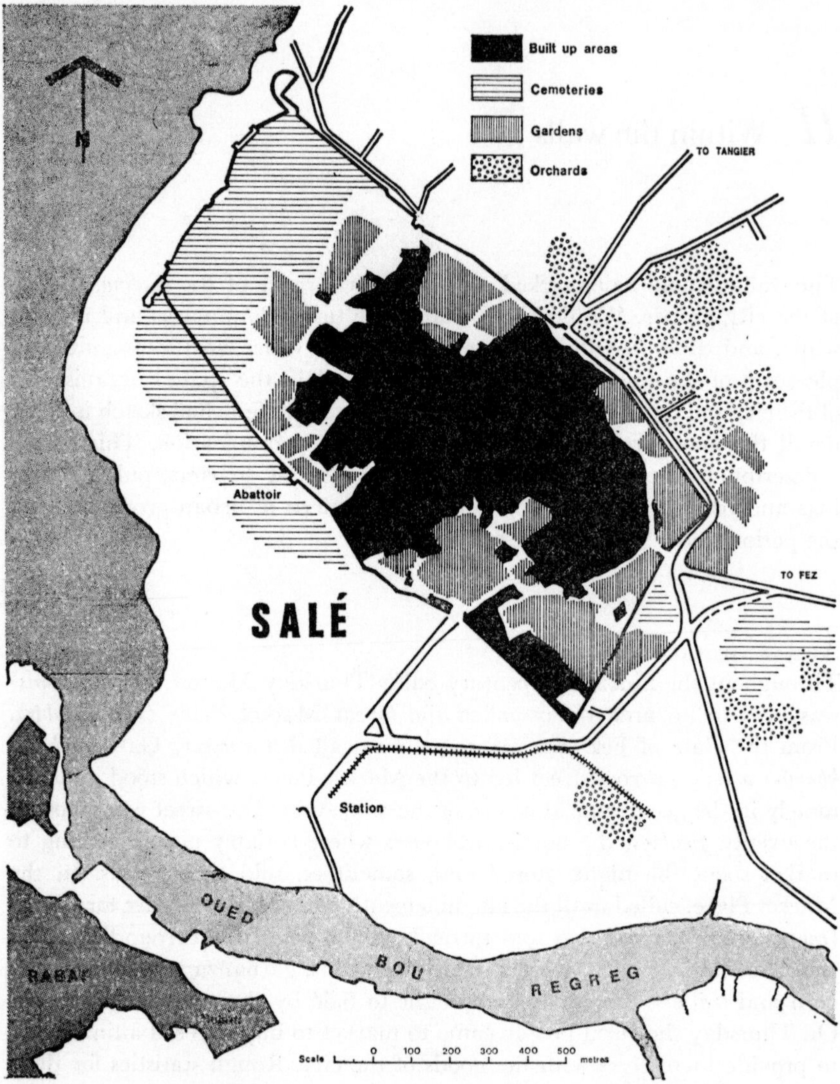

Fig. 5 The Madina of Salé: its cemeteries, gardens, orchards and vineyards

dealing in foodstuffs, about twenty-five altogether, there were half a dozen sellers of pottery and those locally manufactured earthenware cooking utensils famous throughout Morocco as the *tājīn Slawī* (*tājīn* being both the name for the hermetically closed ceramic cooking utensil and the stew in it). Five or six shopkeepers alongside the square sold salt extracted from their marshes along the river. Nearby, on one of the side streets, stood the warehouse of leather and olive oil, where fresh and dried skins for the lucrative tanning business and the olive oil (coll. *zīt bildī*) that formed a basic part of the Slawi diet were bought and sold. A notary from the qadi's court, several measurers and some porters formed the staff of the warehouse and carried out the necessary work involved in transactions.

Close to the noisy, animated market place there were some stately residences, and in the middle of the last century the governor of Salé, Muḥammad b. ʿAbd al-Hādī Znībar, had lived in one of them. Indeed, the flies and smells of the nearby slaughterhouse evidently bothered him so much that he had it moved to an area outside the southern wall of the city. The market provost (coll. *mitḥasib*, cl. *muḥtasib*) also lived nearby and had an office in the square from which he supervised the commercial activities of the market. Near the market place there were lovely streets such as the one that was called Bū Qāʿa, after the family of an administrator of pious endowments who had lived there before his property was confiscated by the sultan Mawlāy Ismāʿīl early in the eighteenth century. By the turn of this century, however, only a few important and respected men still lived near the market place, and the stately houses had become largely inhabited by poor people of recent rural origin. In the 1920s, when a former qadi of Settat returned to his native Salé and bought a house near the market place, his scandalised relatives and friends prevailed on him to move out of a quarter no longer considered respectable. The deterioration of the area around the market place was due, at least in part, to the governor Ibn ʿAbd al-Hādī. In 1851, when a mob pillaged a French ship that had run aground near Salé, the governor isolated the trouble-makers in the areas around the market place, an action which produced the proverb 'Few are the likes of Ibn ʿAbd al-Hādī'.[3]

Movement within the *madīna* took place along a labyrinth of crooked alleyways with odd shops occurring in occasional clusters and a few wider, longer streets concentrating certain crafts. Although an uninitiated visitor, particularly a Westerner, might suffer vertigo and certainly total confusion, the Slawis find the ways of the city both simple and orderly. The basic street plan is relatively clear, once assimilated. From the market place two short streets, The Barbers (*al-ḥajjāmīn*) and The Horseshoers (*as-sammārīn*), lead to the main artery that cuts across Salé from north to south. This street, some ten feet wide and about a mile long, runs from the Gate of Ceuta (bāb sibta) to the New Gate (bāb al-jadīd). Near the Ceuta gate, from which traders left for the north, caravansaries for pack animals were filled with porters, veterinarians, horseshoers, saddle makers, basket weavers and others. Passage through both the Gate of Ceuta and the Gate of Fez was strictly controlled in order to tax the goods that came into and left the city, the collection of taxes being farmed out to the highest bidder who had the title of Owner of the Gates (coll. *mūl l-bībān*).

Entering Salé from the Gate of Ceuta and going along the main street, one passed in sequence workshops of mat makers (*ḥassārīn*) and tinsmiths (*ḥaddādīn*), the stalls of butchers (*sūq al-gazzārīn*), vegetable sellers, and the fish market (*maḥāl al-ḥūt*). A short distance past the spot where the Street of

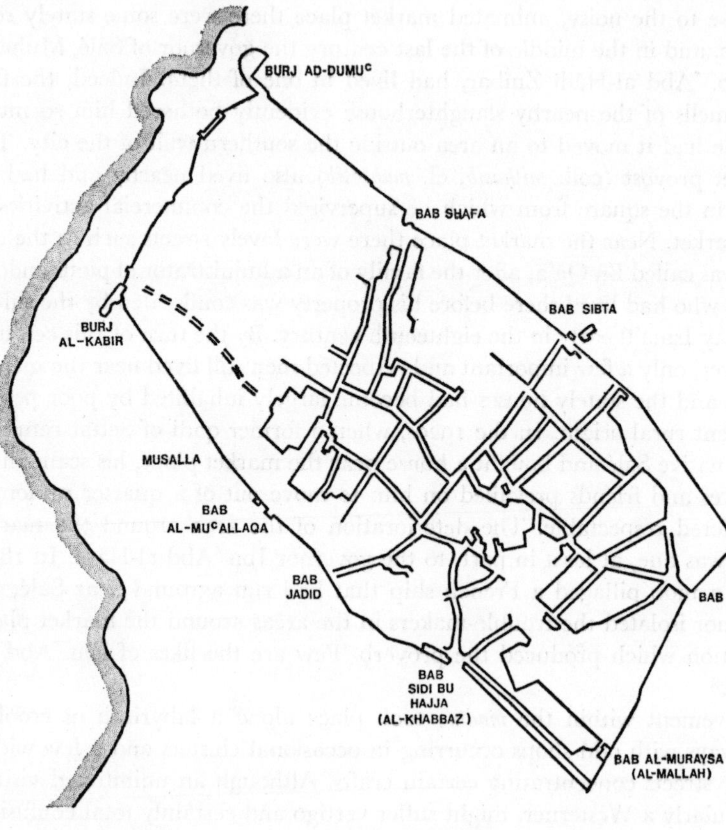

Fig. 6 Salé: main gates and arteries of circulation

Barbers met this artery, another long and busy street ran upwards and westwards towards the Great Mosque. Turning right to go up to the Mosque, one came to the Small Square (*ar-ruḥāyba*), which was filled with butchers and grocers. Then the street narrowed and became the Street of the Makers of Felt Hats (*al-qashshāshīn*), and farther along changed its name again to the Street of Zāwiyat Sīdī Bin ʿĪsā. Beyond, the street became steep and was known as the Incline of the Qadi (*ʿaqbat al-qāḍī*), referring to the nearby house of ʿAbd Allah b. Khaḍrā', the head judge of Fez towards the end of the last century. Walking up this street towards the Great Mosque, one first passed shops of tailors and craftsmen of various kinds. Soon fewer workshops and more private homes appeared. All along the way tens of small lanes and impasses branched off and led to private homes. But let us leave these residential quarters and the Great Mosque for the moment and return to the busy street leading south from the Gate of Ceuta.

Farther along that street an opening on the left led into a lovely large, shaded square called the Thread Market (*sūq al-ghazl*). The women of Salé who specialised in the weaving of rugs or the preparation of yarns gathered there on two mornings each week to buy and sell woollen materials and goods; on three afternoons a week the square became an immense vegetable market. Around the edges of the Thread Market perhaps fifteen merchants had permanent shops for buying and selling woollen goods. In this same square the witnesses of the law court set up their offices and were kept busy preparing documents of testimony and evidence for whoever had need of their services. Here, too, the Administrator of Pious Endowments or Habous (*nāẓir al-ḥabus*) handled matters concerning the large amount of urban property under his jurisdiction. In the afternoon the qadi of the city might hold court in the Thread Market, but on the whole he preferred to judge cases in his home. Later, during the early years of the protectorate, the qadi's court was permanently moved to the Thread Market.[4]

A large entrepôt called the Fundūq Askūr, which had served as a school of medicine in the fourteenth century and is presently the qadi's court, also opened on to the Thread Market. Its main entrance, however, was reached by continuing down the artery from the Gate of Ceuta, and passing the entrance into the Thread Market and a street on the right called the Old Jewish Quarter (*al-mallāḥ al-qadīm*). There one abruptly came to what looked like a dead end. By turning to the left for a few yards and then right again it was nonetheless possible to follow the street further southward. The main entrance to the Fundūq Askūr was just on the left of that bend in the road, while to the right stood an important caravansary called the Courtyard (*al-qāʿa*). In the latter, fresh and clarified butter, honey, raw wool, dried beef, cumin, olives, figs, dates, raisins, walnuts, almonds, henna dye and kat were sold in quantity. Several notaries worked there to keep a record of all purchases—the names of buyer and seller, quantity of merchandise, and prices agreed upon. Thus it was in and around the Grand Market Place and the Thread Market that most products from the countryside came into the hands of the city people.

Retail trade in manufactured goods was carried out on two streets. One of them, the Street of Sellers of Silk Thread, was a long, slightly winding arcade with some fifteen shops on each side which began outside the entrance to the Fundūq Askūr. Most of its shops were owned, until late in the nineteenth century, by Jewish merchants and craftsmen—sellers of gold and

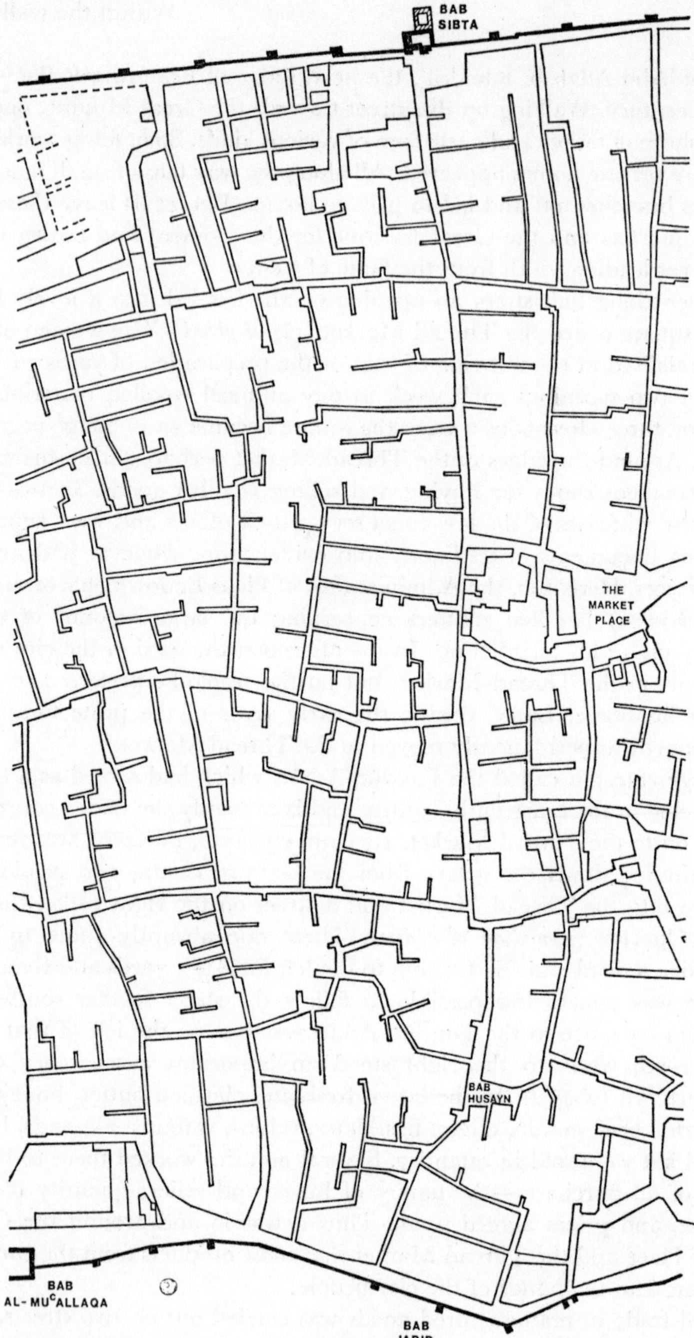

Fig. 7 The commercial area from the Ceuta Gate (Bāb Sibta)

silver, silversmiths and engravers, manufacturers and sellers of silk thread, tailors who worked in velvet and sewed tents for the tribal qa'ids, and cobblers. Several yards before the end of this arcade, where the garden areas began, the other street for retail trade branched off to the left and led back to the Great Market Place. The first half-dozen shops on both its sides belonged to Jewish craftsmen, mostly tinsmiths. Next came the shops of Muslim shoemakers, which extended one after another on both sides of the street as far as the Market Place. About a hundred feet down this Street of the Shoemakers an opening on the left led into a very small arcade called the Bazaar of the Jews (*qaiṣariyyat al-yahūd*), in which some seven or eight Jewish cloth merchants had stores. Slightly further down the street on the right, in another small arcade, called the New Bazaar, about a dozen merchants—Muslims, in this case—sold cloth. Yet farther along, on the left, stood the Bazaar of Columns (*al-qaiṣariyya dhāt as-sawārī*), the main centre for the retail sale of cloth and woollen goods. There were approximately twenty shops in this bazaar and on the two small streets that extended from it.

The Street of the Shoemakers was one of the main and most crowded thoroughfares of the city. Except for one connecting alley where perfumes and spices were sold, all the activities of this street had something to do with the manufacture of shoes. There were several *funduqs* where leather was stored or worked, and tens of shops owned or rented by shoemakers. This, at least, was the case until late into the nineteenth century while the craft still flourished. From around 1890 some of these shops became the property of retail cloth merchants, and from then until the coming of the French in 1912 the retail cloth trade steadily expanded while the production and selling of shoes, as well as silk thread and jewellery, declined drastically. Thus by 1912 the Street of Sellers of Silk Thread and almost half the Street of Shoemakers had come to be considered part of one continuous cloth Bazaar.

This area of about a square mile between the bazaar and the market place was the centre of economic activity in Salé for the great majority of its wholesale and retail merchants and craftsmen. No houses or living quarters broke up the concentration of entrepôts, stores and workshops within this area, and the clamorous activity that filled its streets during the daytime gave way at night to emptiness and silence. Late in the nineteenth century this business district began to grow. The commercial area expanded into the gardens to the south, a complex of new stores rose in the centre of the Great Market Place, and the cloth bazaar continued to increase in size along the Street of the Shoemakers. Changes in the ways of earning a livelihood during the period 1880–1930 altered the landscape of the city. Most of the numerous soap factories and all the countless water and wind mills had by the late 1880s entirely disappeared. The gardens that had been cultivated within the walls of the city had become few and far between.[5] Both the commercial and the residential areas had expanded at the expense of these gardens.

People who became wealthy late in the nineteenth century built houses on those properties within the walls of the city that had formed in the past an agricultural belt between the built-up areas and the ramparts. By 1912 only

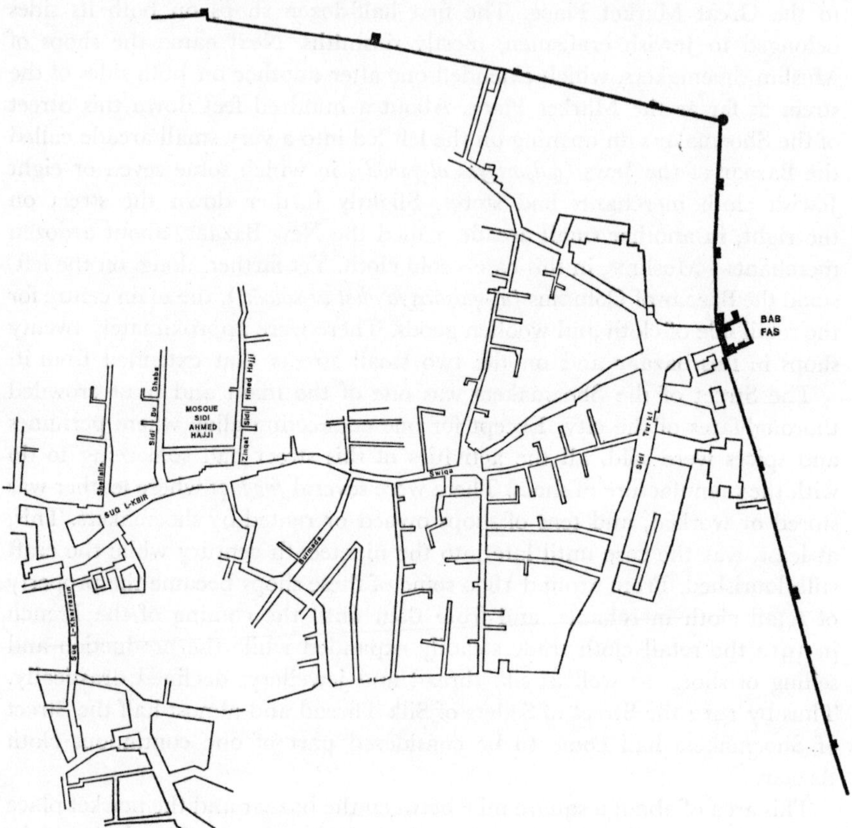

Fig. 8 Entering the market place from the Fez Gate (Bāb Fās)

forty-two irrigated gardens remained in Salé, and by 1930 most of these had been built up.

The quarters

It is difficult to reconstruct with any certitude the pattern of residential quarters in the city over the hundred-year period beginning in 1830. If we judge according to the situation at the end of the century, the area north and east of the commercial centre was inhabited largely by people of rural origin, many of whom came from the hinterland of Salé. To some extent they settled in quarters according to their places of origin. Thus the Ḥuṣayn, Sahūl and Zemmour tended to live near the Small Market (*as-suwayqa*)—a square about a third of the distance up the street leading from the Gate of Fez to the Great Market Place; those from the Doukkala and Chaouia (the inland areas behind Casablanca and El-Jadida) often settled in a quarter known as The Line (*al-ṣaff*)—slightly beyond and to the north of the Small Market; while many of the Swāsa and Sahrāwa (people from the Sus valley and the Sahara or Tafilalt) lived in the caravansaries around the market place. From the market place by way of the Street of the Barbers and on up the Ascent of the Qadi and the Great Mosque represented a similar demarcation. Most of the area to the north of this line, as far as the ramparts, was also populated by relatively new, poor agricultural workers, but these tended to come from the ʿĀmir, Banū Ḥasan and the Gharb. These 'popular' areas and their inhabitants were sometimes considered marginal to the city and its society, although there was no strict separation of the city or of its population into districts. Nonetheless these quarters had a particularly rural feeling about them, and their inhabitants were often referred to as outsiders, *barrānīs*, in contrast to the relatively old, urban society.[6]

The core residential area of the townspeople proper was to the north-west and near the Great Mosque. Muḥammad b. Saʿīd, governor from 1861 to 1892, and his son and successor ʿAbd Allah, who governed from 1892 to 1907, lived here in a sumptuous house. Quite close by, in the quarter of Bāb Ḥuṣayn and on a street named after Salé's governor in the 1840s, Abū ʿAmr Fannīsh, stood the house of the qadi of Salé, Ḥājj ʿAlī ʿAwwād.[7] Since both these officials held court in their own homes, it may be said that the administrative centre of the city was in this general residential area. Most of the high officials and important people lived in this area, with the exception of those, noted before, who at mid-nineteenth century had their homes near the Great Market Place.

The locus of these residential quarters was and is the Great Mosque. At sixty feet above sea level, these quarters and the mosque are at the highest point in the city and one reaches them only after a tiring climb. The Great Mosque towers over Salé, and it equals in size and grandeur the Qarawiyyin of Fez, Morocco's largest and finest mosque. The streets near the Mosque have no shops, only high, whitewashed walls, pierced here and there by large wooden doors usually painted in a dark colour and decorated with enormous nailheads and a circular metal knocker, or a bronze hand of Fatima. These streets are extremely calm and peaceful in contrast to the commercial areas, and the twisting streets and unexpected views of arches and lines of buildings are often strikingly beautiful.

These residential areas—both the northern half of the city predominantly inhabited by those with rural origins and the south-western section of the *madīna*, with its urban-rooted and wealthier population—were loosely divided into quarters (coll. *ḥūma*, pl. *ḥūmāt*). Habous records from 1868

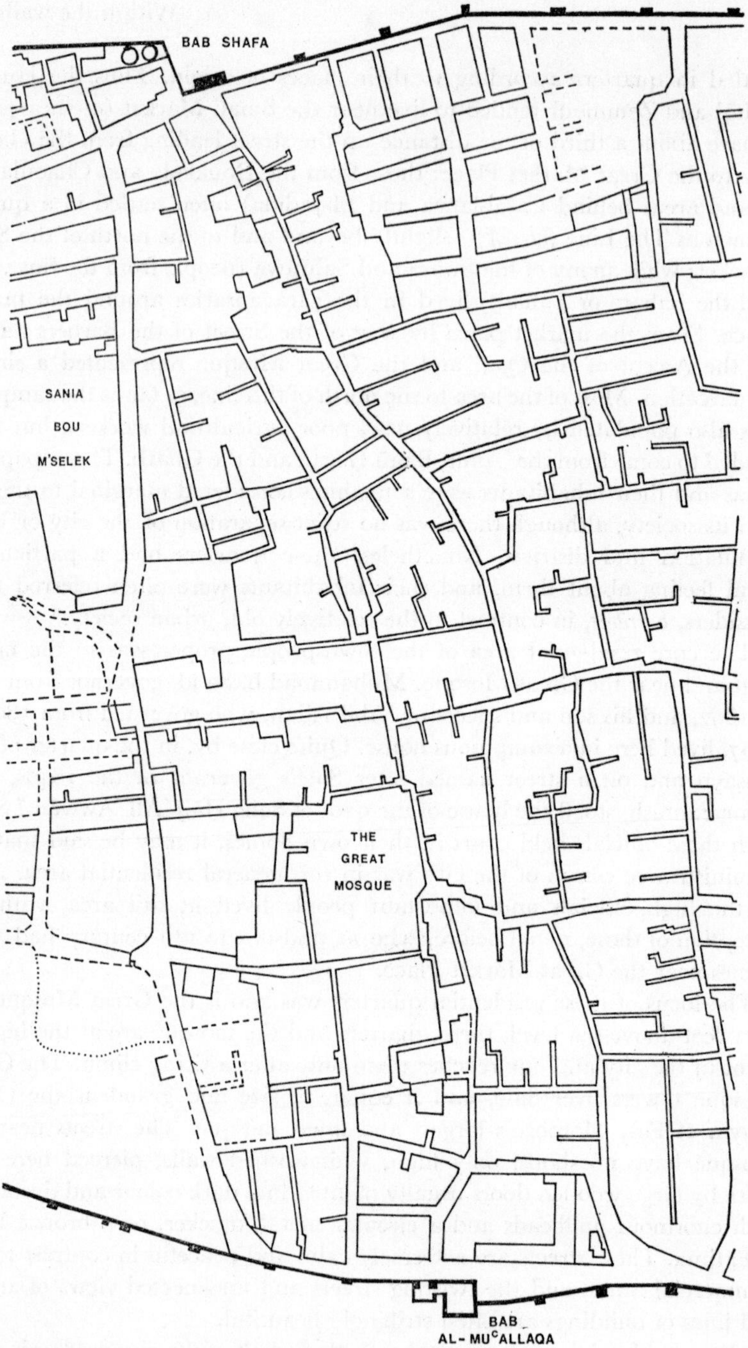

Fig. 9 The residential quarter of the Great Mosque

mention eight quarters in these residential districts:[8] (1) Ṭalʿa, (2) Ra's ash-Shajara, (3) Bāb Ḥuṣayn, (4) al-Mallāḥ al-Qadīm (in Bāb Ḥuṣayn), (5) Bāb Sibta, (6) al-Bulayda (in Bāb Sibta), (7) al-Ṣaff, (8) as-Suwayqa.[9] The French survey of 1918[10] lists five additional quarters: (1) Zanāta, (2) Jazzārīn, (3) Sīdī Mashīsh, (4) Darb ash-Shammākh, (5) Qulayʿa or Bāb Fās. Naciri includes an additional five: (1) Bāb Musaddiq, (2) Qusaṭla, (3) Bāb Shāfa, (4) Darb Khiyār, (5) Bāb Fard.[11]

Some of the discrepancies in these lists are not difficult to explain. All the quarters from the French survey and from Naciri's list were built up after 1868, with the exception of Zanata and Darb Khiyār. The absence of Zanāta in the 1868 Habous list can be explained only by assuming that there simply was no Habous property in that quarter. Darb Khiyār, on the other hand, was probably considered by the Habous authorities as a part of the quarter of al-Bulayda. What we have, then, is a core of nine quarters in the residential areas for the period around 1868, three additional ones by 1918, and four more at a slightly later period.[12]

In the mind of a native Slawi at the turn of this century a neighbourhood or quarter (*ḥūma*) was a vague spatial notion, not an area with exact boundaries, although old people living then told their children and grandchildren that in the past quarters had been closed off from one another by gates. According to Ibn ʿAli, the governor Abū ʿAmr Fannīsh had had these arched stone-and-wood gates built in 1840 following a bombardment by French ships.[13] By 1900 only traces of some of the gates remained, and the quarters lacked a clearly defined identity, spatial or jurisdictional. From the point of view of organisation and administration there were apparently no quarter 'chiefs' (*muqaddim*) in Salé before the French protectorate.[14]

Nonetheless there were vague associations with and hierarchical conceptions about certain neighbourhoods, a feeling of rivalry (*tanāfus*), especially among children, who engaged in forays into respective territories armed with stones. Also, the quarters of Bāb Ḥuṣayn, Ṭalʿa, and Bāb Sibta would celebrate the *ʿAnṣara*, a specifically Moroccan agricultural holiday held in June, each of them lighting a separate bonfire. But for most purposes a quarter meant one or several contiguous streets (coll. *derb*, pl. *drūba*), where friends or kin might live, where boys went to the same Quranic school, met at the same ovens to deliver and pick up bread for their families, grew up together, and perhaps formed lasting friendships. Their fathers often prayed together in the same mosque, perhaps frequented the same religious order; their mothers and sisters visited or chatted from the rooftops. Face-to-face relationships among the inhabitants of the same quarter were likely to be more common and casual than relationships with people living in other neighbourhoods. But such interactions were random and unstructured and did not serve to define the neighbourhood as a meaningful social entity. Every quarter included a heterogeneous mixture of inhabitants from various social networks, kinship groups, occupations or religious orders.

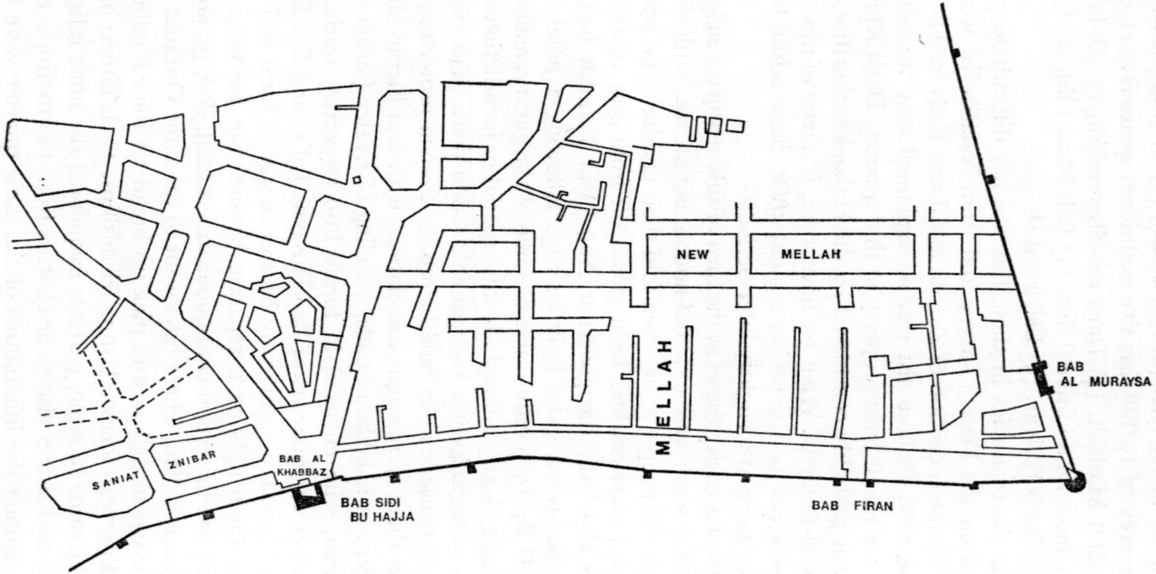

Fig. 10 The Jewish quarter and the new quarter of Sidi Turki

Exceptions to this relatively loose pattern of residence were (1) the Jewish quarter or mellah (*al-mallāḥ*), which had been completely segregated since early in the nineteenth century, and (2) the general division of the city between the poorer, less urban, more rural and more proletarian area in the north-east and the other wealthy urban area in the south-west of the city. Thus religion was one factor in the pattern of residence, life style was another. Separation between townspeople and outsiders was not absolute, yet on the whole each of these groups tended to reside in a separate area, each of which included a set of rather poorly differentiated quarters.[15]

The notion of quarter had no social significance. People brought together by residential proximity did not share a common identity or feel any solidarity on that basis. Agnates, affines, friends or partners might wish to live near-by one another for purposes of convenience, but they rarely managed to do so. Most nuclear families established a new home (coll. *ḍāṛ*, pl. *ḍyuṛ*) wherever they could, depending on the availability of property. The individual house was a closed off, private universe unto itself. Visiting among relatives and friends was widespread, and at times quite informal, but such visits did not create particularistic ties within a quarter. Outside the walls of his house a man could pick and choose on an individual basis those with whom he needed or wanted to interact. The neighbourhood set no boundaries, except those of chance, on his choices.[16]

The interior space of houses

As we have seen, several large arteries stretched across Salé, connecting one central point to another. One of the principal streets leading to the Great Mosque was named at its lower extreme the Old Jewish Quarter, then, farther on, Treetop, and finally the Ascent of the Medersa. Private residences lined both sides of this street, but the only doorways to be seen were those of two or three small mosques, several Quranic schools, a public bath, one or two public ovens, and the shops of a few grocers and sellers of coal. The main entrances to the houses were reached by way of cul-de-sacs that branched off this main street all along its length. Several streets intersected this thoroughfare and they in turn had the same pattern.

The plan of a house seldom departed from the standard model, regardless of size or richness of decor. A single entrance door opened on to a small room and then a corridor. The corridor led to an open-air courtyard, which might include trees or a fountain. On three or four sides of this court were long, narrow rooms with high ceilings and large doors. Columns in the courtyard supported a roof that extended slightly beyond each room, covering part of the court and providing shade. All light and ventilation came from the open court. If the owner of a house was wealthy the interior walls were inlaid with ornamental tiles and the ceilings constructed from sculptured wood. Furnishings, like architecture, tended to be uniform. Low wooden benches with heavy stuffed wool mattresses on them lined the walls of each room and served as sofas during the day and beds at night. There might be large, four-poster, European-type beds at either end of the room if the family had chosen to adopt a style of furnishing that became popular during the later part of the nineteenth century. Coverings for mattresses and the stuffed pillows that adorned them, drapes and curtains were made from brightly embroidered velvet cloth or other fancy materials, if the family could afford them. Wool-stuffed mattresses and ornamental coverings indicated a family's wealth, or at least the wealth of the woman's family, for traditionally a bride received them as gifts from her parents. One or two of these rooms were used to receive guests and to hold celebrations. Other rooms, reserved for the family, allowed the women to sit, talk and sew in complete privacy during the day. At night all rooms were used for sleeping.[17]

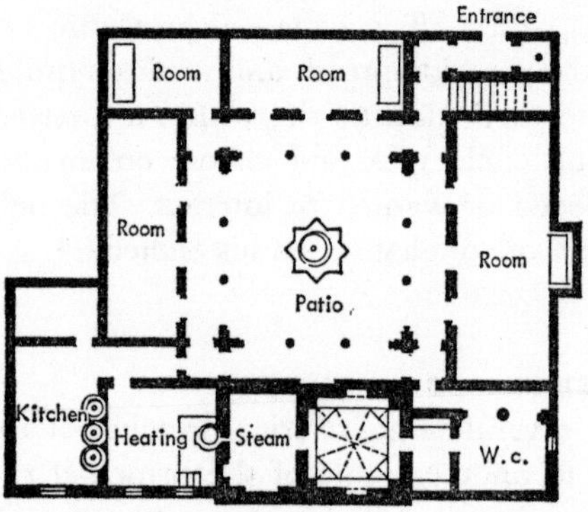

Fig. 11 House layout

An essential part of a house was *ed-dwīra*, that is, one or several small rooms where cooking was done, or a compound of rooms where servants lived and cooked and where food was stored. The most elaborate houses had a garden of fruit trees (*riyāḍ*) connected to the house by a passage (*mduwwiz*), and at the end of the garden a small room where the family or friends took tea. Some houses near the Gate of Ceuta also had a stable (*kherba*) for riding animals, and perhaps cows, sheep and goats. Those families who owned separate fruit or vegetable gardens, within the city or near by, built in them permanent picnic structures (*menzeh*) where they would go on an afternoon excursion or to spend several months during the summer.[18]

In some cases an extended family—a man and wife, their children and young married sons—lived in the same house. Until his death the father controlled the family property, and he might control his sons, married or not, by keeping them under the same roof. When he died the married sons would either divide the house among themselves or separate. Most married men, however, whatever their means, owned their own home, and both the family and the house were referred to by the same word—*ḍāṛ*.

In the part of the city populated by old urban families, and even to some extent in the more rural-like quarters, houses were interspersed so that rich and poor often lived side by side and humble houses stood next to imposing ones. Streets or impasses did not enclose separate economic strata of the city. The differentiation of various areas of the city that has been discussed was based on cultural rather than economic criteria. The good reputation of a certain street or quarter at a given time resulted from the fact that one or several personages of the city lived there. As individuals or their descendants rose or fell in prestige the reputations of streets and quarters fluctuated accordingly. Nonetheless the contrast between the clusters of people and houses around the Great Market Place, as opposed to those around the Great Mosque, remained sharp.

Places of congregation

Ibn Khaldūn described mosques as the 'consolation of Muslims, the desire of their hearts, the sacred asylum of their religion'.[19] The people of Salé appear to have shared this outlook, for scattered about the city were some sixty places of prayer, most of them with minarets. On Friday noon prayers were held in the Great Mosque, in the mosque of Sīdī Ḥmed Ḥajjī near the Market Place and, when the French came, in the Shahba mosque, rebuilt on ancient ruins that may have been the site of the original Great Mosque of the city.

In the mosques men and children prayed, studied and simply met to talk. Scattered throughout the city were tombs of saints and lodges of religious orders which sometimes also served as mosques. In the lodges followers of religious orders would meet daily or several times a week, especially on Friday afternoons. The orders usually associated with urban life—the Darqāwa and the Tijāniyya—had their lodges near the Great Mosque in the area of the old urban population, while another six or seven lodges were indiscriminately spread about all the residential areas.

People also congregated in the twenty caravansaries of Salé, all of which were in the commercial districts or along the arteries leading to them. And they met together in the four public baths (Sng. *ḥammām*) of the city. Water for the mosques, *ḥammāms* and homes was supplied by canals and by twenty-four public wells (sng., *siqqāya*), although only eight of them constantly had water. A few of the wealthiest people in the city built baths and dug wells in their homes, but most people received water from carriers who brought it from wells or near-by springs. After 1912 the protectorate authorities greatly improved the water supply and sewage systems that had been previously supported by the administration of pious endowments.

Most of the buildings and institutions that we normally consider public, such as schools, post offices and municipal buildings were brought to Salé by the French. Many of the mosques had housed schools, of course, but the first government-supported school was opened in 1914, exclusively for the sons of the notables. Postal services had been started several years before the protectorate by Germans in an office near the Gate of Fez and were expanded under the French. The protectorate authorities built the city's first municipality. These buildings did not greatly affect the physical plan of Salé during the first decades of the protectorate, nor did the barracks of the small French community of civil servants and soldiers who settled on the sandy area between the river and the southern walls. While a new European city with all the amenities of modern living rose to satisfy five thousand European settlers across the river in Rabat, the social composition and the outer appearance of Salé changed little. To be sure, a steamer that plied the Bou Regreg and a bridge built several miles upstream made Rabat more accessible to Slawis than ever before. The easy accessibility to the new capital may in part explain the lack of construction and investment in Salé and the consequent image of an unchanging city and society.

The Jewish quarter

The Jewish population of Salé had been moved early in the nineteenth century from their homes interspersed among their Muslim neighbours to the present Jewish quarter or mellah.[20] One of the areas where the Jews used to live came to be called the Old Mellah, in distinction to the New Mellah, which rose on the former site of the old Marinid port at the south-east corner of the city. Ibn ʿAli reports that when the new quarter was constructed in 1807 it contained two hundred houses, more than twenty shops, two ovens and two mills.[21] Its plan resembled the rest of the *madīna*: a long thoroughfare extended from the Gate of the Mellah to the monumental Gate of the Small Port built by the Marinids in the thirteenth century.[22] Along this artery were shops, synagogues and a few houses. From the northern side of the street one could enter any of ten impasses, each one predominantly inhabited by or named after an extended family. Almost all of Salé's Jews carried out their business and affairs in the *madīna* proper or in Rabat. But at night the Gate of the Mellah was shut, and the Jewish quarter became a kind of city within a city.

Empty spaces, cemeteries, ramparts

In 1894 a new quarter was being built in Salé. Separated from the Mellah by a large open space of pasture and irrigated gardens, on land where centuries before shops for the dyeing of leather once stood, it extended as far as the Shahba mosque. This area became the quarter of the Small Fort (*al-quliyʿa*), and soon included the prosperous new business district which spread in the early years of the protectorate south from the Gate of Fez along the street called Sīdī Turkī. The built-up area of Salé had begun to expand into garden areas in the 1880s. When the French arrived forty-two irrigated gardens, covering an area of about thirty-five hectares—over a third of the city's total area—formed a kind of belt which separated the built-up area from the ramparts.[23] By 1930 most of these remaining gardens had been converted into residential or commercial areas, and by the end of the Second World War only a very few still remained.

Old people in the city reported that in the process of digging up gardens to lay foundations, ruins of previous construction were again and again revealed, and in some gardens signs of whole commercial quarters seem to have been found. These reports about layers of civilization within the city suggest the difficulties involved in attempting to reconstruct the history of the physical structure and morphology of a city without the use of archaeological research. Available bits and pieces of oral tradition or written evidence allow us to sketch only the general lines of changing spatial patterns.

Another characteristic of Salé's topography was that the cemetery, of Sīdī Bin ʿĀshir, covered about one-fourth of the intramural area. It extended from the northern to the southern wall, on one side, and from the western wall parallel to the ocean as far as the gardens behind the Great Mosque and the mausoleum of Sīdī ʿAbd Allah b. Ḥassūn. The southern wall (built by the Marinids in the thirteenth century) divided what once had been a single cemetery outside an earlier set of city walls. The cemetery of Sīdī Hishām, outside the wall, has layers of graves superimposed upon one another, and the tombstones on the surface of the ground, some of which have been used to construct the southern wall, go back as far as the thirteenth century. In earlier times Salé may have resembled the spatial pattern common to cities in other parts of the Muslim world in which cemeteries surrounded cities' walls and choked their growth.[24]

The existence of this large cemetery within the walls gave Salé an unusual spatial pattern and also influenced the city's character in another way. The mausoleum of the fourteenth-century mystic Sīdī Bin ʿĀshir was within the cemetery and served to encourage rural people to cross through the city to visit the saint's tomb. Over the centuries pilgrimages to the mausoleum have brought large numbers of people into the city from the surrounding countryside and beyond it. A small sanitarium, built beside the saint's tomb in the eighteenth century and continually enlarged thereafter, and the annual fair held there attracted substantial numbers of pilgrims.[25] The cemetery and its mausoleum contributed to Salé's widespread reputation as a city of religion—of learning and blessedness. The saints buried within its large and small cemeteries, lodges, tombs, and rooms of individual houses were thought to demonstrate that Salé was, as its historians repeatedly emphasised, a city of *awliyāʾ*, of friends of God.

What of the actual shape and size of nineteenth-century Salé, of those formidable walls that caused European travellers to refer to the city literally and figuratively as a fortress of fanaticism?[26] Salé's ramparts, a trapezoid of some 4,700 yards in circumference, have been referred to above as western (facing the ocean), southern (facing the river bank), northern and eastern. In fact the shape of the *madīna* is oriented by and parallels the coastline, which runs north-west to south-east. For Salé's historians their city's orientation was determined by the *qibla,* the direction where lay the Kaʿba of Mecca and to which all Muslims turn at the time of prayer. Thus what I have called the eastern wall is referred to in Arabic documents as the *qibla,* or southern wall, and the other directions follow from that. The two bases of the trapezoid, what I have called the northern and southern walls, were each approximately a mile long, while the wall hugging the reefs of the coast was about six hundred yards and that to the east, pierced by the Gate of Fez, somewhat longer. Constructed from padded clay and red sandstone, some six feet in thickness, these ramparts varied from sixteen to thirty-five feet in height. These limits on the city's space had been fixed during the thirteenth century, even though the walls had often been repaired or fortified.[27]

The Suspended Gate along the western wall[28] opened on to the cemetery of Sīdī Hishām and gave access to the *muṣallā* where prayers were performed on the mornings of the Great and Small Feasts and in cases of drought or eclipses of the sun or moon. The *muṣallā,* a long, white stoned wall adorned only by a simple prayer niche, stood in the middle of the cemetery. When the male Slawis performed prayers there, as I have seen on several occasions, they presented an impressive and dramatic spectacle of a community united by religious bonds. The cemetery also served as a place for promenades and offered a spectacular view of Rabat, the mouth of the Bou Regreg and the Atlantic. The fortifications of the city offered splendid panoramas. At the north-west corner the Great Tower (*burj al-kabīr* or *ar-ruknī,* the Pillar), originally built during the thirteenth century and repaired and fortified with cannons after the French attack of 1861, controlled the approaches to Salé from the ocean. The other end of the western wall, with a view to the ocean and the mouth of the river, was guarded by the Tower of Tears (*burj ad-dumūʿ*), built in 1845.

Between the two forts stood the Old Scaffold (*ṣaqāla al-qadīma*), fortified under Sultan Muḥammad b. ʿAbd Allah (d. 1790). A list of 278 of the artilleryman (*ṭūbjiyya*) who manned these forts in the middle of the nineteenth century suggests that about one-tenth of the adult male population served in this capacity.[29] In 1852 eighteen cannons and two large mortars were brought from England to increase the defences of the city. The Slawis by then were living under the continual threat of bombardment and feared an invasion by Europeans from the sea. All the forts except the one at the Gate of Ceuta (where in the seventeenth century the governor used to hold

a Ḥājj ʿAlī ʿAwwād, qadi *b* Muḥammad aṣ-Ṣubīhī, governor

c Rabbi Raphaël Ankaoua *d* Slawis in a welcoming party for the visit of Kaiser Wilhelm II, Tangier, 1905

Plate 2

a Gate of the Small Port (bāb al-muraysa)

b Aerial view of Salé, *c.* 1950. In the centre, the minaret of the Great Mosque

court) had fortifications. A storehouse for ammunition (*dār al-barūd*), also built at mid-century, was just inside the eastern wall, between the Gate of Fez and the Gate of the Small Port. These nineteenth-century attempts to fortify the defences of the city against an expected French assault, although they proved quite insufficient, demonstrate a will to military resistance which remained strong until late in the century.

Security within the town was carefully regulated and controlled. Of its five gates, all were closed early in the evening, except the Gate of Fez, which remained open later to allow stragglers to return before nightfall. Guards patrolled the streets throughout the night and made sure that everyone found a roof for himself.[30] Visitors to the city without acquaintances stayed in one of the numerous caravansaries, while the poor usually slept in the rooms adjoining the mausoleum of Sīdī Bin ʿĀshir. Most people from outside had friends or relatives with whom they might spend the night.

During the day soldiers controlled entrance to Salé. Anyone bringing products to market would pay the obligatory tax, known troublemakers were not permitted into the city, and outsiders were not allowed to bring in their arms. On several occasions special measures of security were taken, e.g. following attacks by robbers who had ridden into the Bazaar and threatened shopkeepers with their rifles. Prior to the late years of the nineteenth century, when some of the rural people became especially menacing, the Slawis had counted on themselves rather than the soldiers of the governor for protection. Many Slawis kept rifles at home, and if they heard that the tribes were in upheaval and might come to Salé they prepared to defend themselves. At the end of the century about one hundred government soldiers were garrisoned in Dār Bin ʿAttār, near the Bazaar, to protect the city against marauders. But by that time internal tensions and the fear of invasion by one of the European powers had made the city's allegiance to the sultan suspect, and government troops were on hand to quell any disturbances should they arise.

There were several other cemeteries outside the walls of Salé in addition to that of Sīdī Hishām along the river. Along the right side of the beginning of the route to Fez was the cemetery of Sīdī Bil-ʿAbbās, and across from it and a bit farther down was the Jewish cemetery. An earlier Jewish cemetery probably existed above Sīdī Bil-ʿAbbās in Biṭṭāna, but it had been abandoned by the eighteenth century. The area beyond the Gate of Fez near Sīdī Bil-ʿAbbās and the Zāwiyat an-Nussāk which had been settled in the Middle Ages lay in ruins.

To the north of Salé a large and finely built aqueduct, the Wall of Arches (*sūr al-aqwās*), enclosed the gardens to the north of the city and provided an additional rampart. As the post-World War II decade was to show, these gardens outside the walls provided the necessary space for urban growth. The cemeteries just outside the walls did not form a collar round the city which choked its expansion. Construction remained within the walls essentially because population density was not heavy. Even with the urbanisation that accompanied the early years of the protectorate there was for several decades still ample room within the city for growth, by transforming gardens into built-up areas. After 1930, and especially after World War II, the city spread well beyond its walls. By that time, of course, the number of its population had reached over 100,000, an increase of about fivefold.[31]

A note on demography

The society of Salé, judging from the great variety in the origins of its inhabitants, was much more permeable to outside migration than one would suspect. From documents and from interviews with old men I compiled a list of the urban families which were known and respected during the period under study; I soon discovered that the place of origin and date of arrival in the city for most of these ninety families was fairly common knowledge.[32] The majority had migrated from the Moroccan countryside; some had come from other North African cities; and a few traced their origins to Muslim Spain or the Arab east. Their migration to Salé spread back in time over a period of six centuries and in no discernible pattern except that each century, including the nineteenth, had witnessed the arrival of some of these families. The information on migration indicates that the population was continually added to by new arrivals and that these in time became integrated into the social fabric of the community. The city had been open-ended, its society a kind of melting pot. Thus the large-scale migration to Morocco's port cities during the late nineteenth century and the massive urbanisation of the twentieth had been preceded by similar processes, though, to be sure, on a lesser scale. Yet despite this constant movement of population from countryside to city Morocco remained essentially a land of peasants rather than townsmen.

The distribution and growth of population in the country prior to the twentieth century will probably never be known with any certitude.[33] Estimates of the number of inhabitants between 1830 and 1900 vary from three million to eight and a half million. The most reliable estimate seems to be advanced by N. Larras, a French officer who was in Morocco between 1898 and 1906, viz. 4,600,000 (Atlantic plains, 2,200,000; Rif and Atlas mountains, 1,900,000; Sahara, 500,000). Approximately 422,000, or 10·9 per cent of that number, lived in cities.[34] The first estimate by the protectorate authorities, in 1914, gives a population in the French zone of 4,550,000. Of these, the vast majority—approximately 88 per cent—were sedentary villagers, transhumants or nomads. Fewer than 600,000, or 12 per cent, lived in cities.[35] The 1931 census of the French zone showed a population of 5,370,200, of whom 875,000 (16·2 per cent) lived in cities.[36]

The pattern of growth of population and the distribution of people in the countryside and in cities is suggested in tables I and II.[37]

The 'imperial cities', the capitals of political life in nineteenth-century Morocco (Fez, Marrakesh, Meknes and Rabat) contained in 1900 almost half the total urban population. From the economic point of view, Rabat and Salé should be conceived of as a single urban centre—'the port of the Bou Regreg'. The twin cities with their combined population ranked in size just behind Fez and Marrakesh (and, in 1931, Casablanca), and these were the country's largest urban market places. Although until the protectorate period Rabat–Salé was the most populous port in all of Morocco, it handled less maritime commerce than Tetuan (the port of Fez) or Essaouira (the

Table I Population figures (percentages in brackets)

	1900	*1931*	*1971*
A. Total population of Morocco			
	4,600,000	5,370,200[a]	15,379,259
B. Urban population			
	422,000 (10·9)	875,000 (16·2)[a]	5,403,466 (35·1)

C. The urban population of 1931: ethnic composition of the ten largest cities (French zone only)

	Total population	*Muslims*	*Jews*	*Europeans*[b]
Marrakesh	195,122	164,727 (84·5)	21,607 (11)	8,788 (4·5)
Casablanca	163,108	85,167 (52·2)	19,960 (12·3)	57,981 (31·5)
Fez	112,463	90,379 (80)	7,826 (7·3)	14,258 (12·7)
Meknes	57,004	36,466 (63·9)	7,745 (13·7)	12,793 (22·4)
Rabat	55,348	27,986 (50·6)	4,218 (7·6)	23,144 (41·8)
Oujda	30,150	13,164 (43·8)	1,890 (6·2)	15,096 (50)
Safi	26,201	21,253 (81·2)	3,285 (12·5)	1,663 (6·3)
Salé	25,940	22,145 (84·5)	2,387 (9·2)	1,408 (5·4)
Kenitra	21,151	12,886 (60·9)	365 (2·4)	7,900 (36·7)
El Jadida	20,834	15,411 (73·9)	3,288 (15·9)	2,135 (10·2)

[a] French zone only.

[b] Europeans included French, Spanish and Italian. The breakdown of the total population was as follows:

Muslims	5,070,000
Jews	125,000
French	128,200
Spanish	22,700
Italians	12,600
Algerians	11,700

The French population had nearly doubled between 1926 (66,220) and 1931.

Source: see n. 37.

port of Marrakesh). Throughout the late nineteenth century Rabat and Salé were outpaced in demographic growth by other Moroccan cities. Where the overall demographic increase in the coastal cities steadily rose –50 per cent in 1835–65 and more than that from 1865–95—Rabat and Salé showed almost no growth in population.[38]

Table II Urban growth

	1834–36	*1856–57*	*1866–67*	*1900*	*1931*	*1970*
Fez				95,000	112,463	322,327
Marrakesh				60,000	195,122	332,741
Meknes			50,000(?)	20,000	57,004	248,369
Rabat	22,000	25,000	26,000	25,000	55,348	367,620
Salé	14,000			15,000	25,940	155,557
Tetuan	16,000	22,000	21,000	22,000		139,105
Tangier	7,500	10,000	12,000	30,000		187,894
Essaouira (Mogador)	10,000	14,000	16,000	22,000		
Casablanca	700	1,600	6,000	21,000	163,108	1,500,114
El Jadida (Mazagan)	800	1,500	4,000	20,000	20,834	55,501
Azemmour				10,000		
Safi	8,000	10,000	11,000	10,000	26,201	129,113
El-Ksar El-Kbir				10,000		48,262
Oujda				8,000	30,150	175,532
Tarudant				7,000		
Ouezzane				6,000		
Larache	2,500	4,500	5,000	5,000		
Moulay Idris				5,000		
Asilah				4,000		
Demnat				4,000		
Chechaouen				4,000		
Taza				4,000		55,157
Sefrou				4,000		
Amizmiz				3,000		
Beni Mellal				3,000		
Debdou				2,000		
Settat				2,000		
Kenitra					21,151	139,206
Khouribga						73,667
Agadir						61,192

Source: see n. 37.

The number of inhabitants in Salé during the century under study increased from an estimated 14,000 in 1836 to 25,817 (including 1,285 Europeans and 2,387 Jews) in 1931.[39] Excluding Europeans (who did not live in the city before 1912), this represents a growth of approximately 43 per cent. The greatest part of this increase took place during the eighteen years following the beginning of the protectorate in 1912. The first census, carried out in 1913, fixed Salé's population at 18,800, including 1,500 Jews and several hundred Europeans.[40] Thus the number of inhabitants between 1830 and the beginning of the protectorate appears to have increased by about 25 per cent. Ibn ʿAli's manuscript dated 1895 (although internal evidence suggests that at least part of it was written later) estimates that there were three thousand houses in Salé. It is generally thought that a household comprised, on the average, five persons. This would also suggest a figure of approximately 15,000 inhabitants in 1895.[41]

Before the French protectorate had affected the mortality rate in Morocco (by 1930 the annual rate of increase was approaching 3 per cent),[42] the rate of death probably matched or bettered the rate of birth. Sickness and disease acted as powerful restraints on population growth. Epidemics of cholera and plague had reached major proportions in Rabat and Salé in 1855, 1868 and 1877–78, and large numbers of people had died as a result.[43] Rural migration probably replenished an urban population whose numbers diminished because of early deaths. The evidence for migration into and out of the city during this period unfortunately cannot be strengthened by statistics. Yet interviews revealed that among the best known Slawi families in the early years of this century there were an appreciable number, approximately twenty, who had migrated from the countryside during the nineteenth century. This suggests that the urban elite, as well as the total community of townspeople, was not a closed group, and in this respect among others Salé can be characterised as an open-ended city. Moreover tens of families mentioned in documents of the nineteenth century either died out or left Salé permanently, while at least some of the newcomers succeeded in putting down social roots by allying themselves with old families and establishing themselves as an important economic force. Despite the indications of steady movement into and out of the city at all social levels, the old people of Salé whom I interviewed in 1966–67 stated with assurance that at least until 1930 the society of the city had remained closed and exclusive, that in the 'old Salé' one never saw an unfamiliar face and that all had descended from long lines of Slawi families. This contradictory evidence within the oral and written sources will be discussed in the following chapter.

Finally, the population of Salé, though small was relatively dense. In 1918 an average of 240 people per hectare lived in the seventy-five hectares of the *madīna* proper. In the Mellah, an area of four hectares, the average density was 375 people per hectare.[44] With a relatively small population living in limited space, relationships were face-to-face and anonymity was rare indeed. These factors of compactness help to explain how outsiders could become integrated with relative ease into a tightly knit society, and why informants considered the inhabitants of Salé as 'one family' (*ʿāila waḥda*) despite the heterogeneity of the urban population.

Part II The fabric of society

In the four chapters that follow the population of Salé is discussed as a complex community united by certain social and cultural ties, interests and values, and divided by others. Chapter III deals with types or categories of townsmen as described by the traditional historians of the time, and with the kinds of interactions and relationships that gave form to the groupings that are sociologically identifiable from our vantage point. Chapter IV treats the cultural ideals of the community, as embodied in saints and scholars, and seeks to show how ascription by descent and achievement by learning defined the characteristics of these men and the ideals that they represented. In chapter V the beliefs and rituals of the community are discussed as shared values, on the one hand, and as conflicting interpretations of values, on the other. Chapter VI looks at the dominant culture of the community as it was transmitted from generation to generation within the family and through education. Throughout these chapters an attempt has been made to indicate continuities and transformations that marked the social and cultural life of the people living in the city during the century between 1830 and 1930.

III Categories and relationships

All of them [the Slawis], or most, are noble scholars and among their characteristics are a modesty and a dignity of which there are few such examples. Their sons are so well mannered that it is as if they left their mothers' wombs already civilised.

Ibn ʿAlī[1]

Averroes erred when he said, 'prestige belongs to people who are ancient settlers in a town'. I should like to know how long residence in a town can help [anyone to gain prestige] if he does not belong to a group that makes him feared and causes others to obey him. . . . Those without power cannot sway anyone's opinions, and their own opinions are not sought.

Ibn Khaldūn[2]

Within the amalgam of people who comprised the population of Salé between 1830 and 1930 there were various categories and types of individuals. One important means of social identification and classification was by descent, i.e. by determining the origins of particular families. Either by elaborate genealogical charts drawn up by experts on the basis of family documents or through knowledge passed down from father to son, most people had some notion of their origins. A few prominent families traced their roots in the city back into the distant past. Thus, for example, the Msetas boasted that one of their ancestors had been an official of the tenth-century Barghwāṭa kingdom that had ruled the area even before Salé's foundation. The Marīnī family maintained a splendid house that had been lived in continuously by their ancestors since the thirteenth century. The Zwāwīs, who had kept the office of muezzin of the Great Mosque in their family for generations, proudly boasted an ancestor who had been governor of the city in the sixteenth century. And other families like the Maʿnīnū and Fannīsh traced their origins back to Salé's famous corsairs and beyond them to ancestors who had migrated from far-flung corners of the Mediterranean world.[3] But most of the town's population had arrived more recently, and from the rural areas of Morocco nearer to home.

As immigrants from the countryside became urbanised and moved into the central quarters of Salé some of the remaining members of old-established families died out or left the city. Long lists of former Slawi families who had disappeared or declined to only a few remaining noteworthy members were drawn up by Salé's historian, Ibn ʿAli, and still today groups of old men can recite the names of hundreds of such families. There is a lively interest in the inscriptions of tombstones, place names, old documents and legendary tales about families or individuals, because of the information and lore in them concerning the city's former inhabitants. That so many of the prominent men and families of the past have left no descendants fascinates the Slawis and strengthens their pride in the deep-rootedness and continuity of the local family lines that still flourish.

Despite their recognition of the impermanence of family lines and the movement into and out of the community over time, some of the Slawis imagined, or at least claimed, that the social composition and social order of their city have remained fixed and rigid over centuries. Thus, they argued, citing an historical example, the highly skilled and wealthy immigrants from the Iberian Peninsula who had come to Salé early in the seventeenth century had not been allowed to remain there because their moral behaviour did not measure up to the standards of the community. Ibn ʿAli discusses the characteristics and virtues particular to the people of Salé and explains the disappearance of certain families in terms of similar moral imperatives:

It is well known that the Slawis will suffer neither insult nor injustice—even if it leads to their leaving the city . . . Thus today one finds considerable numbers of people of Slawi origin who have sought refuge and settled in Fez because of disgrace or humiliation. One finds in Fez such groups and families [*ṭawāʾif wa-buyūt*] as ʿAṭiya, Bū Qāʿa, Dabbāghīn, Qādirī, Kattānī, awlād ar-Rāʾis, awlād ash-Sharrādī, . . . , etc. Thus only a remnant of Salé's notables and *shurafāʾ* remain there.[4]

These ideal values notwithstanding, identity as a 'Slawi' was assumed and discarded with relative ease. Thus one of the streets of Salé, known as the Mills of the Amghār, was named after a leading family during the nineteenth century, the awlād Amghār. The family who claimed descent from the prophet were from Tīt, an abandoned city south of El-Jadida where one of their ancestors was buried and his tomb venerated.[5] Title deeds show that in 1750 Maḥammad b. ʿAbd as-Salām Amghār 'ar-Ribāṭī' lived in and owned property in Rabat. Another title deed, dated eight years later, indicates the same man living and owning property in Salé and refers to him as 'as-Salāwī'. By the middle of the nineteenth century the awlād Amghār were considered an old and notable local family.[6]

Another example of how residence affected personal identity may be seen in reverse in the case of the awlād Khāliṣ, who migrated to Salé from Ronda in Andalusia after the Reconquista. When al-Hājj Aḥmad b. ʿAbd al-Qādir Khāliṣ, a wealthy merchant, died near the end of the nineteenth century he left no descendants in the city. However, a branch of the family was known to have moved to Rabat a generation or two earlier, and as his nearest relatives they were entitled to inherit the estate. Nonetheless the Rabat branch of the family disclaimed their right to inherit, arguing that none of their ancestors had ever lived in Salé. Apparently they believed that in admitting to Slawi origin they would lose more in the way of status than they stood to gain in wealth from the inheritance.

The urge to identify oneself as a *bona fide* member of the urban community apparently became more compelling as the nineteenth century wore on. The old people of Salé whom I interviewed had been told by their parents and grandparents that most of the people of Salé used to be farmers, that in 'the good old days' everyone had earned his living in one way or another from the land. Among this population of farmers some had distinguished themselves by their piety or learning, and a few had become influential by virtue of their contacts with the *makhzan.* But all the townspeople had shared in their common identity as Slawis. This situation changed, it was said, during the 1860s, when appreciable numbers of people ceased to be able to support themselves by small-scale farming, or otherwise. Those men who succeeded in retaining or consolidating their wealth began to hold themselves and their families aloof from the rest of the population and applied exclusive criteria to determine who was and who was not a Slawi. Genealogies were forged, and extreme airs of superiority were assumed by people who had been in the city only a generation or two, while other families deeply rooted in the city but now poor were said to have died out or to be newcomers or outsiders.[7]

On the basis of documents relating to land ownership or official appointments during the period 1830–1930 I drew up a list of 160 family names and used it in interviews to elicit information about the social structure of Salé and the origins of families.[8] Of these 160 families, 137 were considered old, deep-rooted (*ʿarīqīn*) and respectable Slawi houses. The remaining families were said to have disappeared (seventeen) or not to be real Slawis (six). Slightly less than half of these names were formed from places of origin, either of towns or tribes (e.g. Dukkālī, Ṣubīḥī, Ṭitwāni); a fourth had been named after some famous ancestor (e.g. Bin Saʿīd, Bil-Qādī, Bū ʿAlū, Bū Shaʿara); a dozen had the name of a profession (e.g. Najjār, Ṣabūnjī, Bazzāz); the remaining thirty had surnames that could not be traced but which were considered as of Andalusian origin (e.g. Znībar, Maʿnīnū, Fannīsh).

Certain assumptions were made on the basis of these names as to a person's origin. The last-mentioned group included some of the oldest and most venerable families of the city. Most of those with names evoking places or tribes and many named after an ancestor were considered of rural origin. Those named after a profession were often considered converts of Jewish or Christian origin. Thus, for example, it was said that in the family chest of those named after an ancestor who had been a mat weaver lay his old Christian sailor's cap. Long before the Code of Law in Morocco demanded that every citizen establish a civil status with a surname, Slawis identified themselves by family names.[9] The explanation of one such name is instructive. The grandfather of one of my informants had been born in the rural area behind Casablanca, and as a young man had gone to live in Tetuan. Later he settled in Salé, and people there, remarking that his speech was marked by the accent of Tetuan, gave him the name Ṭitwānī. It stuck as the surname of the family, which later became recognised as one of the leading old families in the city.[10]

The idea that certain families possessed hereditary social and political pre-eminence became current in Salé only in the late nineteenth century, when wealth among some families began to take on a new kind of permanence. The early years of the protectorate encouraged this development because members of families that were considered by the French administration as 'noble' were appointed to positions of influence and offered the best educational opportunities. Yet until the 1870s the social structure of Salé appears to have been relatively undifferentiated in socio-economic classes or cultural categories.

With the emergence in the late nineteenth century of men with new wealth based on commerce and government service, certain families without previous pretensions to high status began to consider themselves alone as members of an extremely refined and old urban civilisation. With exaggerated pride and snobbishness they distinguished their way of life from the primitiveness of others in the city, as well as the surrounding rural population. This did not hinder them, nonetheless, from seeking alliances with powerful rural families when it was in their interest to do so, and it did not mean that upward mobility had become impossible. A perhaps extreme case is that of a man who came to Salé from the Gharb in the late nineteenth century and became the guardian of *makhzan* property. He married into one of the old and respected urban families and, according to the characteristically ambivalent and sarcastic turn of mind of the Slawis, made a perfect fool of himself when he sought to demonstrate his ascent into the bourgeoisie by adopting the attire and style of an urban scholar. By the end of the century the stereotypes of cultural categories had hardened, and they were underpinned by growing cleavages between social groups; but relationships among individuals from different categories and groups continued.

Clientèle groups in the city, alliances between rural and city folk, contractual relations among individuals from the apparently hostile cities of Rabat and Salé, and economic interdependence between Muslims and Jews paid little heed to conventional images of cultural categories. The only absolute constraint reflected by such an image was the fact that marriages between Muslims and Jews were inadmissible, although legally a Muslim man could marry a Jewish woman. Yet individual Jews, collectively referred to at least by some Slawis as 'unmarriables' or 'illegitimates' (coll. *ūlād l-ḥrām*), formed countless economic alliances with individual Muslims. They owned property jointly, lent one another money, and undertook various enterprises co-operatively. A variety of individual relationships existed across cultural barriers, but the stereotypes persisted with a stubborn intensity and could be brought into play under certain circumstances.

The 'people of Salé' formed a community of families which included at one and the same time individuals who by their education, piety or economic position played an important part in the life of the city, and others who achieved no prominence whatsoever. The basic fabric of this community was held together by cross-cutting ties among individuals, and by networks of social relationships. The elite of the community were those important personalities who dominated social networks. Their authority and influence within the community derived from their contractual and kinship ties to other members of society who depended on and supported them, and who in turn had their own followers and dependants. These networks of interdependent coalition groups provided the community of Salé with an unusual capacity for joint action, and a sentiment of consensus which rested on and expressed itself in commonly shared cultural values.

For Salé's late nineteenth-century historian these values were based on the heritage of the past as maintained by the family and the House. Salé's heritage had remained intact, in his view, thanks to the discretion and segregation of its population, and because individual families had lived in separate dwellings and had thus been able to preserve the nobility of their character and behaviour. Decent people lived apart from the poor and the rabble who could not pay the rent of a house, much less own one.[11] Included among those who should be segregated were the poor and needy, those who 'toil endlessly and meet only disdain and must necessarily be envious of and covert the comforts of those above them'. Ibn ʿAli alludes to a kind of latent group conflict by pointing out that the children of those who are comfortable mistreat the children of the poor and that this leads to attacks and hostilities, griefs, hatreds and lasting enmity. In his view the lack of segregation in some of the larger cities of Morocco, overcrowding and insufficient housing had caused a loss of values and the occurrence of evil and disgraceful acts. He argues that where people suffer from poverty and sickness there will be obscenity and a lack of modesty, generosity, consideration and dignity. The Slawis had avoided such a situation, he wrote, and succeeded for the time being in keeping themselves apart; the key to their success was that men ruled over their separate households: the inherited values still dominated, men remained exalted by their children and retained the rights 'to permit and forbid and to give and to take', and every father strengthened his children's sense of modesty (*al-ḥayāʾ*) and the fear born of respect towards him. The distinctiveness and excellence of the people of Salé flowed from these basic virtues.[12]

Ties of interdependence and the sentiment among Slawis that they shared common values served to draw them together and to provide a sense of identity as a unique community. This identity manifested itself to them in various ways. The Slawis saw themselves as a special 'breed' of people, as the following remarks made to me by one of the old itinerant merchants of Salé indicate. 'The Slawis (and perhaps the Fasis) are the best people in Morocco, for they know how to act and to talk in a decent manner, while others—for example, the Rabatis from al-Andalus—by their very nature and almost to a man have an exaggerated opinion of their abilities and importance. The Slawis are immediately recognisable to one another because of their complexion, the colour of their skin and eyes, and their dialect. Furthermore Slawis feel a natural inclination towards each other, even if they have never seen one another before. When they meet outside the city they become immediate friends. And the people of Salé are known for the strength of their opinions. They say what they think and do so with eloquence.'[13]

In addition to this clear-cut self-image in regard to outsiders, there were important cultural or social distinctions within the community of Salé, as recognised by its members. Ibn ʿAli, after having set apart the rural way of life (*al-bādiya*, practised by 'Arabs' or 'Bedouin' *al-ʿarab* or *al-bawādī*, i.e. the rural people), and distinguishing the poor and needy, lists those considered part of the urban way of life (*al-ḥaḍāra*). These are the learned, farmers, craftsmen and merchants, builders, those employed by the government, and those with lineages, i.e. those with a good family name.[14] They are the urban types of people. In another list of the representatives of the community—a declaration of allegiance (*bayʿa*) drawn up by the qadi of Salé in 1822 to recognise Sultan ʿAbd ar-Raḥmān, the signatories mentioned in the document are classified into similar groups: descendants of the Prophet (*ash-shurafāʾ*), personages (*al-aṭrāf*, lit. 'the limbs'), notables (*al-aʿyān*), merchants (*at-tujjār*), learned men (*ʿulamāʾ*), men of known families (*dhawūʾl-buyūt*), holy warriors (*mujāhidūn*), and men of judgement and a firmly established position (*dhawū ʾl-aḥkām wa-ʾṭ-ṭawr ar-rāsikh*).[15] These lists include the main representatives of the urban population and give us an idea of the types of people who were thought of as townsmen.

Other writings, as well as the popular idiom, use a terminology that distinguishes two categories. One of these, *al-ʿāmma*, usually refers to the masses of urban society. Nāṣirī sometimes uses this term to mean all the population of a city: *qāma ʿāmmatu ahli fās ʿalā ʿāmilihā* ('the mass of the people of Fez rose against its governor'); at other times the term means the mass of the populace as distinct from the riff-raff: *fa-ʾl-awwalu tuḥibbuhu l-ʿāmmatu wa-s-sifla* ('and the former is loved by the populace and the riff-raff'); finally, it stipulates the lower classes. The term is then qualified: *al-ʿāmma al-aghmār* ('the ignorant masses'), and these are equated with the 'urban rabble' (*ghawghāʾ ʾl-ḥāḍira*) and the 'rural rabble' (*ghawghāʾ ʾl-ʿarab*) who generally live outside or on the fringes of a city, and periodically harass the townspeople.[16] In speech the term *ʿāmma* may denote the illiterate, or all those of the community who are not descendants of the Prophet, learned scholars or functionaries of the government.[17] These latter made up the other category and were sometimes distinguished as *al-khāṣṣa*, 'the elite of the community', or called *al-wujahā'*—the term favoured in colloquial speech—or *al-aʿyān*, 'the notables'. The members of this group can be defined from the list of notables drawn up by the governor of the city in order to prepare a declaration of allegiance to a new sultan. The list consisted of the names of government officials, ulama, notaries, heads of some of the craft guilds, the leaders of the *shurafā'*, and several other personages of the city. The list of names of the individuals who signed these declarations represents the most prestigious members of the elite at the moment of signing. They were drawn from a pool of the prominent families in the city, known generally as *awlād an-nās* (coll. *ūlād n-nās*), the well born, literally the sons of (important) people.[18]

The general schema that emerges from this discussion of social categories can be visualised as three concentric circles, with the elite or notables in the inner circle, the important families in the middle circle, and in the outer circle the mass of the population, including or excluding at its edge the rabble of the city. Each larger circle could include the smaller circles within it, depending on the circumstances in which the terms were being used. Such a visual model, however, does not reflect the view that Slawis held of their society. As soon as one begins to probe into the sense of these categories one discovers that the relationships among real men have quite another pattern.

Social networks among the well born

In a passage in a poem devoted to the majestic past of Salé and the famous personages who once lived there Ibn ʿAlī writes that the founder of the city was in relation to his brothers and their descendants, the Banū ʿAshara, the centrepiece of their necklace (*wāsiṭat ʿaqdihim*). The metaphor means that the jewel which hangs in the middle of a necklace is incomparably more beautiful and valuable than all the stones along its sides. Thus the ʿAshara family of Salé, who numbered many individuals renowned for their knowledge, bravery, faith and so on, resembled the stones of a necklace. One man, the founder of Salé, excelled all his ascendants and descendants taken together. None rivalled him in either religious knowledge or rank, neither those before him nor those after him. He stood as the centrepiece of the necklace.

Ibn ʿAlī's metaphor makes clear the distinction between the family and the individual. Families important in Salé during the nineteenth and early twentieth centuries considered themselves, and were usually considered by the population, as descendants of an old and proud line. If a man had only recently risen to prominence he invariably vaunted the memory of some ancestor famous for learning, piety or office as a justification for the present eminence of his family name. This was easiest for those families who had already been in the city for several generations or centuries, but anyone who sought status staked out a claim for the historic eminence of his ancestors.

These old families were conceived of as patrilineal groups with real or imagined genealogies going back anywhere from several centuries to the days of the Prophet.[19] Many of them proudly retained the memory of some ancestor who had played an important role in the city's history. Some had inherited the correspondence of the *makhzan* with these ancestors, including decrees that assured the man and his descendants of continued respect and honour and granted them rights and privileges. If a man from one of these families found himself in difficulties he might write to the sultan stating that his ancestor had performed a specific service for the *makhzan*, as testified to by a decree. The sultan might respond by granting him the right to live in a house that was government property, and in effect several families in Salé had been living in government-owned houses on the basis of decrees for generations.[20] However, these cases appear to have been infrequent. Generally a family's past renown, whether attested to by official documents conferring a kind of nobility or not, produced no tangible rewards, economic or social.

Over one hundred families in Salé were identified by my oldest informants as respected and deeply rooted in the city. The members of these patrilineal groups[21] were referred to as *ūlād n-nās*, the well born, or *ahl l-bled*, 'the people of the city'. Each patrilineal group was said to have had a strong feeling of mutual solidarity and a shared sense of identity. Stereotypes of each family often included specific occupations, moral or intellectual qualities and styles of life. A particular family might be said to have distinguished itself by learning, piety, commerce, a certain trade, land holding or government service. Another might be known for its hospitality, avarice, ostentatiousness or humility.

Stories were told to illustrate that families had acted in the past as cohesive groups. For example, the Znībar family had exiled themselves to Rabat early in the eighteenth century because the qa'id ʿAbd al-Ḥāqq Fannīsh, who with his kinsmen and partisans ruled the city independently, had killed one of their members.[22] When the sultan apprehended Fannīsh, the Znībar *family* was given the right to avenge itself, but its members refused to take the blood of other Slawis upon themselves. Then the Fanānsha (pl. of Fannīsh) lost their legal rights as creditors (*dhimma*),[23] had their property confiscated and were exiled from the city. In the written or reported history of Salé this is the only example I have found of a situation of open conflict between cohesive family entities.

The mention of some families sometimes included connotations of group solidarity and remarks about relative size or commonly held characteristics. Thus in the 1920s the Znābra (pl. of Znībar) were considered the 'largest family' in Salé, numbering about three hundred kindred souls, including women and children. The extent of their numbers, in the opinion of some informants, gave them the potential to act effectively as a group. Some streets in Salé also were named after families, e.g. the street of the Maʿanīnūs—Derb Maʿāna (a plural form for the collectivity of Maʿanīnū families).[24] It was thought that all the Maʿanīnū families had once resided together in the street, but no one remembered when. There were other suggestions concerning the importance of patrilineal groups and competition among them. During the last quarter of the nineteenth century, it was said, the ʿAwwāds had surpassed the Znībars in importance because there were more learned men or office holders among them. Repeatedly and with much relish people let fall remarks about petty animosities and jealousies between families, past and present.

These sentiments and memories notwithstanding, I found no evidence of collective action by any patrilineal group or the existence of any effective social and political aggregations along patrilineal lines in the study of the city's social history between 1830 and 1930. Many French writers gave special attention to the 'great families' of Morocco (an expression that erroneously suggested a resemblance to the French aristocracy), and their analyses of the structure of urban society in Morocco became an important element in shaping France's conceptions of and policies towards Moroccans. Indirect rule by protectorate was to be applied by the Moroccan elite, the 'patrician' families whom the journalists, officials and sociologists had discovered. Thus, for example, a small booklet entitled *Les Grandes Familles de Salé* states that twenty high born, influential and wealthy families in the city comprise the elite of the community, and that they alone merit the attention of the authorities.[25] In fact most of the people who belonged to these families had no influence whatsoever. The elite were not leaders of powerful extended families but men who controlled clientèle groups held together by mutual interests, not ties of consanguinity.

A respectable family name in Salé provided its bearer with a potential symbol of prestige, little more. Ibn Khaldūn, five centuries earlier, had noted a similar lack of cohesiveness among urban families and contrasted it with the strong sense of cohesion among tribes. He called the notion of common descent in urban families 'but a delusion of nobility',[26] an expression which aptly describes the Slawis' way of looking at themselves. In nineteenth-century Salé inclusion in a given patronymic and patrilineal category had limited consequences, although it might provide individuals with a sense of belonging to a particular segment of the urban community. As one *contrôleur civil* of Salé remarked, a Slawi would always introduce himself by saying his family name first, to show that he belonged to the city and deserved respect.[27] But it served only as a badge, and did not mean that its bearer was of any consequence.

There were, to be sure, gradations of prestige associated with different family names: e.g. a boy was known as *wild Znībrīya*, 'a son of one of the Znibar girls', because his mother had a family name which carried greater prestige than that of his father. Children of unpretentious social origin were sometimes humiliated in school by the sons of prestigious families, who refused to play with them and who taunted, teased and perhaps attacked them. The boys from these families believed that they formed a group apart, and they did not (or could not) permit the sons of the poor and the uncouth—those without good family names—to enter their circle of friends or their homes. Some men who had been in school between 1900 and 1930 said that in their youth they had painfully experienced a kind of social ostracism among children who thought themselves part of the notability because of their family names. The schoolboys seem to have been caricatures of an illusory aristocratic society that certain families pretended to belong to. The 'delusion of nobility' expressed itself in other ways. Those who belonged to certain patrilineal groups would 'put on airs' and project an exalted sense of self-importance, especially among those less pretentious about their social origins, and the latter might adopt an attitude of meekness and humility. The boy who had been called 'wild Znībrīya' vividly remembered and resented the sight of his father's self-effacing behaviour in the presence of his mother's relatives, 'just because they were Znibars!'[28]

Children unconsciously often caricaturise the behaviour of their parents, and those of Salé seem to offer no exception to this trait of human nature. One informant described an unforgettable social drama from his days in the Quranic school in the early years of this century. It illustrates how the attitudes of children reflected those of their parents. A twelve-year-old son of a high government official used to come to school dressed like a Minister in miniature. His wooden board on which chapters from the Quran were written and memorised was, or seemed, twice as large as those of the other boys. Extremely proud and arrogant, he could memorise any given passage easily and quickly. Next to him in class sat 'wild Znībrīya', the son of a modest shopkeeper. His clothing was simple, and his constant daydreaming and failure to memorise his lessons earned him the reputation of being simple-minded. He repeatedly 'ate the stick', that is, had the soles of his feet beaten by the teacher as punishment for his failures in his classwork. His conceited classmate never ceased to taunt him and call him a 'good-for-nothing thick-skulled peasant'. Finally the shopkeeper's son, in a fit of anger, swore that his tormentor should no longer be able to memorise his lessons; he called on his mother's maternal ancestor, the local saint known as Sīdī Bin ʿĀshir, to carry out the curse. The oath worked effectively, for soon the other boy was crying and begging because he had lost the ability and composure necessary to put his lessons to memory. The curse was then removed. The man who told me this story about himself when he was a boy of ten became well known after this event for the magical powers that he had inherited from his mother's ancestors. The other children stopped their mocking, and people began to come to him to ask his blessing. His father's family had been to no avail, but he found comfort in the blessing of his mother's maternal ancestors.

In a similar manner many people in Salé called upon ancestors for aid or for prestige. The descendants of famous warriors (*mujāhidīn*), no matter how humble their state, prided themselves on the feats of their famous predecessors. They had the uniforms of these ancient sea captains, and some of them wore them in accompanying the governor to the Great Mosque for the Friday-noon prayer. At the procession of the candles, a celebration in honour of Salé's patron saint, Sīdī ʿAbd Allah b. Ḥasūn, which was held on the birthday of the Prophet, these men marched in full regalia, and the memory of their ancestors was also institutionalised by the town crier (*al-barrāḥ*), who, when sent into the streets to announce some important event or proclamation, would begin by shouting, 'There is but one God and Muḥammad is the messenger of God! Sailors! Artillerymen! People of the the city! May you hear only good!' (*lā ilāha illā Allāh wa-Muḥammad rasūl Allah*! *yā ʾl-baḥrīya, yā ʾṭ-ṭūbjīya, yā ahl ʾl-bled mā tismaʿū illā ʾl-khayr in shaʾ Allāh*). This formula was still used in Salé in this century, when the only sailors in the city were those who rowed passengers across the Bou Regreg. Descendants of past heroes still treasured the decrees from the sultans that they had inherited from their warrior ancestors. Almost everyone who was integrated into the city found reasons to be proud of one or another of his paternal or maternal forefathers. Such 'pedigrees' were part of the self-definition of Salé's citizens.

These attitudes, stances and theatrics expressed an attachment to the family, but in practice notions of exclusiveness, the 'delusion of nobility', had a limited role in the mundane business of interacting with other people and of building permanent ties and alliances with them in order to survive in an unstable and often difficult world. However, the attachment to and pride in one's family served a purpose in the forging of links among individuals. Wealth and position in Salé did not automatically confer respect on a man in the eyes of the population. To turn wealth into social status and to become a man whose word counted in the city it was necessary to ally oneself with old families, and with respected people of religion, learning or legitimated authority. There were, especially during the period of economic mobility that marked the late nineteenth century, many men of new wealth who found it necessary or useful to enter into alliances and clientèle groups in order to secure a social position and to increase their material wealth. At the same time such men provided useful allies to individuals who prided themselves on their deep roots in the community. The *savoir-faire*, learning and life style of urban civilisation were a necessary complement to wealth if men wanted to be accepted in the community. People in Salé continually sought security and aggrandisement, and to gain these they had to successfully combine their interests with other men who possessed influence or prestige.

The complementarity of men's needs resulted in a series of arrangements calculated to produce cross-cutting ties among specific personalities and among their families. Links were formed between the rich, the pious and blessed, the learned, and the powerful. Men bound themselves into networks of social relationships which had a latent and sometimes effective sense of coherence and solidarity. These groupings, in turn, had ties with one another and seemed to extend throughout the whole society. The Slawis described the interconnection among people in the city by using a metaphor—the *qādūs*, a waterwheel bucket used for irrigation in their gardens. Thus individuals who originated from a wide variety of families and who had religious, economic or political status or influence became linked in their interests not only with one another but derivationally with a large part of the community.

Marriage alliances were the most favoured means of becoming tied to a powerful individual and thereby to a social network. These alliances wove a net of affinal kin ties among a variety of men and numerous extended families. Most marriages were contracted outside patrilineal lines and usually within the community of Salé. In some cases powerful members of the surrounding countryside arranged marriages for their daughters in the city, and there were occasions when daughters of Slawi families became the wives of outsiders, usually of rural big men. Polygyny was by no means unusual, especially among those forced to travel because of their administrative posts. Concubinage was practised among the wealthy but does not appear to have played a role in furthering ties of alliance.

Marriage possibilities were studied closely to ascertain the effect they could have in adding to a man's wealth, prestige or power, or increasing his allies or protection. The parents of groom and bride arranged the marriage, worked out the details of the contract, determined the amount of bridewealth to be paid by the groom's family and the household belongings to be provided by the family of the bride. The purpose of this exchange was to bind together the interests of two families, not simply two individuals. Sons and daughters were considered as capital to be invested in the establishment of marriage alliances. A man tried to diversify and multiply these alliances, for example by giving one daughter to an important *sharīf*, another to a well known scholar and a third to a wealthy merchant or tribesman, or arranging for his sons to marry into families with socio-economic resources. By spreading his affinal relationships as widely as possible by means of carefully calculated marriages a man sought to establish ties with as wide a variety of individuals as possible. By this process co-operation and certain mutual rights and obligations among relatives could be brought into play. These relationships of affinity were more important for the formation of alliances than those of common origin, occupation or status. In drawing up charts of descent groups and their affinal links, informants repeatedly stressed this fact. Thus the son of the former governor, ʿAbd Allah b. Saʿid, when asked if his father had been a 'friend' (*ṣaḥb*) of the Slawi acting as governor of Casablanca when the French landed in 1907, succinctly and emphatically replied, 'They were not only friends, they were bound together by the closest possible relationship: they were affines [*nsāb*]!'[29]

Ties of marriage within the community influenced the pattern of men's social networks or strengthened solidarities among sets of people who interacted in other ways. The general patterning of these relations was into groups of patrons and clients, a type of social structure aptly called by Eric Wolf 'individual-centered coalitions' which cluster in 'kinship regions'.[30] By entering into such a coalition, through marriage or by other means of alliance, an individual buttressed his social position and status and gained access to economic or political resources controlled by others. Relationships of affinity, business partnerships, ties between teacher and student, drew individuals into coalitions and allowed them to mobilise their energies and to attempt to achieve social mobility. When one individual in such a coalition became better able to grant goods and services than the others a patron–clientèle relationship developed within the group.

This pattern of coalition formation characterised social structure and action in Salé throughout the century from 1830 to 1930. Men vied for socio-economic assets and positions of power in the city at various levels by constantly seeking to enlarge their social networks. A group of allies or clients centred around one man promised no permanence beyond its effectiveness or, at most, the lives of the individuals concerned. However, new groups based on the same pattern regularly emerged in each generation. A man without clients or patron had nowhere to turn in the quest for security or aggrandisement.

The 'big men', the individuals at the centre of even the most important coalitions, did not possess the degree of power that might have enabled them to form a ruling class, an oligarchy or a group of patrician families, because they were in competition with one another. They could not afford to disregard the opinions and sentiments of the rest of the population because competition made them dependent on other people. Thus, for example, the governor needed the legitimation and support of some of the *shurafā'*, the learned, the wealthy, just as they looked to him for patronage. Other men in rivalry with him had their own clientèle groups. Alliances, often strengthened through the bonds of marriage, provided the framework for these relationships. Although several leading figures in the city at a given time might temporarily unite their interests, the conflicts among them were usually intense and recurrent. When dominant groups weakened or ceased to be united by their interests, or simply disappeared because of the death of the individuals who had held them together, new coalitions emerged and contended for positions of influence.

In the chapters that follow there are detailed examples to illustrate these general statements concerning the social structure of Salé, and in the Conclusion the problem of structural analysis is treated once again in more comparative and theoretical terms. The discussion so far has described, on the one hand, the categories according to which Salé's historians and some informants identified people according to origins and styles of life, and, on the other, the social relationships—the networks and coalitions—that characterised actual social groupings. This approach makes it possible to understand the notion of social order that was so important to the Slawis; it also explains the relative fluidity of the city's social structure and the mobility of individuals within its community.

IV Saints and scholars

In the past the people of Salé were extremely attentive in maintaining the nobility of their character, the goodness of their behaviour, the excellence of their virtues, and in following the ordained custom. They were totally conservative and pious in what they ate, drank and wore, and in being satisfied with little. Among them there was pride neither in rank nor in wealth.

There was love for the saints, the family of the House of the Prophet, and they were exalted and respected. There were friendship and ties with them, and love and exaltation of the scholars, because they were the models to be followed and to be listened to. . . .

Ibn ʿAlī[1]

The holy men

Morocco's first independent kingdom was founded at the beginning of the ninth century by Idrīs b. Idrīs b. ʿAbd Allah, descendant of the caliph ʿAlī b. Abī Ṭālib, cousin and son-in-law of the Prophet Muḥammad. The Idrisid dynasty ruled by his descendants remained in power until 985. From then and until the rise of the Saʿadians in 1510 the Berber empires that dominated Morocco during those five centuries did not seek to justify their authority by claiming descent from the Prophet. But the Saʿadians (1510–1659) and their successors, the ʿAlawids, Morocco's present ruling dynasty, were founded and ruled by lines of descendants of the Prophet—*shurafāʾ*.[2] These 'Sharifian' dynasties, as they are called in the historical literature, have dominated Morocco during more than half the period of its Muslim history, and they have drawn legitimation from their genealogical descent from the Prophet.

Lévi-Provençal noted that Morocco has had more authentic or claimed representatives of this religious *noblesse* of descendants of the Prophet than any other country in the Muslim world.[3] Wherever men claimed to be *shurafāʾ*, in the cities or the countryside, and whatever their fortune, they enjoyed—or at least made claims upon—the respect of their countrymen. The authentic *shurafāʾ* of Morocco, as determined by a copious genealogical literature, descend through three branches from a son of al-Ḥasan b. ʿAli b. Abī aṭ-Ṭālib. The genealogies may be represented as follows:

al-Ḥasan b. ʿAlī

al-Ḥasan al-Muthnī

ʿAbd Allah al-Kāmil

Idrīs	Muḥammad an-Nafs az-Zākiya	Mūsā al-Jawn
↓	↓	↓
Idrīsī shurafāʾ	*ʿAlawī shurafāʾ*	*Qādirī shurafāʾ*

Since the eighteenth century some of the ʿAlawi *shurafāʾ* living in Salé became respected and at times venerated by the population, and a number of them enjoyed special rights and privileges. They were exempted from payment of taxes, service in the army, or the judgement of the court of the qaʾid, and a few of them received houses from the government, income from rural farming lands, and the offerings made by pilgrims to certain tombs of saints in the city.

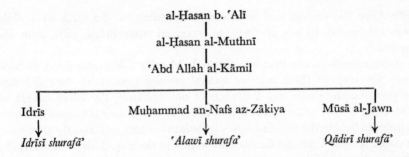

ʿAlawīs resident in Salé divided themselves into several branches. The first family to settle there was the awlād Mawlāy al-Hishām, or awlād Mawlāy ʿAlī ash-Sharīf, direct descendants of the famous sixteenth-century saint buried in the Tafilalt. They reached Salé at the turn of the eighteenth century, when two brothers, sons of an ʿAlawī and a woman of the Zemmour Berber tribes brought a recommendation to the governor of the city from their relative, the sultan Mawlāy Ismāʿīl. The governor gave them rights to the offerings made at the sanctuaries of Sīdī Mūsā and Sīdī 'Bil-ʿAbbās', two of Salé's most frequently visited tombs of saints, and usufruct rights to some of the land of the ʿĀmir tribe. Only one of these brothers left children, and his descendants maintained their rights and privileges and provided the leader (*naqīb*) of the ʿAlawī *shurafāʾ*.[4] Another branch of ʿAlawīs in the city traced their descent back to the sultan Mawlāy Ismāʿīl. Documents in the possession of the family show that one of the sultan's sons came to Salé in 1729 to escape from the conflicts among his brothers over power. According to local tradition he was given a grandiose reception by the population and received a house in the Bāb Ḥuṣayn quarter. He earned his living as a slave merchant and owned a good deal of property, especially near Kenitra among a group of the Banū Ḥasan, where the farming land called ʿ*azīb ash-shurafāʾ* is still in the hands of his descendants. A third branch of ʿAlawī *shurafāʾ* traced its genealogy back to Sultan Sulaymān (1792–1822), who brought them from Meknes to Salé and gave them possession of government property on Derb Maʿāna in the Zanāta quarter. We know little else about individuals from among the ʿAlawī *shurafāʾ* in Salé until the nineteenth century, other than that they were considered the elite among the descendants of the Prophet in the city and prided themselves on being the 'cousins' of the reigning sultans. Every year, during the Great Festival, they received clothes and money as gifts from the sultan, and whenever a wedding or the birth of a child was celebrated by one of them he received appropriate gifts from the palace.[5]

Descendants of the Prophet, through Mawlāy Idrīs, also lived in Salé, but only some of them enjoyed special prestige because of their sharifian origins. Among them was a branch of the Tuhāmīs, the Idrīsī *shurafā'* of Ouezzan. The Wazzāniyya religious order to which they belonged had built a lodge in Salé in the middle of the eighteenth century, and shortly afterwards a noted scholar from the family had settled in the city. This man married a daughter of a well known teacher and soon became highly respected among the local population. His children and their descendants married into some of the leading urban families. The ʿAlamīs of Salé, also Idrīsī *shurafā'*, originated from the Jebel ʿAlam, north of the Gharb, where their famous ancestor Sīdī ʿAbd as-Salām b. Mashīsh (d. 1228) has his tomb. This saint's father, Sīdī Mashīsh, was said to be buried in Salé, and his tomb had long been the object of veneration. The ʿAlamīs whom we later find in Salé probably migrated there in the late seventeenth century during the reign of Mawlāy Ismāʿīl. During the next two centuries their names figured prominently on the lists of captains of the Slawi fleet, and they were considered members of the urban elite. A third and last group of Idrīsī *shurafā'* in the city were the aṭ-Ṭalbīs, whose ancestor Sīdī Aḥmad had migrated there in the seventeenth century from Ksar el-Kbir. Local tradition claims that this shaikh had sent him to Salé to take the place of its patron saint, Sīdī ʿAbd Allah b. Ḥassūn, who had recently died. Instead he became a student of Ibn Ḥassūn's disciple, Sīdī Maḥammad b. Saʿid, from whom he purportedly received a part of the blessing bequeathed by the saint. He was famous for his learning and piety, and when he died a tomb was built in the Ṭalʿa quarter and became a popular shrine. His son, Sīdī Maḥammad, also lived a reputedly saintly, pious and virtuous life, and his tomb rose beside that of his father and likewise became an object of veneration.

The only other group of *shurafā'* about whom there is information is the al-Qādirī family, descendants of the famous twelfth-century saint buried in Baghdad, ʿAbd al-Qādir al-Jilānī. The arrival of the al-Qādirīs in Salé is told in a legendary account according to which three sons of the Baghdad saint migrated to the city. When they died they were buried in a tomb dedicated to their father's memory. The Qādirī religious order has long been important in Salé, as well as in many other places in Morocco and north-west Africa. But there were no relations or contacts between the local lodge of the Qādirī order or the family in Salé and other lodges or descendants of the saint who lived elsewhere.

Thus seven families in Salé enjoyed a special status in society because they were *shurafā'*. This meant that individuals from these families had by birth the potentiality of attaining prestige and reaping material benefits because of their sharifian origins, and that some of them managed to realise that potentiality. In addition to members of these families there were other men in the city who claimed descent from the Prophet, along one of the several genealogical lines. Almost anyone, for example, from the Tafilalt region of south-east Morocco, where the Alawid dynasty originated, could and, it was said, often did claim to be an ʿAlawī. Few of these *shurafā'*, however, attained any renown in the city or came to be considered part of the urban elite on the basis of their religious pedigrees or spiritual gifts during the period under study. Another category of *shurafā'* may be said to have been a part of the city's population. These were families and individuals of sharifian descent who neither claimed nor received prestige because of their noble origins. Thus the Sharqāwīs, Ṣabūnjīs and Bil Ḥasans, some of whom were wealthy and influential, found it unnecessary or useless to draw upon their sharifian origins to increase their social status.

The *shurafā'* of Salé did not form a coherent group in any way. Some of the old urban families, particularly three of ʿAlawi origin, enjoyed certain privileges and rights—gifts from the sultan, access to the use or revenues of government properties, exemptions from taxes and military service. A number of individuals from them were highly esteemed among the population and sometimes called upon to act as negotiators or mediators in difficult or sensitive situations. The governor used them to settle some of the problems and conflicts that arose in the city; they helped to arrange marriages between families; they sorted out squabbles between neighbours and carried out other roles of mediation of this nature. These men were members of the urban elite because of their religious prestige, and this position they owed, at least in part, to their sharifian origins. Respect for the family of the House of the Prophet was one of the qualities that the Slawis valued and it was, in their view, exemplified in their community.

The *ūlād siyyid* of Salé, another category of descendants of saints, were also reputed to possess great spiritual gifts or powers.[6] Their ancestors had been local holy men, and their tombs dotted the landscape of the city and gave it its particular claim to sanctity. Of these saints, three became legendary and of lasting importance: Sīdī ʿAbd Allah b. Ḥassūn (d. 1604), the 'patron saint' called by the Slawis 'sulṭān l-bled'—'the strength (lit. sultan) of the city'; Sīdī al-Ḥājj Aḥmad Bin ʿĀshir (d. 1362), called 'aṭ-Ṭbīb'—'the Healer'; and Sīdī Aḥmad Ḥajjī (d. 1780).[7] The descendants of these saints were the ūlād Bin ʿUmar, who originated from among the Zemmour and claimed descent from Sīdī Bin ʿĀshir, or from his foremost disciple; the Ḥassūnīs, who claimed direct descent from the saint but were said to be from the lineage of his disciple; and the Ḥajjīs, so numerous that they had split into seven separate branches.

These three families received or at least sought the respect of the community; they had rights to offerings made by visitors to the sanctuaries where their ancestors were buried; and they possessed decrees from various sultans recognising their rights to honour and respect by the government and the local population. Besides the yearly pilgrimage fairs to the sanctuaries of their forefathers the Ḥajjīs and Ḥassūnīs formed religious orders (*ṭā'ifa*, pl. *ṭawā'if*) which met weekly in their respective sanctuaries for prayer and the spiritual exercise known as *dhikr*, the repeated mention of specific words or phrases in praise of God. Other men in Salé attended these prayer séances, for the order was not limited to the descendants of the saint, nor did it have a fixed membership. The sanctuaries of these local saints were simply local lodges (*zāwiyas*), meeting places of religious orders that resembled the better-known Sufi lodges spread throughout Morocco and a good part of the Muslim world.

In addition to these three local families there were numerous members of the Nāṣirī family, descendants of Sīdī Muḥammad b. an-Nāṣir, a famous saint of the seventeenth century who was buried in Tamgrūt in the Draʿ valley of southern Morocco. Descendants of the saint and Nāṣirī *zāwiyas* could be found in most Moroccan towns. Their sanctuary in Salé, probably established by immigrants who came there in the eighteenth century, was used exclusively by members of the family. The Nāṣirīs were considered *ūlād siyyid*, although some of them claimed descent from the Prophet's lineage. The family was highly respected in Salé, to the extent that when people passed before their lodge they maintained absolute silence, even groups parading through the streets to the accompaniment of music and shouting in the traditional celebration of a marriage. This show of respect in regard to the Nāṣirī *zāwiya* was presented by Slawis as an example of a particular characteristic of their city and its society—the way in which passions and emotions were controlled because of respect for religion, for the saints and their descendants. Although the veneration of saints was characteristic of most places in Morocco and widespread throughout many Muslim lands, what was perhaps particular to Salé was the association in people's minds between respect for saints and the dignity and decorum of the urban way of life.

Holiness on the wane

The specificity of Moroccan Islam, at least since the sixteenth century, has been described in terms of three principal elements: Sharifism, hagiolatry, and mysticism as reflected in the Sufi orders.[8] Moroccan history during the nineteenth century and the first decades of the twentieth has not yet been studied from the perspective of the interplay and conflicts of these three strands of religious life. The fact is that we still know relatively little about the religious attitudes and tensions, instability and changes among various types of religious strands during this crucial period.[9]

Ibn ʿAli, Salé's local historian at the turn of this century, has written a kind of panegyric to all the saints and scholars who had lived in the city. For him their lives embodied those values that made for the excellence of the city and its society. At the same time he felt that many of these values were undermined by his contemporaries because they no longer regarded the men of religion with sufficient veneration.

The influence and prestige of descendants of the Prophet and of local saints had begun to decline seriously by the 1880s. With the coming of the French protectorate, accompanied by the temporary weakening of the prestige and power of the sharifian dynasty and the demise of the influence of the religious orders, the roles performed by these holy men diminished in scope and importance. A few outstanding personalities of sharifian descent or descendants of local saints continued to act effectively as intermediaries in a variety of situations throughout the protectorate period, but their number and the range of their activities became increasingly limited. Some continued to arrange marriages, settle disputes (often between husband and wife) and give blessings to the sick, but most of these tasks were no longer the private domain of religious experts. Moreover a tendency developed among some elements of the population, particularly the young, to consider *shurafā'* with little respect and sometimes with disdain. Thus, for example, in the 1920s an ʿAlawī who dressed in the finest clothes, behaved rather pompously and lived near the Great Mosque in a house given to him by the *makhzan* was referred to disparagingly by the young Slawis as 'the Sultan of ʿAqba Street'. Another ʿAlawī was pitied because of his naivety—he had no idea of events in the city because 'he did not enter the market place'.[10]

Among those *shurafā'* of Salé who did realise their inherited potentiality of prestige and influence was Sīdī Muḥammad al-Hāshimī aṭ-Ṭālbī (d. 1884). His biography provides an example of the status that a *sharīf* could achieve in the earlier period. He was a fifth-generation descendant of a seventeenth-century saint whose venerated tomb stood in the Ṭalʿa quarter of Salé. One of the sons of his ancestor had earned a reputation for piety and virtue and was also buried and venerated in a tomb in Ṭalʿa. The latter's son, in turn, had served as qadi of Salé under Sultan Sulaymān (1792–1822); the father of Sīdī Muḥammad, a son of the qadi, had only managed to support himself as a poor farmer. Many legends about Sīdī Muḥammad are still told by Slawis, in addition to the information about his life provided in the works of Ibn ʿAlī and Nāṣirī. He was a *shaykh*, or leader of a religious order, and had many disciples. Ibn ʿAlī writes that Ṭālbī alone among his contemporaries resembled in his inner state the great men of earlier generations (*as-salaf*), and that he performed miraculous deeds. The old Slawis say that he had the gift of being able to see into the future (*mukashshaf*); for example, once when asked where he was going he had replied, 'To work for the infidels,' and this was understood as a prediction of the colonial conquest of Morocco. Another incident often related concerned a visit to Salé by Sultan Ḥasan. The sultan began his visit at the sanctuary of Sīdī ʿAbd Allah, then continued to the tomb of Sīdī Aḥmad b. ʿĀshir, where he was greeted by the population; then he asked the governor to bring to him Sīdī Muḥammad al-Hāshimī aṭ-Ṭālbī, for he had noticed Ṭālbī's absence and wanted to receive his blessing. The governor found the saint—dressed in green, the symbolic colour of prophetic descent—and only with great difficulty convinced him that he should greet the sultan. The saint waited in a corner until the sultan came to him, then said, 'May God bless the lifetime of my Lord!' (*Allāh yubārik ʿamr Sīdī*—the most cursory of the customary greeting to the Sultan), to which he added, 'I say this to you in spite of myself.' The saint had shown that, as a descendant of the Prophet, he was equal to the sultan and probably his superior in piety.

For the generation that came of age at the turn of the century the personage of Ṭālbī represented a final testimony to the sanctity of Salé and its saints. He had combined the ideal religious qualities of the past—descent from the Prophet and saints, learning, leadership of a religious order, and had possessed a spiritual ascendancy beyond the secular and religious authority of the sultan. Nāṣirī's eulogy for Ṭālbī describes him in the following way:

[He was] among the pious men [*sulaḥā'*] of the community of Salé. His death came suddenly. He ate a light dinner that night, as was his custom, performed the evening prayer, and recited his private prayers alone in his room . . . when morning came he was dead and no one was at his side. He was nearly eighty, an old man with white hair and beard. An immense crowd from the people of the Two Banks of Salé and Rabat attended his funeral, crowded around his bier, and took turns carrying it so that they should receive a blessing. A prayer for him was held in the Great Mosque of Salé after the noon prayer. He was buried in the room of his house which faces Mecca, and the psalmodists long remained besides his grave. . . .

The sorrow of people because of his death was profound. How could it be otherwise, for he was during his lifetime a luminary for the Two Banks and even beyond them. God the Sublime had honoured him with unparalleled understanding, decency, and gentleness towards his fellow men. Such a man had not been known since the righteous predecessors. . . .

His circle of disciples [*majlis*] was devoted to the teaching of religious science, decent standards, admonition, and the lives of the righteous saints and their inner states. . . . Never was there talk of the futile things of this world or of intrigues. There were only recitations of the Traditions of the Prophet and the acts of the pious, and the like. He regularly carried out his prayers, remained awake at night and recited the Names of God; he spared no effort to do what was good and commended by God. . . . In a word, in his behaviour and character he acted in conformity with the *sunna* of the Prophet and the precepts of the pious ancestors. May God be satisfied with them and reward us for our love of them and others like them. Amen.[11]

Although Ṭālbī was a contemporary of those who wrote about him and only one generation removed from those who gave me oral accounts of his life, the characterisation of the man differed little from the image of other saints of Salé throughout its history. He was a man of great piety, learning and intuition. Through these qualities he realised the potentiality of blessedness inherited from his ancestor buried in Salé and from the Prophet. When Ṭālbī died his house was turned into a sanctuary belonging to the pious endowments, and his tomb became an object of reverence and pilgrimage, like those of the earlier saints of the city. Shortly after the end of World

War I one of the rooms of this house was used for the first Free School in Salé.

It should be emphasised that potential religious qualities rather than actual ones were inherited by descendants of the Prophet and of saintly men, and that these qualities became less valuable and less prevalent in the late nineteenth century and thereafter. Thus, for example, the son of Sīdī Muḥammad aṭ-Ṭalbi was not known for 'saintly' virtues, although his descent may have provided him initially with a basis for gaining the respect of his contemporaries. His path to a position of influence in Salé was marked by several wise marriages—to a daughter of the governor al-Ḥājj Muḥammad b. Saʿid and to a daughter of the wealthy merchant ʿAbd al-Hādī Znībar (following the death of her husband, an ʿAlawī). These alliances later aided him in becoming assistant governor to his brother-in-law, ʿAbd Allah b. Saʿīd, and because of the many prolonged absences of the latter, Ṭālbī was often acting governor of the city. Like others of his generation, he had accumulated considerable wealth by virtue of his official position, bought property and built a new and grandiose house for his family on a former garden area. Later he was entrusted with the Habous of Salé, an appointment revoked in 1915 by the French because of his outspoken animosity towards them. Among the population of Salé Ṭālbī's sharifian descent counted for nothing in their evaluation of his reputation. He enjoyed prestige as an office holder, a man of wealth and connections and an opponent of the French.

The last man in Salé to assume some of the qualities and functions of a traditional saint and to enjoy high status by doing so was Sīdī Aḥmad b. ash-Sharīf al-Qādirī (d. 1921). According to informants, he understood 'things of this world' (namely economics and politics), and yet this did not disqualify him, as it did others, from gaining the love, respect and trust of everyone in the city.[12] al-Qādirī owned and worked some land and supplemented his livelihood by acting as an intermediary in various affairs—the arrangement of marriages, settlement of disputes, arbitration of inheritance, and as a broker for the exchange of properties. For these services, it was said, he received very little recompense, for he was a pious man, an ascetic, a man of the mosque for whom, as one informant phrased it, 'this world [*ad-dunya*] hadn't even the value of spit'. He did, however, also act as a kind of agent for Muḥammad 'Bil-Hàdī' Znībar, the head of customs in Marrakesh during the early years of this century and one of Salé's richest and most powerful personages. He managed all Znībar's local affairs, buying and selling property, collecting rent and storing or delivering goods sent to him from Marrakesh.

In the opinion of his contemporaries Qādirī's role in the community was potentially ambiguous. Basically his reputation rested on the functions he performed as a pious man and a descendant of the Prophet, and yet he was closely involved with the commercial enterprises of a highly important merchant and official. The potential ambiguity between the roles of saint and businessman was resolved in favour of the former because of Qādirī's failure to use his relationship with Znībar to improve his own material situation. In return for his services Qādirī had received little other than the house in which he lived, and when he died he left nothing substantial in the way of inheritance for his children. For the Slawis this was proof of piety, and yet they found it somehow naive and unfair. In consequence a good deal of public opinion was successfully exerted upon Znībar to donate two houses to the children of the deceased. It should be noted that the brothers of Qādirī did not enjoy a similar respect or reputation, despite their common origin. Two of them, like their father, Mawlāy ash-Sharīf, had modest shops in the Great Market Place, while two others managed a living as notaries in the qadi's court. In short, by the turn of the century it had become progressively more difficult and less useful for a man to forge an identity and create a livelihood on the basis of descent from the Prophet or local saints.

The decline in the importance and number of men who assumed these religious roles should not lead us to exaggerate their significance in the two preceding generations, or to dismiss entirely a certain continuity in the values and functions they represented and fulfilled. Descent from the Prophet or from local saints had in the past helped some people to attain positions of social and economic power. Although such individuals had never formed a predominant or even a tightly knit group in the city, they were guardians of sanctuaries, members of official delegations, and in some cases they possessed specific inherited rights to land and other sources of income. Among a relatively large number of men who could claim that they were *shurafā'* or *ūlād siyyid*, few demonstrated qualities and capacities which gave them prestige or functions within the community on that basis. The blessing of God did not adhere indiscriminately to groups of people because of their origins, but rather manifested itself in those individuals who actively, effectively and regularly showed it in their behaviour, piety and mediation among men. One did not have to be a descendant of the Prophet or of a local saint to attain the status and fulfil the role of a holy man, as the biographies of several devoted Sufis prove, but most of those who enjoyed that reputation in nineteenth-century Salé had legitimation by descent. At every level of society there were some people who were identified to a greater or lesser degree as holy men. Thus, for example, a descendant of the patron saint, Sīdī ʿAbdallah b. Ḥassūn, could in the eyes of a handful of men transmit God's blessing and cure the sick by writing verses of the Quran on the inside of a bowl from which water was then drunk. He did not earn his livelihood in that way, but these services allowed him to supplement his modest income as a broker and contributed to his social identity. There were, then, throughout the community, some men who by virtue of their descent and their personalities fulfilled similar roles. As we move forward in time towards 1930 the number of important personalities in the city who were identified in terms of their religious prestige and because of their origins dwindled. For some people the past seemed a golden age, partly because then the behaviour and functions of the *shurfā'* and *ūlād siyyid* had been deemed worthy of their origins. It had been a time when men knew and deserved their place in society.

The ulama or learned men

Another category of people was included among the religious elite. They were the ulama, that is to say those men who distinguished themselves by their knowledge of the Islamic sciences and, as a consequence, enjoyed prestige and influence among their contemporaries.[13] The ulama of Salé, like the descendants of the prophet and the saints in the city, did not form among themselves an effective group of any kind. In each generation a small number of individuals who excelled in their knowledge of the religious sciences gained a reputation such that people identified them as ulama. Their specialised knowledge made them experts in Islamic law, 'the people of learning, religion, and insight', those responsible for 'tying and untying' matters of religion. It was a title bestowed by usage and not by any formal procedure of recognition, and was neither inherited nor ascribed.[14]

The ulama of Salé who signed an oath of allegiance for the investiture of a new sultan were chosen by the governor of the city on the basis of their recognised eminence as religious scholars. These men had studied for many years with the best teachers in the city, and perhaps in Fez, and themselves taught the religious sciences in Salé's mosques. Some held important offices such as qadi, khatib or imam in one of the Friday mosques, while others worked as teachers, legal experts or law clerks. Except for the choice of certain ulama by the governor to sign the proclamation recognising a sultan, no list of their names ever appeared, and it would have been difficult to establish a consensus of opinion at any given time concerning their identity.

The biography of the most famous scholar in Salé during the late nineteenth century, Aḥmad b. Khālid an-Nāṣirī (d. 1897), although not in all ways typical of the ulama, nonetheless reflects many features common to their various careers.[15] The Nàṣirīs were descendants of the seventeenth-century saint buried in Tamgrūt who had played an important role in the history of southern Morocco.[16] Members of the family spread throughout Morocco, often establishing lodges of the Nàṣiriyya religious order wherever they settled. Khālid, a descendant of the saint's brother, reached Salé in 1805 and soon began to trade in the Gharb. With the death of his first wife, who came from a wealthy Nāṣiri family in Tangier, he inherited property in the north. Then he acquired further land and usufruct rights to farms in that area, and later settled in Larache where he married the daughter of an ʿAlawī *sharīf*. Finally in 1834 he returned to Salé.

His son Aḥmad was born in the town. Because of his father's urging and his own talent he became an educated man, going through all the stages of the traditional Moroccan system of learning.[17] After memorising the Quran according to several methods of recitation, he began to study the religious sciences. Eventually he completed his education by attending all the courses that were offered in the mosques of the city. During the middle of the nineteenth century, it should be noted, experienced teachers who had studied with the finest scholars of the Qarawīyin University in Fez were giving courses in Salé.[18] The study of the Islamic religious sciences was considered a means of establishing a connection with the teaching of the Prophet. Scholars stood as links in a chain, each attached to the preceding generation, and ultimately leading back to the teachings of the Prophet himself.[19] Nāṣirī's teachers were all outstanding ulama, and many held official legal and administrative positions, such as qadi, *muḥtasib*, and imam to Sultan ʿAbd ar-Raḥmān. Soon he too established himself as one of the ulama of the city.

According to Nāṣirī's biographer, his gifts of eloquence, memory and intelligence, his irreproachable comportment, honesty, intelligence and learning soon recommended him for government service. After some reluctance to abandon his studies and become an official, he began a long and varied administrative career.[20] Nāṣirī's advancement in official positions shows how a bureaucratic career could be forged. He began as a notary in Salé and then became deputy to the qadi, al-ʿArabī b. Manṣūr. When his teacher and father-in-law, Abū Bakr ʿAwwād, became qadi, Nāṣirī was entrusted with the administration of pious endowments. Soon he was travelling with the qadi to other cities and meeting various ulama and leading personalities of the kingdom. In 1875, at the age of forty, there began a series of appointments to positions within the sharifian administration. He served as either notary or customs director in Casablanca, Marrakesh, Mazagan, Tangier and Fez, and returned to teach and write in Salé only shortly before his death in 1897.[21]

Nāṣirī, like the other ulama of nineteenth-century Salé, had inherited no special right or calling to religious knowledge. Education had offered him an unrestricted, practical means of gaining a livelihood and with it the possibility of winning for himself prestige, patrons and clients, and, ultimately, entrance into government service. In nineteenth-century Morocco men with religious knowledge filled administrative, financial and judicial positions in the government, and among the individuals considered most suitable for these positions were ulama and merchants from Salé.[22]

These scholars enjoyed a prestige similar to that which belonged to workers of miracles and wonders, the descendants of the Prophet and the saints who showed proof of their gift of blessedness. The difference, as one informant put it, was that although the scholars were learned, pious and decent people, one could not seek their religious protection.[23] The learned, however, had their own invaluable specialisation, for they were the custo-

a Sanctuary of Sīdī ʿAbd Allah b. Hassûn, *c.* 1920

b The city and its terraces, *c.* 1920

c A city and a people dressed in white

Plate 4

a Street in residential area leading to the Great Mosque *b* Entrance to the Great Mosque; to the left, the Merinid Madrasa

c The Great Market Place, *c.* 1920

dians of religious knowledge and the experts in Islamic law. Religious studies provided a man with prestige and practical knowledge, allowed him to interpret the law and gave him access to the powerful. For these reasons people searched after the friendship and kinship of scholars and sought alliances with them.

Learning, rather than blessedness or piety, became an increasingly important means to social and economic betterment during the century between 1830 and 1930. Although the learned had always enjoyed the favour of the Makhzan and its appointments to administrative positions, opportunities for government service became more widespread from the 1860s onwards. At the same time diminishing resources in Salé, coupled with the opening up of new ports to European commerce, added incentive to an investment in learning. Slawis with a religious education rose from humble origins to rewarding government posts. As an avenue to social advancement religious studies attracted mainly the sons of the disinherited and the humble, at least until late into the nineteenth century. Few scholars in the city came from old and wealthy families renowned for the religious knowledge of their forebears. Only from the turn of the century onwards do we find important men encouraging their sons to pursue their studies in order to become scholars, and then usually only one son is given such encouragement. In the previous generation men of wealth and political power sought to ally themselves through marriage ties or in coalitions with individual scholars. Learning then was an adjunct to, not a means of attaining, influence in the city. By the last decades of the century the ulama had attained a much greater role and stake in economic and political life.

In discussing the role of the educated and literate in nineteenth-century Salé it should be noted that the ulama had no monopoly of learning. According to the old men of the city, in the past many people who earned their living in the market place or from the land had studied the basic principles of religion, and knew how to read, to write and to figure; some of the merchants, artisans and farmers were known to have personal libraries and a continued interest in book learning. Moreover both the literate and the illiterate sometimes attended circles of prayer and of learning which were held at night in the lodges and mosques of the city.[24] In Salé today it is fairly common to see bazaar shop owners in their seventies and eighties reading the Quran, books of law, history and literature while they await customers, and informants claim that their fathers and grandfathers read no less than they do. A former itinerant trader, now in his seventies, studied until he was twenty with the hope of becoming a scholar, and his case was by no means unique. Only when his father became ill was he forced to abandon his studies and take his place as an itinerant trader. Interviews among old people indicate that literacy was much more widespread than we normally assume it to have been in pre-industrial cities such as Salé.

The fact that learning went beyond a small circle of scholars and that a number of men had some pretensions to and great respect for written knowledge increased the prestige and influence of the ulama and discouraged their isolation from the rest of the community. The ulama were masters of the religious sciences and law, but for most of the community they also defined the normative rules of religious faith and practice. At the same time they set the standards of correct urban behaviour in dress, speech, manners, and so on. The circumstances which in the late nineteenth century had placed the ulama within the mainstream of social life seemed significantly different from an earlier situation in which they had been rather reclusive and isolated. Ibn ʿAlī, with typical disapproval, complains that in his time the qualities of scholars and the values of religious learning had been undermined and become debased. In his biography of the qadi al-ʿArabī b. Manṣūr (d. 1868) he writes that Ibn Manṣūr had been the 'last just qadi of Salé'. Since his death no one had been able to awaken such fear and respect among the population.[25] Stories about this qadi are still repeated with awe. People say that he passed along a tunnel from his house to the court so that he would not see or be seen by anyone in the streets, and that in court he judged people from behind a curtain lest they be relatives or important personages and so influence his judgement in their favour. Because of his highmindedness and independence he was even able to decide against the sultan in a particular dispute related to land ownership in the city. These anecdotes glorifying the scholars of yore are an expression of criticism by some members of the community against the worldly appetites and pursuits of the ulama of the late nineteenth century. They do not, however, question the rights and duties of the ulama to define the rules of religion and morality.

Although the qualities of isolation and reclusiveness no longer adhered to the scholars of Salé, their prestige and influence within the community were not, on the whole, adversely affected. Indeed, as the image of the scholar changed, his influence increased. Learning had become a marketable commodity in the city from the 1870s, to the extent that by 1906 Rabat and Salé could be called a 'Makhzan nursery for officials'.[26] By then the ulama had entered fully into the mainstream of Morocco's social, economic and political life. During this process the nature of education in the intellectual capitals had slowly begun to change. An interest in belles-lettres had developed at the expense of pure religious science, to the extent that the reign of Sultan Ḥasan can be said to mark the beginning of a renaissance in Moroccan literature.[27] Books began to be lithographed and typographically reproduced in Fez, and booksellers carried Arabic works printed at Būlāq in Egypt and at Constantinople, and volumes from the Bibliotheca Arabico-Hispana. At the same time contact with a growing number of Europeans in the port cities excited the intellectual curiosity of some scholars, if not their sympathy. As I shall show below, the situation in nineteenth-century Morocco—the profound political and economic effects of the expansion of the European powers and the cultural challenges by external ideas—awakened the deepest hopes and fears of the ulama.

Early manifestations of the literary renaissance took the form of modifications in linguistic usage and an interest in history and poetry, traditionally looked down upon by the scholars. The correspondence among scholars of the late nineteenth century was filled with discussions about literature, with poems, linguistic arguments, etc.[28] There were also written expressions of the need for religious reform. Nāṣirī, as will be seen later in detail, was ardently opposed to certain of the religious orders. Writing in a tone reminiscent of the eighteenth-century Wahhābī movement, whose ideas of restoring the purity of early Islam had undoubtedly influenced him, he called for the strict following of the principles of the *sunna*—the established custom of the Muslim community. He attacked the practices of heterodox religious orders in the most violent terms and held them responsible for the decadence of religion. Religious reformism was perhaps still a minor element in the evolving ideology and identity of the ulama. No doubt the majority of the population continued to demand that they should perpetuate traditional religious life in all its facets. At the same time the ulama had become immersed in the new economic and political realities of the country, and their ideas were changing.

The respect and influence enjoyed by the ulama increased among the Slawis during the last decades of the nineteenth century as they became more involved in economic and political affairs. Thus, for example, al-Ḥājj al-ʿArabī b. Saʿīd (d. 1891), brother of the governor al-Ḥājj Muḥammad, an extremely wealthy landowner and man of his times, was also a famous scholar and teacher in Salé. Ibn ʿAlī describes him as his spiritual guide (*shaykh*) and says that his 'sign' (*baraka*) appeared to most of those who studied with him or attended his circle, because he was a great scholar, shaykh and notable.[29] The image of the traditional scholar in Salé maintained many of the old values, despite the changing conditions and styles of life. al-Ḥājj aṭ-Ṭayyib ʿAwwād (d. *c.* 1914), was a typical example of a scholar who entered the service of the Makhzan and made his fortune. ʿAwwād, a jurist and government official, is described by his son, writing in 1964, as 'among the best of those extraordinary men of erudition, religiosity, nobility, morality and sentiments of real patriotism which Salé produced'. As a young man he had read the collections of poems of the ancients and moderns and devoted himself to the study of Arabic, its styles and diversity. He distinguished himself early as a writer and poet, and continued throughout his life to write literary articles and poems in various rhymes and metres. He opened his library to students and scholars who came from Tetuan, Fez and Mali, held long discussions and carried on an active and continuous correspondence with them. The biography relates how the scholars of Salé used to meet to discuss various matters. ʿAwwād kept a diary on discussions of poetry and linguistic arguments that took place on these occasions and included passages of letters dealing with such matters. He noted, for example, his conversations with the *muftī* aṭ-Ṭayyib an-Nāṣirī, who had criticised the terminology in the preface that he had written to the oath of allegiance to Sultan ʿAbd al-ʿAzīz. (The scholars of Salé had met at the home of the qadi and elected Ḥājj Ṭayyib ʿAwwād to draw up the document.) ʿAwwād undertook the pilgrimage to the Hijaz, met the great scholars of the East, and later wrote a travel book about his experiences. He followed the Tijānī religious order and its shaykh, 'the knower of God, the saint, the righteous, the scholar of *Ḥadīth*', Sīdī al-ʿArabī b. Sa'īḥ, of Rabat, and was educated by him and by Aḥmad b. Mūsā, a student of Salé's best teachers and himself a disciple of Ibn Sa'iḥ.[30]

These biographies show the extent to which the traditional view of the scholar was perpetuated while subtly incorporating new values such as literary accomplishments and patriotism. Although these scholars were men of their times in every way, their biographies interpret their lives according to ancient, tried and trusted stereotypes. In the conception of religious science as an unbroken chain the scholars of Salé continued to represent the links of the chain. However well they might succeed in taking advantage of new economic possibilities in the administration, commerce, the buying up of lands, and whatever new ideas and values they might be aware of and support, Salé's scholars maintained an old and idealised image in people's minds and by their own conscious endeavours.[31]

The opportunities available to the would-be ulama to achieve social status differed from those available to would-be holy men, for the scholar depended for his prestige on acquired knowledge rather than on descent. Scholars, like holy men, had only the potentiality for acquiring wealth, influence and authority—a potentiality that had to be realised by the force of personality and the strength of alliances and contacts. The retiring scholar who did not or could not use his position to advantage was respected but considered ineffective in dealing with the realities of this world.

An example of a scholar who did not—in fact refused to—attain worldly advantages was Aḥmad 'Bil-Fqih' (b. al-Faqīh) al-Jarīrī (d. *c.* 1930). His father, who had been a qadi in Salé, left him a substantial inheritance, which he failed to use to his benefit. Years after French troops had appropriated some of his land without payment, some of the townspeople succeeded in bringing pressure on the protectorate authorities to indemnify him. When they informed Bil Fqih he promptly refused the payment and argued that whoever gave land to the enemy no longer deserved the protection of God and His Prophet. The Slawis found his attitude highly principled but innocent, indeed somewhat foolish in practice. They felt similarly about his refusal to accept payment for drawing up documents or for giving judicial decisions, and about his extreme simplicity in dress and diet. These were admirable qualities and identified him as an ascetic man (*rajul zāhid*), respected and beloved, but out of step with the times. The pasha of Salé invited him to his home several times a year when visiting scholars came from other cities. Otherwise he had little contact with the urban elite, and the range of his influence within the city was very slight. In contrast to Bil Fqih, other scholars of Salé had achieved rank and status and had derived wealth, influence and authority from their religious learning.

The modernisation of education

Until 1912 the only kind of acquired knowledge by which an individual could advance in the society of Salé was religious learning. Secular education or the knowledge of foreign languages and sciences was non-existent. Before the beginning of the protectorate the *madīna* of Salé remained more or less isolated from contact with Europeans. Although some of those who worked in the ports or had participated in delegations to Tangier or Europe had seen and known Europeans, and despite the fact that Arabic newspapers from the East and from America were being read to some extent, hostility to modern ideas remained strong. The only trained doctor in Salé, a Syrian, had an extremely limited knowledge of modern medicine. From time to time an English doctor from the Protestant mission in Rabat would be called to Salé, but he and his knowledge were viewed with the greatest suspicion. Although some Slawis were under the legal protection of European powers and others had constant contact with Europeans through their commerce in Rabat, the people of the city had no desire whatsoever to emulate the ways of thinking or way of life in Europe.

Shortly after the beginning of the protectorate two French schools opened in Salé. One belonged to the Alliance Israelite. It was attended, at first poorly and reluctantly, by some of the Jewish children in the city. The other school was established by the French government for the sons of Great Families and situated in a house in Bāb Ḥuṣayn. The director had been carefully selected so as to be acceptable to the Slawis. The son of a respected qadi from Fez, he had studied French in Tangier, probably in an Alliance Israelite school. The first group of students in Salé's new school numbered about ten boys, all over the age of fifteen and already educated to some extent in the religious sciences. They included two sons of the Pasha, Ṭayyib aṣ-Ṣubīḥī, two sons of the historian Aḥmad an-Nāṣirī, and several other sons of prominent personages in the city. From the beginning, then, the French succeeded in convincing some of the town's notables that it was in their interest to have their sons given a French education. Apparently these men were a small minority, for most of the notables refused at that time to allow their boys to attend the school. Many boys in the city wanted to study in the French school, but few managed to win the approval of their parents.

Within a year the French authorities moved to a larger building—the famous House of Bin ʿAṭṭār.[32] The purpose of this School for Sons of Notables (*madrasat abnāʾ al-aʿyān*) was to give a French education to those who would become the elite of the next generation. The number of students soon doubled to about twenty, but opposition to the school remained strong. A new director, an Algerian of French citizenship, was appointed. Rumours soon spread that his French mother, following the early death of her Algerian, Muslim husband, had brought him up as a Christian, and opposition to the school grew. Nonetheless a Tunisian teacher, said to be a good Muslim, won the respect of some of the influential Slawis and even began to give French lessons to the Pasha at that time, Ḥājj Muḥammad aṣ-Ṣubīḥī. An attempt was made to end the growing resentment over secular education: one classroom hour a day and several hours in the afternoon following classes would be spent on studying Arabic. But otherwise the curriculum paralleled that of the French primary school.

Opposition to European civilisation had been a vague but forceful sentiment long before the presence of French schools. When some children in the city actually began receiving a French education certain Slawis saw a direct threat to their religion, to their very existence as Muslims. The education of the past became idealised: it had ensured the transmission of religious knowledge from generation to generation, from scholar to student, continuing that unbreakable chain from the Prophet to his people; the past scholars of the community had given constant proof of the continuity and identification of the Muslim community of Salé and had been the backbones and guardians of cultural values. The Slawis believed that education in the French school would eventually lead to the establishment of the religion and civilisation of Christian Europe in the place of Islam. Those who had been trained in the religious sciences would be replaced by others instructed only in the sciences of an alien culture, itself embedded in an alien religion.[33]

Seen from another angle, however, education was highly valued for pragmatic reasons. In the past it had opened up important avenues to economic and social advancement. Many leading individuals had derived much of their prestige, wealth and power from their education. It became quite clear that under the colonial regime an education in French schools would be advantageous in dealing with the authorities and in gaining access to resources controlled by a colonial-dominated administration and economy. These conflicting feelings and attitudes in regard to education gave rise to an ambiguous attitude towards the French schools, and explain why only a limited number of young Slawis managed to attend the French school. One informant explained that his particular case was not at all unusual: his father forbade him to attend the school and insisted that he continue in the Quranic *msīd*. Nonetheless he contrived to study in the French school in the afternoons after leaving the *msīd*. In his own words, he 'felt that he had to know the Nazarenes' language and to understand their ways'.

In 1921 some of the leading personalities of Salé gathered together and arranged for the opening of a Free School.[34] Its purpose was to give instruction in the religious sciences and to provide instruction in Islamic history and in mathematics. All subjects were to be taught in Arabic, but according to modern methods borrowed from French schools. Free Schools had already opened in Fez and some other cities. Their aim was to undermine the attraction of the French schools and to safeguard the religion and cultural heritage of Islam.[35] In 1922 the Free School in Salé outgrew its premises, and a house next door to the tomb of Sīdī 'l-Hāshimī aṭ-Ṭalbī (after whom the school was named) was donated to the Habous by Aḥmad aṣ-Ṣabūnjī to accommodate the growing number of students. Income from the rental of a near-by house owned by the former governor, ʿAbd Allah b. Saʿid, was donated by him to pay teachers' salaries. In 1924 the French claimed that ideas hostile to them were being spread in this and other schools subsequently opened. They expanded the School for the Sons of Notables so that it included more students and devoted additional hours to the study of Arabic. In 1925 seventy-four students were enrolled in the French school, and five Slawis were studying in the French Collège of Rabat. They were, according to the *contrôleur civil* of Salé, 'completely adapted to our civilisation'.[36] Yet the Free Schools, however brief their existence, had succeeded in giving their students a modern Muslim education in Arabic.

The generation of Slawis educated after 1912 were, then, of three types: (1) those who had followed a traditional education in a Quranic school and then studied with well known scholars in Salé or Fez; (2) those who went into the French school after some traditional studies; and (3) those who went from the Quranic school into the Free Schools. All these individuals possessed or were on the way to acquiring through their studies the potentiality for upward social mobility which had previously been reserved to the traditional scholar.

Many of these young men became impatient and dissatisfied with the dwindling opportunities open to those with an education, particularly from the mid-1920s onward. They and their counterparts in other cities were to be in the forefront of the nationalist movement that was to emerge after 1930.[37] Education continued to be the hallmark of the elite, but in the guise of the tarbouch rather than the turban. By 1927 the young and educated had developed new styles of life and expanded their intellectual horizons. They had formed a literary club and held regular meetings to discuss contemporary political and cultural trends in the Arab and Muslim world. They read a variety of newspapers, magazines and books written in Arabic and French, and put out their own weekly news sheet. Their most radical departure from the stereotyped educated man of the preceding generation took place in 1930, when they organised themselves into a theatre troupe and performed an Arabic play about Harūn ar-Rashīd, the famous Abbasid caliph of ninth-century Baghdad. The educated elite of Salé in 1930 communicated the meanings of Islamic culture to the community, just as men of learning had in the preceding two generations. But the meanings of that culture had changed appreciably.

Summary

Descent from the Prophet or from an acknowledged saint, and reputation as a scholar in the religious sciences, had provided men with opportunities to reach high positions in the society of Salé during the early decades of the century between 1830 and 1930. From the 1860s onward, saintly men or unworldly, pious scholars became less influential, even if the values that they represented continued to be exalted. A different type of educated and respected man emerged in Salé and entered the ranks of the elite, particularly in the 1880s. He was immersed in the administrative affairs of the central government, concerned with the political, economic and social life of his times, and influenced by the new cultural styles and ideas of the budding Arab renaissance.

Among the generation that grew up during the first decades under the French protectorate this neo-traditional type of scholar became less common and less predominant. The new generation replaced him with another kind of educated man, one shaped either in a French or in a renovated Arabic school. He too looked to the bureaucracy of the central government for employment. But an administration dominated by the rules and styles of a colonial power would not and could not accommodate and integrate sufficient numbers of educated young Moroccans. Once again, and yet more dramatically, the intellectual horizons of the educated had broadened. Religion and education, the defintion of Islamic culture, had been altered in their content and in their form. A strain of secularism had taken root, and though it was affected by and sometimes articulated in the terminology of Islam and religious learning, it was to grow and shape the aspirations and behaviour of the new elite and to help produce modern mass nationalism.

V Religious practice and belief

To speak of cultural inertia is to overlook the concrete interests and privileges that are served by indoctrination, education and the entire complicated process of transmitting culture from one generation to another.

Barrington Moore[1]

The old people of Salé interviewed in 1966–67 interpreted the experiences of their generation by employing the terms and symbols of religion. They wanted to emphasise to me that despite the economic and political difficulties they had faced and the temptations to compromise with the values and way of life of the French, they had remained faithful to the religion and culture of their predecessors and their ancestors. One man in his seventies expressed this to me by a parable. 'A wealthy merchant wanted to marry the beautiful daughter of a poor servant of God, a sufi. He went to the girl's father and offered a handsome dowry for her hand. The offer was accepted by the sufi on condition that the merchant exchange his fine clothes for coarse ones and spend seven days and nights in solitude, prayer and fasting. The merchant agreed. When the week had ended the sufi came to him and said that he could now marry the girl and return to his former way of life. The merchant replied that he no longer wished anything other than to pursue the sufi way.'

The old man explained the parable to me. Men come to depend on their way of life because of habit and routine. These are what determine how a man lives. The merchant had become dependent on luxury until he was transformed by the experience of piety. The changes that had taken place in Salé because of the French protectorate were analogous. 'When I grew up,' he explained, 'every aspect of a person's life in Salé—his work, customs, social relationships and ideas—was determined by Islam. There was continuity between the lives of our fathers' fathers' fathers' generations and my own. We made do with what we had. There was a permanent quality to the way we lived and to the conditions of our lives. It was like the *qādūs*, the bucket of the waterwheel which raised subterranean water for irrigation in out gardens.[2] When the French came their signs of progress, such as hospitals, roads, schools, etc., and their ways of thinking and humane ideas did, of course, make a strong impression on us. But soon enough we realised that the French were sons of Adam, just like us; that in each of them there was good and evil, just as there was in each of us and in every man since Creation. But all of that we had known from Islam. Its eternal validity had nothing to gain from the lessons of Christianity.'

The way in which the old man's explanations construe the experience of several generations is straightforward and polemical, and contains elements of the familiar contrast in polemics between Western materialism and Eastern spiritualism. He faithfully and nostalgically idealises a past when the tenets and practices of religion appear to him to have provided absolute harmony in the lives and affairs of men. French domination over Morocco is interpreted as a temporary challenge by an alien religion and way of life. It impresses and seduces the Moroccans, causes them momentarily to lose self-confidence. The rich merchant in the parable has the trappings of materialism and is supposed to represent the colonised Moroccan. When he wants to marry the beautiful daughter of a 'real'—that is, a pious, ideal—Muslim, he comes to realise the worth of the religion which he has neglected. Marriage and religion force him to change his ways and return to the fold of his community. Family and belief reassert themselves as the sources of identity and authenticity.

In the present chapter I want to show why most Slawis subscribed to so schematised and categorical a view of the changes that took place between 1830 and 1930, and why they conceived of cultural values as more homogeneous and consistent than they possibly could have been. There is an implicit argument here: that religion provided the vocabulary and symbolism, the cultural concepts, by means of which reality was perceived and social change experienced.

The texture of religious life in Salé during this century and the ways in which its values were inculcated among the community, young and old, men and women, can be only briefly sketched within the context of this study.[3] My concern here is with the beliefs, practices and institutions of Islam as they were encapsulated within the daily lives of the people of the city. This view of Islam does not represent the precepts and dogmas codified in the literature of the Malikite school of law, which can be called the orthodoxy of the Maghrib. Rather it seeks to look sociologically at metaphysical thoughts and symbols, psychological attitudes, established norms and daily habits, all of which were considered by the Slawis as parts of their religious life.

The dominant cultural values of Salé were anchored in the religion of Islam.[4] From birth to death the Slawis repeatedly heard and declared the name of God and of the last of His prophets, Muḥammad. When a child was born the midwife or father whispered into his ear the *shahāda*, the declaration of faith of Islam: 'There is but one God and Muhammad is the messenger of God.' When death had descended on a man, chanters of the Quran and teachers came and recited to him the same declaration of faith, so that his soul might depart hearing those words. From cradle to grave people breathed the social air of religion. Tens of mosques, lodges, sanctuaries and tombs of descendants of the Prophet Muḥammad and local saints dotted the landscape of the city. The blessing of God was part and parcel of everyday life, and so too was the fear of God, of damnation in the hereafter.

Religious faith and fear of God influenced people in many aspects of their everyday behaviour. Most social constraints and sanctions were couched in the terms and given the force of religion. For example, paternal authority was backed by the father's ability to apply an ultimate sanction. If he cursed his son by pronouncing the formula 'May God heap wrath upon you!' (*Allah yiskhaṭ ʿalīk*) the boy was effectively banished from the family and exiled from the city. In this way parental and Divine malediction became one and the same, and the displeasure of one's father potentially involved the wrath of God.[5] In general, people in Salé believed that blessings, invocations and curses had real effects. In their view of life the supernatural and the miraculous were intrinsically woven into mundane affairs, and God and Satan actively participated in this world.

Religion was looked to for the explanation of the meaning of life. It was believed that God in His infinite wisdom knew and controlled past and future: He determined the three principal conditions of man—his material situation, the duration of his lifetime and his state after death. The consequences of this religious view did not predispose men to fatalism. They did not renounce their fate to God. Rather they *assumed* His grace towards them provided their actions conformed to His laws.

The religious devotion of individuals must have varied between piety and mere formalism. The fear of God, moreover, whether spontaneous or induced, could not have occupied a man's every waking thought. Indeed, religious faith according to the tenets of Islam encourages active participation in the here and now—*ad-dunyā*—provided that it is complemented by preparation for the hereafter—*al-akhīra*. Endeavours towards worldly material benefits were to be accompanied by 'investments' in the world to come, the life after death. A younger man, remiss in his spiritual duties, would make up for his negligence later in life. It was considered commonplace and natural that older men, those who approached death, worried more about the afterlife than others, especially if they had neglected God and His law in their younger days.

The intensity of an individual's faith and devotion did not necessarily reflect their content. Beliefs and practices varied between simple and complex, intuitive and learned. They differed according to groups—men and women, old and young, literate and illiterate, city people and outsiders. Yet beyond these important social differences were shared values, a common commitment to a set of symbols, an inclusive cultural framework that defined membership and participation in a community. The fact that all but a small minority of the city's population identified themselves as Muslims was a significant factor in the social integration and harmony that characterised Salé as a community. Of course, these are relative statements: the individual members of the city rarely acted as an integrated social body, their shared cultural values were only sometimes expressed in communal manifestations, and religious symbols could at times express not consensus but social frictions and conflicts. Nonetheless an examination of the avilable evidence relating to everyday affairs, on the one hand, and to moments of crisis, on the other, shows that shared religious norms and values permeated routine activities and conditioned reactions to and perceptions of critical experiences and events.

Religion and time

On the simplest level, religious practice influenced the rhythm of life and the sense of time. The five daily prayers carried out by the great majority of adult men influenced the order and sequence of the day, the hours of sleeping, eating and working. The times of prayer—sunrise, mid-day, mid-afternoon, sunset and evening—regulated and ritualised the daily flow of time. Prayer also culminated the week. On Friday mornings men made their weekly visit to the public bath in anticipation of the noon prayer. Work came to a halt while they bathed and put on their best clothes. At the same time their wives busily prepared the special meal to be served at home after the prayer. Just before noon the gates of the city were locked, and the governor began to lead his entourage to the mosque. The two Friday mosques were filled by Slawis and by hundreds of people who came from the surrounding countryside. During the time of prayer there was a deeply felt sense of the equality of all Muslims. Informants repeatedly stressed that at these moments every man experienced an awareness that he was God's servant, and that in His house no social distinctions existed.

The noon prayer in the Great Mosque did not make Friday into a day of rest comparable to the traditional Saturday sabbath of Judaism or Sunday of Christianity. Immediately after prayer, mundane affairs animated the square in front of the main entrance to the mosque. Profane and sacred space and activities, religion and worldly life (*dīn and dunyā*) existed side by side. Auctioneers of property greeted the crowd emerging from the mosque by proclaiming the availability and prices of various plots of land and buildings.[6] Afterwards people returned to their homes, ate a copious meal whose menu was more or less established by tradition, and retired for a siesta. In the late afternoon most of the shops opened as usual and enjoyed especially active business. In the early evening women and small children often strolled in the city, visiting the tombs of saints and winding their ways through the graveyards by the sea to catch a glimpse of the sunset. Friday evenings, too, brought a larger number of men than usual to the lodges of the religious orders for prayer and study. It was the only day during the week when routine changed slightly, and the pace of life, normally slow in any case, became very relaxed.

The passage of time during the year followed the rhythm of religious celebrations. Most months of the Muslim lunar calendar were known in Salé according to the names of the holidays during which they fell, rather than by their formal names.[7] They were called in the colloquial:

1 l-ʿāshōr.
2 shāyeʿ l-āshōr ('Following the ʿāshōr').
3 l-mūlūd.
4 shāyeʿ l-mūlūd.
5 jumād el-luwwel.
6 jumād et-tānī.
7 rjeb.
8 shaʿbān.
9 ramḍān.
10 shhâr fṭōr.
11 bīn la-ʿayād ('Between the Holidays').
12 l-ʿīd le-kbīr.

The first month of the year was marked by a joyous celebration. According to a proverb, 'When ʿĀshūrā' comes, people celebrate with their children in the cities and the villages' (*ida jat ʿāshōrā, n-nās ifarḥū b-ūlādhum, fī l-mdūn u-l-qōrā'*).

l-ʿāshōr referred to the tenth day (*nhār ʿāshōrā*, cl. *ʿāshūrā'*) of the month properly called Muḥarram. It was a day of fasting and almsgiving in commemoration of the seventh-century martyrdom of al-Ḥusayn, the son of the caliph ʿAlī b. Ṭālib.[8] In Salé, as well as in the rest of Morocco, it was a day of joy rather than of mourning.

The Day of the Prophet, the Day of the Saint

The festival of the *mūlūd* (cl. *mawlid* or *mawlūd*) fell on the twelfth day of the month of *rabīʿ 'l-awwal*.[9] In Salé it commemorated both the death and the birth of the Prophet Muḥammad, as well as the festival of Salé's patron saint, Sīdī ʿAbd Allah b. Ḥassūn. It began a week of celebrations, which included pilgrimage fairs (*mūsim*, cl. *mawsim*, lit. 'season')—in honour of the city's most important saints. On the eve of the *mūlūd* a very old and famous tradition was carried out—the Procession of Candles (*dōr ash-shmāʿ*), a pilgrimage to the sanctuary of Sīdī ʿAbd Allah. A Saʿadian sultan of the sixteenth century, Aḥmad adh-Dhahabī, is thought to have brought this ceremony to Morocco, modelling it on the torchlight procession introduced into the Ottoman empire by the sultan Murad III (d. 1588).[10] Initially performed in Fez, Marrakesh and Salé, it continued only in Salé, and there it became associated with the patron saint of the city. The procession and its preparations were financed by income from a garden that had been donated for the purpose either by a disciple of the patron saint or by a rich widow.

Within the sanctuary of Sīdī ʿAbd Allah stood six wax constructions some ten feet in length and four or five feet in diameter, and two slightly smaller ones. Each of these 'candles' was a finely sculptured wax tapestry of various colours and shapes, each a sort of unique kaleidoscope. Every year after the ʿĀshūrāʾ the candles were taken from the sanctuary to the house of a Slawi master artisan in order to be prepared for the procession. The artisan who carried out this work in the 1940s had learned to do so from his maternal grandmother. (She was from an old Slawi family, the ūlād al-Mīr, which had specialised in this art for generations.) Normally he worked as a druggist, but for two months of the year he and his family were paid from the city's fund of pious endowments to devote all their time and energy to preparing the candles for the celebration.[11]

The procession was led by the head of the Ḥassūnī family and religious order. He was followed by others who claimed descent from Sīdī ʿAbd Allah and by the boat rowers of Salé. They all gathered together on the eve of the *mūlūd* in the Great Market Place of the city. Dressed in multi-coloured embroidered uniforms, said to have been handed down to them by their corsair ancestors, they were still called 'artillerymen and sailors' (*ṭūbjiyya u-baḥriyya*).[12] A group of musicians and other members of the religious order joined these people, and together they formed an impressive military type of parade. Streets along the route of the procession were crowded with onlookers. Those in the procession first visited the sanctuary of another local saint, Sīdī Aḥmad Ḥajjī, near the Great Market Place; then they descended the Street of the Shoemakers into the Bazaar, passed along the Street of the Silk Threaders, by the former hotel–warehouse for olive oil and through the Old Jewish Quarter, and climbed the Ascent of the Madrasa until they reached the Great Mosque. From there the procession, by this time followed by most of the inhabitants of the city, turned to the left, continued past the Tijānī lodge and descended to the right towards the cemetery of Sīdī Bīn ʿĀshir and the ocean. Just before reaching the cemetery, at the end of the built-up area, stood the sanctuary of Sīdī ʿAbd Allah b. Ḥasūn, and next to it a house called *dār ash-shamaʿ*, the House of Candles. The procession made several turns around the house, recalling the perambulations around the Kaʿba in Mecca during the pilgrimage.[13] Finally the candles were taken into the sanctuary, where they remained hanging for the next ten months.

That night a ceremonial meal called *gisʿa* (the name of a wooden eating platter) was served to the descendants of the saint, the 'artillerymen and sailors', the members of the religious order and the poor. From the platter, filled with couscous and roasted lamb that had been sacrificed for the occasion, groups of some twenty men took turns eating. Afterwards and throughout the night the men chanted prayers and panegyric poems in honour of the Prophet, while in the background an orchestra played Andalusian music, and tea and cakes were served to visitors. In Salé the birthday of the prophet had become the occasion for the celebration to honour the local patron saint. Orthodox and popular religion had been combined into a kind of local patriotic fête, much like the celebration of marriages in the city. It was as if prophet and saint had been turned into members of the Slawi family.

The prayer for rain

Another example of how Salé's saints had been internalised into the community may be seen in respect of the orthodox practice of the prayer for rain, *ṣalāt al-istisqā'*, sometimes called in Morocco *al-laṭīf* (meaning an invocation of God 'the Benevolent'). The recitation of this prayer took place at no fixed time. Usually it was held because of drought or famine, or in the event of a natural calamity such as an earthquake or an eclipse of the sun.[14] The prayer was performed out of doors at the *muṣallā*, the long white wall with a prayer niche in it, situated in the large cemetery separating Salé from the river.

After the completion of the prayer according to the orthodox practices stipulated in the books of law, the Slawis introduced some local innovations. They would march through the city barefoot, stopping to visit the sanctuaries of the saints, Sīdī Aḥmad b. ʿĀshir, Sīdī ʿAbd Allah and Sīdī Mūsā ad-Dukkālī. At the same time the Jews of the city went to their synagogues to pray for rain according to their ritual. Afterwards they walked to the Jewish cemetery and chanted the psalms of David over the tombs of their ṣaints. Everyone, Jew and Muslim, had fasted throughout the day.[15] When I asked people why, following the orthodox practice of this prayer, they visited the tombs of the city's saints, they replied that the ways and secrets of God were infinite and that by visiting these sanctuaries no harm could be done, but some good might result.[16]

After the procession through the city and the visiting of the Saints, people went to the mosques, performed the formal prayers, and then chanted to the melody of the *Burda*, a famous song praising the prophet, the following verses one hundred times:

yā 'l-laṭīf fī-'l-azal, anta 'l-laṭīf wa-lam tazal; alṭaf binā fī mā nazal, bi-ḥurmati 'l-Qurʿān wa-'alā man nazal

[Oh God, the Benevolent in all times. You are the Benevolent and have not ceased to be; be benevolent to us in what is to come, in respect for the Quran and him to whom it was revealed.]

Although the recitation of these verses, called *al-laṭīf*, was not itself the prayer for rain, it came to be associated with droughts and with all crisis situations.

The recitation of the word *al-laṭīf* was also part of the litany in mosques and lodges of religious orders. Early each morning teachers and ulama would gather in mosques and, sitting back-to-back so as not to be distracted, chant the words *yā 'l laṭīf* a fixed number of times.[17] During grave crises the *laṭīf* was recited in all mosques, the number of recitations being divided among them. Usually a recitation of the 'great' *laṭīf* came about because of an order by the sultan to the qadis of the empire. The formula was used by governments at various times, as an invocation to God, e.g. to bring rain, to stave off an expected evil, to expel invaders from Morocco, to stop the French invasion of 1911. Used in this way, it resembled the litany (*dhikr*) of religious orders, and it could be—and indeed was—used as a prayer, or as a political symbol. Thus in 1930 the young men of Salé used the recitation of the *laṭīf* to protest against the Dahir Berbère. They went a step further in tailoring the prayer to specific aims, actually changing the words so that they ended with the phrase 'do not separate us from our Berber brothers'.[18] When the *laṭīf* began to be recited for modern nationalist purposes in the 1930s it evoked symbols associated with the prayer for rain, visits to the tombs of local saints and the recitations of the religious orders. All these communal religious experiences, while serving specific purposes, also acted to tighten the threads that tied the people of Salé to one another.

The festivals

Besides the prayer for rain, held only when necessary, the *ṣālāt al-ʿīd*, the public prayers on the mornings of the two annual festivals, also took place in the same cemetery outside the town. The 'Little Festival' (*ʿīd as-saghīr*, or *ʿīd l-fṭor*, cl. *al-fiṭr*, the 'Festival of the Breaking of the Fast'), as it was usually called in Morocco, marked the end of Ramadan, the month of fast that is a basic obligation for all Muslims.[19] Every man and boy in the city attended the morning prayer on that day, and, if he could afford to, wore new clothes and shoes. The poor of the city lined the main streets leading to the cemetery and the paths within it, for it was a day of charity as well as rejoicing. Following the prayer, people returned to their homes to eat various traditional holiday foods. The celebration and vacation from work continued for seven days. It was a time of mutual visits among relatives and friends, of hospitality and generosity. During the week many marriages took place, for it was said that only the poor or miserly married during the month of Ramadan in order to escape the costs of large-scale celebrations.

The festival brought to an end the onerous and wearisome month of fast. All adult members of the community, from religious conviction or social pressure, abstained from food and drink during the hours of fast from daybreak to sundown. The pace of work slowed perceptibly because of the daytime fast and the long wakeful nights given over to feasting and prayer. In the mornings the city was partly deserted. People came to life slowly in the afternoons but never fully participated in their normal working activities. After the evening meal that broke the day's fast the city began to stir and its inhabitants regained their energy. During most of the night they visited friends or prayed and studied in the mosques and lodges. Just before sunrise there was a final meal before the fast began again. Most people would then sleep through the morning.

Ramadan was a period of religious fervour and sacrifice. Participation in the fast was considered a means of purification and expiation, a way of gaining God's blessing and grace and ensuring for oneself a place in paradise. Perhaps more than any other factor it defined who belonged to the community of Islam. Ramadan did not simply define a religious community, it also offered people opportunities to spend agreeable evenings in one another's company and to escape the normal routines of work. In Salé the fast and its culmination in the Little Festival offer an example of what Jacques Berque has called the 'intrinsic duration' of a particular way of life.[20]

To a lesser degree the Great Festival (*ʿīd al-kabīr*) was an integral part of the annual rhythm of life in Salé. On that day, the tenth day of the month of pilgrimage, *dhū ʾl-ḥijjah,* the entire Muslim world celebrated along with the pilgrims assembled at Mina the annual sacrificial feast. Just as for the prayer for rain and the Little Festival, the Slawis carried out ablutions and prayers at the *muṣallā*. Early in the morning straw mats were brought to the cemetery. Around 8.0 a.m. the people of the city began to arrive. Soon the area was filled with men, most of whom were accompanied by their sons, and a small number of women who sat far to the rear of the men. For a while the congregation chanted in unison, 'There is no god but God. God is most great. Praise be to God and glory to God. There is no power and no strength, but in God!' Then the qadi of the city led the prayer of two bowings, greeted the assembly, ascended the portable wooden steps (*minbar*), and delivered a sermon (*khuṭba*). Next he retreated behind the prayer niche to sacrifice the first sheep killed that day in Salé. As the men of the city returned to their homes through the cemetery they bought sweets and gave alms to the poor who lined the way. In each home a sheep was sacrificed on that morning, either by someone in the household or by a butcher who made the rounds through the city. On that day almost half the sheep consumed in Salé during the entire year were slaughtered.[21] According to tradition, parts of the sheep were prepared and eaten at special times on that day of the festival and throughout the following week. Some of the meat was preserved and set aside for other celebrations during the year. Once again households reciprocally visited one another to renew and strengthen ties of kinship and friendship.

The celebrations of the two festivals in Salé seem to be standard manifestations of the religion and customs of Muslims throughout the world. Thus there is little point in dwelling on ethnographic description, except in so far as it might further our understanding of the particular cultural symbols and self-view of Slawi society. One finds in Salé no evidence of those embellished celebrations of the festivals that exist in rural areas of Morocco, so minutely and fascinatingly depicted over forty years ago by Westermarck. The Slawis had particular customs in their prayers for rain and their combined celebration of the anniversary of the prophet and the local patron saint, but the practices associated with the two festivals lacked any peculiarities in respect to Islamic tradition. These rituals contributed to binding the community together, and played an important role in reinforcing the symbols and values of a commonly shared culture. Prayers and celebrations provided form and content to religious beliefs and influenced the rhythm and cycles of time as perceived and experienced by the people of the city. The relative sobriety and lack of embellishment in the celebration of these festivals strengthened a particular pride among Slawis in their religious propriety and exemplary piety. For the leaders of the community, their city showed itself in this way to be a model of decent, orthodox Islamic practice.

Rites of passage

Apart from the daily and yearly prayers and religious celebrations, a series of rituals of a different sort marked an individual's life. In elaborate rites of passage the natural events of life—birth, maturity, marriage, death—were imbued with the cultural symbols of religion. The all-embracing quality of religion in Islamic theology, and its capacity to comprehend the totality of existence, have been described and analysed in general studies of Islam.[22] Particular studies of manifestations of religion and magic in parts of the Muslim world (usually presented as catalogue-like collections of ritual and belief, the best example for Morocco being the work of Westermarck) complement these overviews. Yet few detailed investigations of individual towns or villages actually show how the practices and cultural symbols of Islam entered into people's everyday lives.

A description of rites of passage based on material from Salé provides a framework for understanding how religion was experienced and what were its symbols, values and customs.[23] Nefissa Zerdoumi has described how the atmosphere of giving birth in Tlemsen was filled with mystery, magic and religiosity. The child was considered an angel come from heaven and did not really become part of the family until after a series of ritual ceremonies.[24] In Salé the situation was very much the same. When a woman began to feel labour pains she called to God and the Prophet for their help, for God, it was said, would liberate the baby from its mother. In case of a difficult delivery a scarf belonging to the woman would be attached to the minaret of a near-by mosque by the muezzin, so that passers-by would see it and call out, 'May God deliver her!' When the baby was born the father came to whisper into its ear the *shahāda*, the Muslim creed. Then the baby was swaddled and his eyes and eyebrows blackened with kohl. These practices, the women of Salé believed, were stipulated by Islamic law.

According to a proverb current in Salé, one can be certain of only two things in this world. 'Marriage and death are inevitable.'[25] The Slawis, like most Moroccans, had developed elaborate ways to arrange and celebrate their marriages.[26] These arrangements and celebrations were carried out in strict accordance with the acceptable model of behaviour in Salé, 'the consecrated tradition' (*l-qāʾida*),[27] and they were closely tied to religious symbols and to the values of kinship solidarity.

The dominant *motif* in the marriage ritual was the modesty of the bride. The term for this quality of modesty, reserve, decency was *liḥya* (cl. *al-ḥayaʾ*), and it expressed the most essential element of what was considered decent behaviour for both men and women. For a girl it meant that she must remain hidden away (*ḥajba*) before her marriage, and that she could not leave the house for an extended period of time after the consummation of the marriage. But more than that, it was a whole way of behaviour, a sense of self-respect with overtones of piety and morality. Marriage followed by parenthood was the threshold into adult life, and full participation in adult life meant following these strict rules and codes of decency.

To appreciate these aspects of marriage let us consider one of the prevalent customs associated with marriage. On the day before the first festival to fall after the marriage (provided that at least three months have passed), the bride leaves her seclusion for the first time for a celebration called the 'greeting' (*s-slām*). The bride's male relatives who are allowed to see her—paternal and maternal uncles, husbands of her aunts, and some male relatives of the groom—come to visit her and give her gifts. She 'goes out to them'[28] and receives their gifts (also called *s-slām*). The bride wears no make-up, dresses simply and behaves as shyly as a young virgin. It would be considered shameful for her to appear to her father or male relatives except in this fashion. On the festival the next day the bride's father offers hospitality to his relatives and to those of his son-in-law. They remain there two or three days, 'enjoying themselves with water and pasturage [a Quranic allusion to plenty] and laughing and talking about the bride with hennaed hands'. With this celebration the bride and groom are considered to have taken their places as full members of the Muslim community and to have become responsible before God for all their actions from then until their deaths. This aspect of marriage, celebrated along with a religious holiday, represents initiation into complete religious majority.[29]

Malinowski has written that 'of all the sources of religion the supreme and final crisis of life—death—is of the greatest importance'.[30] The death rites practised in Salé illustrate how religion gave meaning to people's lives. In the narrative that I have recorded, death was described as something that 'settles on' a man. When that happened his family brought to his bedside the religious students and teachers of the city, and they repeated to him the

Muslim profession of faith, the *shahāda*: 'This is what a man should repeat or at least hear when he enters life and when he departs from it.' The dying man was given drops of honey and water so that the agony of death would be easy for him.[31] Religious passages were chanted 'until the man's soul departs there among them'. No one should scream or cry, for 'those who fear God and know what exists between them and Him' must control their emotions. On that night the corpse was closed in a room 'to be left alone with God'.

On the following day the family bought a shroud and balms from the students. (The Slawis say that Islamic law has given them three balms (coll. *leḥnōṭāt*) for this world: for the naming ceremony on the seventh day after birth, for marriage, and for death.) The men of the family went to the mosque where the shroud was sewn, while the women remained in the house to prepare the mixture of balm, dried roses, cinnamon, cloves, saffron, camphor —'the fragrant perfumes of this world decreed by law, because they come from Paradise'.

Every detail of these rites was carried out in strict accordance with the Slawis' conception of Islamic law: 'Those who are honest know the obligations of God!' The specialists who washed the dead followed the law perfectly—'the detailed process that is prescribed from beginning to end'. The corpse was washed so that it would be ritually pure, was wrapped in the shroud, placed in the coffin, and sprinkled with the mixture that had been prepared. Meanwhile the public crier had gone to the city to proclaim the consecrated formula: 'There is but one God. Muḥammed is the messenger of God. So-and-so has just died!' Then the relatives and friends of the deceased gathered with the religious students around the coffin, which had been covered with a cloth from the tomb of some saint in Salé or one brought from Mecca. The students chanted, and the relatives of the deceased distributed money to them and to the poor.

Later in the day the coffin was carried in a procession through the streets and to the cemetery, and people joined in reciting religious verses. 'Among real believers,' the Slawis insisted, 'there is no wailing or crying, for if the dead man were to hear them he would be shocked. Crying out for mercy is forgivable, but screams and wailing are only for the ignorant!' When the procession reached the cemetery the dead man was lowered into the grave while the students continued their chants.

The family of the deceased returned to his house, sacrificed several sheep and prepared a special meal of soup, honey, butter, olives and radishes. This meal, with its various courses, was also considered part of prescribed Law. In the evening another meal, 'The dinner of the grave' (coll. *leʿsha d-leqbar*), was served. The next morning the family once again provided a traditional meal—bread, figs, dates, a hot thick, soup and coffee, and throughout the day those who came to offer their condolences had to partake of food.[32] On the following day, 'the day of kneading' (coll. *leʿjin*, in the female dialect *leʿzin*), friends and relatives of the deceased went to the baker and ordered, according to their means, loaves of bread. At the grave half of these loaves were distributed along with figs and dates to the poor and to students. The other half was given to the women of the deceased's household, who divided it among their relatives and the poor. Similar ritual practices followed on the third day after death. Afterwards, on the following three Fridays and Mondays, people came to offer their condolences and to partake in a meal of remembrance.

These rites of funerals and mourning in Salé differ only in detail from other places in Morocco, and they are largely in agreement with the tenets of Islam.[33] During four months and ten days the widow of the deceased wore only white. The Slawis say that in this case, as in all others, they do 'what God has decreed'. The widow did not leave her house, see any men, or look into a mirror. God, it is said, demands these things. It is 'God's right' (*ḥaqq Allah*). When the period of mourning had finished, students and guests again gathered to recite prayers and to eat together. On this day of lamentation (*n-nʿī*, cl. *an-naʿy*) the relations of the widow brought her gifts of new clothing. She gave away her clothes of mourning and put on new ones. Then, as one old woman phrased it, 'the widow sits in her home and praises God. If she has children [to support her] she praises God, and if she has had none the inheritors come and carry off their portions.'

These rites of death illustrate the all-embracing framework of religion in Salé. People believed that every action that took place in these situations had been stipulated by Islamic law and consecrated by tradition. The functions of religion in this context were cultural, social and psychological. From religion came the ordered beliefs, symbols and values of the community. At these moments Islam reinforced the ties among individuals and satisfied the demands of the individual for inner security—for a stable, comprehensive, coercible world in the face of 'the final crisis of life'.

A moral framework underlying social arrangements

The emphasis placed on religion in Salé shows that the practices and beliefs of the townsmen, although widespread in the Muslim world, played an especially crucial role in the Slawis' self-view concerning the cultural superiority and social integration of their community. The Slawis' essential claim to uniqueness and fame was the unity and coherence of their society and the exacting quality of their adherence to the correct religious rules and values. They repeatedly used the analogy of their irrigation system, the water buckets that perennially drew from the wells and fed the soil. This image of harmony expressed for them the ideal characteristics of their society and their culture. To be sure, social and cultural tensions and differences existed. Thus, for example, the description of death rites taken from women deeply rooted in the old families of the city emphasised that only those ignorant of religion screamed and wailed.[34] Some of the population practised other customs and no doubt expressed their grief much more dramatically. They were outsiders (*barrānī-s*), and did not always share the cultural values of, or the sense of inclusion in, the community. This separation between groups, a permanent feature of city life, reflected the constant movement into Salé of new inhabitants. The relative ease of assimilation into Slawi society and adoption of its values never put an end to these differences and tensions, because new population continually arrived and remained marginal. There were always some outsiders a step behind those who had integrated themselves into the community. The integrated Slawis, especially the religious leaders among them, felt themselves responsible for leading other elements of the city's population to the practices and beliefs of what they considered the true path of Islam. Their criticism of the outsiders exerted a strong pressure towards assimilation, but it also intensified conflicts.

In addition to the rituals of prayers and celebrations throughout the year, the rites of passage and the constant use of religious symbols and formulae in conversation and everyday activities, some aspect of religion was laced into almost every social or psychological situation. Thus, for example, a long voyage was celebrated as if it were the pilgrimage by a special repast called 'the leave-taking' (*l-widāʿ*). The guests included relatives and friends of the traveller and, depending on his means and social status, co-workers or petty officials or leading personalities of the city. On these occasions people ate together, and religious students came to chant prayers and litanies. The atmosphere resembled in its sounds, smells and tastes that of the rites of marriage and death, with the social ties and cultural values of the city as underlying themes. The older men, dressed conservatively and immaculately, silently reclined on thick woollen pillows and mattresses. The young greeted them, kissing their hands or shoulders, and then retired to another part of the room to huddle together in whispered animation. The women remained in another room, from time to time echoing their high-pitched trills (*zghārīt*, or 'yoo-yoos') through the house. This carefully controlled behaviour stemmed from the assurance held by people that the right behaviour for such occasions was dictated by the tenets of religion.

The religious tenor of life was apparent in the most informal of situations and among all groups of people. The recitation of secular poetry may serve as an illustration. Salé was one of four cities in Morocco famous for its composers and reciters of *malḥūn*, a poetical form using a stylised version of the spoken language. Four groups of some thirty to forty men would meet each Thursday night for the purpose of reciting, singing or simply listening to these poems.[35] Most of them described the historical exploits of Arab heroes of the past, or the virtues of love and the fair sex.[36] Although this form of poetry was old and highly developed, those who frequented the weekly circles were not considered 'decent' men. Other people suspected them of lacking morality and piety, and accused them of being men of bad character and chronic smokers of hashish. Yet even these meetings attested to the all-encompassing religious sysmbols of Islam. They began with praise to God and ended with the recitation of the opening verse of the Quran.

The fact that religion was inherent in so much of routine behaviour and activities in Salé fit the Islamic ideal in a curious way. The Muslim scholars said that Islam embraced not only a system of beliefs and practices but also a complete code of rules to regulate every aspect of an individual's existence. The Sharīʿa was a comprehensive code for a total way of life, subsuming all legal and social transactions as well as personal behaviour.[37] The Slawis conceived of their conduct and customs in accordance with this principle, but often in effect the process of logic was reversed so that most everyday actions received a religious value and justification, whether in actual fact prescribed by Islam or not.[38] In effect the people of the city did not distinguish between social norms and religion. Few of them knew the tenets and codes of normative orthodox Islam as defined by the Malikite school of law. Nonetheless most were convinced or at least claimed that every aspect of their individual lives followed the letter and the spirit of that law. The norms and values of the community *were* Islamic law for those who accepted them. They expected all those who lived in Salé, when adult, and if fully possessed of their mental faculties, to adhere to the code of morals of the city, i.e. to what they defined as Islamic law. There were considerable social pressures and constraints to ensure that men acted 'religiously', that is, that they conformed to the way of life which prevailed in the city.

VI Cultural tenacity

'adāt d-būk, ma yaghlabūk! If you follow your father's ways, they won't get the better of you!

Family life and socialisation

In the preceding chapter I argued that the Slawis considered the totality of their social conduct as a true reflection of the Islamic way of life and that adherence to religious beliefs and practices had become a matter of habit and second nature to them. The perpetuation of these norms and values took place in the first instance and most crucially in the home. There the family instilled in the young the rules of behaviour that represented in the community the dictates of an inseparable whole—religion, law and morality.

Households consisted, in some cases, of conjugal nuclear families and, in others, of extended families. A conjugal household formed when a newly married couple needed more space and could afford to buy a house of their own. Until able to do so the couple normally remained in the household of the husband's father. If that house was large enough they would usually continue to live there as long as there was sufficient space for their numbers. There was no regular pattern for the establishment of new households, but rather a constant separation of domestic families into conjugal ones, on the one hand, and extension from conjugal into domestic units, on the other. Differences of status and wealth, traditions of particular families, personal circumstances and the availability of property, all served to influence the type of household and the cycles that it passed through. Judging by the records of property ownership, prior to the expansion in construction of the late 1800s small houses changed ownership frequently, while larger and more expensive dwellings remained in the same families over generations. This perhaps suggests differences in family structure in accordance with wealth and status differentials. However, since the last decades of the nineteenth century there has been large-scale construction and occupancy of single houses by young married men setting up their own family households.

When a man married, had children and lived in his own house he was considered the 'master of a family'—*mūl eḍ-ḍār*; the term *eḍ-ḍār* denoted both the house and the family. The family unit (*eḍ-ḍār*, *l-ʿaʾila* or *l-baīt*) was the inner core of a series of increasingly large concentric circles that could conceivably include all of a man's patrilineal relatives. In effect most people traced their descent back only two or three generations so as to include a number of specific and vague relatives of varying degree and nature. People were known first and foremost by their family name. No one was ever only himself, but was always someone's son, brother or cousin. Women, even when married, continued to belong to their paternal families as well as to their husbands'. Thus an obituary notice, in announcing the death of a woman, would mention her family name first and then the name of her husband.[1]

A man's family and his home were considered a kind of sanctuary in which the integrity of women and small children was protected. The division of internal space in the house, the small, intimate rooms, served to seclude women and children further, particularly the girls of the household. The sexual differentiation reflected in divisions of space within the house also had economic and social aspects. Women carried out all household tasks and led a separate social life, and the house provided the focus for almost all their activities. A man, on the other hand, spent most of his time outside the home. Boys, once they began to frequent school, and especially when they reached puberty, separated themselves from the feminine environment of the home and spent most of their time in the streets and environs of the city. Strong ties of sentiment united the various members of the family, but its homogeneity and harmony as a unit manifested itself only *vis-à-vis* others. All those not members of the family or inmates of the house were termed *barranīyīn*—outsiders and intruders, the same term used to describe the marginal people living on the fringes of the old-established population. If someone could enter another man's house he had to be a relative or be given the respect of and addressed as a kinsman.

In principle a man ruled over his household. He was provider, master and guide, the dominant personality of an authoritarian and patriarchal family regime. His wife and children understood filial piety as an obligation of Divine inspiration. Complete subordination and obedience to the absolute authority of the father was considered the duty of every son. Fathers, paternal uncles and grandfathers were, according to my informants and to the written sources, always the objects of respect, emulation and affection. There is, however, some evidence to the contrary: according to a psychologist from Salé, parents, and particularly fathers, inspired among their children sentiments of fear, sometimes hatred; rarely love and almost never admiration.[2]

The hierarchy of authority within the family was clearly ordered and dominated by males. Predominance belonged to the father, and then, in descending order, authority and respect belonged to the eldest son, to the younger sons and, finally, to the daughters. The relationships between the various members of the family were marked by subordination, reserve and a usually hidden hostility, particularly amongst brothers and sisters. The mother had a less clearly defined role, being at once female and parent. In her behaviour towards her husband she accepted her dependence and claustration with resignation. With others she might express pride in her husband's exercise of authority, his manliness, but she also knew that a certain realm of authority belonged to her. She was entrusted with the house and the responsibility of maintaining and preserving the customary ways of family life. Moreover the mother assured the uninterrupted transmission of cultural traditions through the education of her children.[3]

In regard to child-rearing and socialisation, young children were under the absolute control of women. Until the age of seven or eight the father of a child remained apparently indifferent and external to his upbringing. During the first few years until weaning, a baby was in almost permanent contact with his mother. He slept in the same room and sometimes in the same bed, was fed whenever he cried, and spent most of the day on the back of his mother, grandmother, aunt, housekeeper or sister. All the evidence available indicates that warmth and affection characterised this period of childhood, creating a bond of confidence and intimacy between mother and child.

Children learned to talk from women. Boys, until they entered school, spoke with the characteristic features of feminine speech, a 'bad habit', forcibly, if need be, unlearned in school. Little girls soon learned from their mothers, along with the household tasks, the obligations of womanhood: isolation, docility, the reverent fear of man, the meanings of honour and shame. A girl remained with her mother and the older women of the household until acquired by a groom and his family. The whole of her life until then was considered a period of upbringing—*tarbiyya*, a term that denotes at one and the same time infancy, education and good manners.[4]

In educating her children a mother taught them to submit to the sacred rules of religion, law and morality in order to gain the benediction (*baraka*) and satisfaction (*riḍā*) of God and parents, and to escape their malediction (*sukhṭ*). These stringent rules of conduct were taught with the conviction that no gesture was indifferent and that good manners could be acquired only through fear and suffering.

The child learned at first, by the 'apprenticeship of mechanisms',[5] such things as cleanliness, respect for bread, attitudes of deference towards parents, discretion and modesty towards strangers, charity to the poor. A mother scolded and punished her child if he disobeyed the rules. She reinforced these sanctions by recounting legends in which mysterious powers punished those who disobeyed the complicated and minute code of behaviour which regulated every aspect of daily life and whose imperative character came from belief and tradition. In such a way a child came to observe customary habits, the gestures that had to be accomplished, the formulae pronounced to assure the success of various activities or to divert evil influences. And he learned to refrain from acts considered illicit and forbidden (*ḥarām*) according to religious prescriptions, and from what was shameful and contrary to morality and decency.

In this process of socialisation norms and cultural values which prevailed in Salé became accepted and internalised. A boy took on lifetime habits, kissing the hand of his father, his teachers, or any important or respected person, or picking up a piece of bread that had fallen to the ground and putting it in a clean place. He showed humility, respect and deference to those he looked up to and would demand the same from those who he felt should treat him in such a way. He learned that men fixed the tone of their voices, adjusted their glances and gestures to maintain a cloak of dignity and forge a reputation as someone feared and respected. By imitation, memorisation, participation in rituals and observation children acquired the knowledge of *l-qa'ida*, the code of *savoir vivre* which constituted the essential basis of education.

Politeness, discretion, propriety, decency, cleanliness, ways of cooking, table manners and rules of dress all formed part of that extremely refined code of *savoir vivre* which occupied so predominant a place in social relations and moral judgements. Whatever caused shame and could irritate or inconvenience someone was considered impolite. A courteous and refined man (*ḍrīf*) evinced in his behaviour a combination of attitudes, gestures and words which made his relations with others harmonious, amiable and so natural that they seemed spontaneous. This refinement was considered the hallmark of townsmen in cities such as Salé, Rabat, Fez, Tetuan or Tlemsen, and it characterised most of the ideal qualities of a man of virtue, delicacy in negotiations (*es-siyyāsa*), finesse in language and liveliness of wit (*l-ḥdāqa*), and modesty, reserve and decency (*l-iḥya*). A girl of refinement was supposed to possess some of these qualities, but most of all she needed a sense of modesty (*l-ḥishma*). That meant being homebound and morally beyond reproach, for a girl's honour depended on her virginity.

The arts of conversation and humour, if practised at the right time and place, were highly esteemed. Formalised and rather elaborate greetings and embracing of relatives or close friends of the same sex marked almost all social relations. The shaking of hands, followed by the movement of the hand to the lips or heart, both in greeting and parting from someone, besides representing an act of simple politeness was said to have a religious significance and to assure happiness and success in one's dealings. In conversation a polite man faced and gave his full attention to his interlocutor and did not interrupt him unless absolutely necessary. An intricate play of religious and proverbial expressions, aphorisms and clichés and a wide use of euphemisms characterised an amiable conversation. Formulae containing the name of God were invoked regularly and made up an indispensable part of polite conversation: they were used to express the hope that a future project would succeed, or to communicate satisfaction, relief, gratitude, etc.

Discretion, children learned, meant not to run, speak loudly, whistle, sing, yawn or say the wrong thing. Nefissa Zerdoumi cites the proverb 'Flies don't enter a closed mouth!' and explains that not only flies but germs and demons were said to enter people by their mouths. Silence was healthy as well as golden. Discretion also meant respect and lack of familiarity towards elders, separated from younger people by an impassable 'yellow line', a 'wall of bricks', which maintained everyone in his rightful place.[6]

Rules derived from religious law or custom set down a variety of recommendations and interdictions concerning the preparation and eating of foods. Even the etiquette of meals had a somewhat consecrated character: removing one's shoes before entering the room (as before entering the mosque), bending one's knees to gather cross-legged on the floor around the common plate of food, the declaration of the *basmalah* ('in the name of God') before touching one's food, eating with only the right hand, taking only that part in front of one and eating it quickly and without mess, washing the fingers and rinsing the mouth after the meal. These table manners were taught to children early in their lives and strictly enforced. Only when a boy had matured and learned how to behave at table could he hope to eat in the company of his father and older brothers and relatives. In the household men ate separately, and usually first, while the women sat in the corner or in another room and waited for their share.

Cleanliness and notions of purity also formed an important part of the code of morality. Zerdoumi quotes a proverb that would have equally expressed the sentiments of the Slawis: 'Hunger comes from God and dirtiness comes from the devil.'[7] One had to be clean to obtain Divine favour. Ablutions before entering the mosque were necessary, otherwise prayer had no value. Like the visits to the Turkish bath (*ḥammām*), ablutions made fatigue, aches and pains and bad luck disappear. They made one closer to God. Impurity was defined by failure to conform to conventional rules of personal hygiene and dietary laws. If a man did not, for example, shave his head and cut his nails, or if he ate the flesh of pigs, he was considered to have lost his human dignity and to have become like an animal.

The socio-religious constraints of the community that ensured cultural conformity were most clearly articulated in the concept of *ḥashūma*—the recognition of that which is reprehensible. This recognition was the touchstone of good upbringing and civility, and its absence signified that a person lacked religion, modesty, dignity, honour and reason. In effect it meant that he had to experience and show embarrassment in numerous circumstances of individual, family and social life, particularly in matters touching upon sexual segregation and paternal authority. The internalisation of those values, tied to the recognition of what was reprehensible, the learning of the 'good' by exclusion of the bad, provided the basis for the later stages of education in Salé.

Ideas about human nature

The Slawis held strict and explicit ideas about how to bring up their children. These ideas were usually associated with a theory of human nature which almost all my informants could articulate with some degree of sophistication. I want now to discuss the 'stages of life' as described to me by informants. I have relied in particular on the descriptions and explanations of an old itinerant trader from a family long established in the city. He was a man of limited education, but had read a few of the classics of moral literature which in their nineteenth-century Egyptian edition enjoyed a fairly widespread distribution in Morocco. He claimed that whatever he had read only repeated what were common knowledge and shared ideas about moral education among the Slawis, and indeed other interviews justified this claim.

The life of a man was perceived in terms of phases (*ṭawr*, pl. *aṭwār*): infancy, childhood, adolescence, and maturity (*tarbiyya*, *ṭufūliyya*, *murāḥaqa*, and *rushd* or *bulūgh*). During the first phase the child grew from a helpless baby, completely dependent upon his mother, into a boy: 'the child is a guest for seven years' (*l-wild dīf sbaʿt snīn*), and he should be treated with complete indulgence. During the next phase, that of childhood, 'the child is a slave' (*l-wild ʿabd*), and to be treated harshly, beaten when disobedient and constantly watched and questioned. Parents forced their eight- to twelve-year-olds to perform difficult tasks and to assume responsibilities. Boys began to attend the *msīd*, or Quranic school, and learned to pray, perhaps even accompanying their fathers from time to time to the mosque. Although the regular recitation of prayers was not yet demanded of boys this age, pressure towards full conformity to religious obligations began. Moreover parents of a boy who prayed regularly before maturity would, it was believed, be rewarded on the Day of Judgement.

After puberty, and until maturity, 'the child is a minister' (*l-wild wazīr*). The child should execute his father's orders, ask questions, observe and learn to understand the matters of this world and of religion. During this phase the boy learned a craft or, if he was fortunate, continued his studies. By the time he reached maturity he was supposed to be able to stand on his own feet and to be prepared for marriage. The formation of his moral and intellectual qualities was considered to be complete. If at this time the young man was incapable of managing things on his own, then there was no further hope for him. If, on the other hand, he had proved himself and acquired the qualities of manliness and virtue, then his father considered him as a friend and trusted him completely to act on his own in a manner that would not bring dishonour upon the family. With maturity and marriage the responsibilities of manhood were assumed. Total acceptance by the community as a 'full man' (coll. *sīd*, cl. *sayyid*) was not attained until he became a father, or made the pilgrimage, or until his beard and hair whitened. Only then did others consider him a complete man with noble qualities, one who knew how to conduct his affairs and maintain a household.

This view of the stages of life rested on a theory of human nature that distinguished between two kinds of intelligence: innate intelligence given by God (coll. *l-ʿaql l-mūhūb*, cl. *mawhūb*, 'granted'), and acquired intelligence that came from experience and learning (coll. *l-ʿaql l-iktisābī*). Only by a successful transition through the stages of life outlined above could a man gain acquired intelligence and come to possess the ability to reason. Without it he would know neither how to act in this world nor how to prepare himself for the hereafter: there would be, according to my informants, 'no difference between him and a donkey'.

The theory of socialisation described by my informant presents us with a schematised, ideal type of personality. Like the preceding account of religion and cultural values, it assumes a collective morality and world view shared by and amongst all members of Salé's community. This uniform view of common characteristics fails to take into account the diversity of ideas in a society.[8] It emphasises certain qualities that individuals should possess in order to pursue what are defined as the essential purposes of human life. These ideal qualities tell us a good deal about the values that people held. But to see culture as a determinant and personality as an effect it is necessary to draw on examples, and these show a diversity of ideas within the society.

The first example concerns the belief system of women and the way in which it influenced children. A man born in Salé around 1910 provided the details of the account. His father, a shopkeeper of modest means, came from an old, if little known, Slawi family. His mother, on the other hand, belonged to a powerful family in the city, the Znībars. When he was a young boy his mother used to impress on him the efficacy of the *baraka* of the saints, particularly of her maternal ancestor, Sīdī Aḥmad b. ʿĀshir. She told him that as a young girl she had witnessed through her back window (which gave on to one of the lodges of a religious order) virulent arguments concerning religious orders between the qadi of Salé, ʿAbd Allah b. Khaḍrā, and the historian Aḥmad an-Nāṣirī. She interpreted Ibn Khaḍrā's position as being favourable to the orders and thus supporting her sentiments about Salé's saints. This fervent belief of hers proved to be 'true', my informant assured me, in later events.

Around 1920 his mother, who was pregnant with twins, became quite ill. The traditional cures that she underwent failed, but she would not agree to the urgings of the family that she visit a European doctor. As a married woman she refused to leave the house. Eventually her brother, then a religious official in Fez, insisted that she go to the doctor. Since he was highly respected and a man of authority in the family, he prevailed upon her to visit the doctor the next day. That night she dreamed that she visited her maternal ancestor, Sīdī Bin ʿĀshir. The inside of the mausoleum had changed since her previous visits as a girl. A man was sitting there with the hood of his cloak pulled down over his eyes. In front of him were glasses filled with oil. After she spoke to him he offered her a glass with a little oil. She drank it, and all her pains disappeared. Then she awoke from the dream, and with great joy found herself completely recovered. The next day her husband allowed her to visit the saint's tomb. She found it just as it had been in her dream. This account illustrates how faith in the blessing of the saints was a primary element in the beliefs, values and symbols of women and the children under their influence. The personalities of people in Salé and the emotional content of their beliefs were shaped by such experiences during the early years they spent in the nest of female society.

At some point in their lives all boys suffered the trauma of removal from female society into the society of men. A father put his son into the Quranic school some time between the ages of three and seven. Handing him over to the teacher, he pronounced a stock phrase: 'He is now your son, his education belongs to you. Hit him. If you should kill him, I will bury him!'[9] Although not to be taken literally, the phrase expresses the role of the Quranic teacher and the seriousness attached to a boy's religious and moral education. The teacher had unlimited authority and was a sort of accomplice to the father's exercise of repression.[10] In the *msīd* a boy was to learn by heart and in his heart the sacred words of the Quran. But he was also to be taught total submission to the authority of adults. The experience in the *msīd* made a boy feel the rigour of social constraint. Teachers and fathers acted towards boys of this age with the conviction that religious learning and morality could be acquired only through fear and suffering. The Slawis were convinced that their community exemplified the real values of Islam, particularly in regard to the respect of the young for their elders. The total dependence in word and deed of the young on the old was considered the very basis of natural order, of the customary way of doing things, of Islam and of its civilisation.

Advanced education

Boys went to the Quranic schools to learn how to behave in the company of men. If they continued to attend these institutions long enough they became literate, at least in the rudiments of reading and writing. The Slawis claimed that literacy was widespread in their city. I would estimate that approximately one-third of the male population attended Quranic schools, but there is no evidence that would allow for a reliable conjecture about the proportion of the population able to read and write at any point in time.[11]

A few girls learned to pray and to read the Quran at home or in the house of a woman teacher. They belonged to families which had a reputation for learning and the means to employ a teacher, or the availability of one at home. But as far as we know they never used their knowledge to earn a livelihood. The vast majority of girls stayed at home with the women, perfecting the arts they would practice as wives and mothers—housekeeping, cooking, sewing, caring for children. Most of them also received a strict, if informal, training in deportment, so that they learned the graces and the ideals of femininity—modesty, patience and servitude.

All parents arranged the marriages of their children, often with a view to maintaining, consolidating or enhancing their interests and social position by an alliance with another family. In the carefully weighed decisions that led to the arrangements the reputation for literacy and social graces of a prospective groom or bride, or their parents, represented an important calculation. Marriage alliances were, as we have seen, a primary means of creating assets and a fundamental aspect of social, economic and political behaviour. The educated held a strong card in the intricate play and negotiations of marital arrangements. The daughter of an educated man, once married, would bring to her husband and his family not only access to people of knowledge but the prestige of the most esteemed style of life in the city as well. She would be expected to know how to care for a home and to provide her children with an exemplary moral education. Similar advantages of prestige and life style accrued to a girl's family when she was married to a man of education.

When the Slawis proudly vaunted the excellence of their community they justified themselves primarily by referring to the glorious past of the city as a centre of learning. The local historian Ibn ʿAlī documents this contention by showing that the people of Salé had a full share in the study of the sciences of Islam and of the ancient philosophers, and by exhaustively listing the subjects that had been taught in the city and the names of famous local scholars.[12] Between 1830 and 1930 Salé continued to be considered as the second most important intellectual centre in Morocco after Fez. In fact the two intellectual luminaries of the city during the second half of the nineteenth century, Aḥmad an-Nāṣirī and ʿAbd Allah b. Khaḍrā, had undertaken all their studies in Salé because the teachers there were unrivalled, even in Fez.

The biography of a leading teacher over the past half-century shows the perseverance of the classical pattern of education and the 'type' of person it produced. Aḥmad b. ʿAbd an-Nabī, born around 1883, first studied in several Quranic schools. At about the age of fourteen he began attending the lectures given in the mosques and lodges by the half-dozen most reputed scholars of the time in Salé. After six years of following these courses he felt that he had nothing further to learn in his home city. He went to Fez to study at the Qarawīyin, the main centre of learning in the whole of Morocco.[13] At the turn of the century about ten young men from Salé were living and studying in Fez. Most were later to attain important positions in the religious or political life of their native city. Among them was Muḥammad aṣ-Ṣubīḥī, subsequently appointed to replace his father as governor, and his cousin, Aḥmad, who was to become market provost (*muḥtasib*) in Salé, and then administrator of pious endowments in Meknes. They lived in a house rented for them by their parents. Each of the Slawis students studying in Fez lived according to his family's means. Bin ʿAbd an-Nabī had to support himself, because his father, an itinerant merchant, had died many years earlier and left him nothing. He worked as a copyist and lived in a hostel, the Medersa aṣ-Ṣaffarīn. When, after eight years of study, he found that he had heard all that the scholars of Fez had to say he returned home.

His first job in Salé was as a teacher in a Quranic school, but soon he was also lecturing at night. Within a few years he had gained a reputation as one of the most learned scholars of the city. Now he earned his living by teaching older boys and adults and by advising people on legal matters. Throughout his life he continued to earn his living in this way, and most of that first generation of Slawis who received any religious education after the beginning of the French protectorate studied with him at one time or another. Bin ʿAbd an-Nabī provided the ideal type of traditional education in Salé, more or less from the beginning of the protectorate era until its end. Many Slawis considered him the perfect religious scholar, because he never compromised his ideals or allowed himself to be tempted by fashions, government service or politics.

Along with these continuities in education, the cultural horizons of Salé changed during the period under study, particularly during the second half of the century that began in 1830. The intellectual renaissance of the late nineteenth century, the establishment of the French protectorate and its schools, the development of modern Arabic educational institutions, the spread of Islamic reformism and the beginnings of political nationalism had all taken place by 1930, but they had not altered in a radical manner the traditional roles of the family and religious education. Some young men were influenced by alternative cultural ideas and practices, but their lives continued to be deeply influenced by the relative stability of the patriarchally dominated family. Their elders still maintained authority, demanded cultural conformity and exercised social sanctions. Discipline and submission to authority continued to be the principal effects of socialisation and education. The internalisation of the prevailing code of morality and teachings of Islam still constituted the bases of religion and the meaning of life. This culture was not a seamless cloth, but for all that its bits and patches held together tenaciously, and they formed a pattern in which a variety of ideas, beliefs and practices fitted together.

The religious orders

Llī mā ʿindu-sh shīkh, esh-shīṭān huwa shīkhu. Whoever has no shaykh (religious guide), Satan is his shaykh!

Sufi mysticism had taken root and become an integral part of religious life in Morocco since at least the fourteenth century. In nineteenth-century Salé Sufism existed within the framework of the religious orders and within the walls of their various lodges. The men who frequented the orders bore little resemblance, however, to the Sufis of old. They did not devote their lives to the disciplined 'way' of their masters, nor live together supported by endowments and charity in a convent-like atmosphere. The Sufi lodge (*zāwiya*), once a hermitage or school, had been transformed during the centuries into a meeting place that catered to the congregational needs of various sections of the urban population. Mother houses or branch settlements of religious orders, they fulfilled a variety of functions for the local community.

Most of the large lodges contained a separate room for prayer, the mausoleum of a saint which was covered by a dome (*qubba*), a room set aside for recitations or celebrations, a Quranic school, and rooms for guests—pilgrims, travellers or students. A cemetery, with the tombs of people from the city who had wanted and been able to afford burial in it, usually adjoined the lodge.

According to the old men of Salé, every adult male used to attend the meetings of one of the religious orders regularly.[14] Fifteen orders (*ṭā'ifa*, pl. *ṭawā'if*) had lodges in the city, most of which constituted branches that were widespread throughout Morocco and sometimes beyond.[15] Two groups were particular to Salé, the Ḥassūniyīn and the Ḥajjīyīn, and they met in the tombs of the local saints from whom they took their names. In the evening, after they had finished their work, many of the townsmen went to lodges to perform the evening prayer. The prayer was followed by liturgical recitations and litanies specific to each order, the incessant repetition of certain words or phrases in praise and remembrance of God (*dhikr*), or the recitation of Quranic passages.

The tenor of these meetings varied from calm to frenetic, depending on the identity of the order and its adherents. The old-established population of Salé tended to visit six or seven particular lodges. These they considered to be like themselves, that is, more dignified and more orthodox in their practices than the lodges where those whom they termed the ignorant masses participated in ecstasy-inducing recitations. The Darqāwiyya, Tijāniyya and Kattāniyya religious orders had a reputation for controlled decorum, while the ʿAisāwiyya, for example, was said to be gross and violent in its proceedings. In short, there appear to have been two categories of religious orders in Salé, and these paralleled two sorts of people—*bona fide* Slawis and outsiders.

Aside from this overall distinction, affiliation to orders reflected no clear pattern. Among both groups of people, members of the same family or occupation often followed different orders. I recorded many cases of brothers, fathers and sons, men of the same neighbourhood and trade, whose ties of kinship, residence or trade did not extend to their common participation in the activities of any single lodge. A few families stated that for many generations they had been followers of a particular order. This was the case with the Ḥassūnīs and Ḥajjīs, descendants of local saints in whose names lodges had been established. The only way in which the affiliation to lodges reflected to some extent an important aspect of the city's social structure was the tendency of clientèle groups to meet in particular lodges. Among some people on the pale of the Slawi community the attachment to lodges and their shaykhs was extremely close. The Slawis, on the other hand, expressed little sense of identity or group cohesion along the lines of the religious orders. On the basis of the evidence from Salé for this period one must be wary of any generalisations about the social or political functions of religious orders in Morocco, or for that matter anywhere in the Muslim world.

The information collected from field research in Salé about the orders is sparse and inconclusive. Only the Tijāniyya and Darqāwiyya were described to me in any detail. Some of the more important coalition groups described in chapter III often visited these particular orders. After prayer and recitations the men present in these lodges would split up into groups and discuss matters of common interest. This was the case among the Tijāniyya, in particular during the critical period between the death of Sultan Ḥasan in 1894 and the beginning of the protectorate in 1912. These informal meetings offered occasions for the exchange of information about the economic and political conditions of the country according to the latest rumours and to reports from the Eastern Arabic press. And on these occasions men simply discussed the mundane affairs of the city.

The limited information at hand suggests that the religious orders offered men opportunities of creating and strengthening the bonds among them. More than the patrilineal family, the quarter or the guild, the religious orders offered a framework within which groups holding common values and interests could come together at a fixed time and place. These religious orders, moreover, were not for the most part unique to Salé. The followers of a given lodge were 'brothers' of their counterparts throughout Morocco, and sometimes beyond. Especially in regard to Rabat and Salé, this sense of brotherhood could override an otherwise chauvinistic, local solidarity.

There is little evidence that the religious orders provided effective institutional bases for any concerted action, religious, political or other. Only the ill-fated Kattānīyya order showed a vague, short-lived tendency towards political manœuvring. After its foundation in Fez late in the nineteenth century the Kattānīyya took root in Salé and gained the support of some of the leading personalities in the city. When in 1908 Muḥammad b. ʿAbd al-Kabīr al-Kattānī, the leader of the order, was imprisoned and died at the hands of the central government, his family sought refuge among their powerful friends in the city. But the government closed the order's lodges throughout the country, and the followers in Salé abandoned Kattānī's cause.[16]

Many of the town's lodges played an important role as centres of religious education and prayer. At certain times of the year, especially during the nights of Ramadan, the ulama of the city gave courses in those lodges that were attended by the established urban population. Throughout the year, on Thursday nights and Friday afternoons, most religious orders carried out prayer meetings which might include 'séances' (*ḥaḍra*) of recitations, litanies or sermons of admonition, depending on the practices of the individual lodge. And finally, as described above, in some cases annual religious festivals coincided with celebrations by particular lodges in honour of the saints in whose name they had been founded.

The religious orders provided for the social and religious needs of various segments of the community. All the activities mentioned so far were participated in by men in groups. But the lodges also satisfied the personal needs of individuals. Thus a man who regularly attended the meetings of a particular order might also use the premises of that lodge to celebrate events and rites of a personal nature, like his return from the pilgrimage, the circumcision of his children or the burial of a member of his family. On these occasions the lodge became a gathering place for a man, his family and friends.

Individuals also came to the lodges at times when there were no formal meetings, simply to pray or to meditate. In many cases they believed that the saints who had founded the order 'worked' on their behalf and acted for them as effective intermediaries to God. Some informants stated that at moments of crisis in their personal lives they would go to their lodge to speak with their saint. Others made a habit of visiting various lodges so that they could know how to gain the intercession of several saints. Those who denied the capacity of intercession might still go to a lodge to pray in solitude or to carry out their obligatory daily prayers. For them the intention of prayer (*nīya*), whether in a mosque, a lodge or elsewhere, defined a man's piety. The ignorant, it was said, might seek intercession by the saints, but they were nonetheless sincere Muslims in their intention. Many women also visited some of the lodges individually, especially those that served as burial grounds. But here again the religious orders differed in their practices: some accepted burials and visits by women, others did not.

To some extent the religious orders did, of course, reflect the social structure of the city. Some tended to be frequented by established townsmen, while others drew their adherents from the marginal people of the population. The former groups included the cultural and religious elite of the city, and to some extent literacy set the tone of those lodges and their followers. The latter group, though perhaps comprising lower-status elements of the deeply rooted urban population, was characterised by a rural ethos and a following who were illiterate and mostly of peasant background. This division of the orders into two types served to legitimate and reinforce the dichotomy in social structure that has been noted before. The consequence was that those not deeply enmeshed in the activities and institutions of the bourgeoisie were considered as 'outsiders', both socially and religiously.

It is necessary to draw a thin line here. Clearly, religious dissension as expressed by the various religious orders played some role in the life of Salé's community during the period, just as it did in Morocco's history. But the nature of this dissension must be clarified so as not to give more weight to the functions and significance of the orders than the evidence will bear. The situation of the orders in Salé does not support the generally accepted view that Moroccans reacted to the events of the late nineteenth century by seeking refuge in a proliferation of mystical religious orders that had military and political inclinations.[17] The information on this question in Salé is more limited than one would like, but sufficient for a cautious interpretation of religious dissensions and the roles of the orders.

A passage in the history of Nāṣirī discusses the lack of propriety of the religious orders that appealed to the people of the countryside.[18] Although Nāṣirī may have been either a partisan of a particular order or opposed in principle to all religious orders, he explicitly limited his attack to orders of a rural character.[19] He focused his criticism on the nature of the relationship between the orders' followers and their particular shaykhs—whether already deceased or still alive. The followers of the orders, he says, turned to their shaykhs for aid or refuge, especially at moments of distress. Each group believed that its shaykh alone could benefit or harm mankind. Thus, according to Salé's historian, a very tense situation had arisen during the nineteenth century. The Muslim community had split itself into many groups, with every city or village containing numerous religious orders. Nāṣirī points out that the 'shameful propaganda' of these orders had existed in Morocco since the tenth century A.H. (1495–1592), but that such ideas were unknown to the 'venerable forefathers of Islam', those who provided the model for the behaviour of all Muslims. Moreover, he argued, the sectarianism of the orders opposed the very tenets of Islam, the unity of the community, and the unique existence of God. Muslims who were orthodox in their beliefs should regard those individuals who possessed great intuition and piety as 'the teeth of a comb', beloved because of and for God. They should love the shaykhs licitly, that is, according to Islamic law, and not with the love of partisanship or by attributing to them qualities that belong only to God.[20]

Those accused of being sectarians, of following the errors of certain religious orders, were called the 'lowly' or 'common people' (*ṭaghām*): they met at special places and times and took part in séances—a heretical practice (*bidʿa*) which, misusing Sufi terminology, they called 'the presence' (*al-ḥaḍra*). Nāṣirī reports that these people took over lodges in the name of some shaykhs and turned them into prayer mosques, and there they danced and sang to the accompaniment of various instruments, sometimes even burning fires to honour their leaders. During these séances the followers of the orders lost themselves in such activities for long periods of time, and in this state of confusion they believed that their 'way' was closer to God.[21]

Nāṣirī goes on to elaborate the ignorance, uselessness and sinfulness of such people, describing how by their practices at the tombs of saints they imitated the customs associated with the holy Kaʿba of Mecca: tombs were covered, rertain limits around them were made inviolable, and animals were brought to them as sacrifices. The yearly pilgrimage fairs to these tombs also come under attack by the historian. He considered them illegal and stated that during the course of the fairs moral abominations and scandals took place, especially among the rural people. In the final analysis he considered that the followers of these religious orders were not true believers: by associating the name of God with the names of saints in verses of praise, oaths, entreaties for compassion, and the like, and by adding the name of a servant to the name of his Master by the conjunction 'and', they partook of polytheism.[22]

Given the lacunae in our information both about the development of urban and rural religious orders in nineteenth-century Morocco and about the spread of reformist ideas among scholars, it is difficult to draw sociological conclusions from Nāṣirī's remarks. Yet this was a period of profound economic change and increasing social differentiation in Salé. Nāṣirī's position seems to indicate growing dissension between the wealthy and literate inhabitants of the city and their allies on the one hand, and the groups on the margins of and outside urban society on the other. The latter, treated as aliens and heretics, were attacked on religious grounds because of their adherence to the practices of certain religious orders. Moreover in a period of uncertainty and upheaval the attraction of the ecstatic orders may have represented a reflex and a refuge to the poor and illiterate on the fringes of the city and in the countryside.

Those who profited from economic change responded differently. Criticism of orders that were popular among the masses was used by the educated urban elite as a means of increasing their social prestige and influence as custodians of the religious tradition. The main object of their propaganda was the central government. The ideology of reformism, that is, a return to the orthodoxy of the venerable forefathers, served a double purpose: it attacked factionalism by calling it heresy, and at the same time defended the moral fibre of the Islamic community. The urban elite made themselves spokesmen for these policies, arguing that a return to orthodoxy, which they alone could ensure, was the only way to protect Morocco from the insidious and harmful consequences of European civilisation. Thus an-Nāṣirī's position is an early expression in Morocco of the two tendencies—internal reform and external defence—that were to mark the development of much of modern Islamic thought.[23]

Reformist ideology had a significant influence on the growth of modern nationalism in Morocco from the 1920s onwards. In Salé, an important centre of the national movement, all the religious orders seem to have fallen into disgrace as a consequence of these political developments. This partly explains the lack of documentation available on the subject. Nonetheless the orders had clearly provided frameworks for the gatherings of social groups, and they had fulfilled religious and cultural needs.

Gellner has suggested that the Sufi religious orders in rural Morocco were a *substitute* for the legalistic Islam of the ulama, while the urban orders, on the other hand, acted as an *alternative* to the orthodoxy of the ulama.[24] As far as Salé is concerned I would argue that the popular orders complemented the religious life of their followers, while the orders frequented by the established urban population supplemented their religion. In both cases the social and cultural influences of the lodges were marked, particularly in what may be termed the continuing education of adults.

The ideals of Sufism and asceticism did not lose all meaning in the city. In the 1960s people still talked with admiration and enthusiasm about the revered and saintly men whom they had known. One of these, l-Fqih Bin ʿAbūd, was often mentioned. He had come to Salé in the late nineteenth century because it still exerted its attraction as a place of withdrawal from the world for mystical purposes. He spent his days in the lodge of the Darqāwā religious order, reading and meditating. Because he had previously been a teacher of the law, people sometimes came to him for legal advice, and he appears to have lived from the fees they gave him. In the evenings he held a circle of learning in which he taught the religious sciences and the works of the famous mystics of Islam. Among his disciples on these occasions were some of the city's most highly respected scholars, officials and men of affairs. They would sit at his feet like small children beside their father.

Part III The disruption of economic life

The occupation of Algeria disrupted the unity of North Africa and made it submit to the same economic laws and the same juridic principles, whoever might be the reigning sovereigns.[1]

When the French occupation of Algeria began in 1830 Salé was a small city with a viable and self-sustaining economy. During the next century extensive and unprecedented transformations resulting from the incorporation of Morocco into the world capitalist system profoundly affected the ways in which the people of the city earned their livelihoods. This period of economic change and the social consequences that accompanied it may be divided for analytical purposes into three main phases.

1. Between approximately 1830 and 1865 raw cotton, cotton cloth and manufactured cotton goods from Europe increasingly penetrated the Moroccan market and caused the gradual abandonment of cotton farming and manufacture in and around Salé. The growth, production and sale of cotton and its products, until then the principal economic activities of most of the population, eventually came to a stop. The city began to depend on the consumption, processing and trade of a variety of goods imported from Europe. Local resources no longer provided the basis of the economic well-being of the majority of the population.

2. From around 1865 until 1900 the pre-colonial economic penetration of Morocco intensified and led to a growing dependence on European and international market conditions. It was a period of monetary instability and crises, of sudden and yet recurrent phases of prosperity and depression. The craftsmen who formed the majority of Salé's labour force became increasingly impoverished. At the same time a small group of merchants and government servants gained control of most property and wealth in the city.

3. From approximately 1900 until 1930 Morocco became wholly dependent on foreign powers, both economically and politically. In Salé during the first half of this period (until the beginning of the French protectorate in 1912) the tendencies of the previous phase were accentuated; the economic conditions of craftsmen declined yet further, while the new urban capitalists retained or increased their wealth. During the first eighteen years of the

protectorate (1912–30) the overall economic expansion of the country had limited effects in the city. Some merchants, officials and craftsmen benefited from the presence of the French and the development of the new capital at Rabat, but for the bulk of the labour force the general standard of living declined because of continual currency depreciation and the rise in the cost of living. By 1925 the majority of the townspeople were suffering prematurely from the initial effects of the world depression.

In the next three chapters I present an elaboration of this scheme, along with detailed material on the various sectors of economic life in Salé. The information and conclusions that will be presented have been drawn from bits and pieces of written evidence and from oral testimony supplied by the oldest and most reliable informants in the town. This material and my interpretation have been measured against and supplemented by J.-L. Miège's monumental thesis on European economic penetration in Morocco for the period 1830–94. Miège's view of socio-economic change in Morocco during this period is based almost entirely on European sources. On the whole the indigenous written and oral sources used in this case study of Salé substantiate as well as illustrate many of his conclusions.

VII Free trade and imperialism

When we look at economic conditions at the beginning of the period under study we find the Slawis apparently indifferent to maritime trade. On the whole they drew their sustenance from their own soil and from overland trade in the city's hinterland and beyond.

The port of Rabat–Salé had by this time lost its predominant role as a centre of commerce to Tangier and the newly founded port of Mogador.[2] Piracy and the maritime trade associated with it had already ceased to be remunerative several decades before the 1818 treaty with the European nations in which Morocco's sultan promised to respect the freedom of the seas and disarm his warships. Although some of the town's products were still transported to other ports and sold there to European importers, local maritime trade had declined to almost nothing. In its place the Slawis had turned the direction of their economic activities towards the interior and established tightly knit bonds of trade with the rich rural areas north and west of the city.

Most of the people drew their livelihood from farming and crafts, and trade in locally produced goods. The most important economic resources of the city at that time were, in descending order: (1) cotton and linen and their manufactured products; (2) leather tanning and its products; (3) fired clay and the pottery made from it; (4) grapes and the manufacture from them of a sort of jam called *as-sāmit*; (5) straw mats made from locally grown reeds.[3]

The cotton industry was highly developed and provided work for a good part of the population.[4] Until the 1830s all the raw cotton used in manufacturing cloth was grown and processed in and around the city. The ways of processing raw cotton fibre into textiles vary, of course, according to the level of technology and the machinery available. Apparently the Slawis practised a system in which almost every step of production—the spinning of thread, dyeing it and weaving it into cloth—was carried out by specialists working individually or in small domestic units. Farmers picked the cotton and had it auctioned at market. It was sold in small bundles, then cleaned, dried and auctioned again. Women often then bought the cotton, carded it and sold it once more in the open market to others for spinning. Finally weavers purchased the processed thread, wove it into cloth, and in turn had the greater part of it auctioned to wholesalers or garment makers. This general pattern of production and sale seems to have been the rule for all crafts and for the buying and selling of products.[5]

Until mid-century most of Salé's economy seems to have revolved around the textile industry in one way or another. According to Ibn ʿAlī workshops for the weaving of cotton and linen cloth alone numbered some six hundred. This is a fabulous figure, and one is not sure what it actually represents in terms of the size of the industry. But clearly the manufacture of cotton cloth occupied the central position in the city's economy. Moreover many people in shops and at home were engaged in sewing and embroidering garments from locally manufactured fabrics, both for the internal commerce of the city and for the rural markets. The cloth and garments made in Salé gave the population a reputation for economic self-sufficiency and well-being. Sultan ʿAbd ar-Raḥmān (1822–59) is said to have been extremely impressed by the multitude of Slawis who came to greet him during one of his visits to Rabat–Salé. All the Slawis wore white, locally produced linen clothes—shirts, vests, trousers, belts, turbans and cloaks. The sultan was prompted to remark at this manifestation of pomp for his benefit that the people of Salé were shrouded while still alive.[6]

At approximately the same time that Salé and the rest of Morocco enjoyed relative economic stability and prosperity the industrial revolution of Western Europe began increasingly to look to the Middle East and North Africa for raw materials for its industries and new markets for its products. In Britain Lancashire cottons had between 1770 and 1840 provided the cradle for modern industrialism. Morocco, although drawn out of political isolation by the French conquest of Algeria in 1830, still managed to keep most of its resources within the country and its markets relatively closed to European products until the 1850s. Exports were formally banned on religious grounds, while a 50 per cent duty was imposed on imports of manufactured goods. Most of the limited foreign trade passed through Mogador and Tangier to Gibraltar and was under strict government control. The government protected the local cotton handicraft industry, but at the cost of lowering duty on the import of raw cotton fibre.[7]

By 1854 the *makhzan* was anxious to increase its revenues and became less hostile to European pressures in favour of free trade. France needed cereals and woollens for its army in the Crimea and turned to Morocco. The purchase of Moroccan wheat by French merchants caused prices to rise abruptly, and the extension of cultivation was paralleled by an increase in the government tithe on crops and the duty on exportation. Within a few years the government no longer even attempted to maintain protective tariffs. In 1856 an Anglo-Moroccan commercial treaty removed all restrictions on trade, except on arms, ammunitions and tobacco, and fixed import duties at 10 per cent *ad valorem.* The sultan no longer sought nor was able to control commercial relations with Europe, but only hoped to increase the government revenue by encouraging the development of trade.[8]

Within a few years British merchants were exporting large quantities of raw cotton and cotton cloth into Morocco. Cotton farming in Salé had already begun to decline because the raw cotton fibre imported through Gibraltar was of better quality and, even with protective tariffs, no more expensive. With the reduction of tariffs the Slawis could no longer even compete with the prices of British manufactured cotton goods, which between 1856 and 1865 made up over 50 per cent of Morocco's imports.[9] The end of cotton farming and the textile industry in Salé was averted for a few years by the American civil war, which cut off the supply of raw fibre to the Lancashire mills. Once the war ended, the supply to the mills was resumed. Within a few years the renewed trade in imported British cottons had led to the complete demise of Salé's plantations and handicraft industry. The Slawis lost more than their cotton industry to European commercial expansion in Morocco. The resources on which they depended rose steeply in price because of the demand for them on the international market. Thus, for example, agents working for merchants in France and Spain purchased large quantities of cork oak wood from the nearby Mamora Forest and leather, wax and wheat from the Gharb. Nonetheless economic conditions in the city appear to have remained relatively stable and tolerable until around 1865.

Ibn ʿAlī reports that during the first part of the reign of Muḥammad b. ʿAbd ar-Raḥmān (1859–73) prices in Rabat and Salé were low, while the value of buildings and land rose. Some people began to accumulate wealth, to have elegant clothes, and to enjoy luxury goods. Beautiful houses were built, with inlaid mosaics, marble, and magnificent sculptured and engraved wood and plaster.[10] These were the beginnings of new wealth accompanied by a more conspicuous style of living. During that period Ibn ʿAlī's father was among some thirty men from Salé who began to sell the imported goods of Europe throughout the rural markets of the Gharb. At the same time Jewish itinerant traders from Salé had taken to trading these products among the tribes of the Sebou and east of the city. These traders bought goods from kinsmen or associates who had established wholesale houses in Rabat. If they sold sewn garments they employed their families or neighbours to make them. New methods of organisation and division of labour began to appear.

In 1865 almost 2·2 million pounds of wool were exported from Rabat. Its price had risen 400 per cent in twenty-five years. While some merchants and officials from Salé profited from this burgeoning commerce, craftsmen suffered from the disappearance and expensiveness of their primary material. Conflicts of interest among various groups sparked social antagonisms, but for the most part these found expression in outbursts of xenophobic feeling rather than in civil strife.[11]

By 1865 it was clear that the prosperity that came with European economic expansion had not affected most of the urban population of Salé. Only a limited number of people had adapted successfully to the changes in economic processes. In the long run these changes would cause the impoverishment of the majority of Salé's population and the enrichment of a small minority. Only the latter successfully gained access to hard capital through commerce, and within a generation the ownership of most of the crops, goods and property in Salé would be in their hands.

The temporary boom of these early years of economic penetration was accompanied by increasingly hazardous economic conditions in the countryside. In consequence many people migrated to the cities. The growth in absolute numbers of the population of Salé during the nineteenth century was, as I have shown, relatively slight. But taking into account famines and epidemics, the relative stability in numbers of population can be explained only on the basis of migration from the countryside into the city. Crop failures, drought and famine in 1850 and the late 1860s and 1870s pushed large numbers of hungry rural people into the coastal cities. Salé, like Rabat and Tangier, received fewer migrants than the new, developing port cities, but the proportion of inhabitants from rural origins certainly increased.[12]

In 1867 there was a failure of crops throughout Morocco. But already a year earlier the tribes around Salé had attacked the city, pillaged its gardens and cut off its communications. Although perhaps encouraged to these acts by news of the Sultan's sickness, their harvests had been steadily bad since the famine of 1864.[13] Once again in 1867–68 locusts and drought caused wheat prices to rise some 60 per cent, and many rural areas were politically unstable. Continued misery and penury throughout the countryside created serious pressures of migration into the cities, as well as affecting food supplies.

At virtually the same time Europe was undergoing an economic crisis caused by overproduction. As a result, wool, now Morocco's most important export, decreased sharply in value. Local merchants were hard hit and severely pressed by their creditors. Simultaneously interest rates rose sharply. Imported merchandise unloaded at rock-bottom prices made it absolutely impossible for local artisans to compete with these goods in an already dwindling market.

The conjuncture of local Moroccan and European crises was to become a regular pattern throughout the rest of the century. These crises led to accelerated and interconnected changes: urbanisation, new commercial axes, the ascendancy of urban capitalism, social tension, and finally financial crisis. Rural farmers abandoned their fields for the cities, small merchants were ruined, artisans were unable to make a living. The only people who profited from this situation were those with ready cash who could buy up and store food surpluses and speculate in land. A small number of men with capital and commercial skills succeeded in concentrating and consolidating wealth as a result of the rise of urban capitalism and the subsequent economic crises.[14]

The domination of the city's economy by a small number of people was a gradual process that took place during a period of intermittent crisis and prosperity. The occupation of Tetouan in 1860, the subsequent indemnity to Spain, the growing debts of the Moroccan government to the European powers and the spread of the protégé system further weakened the country, politically and economically. At the same time the diplomatic neutralisation of the country by the European powers made it unable to defend itself against further economic penetration and dependence. The periods of prosperity that separated crises led some people in Salé to think that the free play of world market forces might be advantageous to them. For most of the people concerned these were false hopes.

Take, for example, some of the phases of decline and prosperity during the second period that I have defined, 1865–1900. The years 1871–75 were excellent for agriculture and for commerce. Low taxes and the high prices paid for Moroccan exports, especially wool and wheat, stimulated trade with Europe and the internal market. Large quantities of tea, sugar and cotton found ready buyers in both rural and urban markets.[15] 'In 1875,' Nāṣirī reports, 'prosperity had returned, security had been re-established, life had become easier, and prices had fallen to a large degree . . .'[16] However, the economic situation took a downward plunge in a prolonged crisis from 1877 to 1886. It began with a crop failure because of drought and was followed by invasions of locust that devoured whatever crops had survived. Wheat prices sky-rocketed some 300 per cent within a few weeks after the beginning of the 1878 harvest. Animals, lacking pasturage, died by the thousands, and those that survived were sold at minimal prices because the farmers could no longer feed them. A familiar chain of catastrophes was soon unravelling: famine, epidemics of cholera and smallpox, sickness and death, and the paralysis of economic life. For the next seven years Morocco experienced a 'subsistence crisis'—soaring prices, scarcity, migration of population due to famine, misery, and finally social and political conflicts—'the troubles born of despair'.[17]

The insufficiency of government revenues and the steady depreciation of local currency were two of the principal features of Morocco's path to economic ruin. The rising costs of government indebtedness to the European powers have been described along general lines in some recent studies of Moroccan and North African history.[18] But detailed studies tracing the effects of inflation and monetary disorder are greatly lacking.[19] It is clear, however, that the exchange rate of Moroccan silver currency fell drastically throughout the period under discussion. The coin of exchange was the silver ūqiyya (also called dirhām). In principle ten ūqiyya weighed ten ounces in silver and were equivalent to the Spanish réal douro or five French francs.

In fact the ūqiyya was continuously declining in value. In 1844 the réal was worth fifteen ūqiyya, in 1876 between fifty-three and sixty-three ūqiyya, and by the end of the century 140 ūqiyya.[20] The overall depreciation in the value of the Moroccan currency during a seventy-year period was of the order of 140 per cent.

Once again some individuals in Salé profited from these conditions. Because of the growing insecurity of the route between Casablanca and Rabat merchants in Rabat and Salé entered into direct commercial relations with Marseilles, by-passing their former intermediaries both at Gibraltar and at Casablanca.[21] Hard currency was again at a premium. Those who could mobilise capital bought up property at advantageous prices and lent money at ruinous rates of interest. Those who had begun to grow wealthy in the 1860s consolidated their fortunes. They were joined in their economic domination of the city by a few men who had utilised their assets to speculate in wheat, especially during the great famine of 1878. The land records for these years show that much of the city's property was bought by these men during this period of economic upheaval.[22]

The rise of this type of urban capitalism in Salé reflected what was happening in all the important coastal cities of Morocco. The scarcity of hard currency during the periods of crisis made the farmer, the small merchant and the artisan progressively more dependent on the loans and credit of the wealthy. The interest demanded was usurious—anywhere from the normal 50 or 60 per cent a year to 200 per cent during crises. Property held as collateral was surrendered if the crop did not come in or the merchandise went unsold. Wealth which had previously been transitory became, in the hands of the few, more stable and permanent. If a man could amass some capital, find protection in associations with Europeans or their protégés, and invest in property or loans or speculate in the exchange of merchandise or currencies, he was fairly well assured of maintaining his wealth. This tendency towards the monopolisation of wealth by a relatively small number of people accompanied by the impoverishment of most of the population intensified during the last decades of the nineteenth century.

Ibn ʿAlī saw in the decline of Salé's cotton industry a symptom of the general deterioration of local crafts and the impoverishment of craftsmen. By 1870 Morocco was importing cotton goods to the value of thirteen million francs annually. In Salé everyone had taken to wearing clothes made from imported fabrics. Moreover other manufactured goods from Europe had also disrupted industries and changed habits of consumption.[23] The bazaars began to include European-made woollens, shoes, umbrellas. Tea and sugar, never used previously by the majority of the population, became a staple part of the townsmen's diet (and absorbed between a quarter and a third of Morocco's expenditure on imported goods). Appreciable quantities of such items as candles, paraffin, building materials, cutlery, noodles and wine found buyers in the country's market places. Furthermore European manufacturers, imitating Moroccan styles, produced and shipped to Morocco such things as fezes, pottery, brocaded cloth, silks, pillows, moquettes.[24] Salé's craftsmen could not compete with the cheapness and in some cases the quality of these European goods. Most of them tried to move into crafts which still found some market, however limited, for their products. A few managed to become itinerant traders in the countryside, where goods handled by Slawis, whether locally manufactured or imported, still had a ready market.

Behind the screen of the few Moroccans able to take advantage of trade with Europe were the vast transport and industrial enterprises of Europe, the competition of expanding industries seeking out new markets, and the privileged foreign merchants. In effect the coastal cities of Morocco became annexed to the commercial hegemony of Europe, its market economy, steamships and investment capital. The interior of the country, on the other hand, largely retained its traditional economy and became gradually poorer and more isolated. Morocco's traditional internal routes of trade and caravans with the Sahara, black Africa and Algeria were disrupted and finally ruined by the political and economic consequences of European industrial and political domination.

After the death of Sultan Ḥasan I in 1894 the Moroccan government lost whatever hope it might have had of controlling European economic penetration further or indeed of retaining for long the country's political independence. Between 1894 and 1912 the country's economic and political vulnerabilities and weaknesses increased. The European powers contrived treaties among themselves in order to divide the spoils. Foreigners arrived in growing numbers. More and more people sought and gained foreign consular protection. Money was continually devalued. Duties on goods and the taxes on the acquisition of land went uncontrolled. Political strife, rebellion and foreign intervention became common, and gradually the Moroccan government, the Makhzan, lost effective rule over the country.

Morocco on the eve of the establishment of the French and Spanish protectorates seems to most observers to have remained unchanged, permanent, immutable through the preceding decades of turmoil, and Salé is often cited as the outstanding example of the country's timelessness, its imperviousness to change. All the travellers and scholars described Salé during the early years of the protectorate period as a hermetically closed, fanatical society, a kind of carry-over of medieval life. It is true that Salé still had the image and many attributes of a city of religion and learning. The Slawis maintained traditional styles of life and values more, for example, than the populations of Mogador and Casablanca did or could. Moreover, in contrast to other port cities, it remained closed and hostile to European settlement. Nonetheless the Slawis had profoundly experienced the same economic and social transformations that affected the inhabitants of the large cities of the interior or the coast. Far from being self-enclosed, their economic survival had depended on the trade of manufactured products and the import–export commerce of its port.

The economic upheaval caused by European commercial penetration from 1830 onwards deeply affected the ways of earning a livelihood and the standard of living of Salé's population. These effects, some of which have been mentioned above, will be elaborated upon in the following chapters. However, several other points have to be made first to complete our overview of the economic changes that took place in Morocco between 1830 and 1930 owing to free trade and imperialism. During this period, and particularly after the 1860s, the bureaucracy of the central government grew dramatically. The Slawis gained many of the newly created appointments in the customs services of the more active ports. These officials, on the whole, did very well for themselves; some of them became wealthy and influential men in government circles. Wherever and for however long they served, the great majority retained roots in Salé and ultimately returned there. The power of these government functionaries, local authorities and certain wealthy merchants grew as the internal Moroccan crisis of 1894–1912 unfolded. When the French protectorate was established in 1912 the city's wealth lay in the hands of this small group of men. At the same time the mass of the population had been reduced to eking out a living as small traders or craftsmen.

During the first two decades of the protectorate economic change in Morocco accelerated and had wider social ramifications than in the past. Already by 1912 Rabat had replaced Fez as the country's political capital.[25] A bridge was constructed several miles upstream to ease communication and transport between the two cities, Rabat and Salé. But it had the adverse effect, from the Slawis' point of view, of allowing direct travel between Fez and Rabat without having to pass through their city. In consequence Salé declined as a centre of movement and communication and began to become a dependant of Rabat.

To be sure, some of the population of Salé gained immediate advantage from Rabat's development. Thus some thirty Slawis, because of their educational qualifications, received posts in the indigenous administration set up and expanded by the French; a few of them were appointed to important positions. Under the protectorate Moroccan government officials earned high and regularly paid salaries. Thus, for example, in 1914 a Slawi member of the Court of Appeal in Rabat received 1,200 francs a month. It was a very large sum of money at the time, and some people in the city today see those salaries as the origins of the fortunes of certain families.

Artisans who did any work associated with the building trades found in the new capital of Rabat a boom town. Slawi builders, masons and carpenters enjoyed a good reputation and were given priority in much of the building going on in the capital. And some construction also took place in Salé itself, such that by 1930 many of the city's irrigated vegetable gardens had been built up, as well as a small European quarter. Some merchants of Salé prospered from the growing trade based on the importation and distribution of European goods. In the earlier period a small nucleus of merchants had provided Salé's itinerant traders with goods to sell in the rural markets. In the 1920s a growing number of retail merchants had set up shops in the bazaar and sold directly to the rural people. Some Slawis also participated in various ways in the beginning of the development of Port Lyautey (Kenitra), which by the late 1920s had become an important commercial centre, directly serving the markets of the Gharb.

A significant effect of the protectorate was that more people from the countryside came to Salé's markets and bazaars and that fewer Slawis searched for their livelihood in the rural markets. In part this reversal in the pattern of commerce resulted from the roads and transport system created by the French. Salé's Thursday market was moved twice—in 1912 from within the city to outside the Gate of Fez, and in 1926, to its present site along the route to Meknes—to accommodate the growing number of rural people at the market. The permanent population of the city also increased between 1912 and 1930, partly because of migration from rural areas. Many of the shopkeepers, whose numbers in the city grew appreciably in the early decades of the protectorate, were immigrants from the south; others had been itinerant peddlers who found that it no longer paid them to ply the rural circuits. By the 1920s craftsmen and their sons had also begun to open stores and shops in the bazaar to sell European goods, particularly cloth. But the growth of the bazaar and retail trading in general was offset by the loss of markets in the Gharb, which now came to have its own important commercial centres.[26]

The expansion of commerce in Salé and the opportunities available because of Rabat's development improved the lot of only a small part of the city's population. Approximately half the labour force remained artisans of one sort or another. The viability of most crafts had already been severely undermined by an increasing flow of imported products. With the establishment of the protectorate the economic situation of the majority of craftsmen worsened still further. They suffered in particular from new tax laws and an expanding flood of cheap imported goods. By 1930, moreover, basic tastes and patterns of consumption had begun to change slowly but surely. Some of the young students had taken to wearing European-manufactured clothes; imported linoleum began to appear and replaced straw mats; machine-manufactured carpets from Manchester decorated the homes of the wealthy rather than local carpets; European-made farming tools and metal instruments such as locks and knives found a readier market than those made locally; with modern means of transport, horses lost much of their utility, and the rural notables spent less on the traditional paraphernalia made by Slawi craftsmen; and all the various trades connected with packing and caring for animals rapidly declined. In the late 1920s these were significant economic trends. Within a decade they had completely undermined most of the city's traditional crafts.[27]

After 1925 the situation of relative prosperity enjoyed by a minority of the population began to decline.[28] Three consecutive years of drought between 1927 and 1930 brought the economic life of the city to a standstill. Those with capital had over-extended their investments and were unable to come up with the hard cash necessary to save themselves. During the crash of the 'thirties about a quarter of Salé's merchants had to leave the city, while small merchants and artisans were reduced to subsistence level.[29] The markets had already been flooded with cheap Japanese goods, and most of the products still manufactured in Salé found few buyers. The Slawis remember the world crisis that began in 1930 as the 'Year of Japan' (*ʿām yabūn*). For them it marked the culmination of that process of economic ruin and destitution that had begun a century earlier.

The three generations which more or less span the century from 1830 to 1930 experienced, on the whole, continually worsening economic conditions. The most apparent symptom of this was the progressive rise in prices and devaluation of money. The pattern was not altered during the first eighteen years of the French protectorate. Indeed, the facts and figures for the period between 1914 and 1929 show a sixfold increase in the general cost of living in Morocco.[30] By 1926 the rapid capital investment of the French administration and the costs of the war in the Rif against ʿAbd al-Karīm had driven prices high enough to make a ceiling on them necessary. The position was further aggravated by the flight of European capital to Morocco in the early 1930s.

Economic activity in Morocco undoubtedly expanded on account of the presence of the French protectorate. But for the most part it was the growing population of European settlers who profited from economic development. By 1925 Casablanca, the centre of European settlement, was handling 70 per cent of Morocco's foreign trade. The economy of the country had been almost completely assimilated to that of France, and Europeans controlled all its important sectors. In the countryside cereal crops and viticulture were encouraged because of their marketability in Europe, and to some extent Moroccan agriculture became almost totally dependent on overseas markets. In the late 1920s a surplus of wheat and grapes in Europe, the droughts and locusts in Morocco and land expropriations by colonists under the guise of 'public utility' ruined many farmers, spurred urbanisation and added to pressures on dwindling resources. The pre-colonial period, from 1830 to 1912, had been marked by increasing economic and political interventionism on the part of the European powers. The first decade of the colonial period had completed this process. In most ways the Moroccan economy had become an adjunct of France, exporting its raw materials and importing the finished products of Europe.

VIII The impoverishment of the many

ḥarfa d-būk ma yaghlabūk! If you follow your father' craft they won't get the better of you!

yetqāḍa mal jeddīh, utebqa ṣenʿāt līddīh. The wealth of one's forefathers is dissipated, but the workmanship of one's hands remains.

The crafts

The Slawis were brought up with the notion that a man should imitate his father in all his actions, including the way in which he went about earning his livelihood. In fact the chances for this kind of occupational continuity from generation to generation became quite limited from the late 1860s onwards. The majority of the population during the century under study worked as craftsmen, but changing economic conditions undermined the viability which many of the crafts had enjoyed in the past. In particular the collapse of cotton farming and the decline in the manufacture of fabrics forced large numbers of people to take up other crafts. But these crafts soon followed suit, declining rapidly in the face of a growing volume and variety of imported goods.

Facts and figures on these changes, though sometimes meagre and invariably uneven, make it possible at least to outline some aspects of the lives of working people.[1] In 1858 the French consul in Rabat described Salé as an important manufacturing city which surpassed its neighbour across the river in productivity. Fourteen years later, in 1872, the combined production of Rabat and Salé still ranked second in volume, following Fez, for all of Morocco, despite the decline of the cotton industry. The leading manufactured goods were now babouches (Turkish slippers), pottery and cloth, in that order.

Shoemaking had replaced weaving as the primary industry. Shoemakers (*kharrāza*) had traditionally been wealthy and powerful members of society in both Rabat and Salé. In the 1850s and 1860s there were about 150 workshops in the two cities, employing approximately 1,500 workers. In 1872 the sources mention 700 shops, with 3,000 workers. At the end of our period, however, the craft had declined appreciably, and the 1924 census lists 116 shoemakers in Salé (sixty-seven masters, seven workers and forty-two apprentices).[2]

The decline of this branch of manufacturing was not, at least in the first instance, a result of the importation of European shoes. (This was to be the case in the 1920s, when Japanese plastic shoes flooded the market.) Rather it stemmed from the closing of markets in the Arab East and in sub-Saharan Africa, and from the competition of other cities. During most of the nineteenth century Slawis excelled in working leather, not only into babouches but into other objects such as bags, sacks, wallets, powder flasks, etc. Leather products from both Rabat and Salé found ready markets throughout Morocco. Those who practised this craft had come almost exclusively from the established population, and their occupation was considered a noble one. But by the end of the 1920s there were only a few of the old master craftsmen in the city and little was left of the reputation for nobility that had been attached to the craft.

The suppliers of leather and tanners (*dabbāgha*), along with the owners of cotton farms, had been among the richest and most prestigious people in the city. In the 1850s there were some forty tanneries in Rabat and Salé, and they employed almost 200 men. Ibn ʿAli reports that the tanning and dyeing of leather and the way in which it was made into babouches and other products had long been a local speciality. When, however, in the 1880s Fez, Marrakesh and Tetuan began to compete in these industries the tanners of Salé suffered from the competition. Whereas the leather goods exported from the city had once equalled the total production in all other Moroccan cities, tanning and the crafts associated with the working of leather became seasonal and completely dependent on the availability of money in the rural markets. Still, tanned skins fetched good prices in Fez, where they were dyed, and the tanning industry retained an important, if diminished, role.

The potters of Salé and Rabat at the mid-nineteenth century and until the crisis of the 1870s numbered about 200, and they ran some forty workshops. Salé pottery was of a special kind and was widely sold throughout the country. Indeed, the generic name in Fez for the container used to cook all sorts of stews still derives from the Salé model (viz. *tajīn slawī*). The production of pottery also declined, however, and the 1924 census lists no potters at all in the city.[3] Seven merchants sold pottery, tar and salt in the Great Market. Most of them earned a modest living, although they were descendants of formally prestigious and wealthy craftsmen.

I have mentioned before the primary importance of the cloth-weaving industry. The weaving of wool for winter cloaks, long a speciality, declined less dramatically than the occupation of cloth weaving. In 1858 there were fifty-three workshops for weaving cloth and wool in Rabat and Salé, where during the previous generation, if we are to believe Ibn ʿAlī, there had been 600 in the latter alone for the manufacture of cloth. Other crafts associated with the preparation of cloth and clothing, such as dyeing, the making of brocade, tassels and lace, the embroidery of coloured silk, etc., all declined. By 1885 the trade of weaving cloth, as distinct from wool, had almost entirely disappeared in the two cities because of the massive importation of European, essentially English, cottons. In 1924 the census of crafts counted twenty-five master weavers in the city, almost all of whom worked with wool.

A few crafts, however, did continue to prosper during the pre-colonial and colonial periods. Thus straw mats made in Salé still today decorate the walls and floors of most of the mosques and sanctuaries of Morocco, and as far away as Senegal. In 1865 some 25,000 mats of various kinds were woven and sold in the two cities by 250 workers employed in twenty-nine workshops. In 1872 there were about a hundred workers in sixteen workshops, most of them in Salé. By 1913 we find an increase: thirty workshops in Salé and more than 200 workers (approximately one-fourth masters, one-fourth workers, and half apprentices). According to one estimate some 3,000 metres of these mats were produced each month. Rush from swampy areas of the Banū Ḥasan and the Zemmour was cut green at the end of each month, brought to Salé, dried in the sun and stored. Later it was washed, then dyed and woven into ornate patterns.[4] The art of weaving mats is said to have been brought to Salé by emigrants from Islamic Spain, and since then it has remained a speciality.[5]

Another group of craftsmen who did not suffer from the competition of European goods were builders and those who practised other specialised crafts related to construction and decoration.[6] Master builders from Salé were often hired by the government to build palaces and public buildings throughout the country, and many of them prospered through their participation in the expansion of Casablanca and Rabat during the early years of the protectorate. In other cities of Morocco a master builder produced a plan, as would an architect, and it was up to the owner of the property to hire individually each of the craftsmen necessary for the various tasks. But builders from Salé both designed and constructed themselves and they had an excellent reputation for imaginativeness and aesthetic taste, as well as for competence. Indeed, throughout the period under study some of the wealthiest and most respected men in Salé were builders. Their expertise had an additional dimension which partly explains the prestige they enjoyed. The qadi called upon them to delimit property being sold or divided because of inheritance. In effect some of them spent more of their time as court experts than as builders, and their influence in the city resulted from their knowledge and judgement of important affairs concerning property. Building was a highly specialised craft, and its practitioners, if they did not originate from the city, found integration into the urban community easy, and they often rose quickly in status.

Finally, among those industries that remained prosperous one should mention the weaving of wool blankets, rugs and carpets. These were made in Salé but sold in the market of Rabat.[7] At mid-nineteenth century the carpets enjoyed a good local market and were sold in the interior of the country, transported into the Sudan, and exported to Europe. Orders from the palace retinue and foreign consuls alone kept some of the workshops in constant production. In 1855 there were twelve workshops which produced 840 rugs. Ten years later we find thirty workshops. In all cases the weaving of carpets seems to have been carried out by women.[8] Although I have not found figures for later years, informants in Salé spoke of a steady rise in the manufacturing of these items, especially after the beginning of the protectorate, when different methods of design and dyeing began to be used and expanding European markets opened up.

The processing of wool—washing and dyeing it, and making into yarn—was almost entirely done by women. Still today in Salé the Thread Market is filled two mornings each week with women buying and selling wool and yarn, and on two afternoons the little side streets lying off the Bazaar are lined with women waiting for their carpets to be auctioned. These women work at home, usually with the help of other women in their households. There have been, however, factories owned by wealthy women weavers who employed other women, but especially female slaves and young girls between the ages of five and fifteen.

In 1855 the total value of products manufactured in 350 workshops in Rabat and Salé had been 4,828,000 francs. Ten years later, in 1865, the number of workshops had increased to 383 but the total value of products had declined to 1,618,000 francs. The relative importance of the various handicraft industries in 1865 is shown in table III. The most important industry in terms of the value of its products was woollens, which, unlike cotton cloth, was not affected by European imports until very much later. Next in gross value, but employing a much greater number of workers, was the babouche industry. Woollens and babouches accounted for almost two-thirds of the total value of manufactured goods, and most of the remainder fell to the production of leather and pottery. At least half these industries were situated in Salé, which at that time had a population of approximately 15,000, and they probably absorbed slightly more than half the city's adult male population. Over half of these appear to have been involved in the manufacturing of babouches. Most of the rest worked as tanners, weavers of woollens, mat makers or potters.

These craftsmen, who formed the majority of the city's labour force, earned an average salary of 0·53 francs a day. Master workers (*mʿallim*, pl. *mʿallimīn*), after paying the overhead costs of their workshops, usually earned only slightly more than their journeymen (*ṣānaʿ*, pl. *ṣunnāʿ*). The best paid workers, the jewellers and dyers, with an average income of 0·75 francs a day, were small in number. Most of the jewellers came from the Jewish community, for in nineteenth-century Morocco the Jews specialised in the working of metals, much as they had in many parts of the medieval Muslim world. The largest cotton weavers, though now few in number, enjoyed a

Table III Manufacturing industries of Rabat and Salé (1865)

Item	*Existing workshops*	*Workshops in use*	*Number of items made*	*Value (francs)*	*Value per item (francs)*	*Workers*	*Per diem salary (francs)*
Arms	24	24	5,000	150,000	30·0	95	0·45
Babouches	250	150	147,000	452,000	3·0	2,025	0·45
Mats	29	29	25,000	35,000	1·0	250	0·45
Saddles	13	13	500	16,000	29·1	40	0·50
Rugs	30	30	350	36,000	102·9	68	0·50
Cotton cloth	28	15	45,000	45,000	1·0	80	0·60
Woollens	27	26	95,000	620,000	6·5	300	0·50
Jewellery	12	12	2,000	14,000	7·0	40	0·75
Pottery	35	32	500,000	100,000	0·5	250	0·40
Tanneries	40	40	80,000	150,000	1·9	400	0·50
Dyers	15	12				40	0·75
Totals	503	383	899,850	1,618,000		3,588	0·40–0·75

Source: Adapted from Miège, *op. cit.*, p. 178.

relatively good salary of 0·60 francs. The larger part of the workers had a daily income of 0·45 or 0·50 francs—rather low even for those days.

The income of these people probably did not allow them to live well at all, judging by some prices of goods that are available from other sources. Figuring on the basis of the average pay of 0·53 francs per day over a maximum figure of 365 days, one comes up with an annual income of 192·45 francs.[9] Such a sum would have bought almost nothing. In 1855 the food budget for a relatively wealthy artisan in Tangier with a family of four amounted to 956·35 francs.[10] Basic cereals for bread, couscous and rice alone came to over 130 francs. This artisan was considered to be well off, but even the sum that he spent on basic foods—not to speak of the costs of rent, clothing and other essentials—suggests that the buying power of workers in Salé was very meagre. Thus to buy a pair of babouches at the going price of three francs demanded almost six days' salary. These workers must have had additional income from property or interests of one sort or another, but the amount of their income and the indications of prices suggest that they had a very low level of living.

Despite the increasingly precarious economic situation of craftsmen after 1865, most Slawis found no alternative way of supporting themselves. They did, however, move from one craft to another as these improved or declined in importance. Of course, an older man was unlikely to change his livelihood if he had become a craftsman after long years of apprenticeship. But if he believed that his craft was no longer viable or profitable he would apprentice his son to a master artisan of another, more flourishing handicraft industry. This might be done through ties of kinship, or friendship, for example by sending a son to learn the trade of his mother's brother. In other cases a man, though he had learned a craft from his father, might begin to work in the trade of his wife's family once he was married, if that trade was more remunerative than his own. The ideal preference for following one's father's trade was a deeply ingrained attitude among Slawis. Yet economic realities of the period changed practices, if not ideals. Within certain limits the Slawis learned to be adaptive and practical in choosing trades. This becomes clear if we look at the relative number of masters, workers and apprentices. Thus, for example, makers of straw mats and masons were still prosperous in 1919, and continued to include large numbers of apprentices and workers in relation to masters. In contrast, among the declining shoemakers and tanners there were few apprentices. Crafts whose products no longer found a ready market ceased to attract young men, and when the old masters died no one replaced them.[11]

Among the old artisans whom I interviewed in Salé few had followed the crafts of their fathers. My neighbour, a respected if poor carpenter of seventy years of age, was a typical case. When he was a small boy, around the turn of the century, his father had barely managed to eke out a living as a shoemaker. 'In those days,' he said, 'many people were poor; they did not die of hunger, thanks to the fact that vegetables from Salé's gardens were plentiful and cheap. Shoemakers had a saying about themselves: "I've but 100 Hassani coins and my pair of babouches" [*ma ʿindīsh ghīr miʾat ḥasanī wa-l-bilgha dyalī*]. Because of his poverty my father had me learn carpentry from a friend of his who was doing well.'[12] This man did not, in fact, manage to do very well, but by working as a carpenter rather than a shoemaker he had probably saved himself from abject poverty.

In the early years of this century most Slawis still supported themselves by working in handicraft industries. They were, however, on the edge of poverty well before the world crash of 1930. The change from one craft to another had allowed people to subsist and to maintain most of their customs and traditions. They had retained the dignity of work but had lost most of their prerogatives and the ability to protect their economic interests. There is little doubt that the economic situation of the craftsmen bred discontent. For a traveller of the 1890s 'the old pirate town seems given over to shoemaking and fanaticism'.[13] In the late 1930s the Contrôleur Civil characterised Salé's craftsmen as 'an anxious working class which was hostile to innovation that might trouble its interests'.[14] In effect the conditions and mood of most people who earned their living in handicraft industries had significantly worsened. The first generation to suffer economic upheavals because of the penetration of European goods became much poorer, but certainly not pitiful or lacking in pride. In the late nineteenth-century language of Kipling's *The White Man's Burden* ('silent, sullen people', with their 'heathen folly') the Slawis appeared to Europeans as 'fanatic shoemakers'. From the vantage point of the historian they appear to have maintained their social and cultural ideals and their self-confidence, despite impoverishment. The next generation of the city's craftsmen and manufacturers had, in the view of some French administrators of the 1930s, become a class of proletarians with a potential or real consciousness of their own dissatisfaction. Salé's working class was on the whole poorer, indeed in some cases indigent, and many had lost confidence in themselves. Nonetheless, traditional ideals about religion and politics were re-interpreted rather than replaced. Men continued to think and act as individuals, families and coalitions of patrons and clients, and did not attain the consciousness of belonging to a socio-economic class.

The organisation of labour (guilds)

The once held idea that Muslim cities were characterised by corporate groups which expressed ethnic, religious or professional solidarities no longer appears justifiable. In particular, recent research has discredited Massignon's argument that a socio-religious institution, viz. the professional corporation or guild, dominated urban life. The case of Salé substantiates doubts expressed by Hourani as to the independence of Islamic guilds at any time or place.[15] 'Guilds', i.e. associations of persons with common professional interests, existed in Salé, but they had a particular and limited role throughout the period under discussion.

Most of the master craftsmen, workers and apprentices were affiliated to groups, called in the dialect *ḥanṭa*, pl. *ḥnāṭī*. Formally these groups were divided into two main categories: (1) craftsmen and artisans (*ahl al-ḥirāf wa-'ṣ-ṣanāiʿ*) and (2) itinerant traders and shopkeepers (*sāḥāt al-aswāq wa-ahl al-ḥawānit*). In practice this formal distinction between industry and commerce gave rise to no solidarities within the framework of the guilds among artisans *vis-à-vis* merchants.

Separately or together, these guilds had no civil personality or corporate identity. There was, however, legal recognition of some of the obligations and privileges pertaining to various occupations, and these were codified in customary law (*ʿurf*), that is, in the collection of judicial questions (*nawāzil*) referring to economic life and the responses to them (*fatāwā*) by men learned in law. These responses or decisions, especially those rendered by legal experts in Fez, were binding in most of the cities of Morocco. But Rabat and Salé had accumulated their own corpus of customary law, with specific rulings relating to various occupations. Unfortunately this literature remains unexploited because of the inaccessibility of the relevant collections of texts.

In addition to these rules and regulations specific to the practice of many occupations, the members of a 'guild' sometimes acted together for their mutual benefit. An example from a period which long precedes the scope of this study, the sixteenth century, illustrates principles which, according to informants, were still operative during the nineteenth century: the cloth merchants of Salé, constantly and without warning, were taxed by the *makhzan*. Finally they agreed among themselves that each time they purchased cloth they would put one *dirhām* into a common treasury. This money would be used to meet unexpected exactions by the central government. However, the weavers of the city objected to the plan. They claimed that it would be at their expense, since the merchants would surely pay them one *dirhām* less on each purchase so that, in effect, they would be paying the tax. The qadi of the city, when called upon to make a decision, argued that the weavers had no right to money that the merchants might want to put aside. The weavers then demanded that the *muftī* of Fez consider the same case, and he decided in their favour.[16] In this example the members of two occupational groups defended their opposing interests by banding together against one another. This kind of spontaneous solidarity of people who followed the same line of work manifested itself on several occasions during the nineteenth century, but never within the framework of co-ordinated action by the occupational group itself.[17]

The mundane day-to-day activities in the economic life of Salé showed no real evidence of organisation among these groups, but they did carry out certain group functions. For example, collections of money were made from time to time among a particular group of craftsmen in order to help one of their members afford an unexpected obligation, such as a wedding or funeral, or to assist one of them if he was unable to continue working because of an accident or poor health. Shoemakers would help a newcomer to the craft set up shop, and tanners made a collection among themselves for indigent *shurafāʾ* passing through the city.[18] Many craftsmen contributed towards the expenses for an annual picnic held by their groups. More important was the matter of taxation, and here these occupational groups played an important role. Many of them offered gifts (*hadīya*) to the sultan on the occasion of religious festivals. This gift, demanded from them as a group by the authorities of the city, was bought from obligatory contributions by individual members. In 1890 the 'gift' was transformed into a direct money tax, and by 1904 its amount had been increased about twentyfold.[19] Precise information on the amounts and methods of payment is lacking, but apparently both were highly arbitrary. In the pre-colonial period, I was told, certain guilds had to produce gifts in cash whenever the governor of the city appeared before the sultan.

Most of the guilds had a chief (coll. *l-amīn*)[20] and an assistant to him (*khalīfa*). The chief was chosen by acclamation by the members of the guild and then approved by the market provost (*muḥtasib*). He collected the various contributions from members after the most respected personalities had determined its amount, and he represented the guild *vis-à-vis* the authorities of the city. If there were complaints against a member of the guild by the authorities or by an individual, or if disputes arose among members of the guild, the chief would act as an intermediary between the parties. He also acted as a guarantor in acts of surety (*ḍamāna*) for members of the guild who were not yet recognised as Slawis, i.e. were new to the city, not yet married, or not property owners. The surety was usually written up in a legal notarised act such as the following: 'The master forger as-Slawī guarantees with money and security any possible accidental losses of property to the clients so-and-so. This surety is further guaranteed by the chief of the forgers in Salé, the master Ibn ʿAisā as-Sammār.'[21] In some cases the guild as a whole might make a legalised agreement, for example with the administration of pious endowments for the rental of land. Thus we find a quarry rented to the guild of potters, which then divided it equally among its artisans.[22]

A degree of official control over economic life was exercised through the guilds by the *muḥtasib*, a kind of market inspector who in medieval Muslim towns had regulated most economic affairs, as well as supervising public morality. Officially the *muḥtasib* of Salé policed the market, fixed prices and checked weights and measures, and did this through the chiefs of the guilds. In practice, however, he did little more than arbitrate in disputes that took place between buyers and sellars. Such, at least, was the case since the late nineteenth century.

The office of *muḥtasib* in Salé and the structure of the guilds had apparently been more significant in the city's economic and social life before the growing dependence on European goods. Prior to the 1850s these institutions may have defined economic rules and regulations with greater rigour. Thus a document from Salé dated 1225 A.H./1810 A.D. shows members of the guilds juridicially recognised as a group and the *muḥtasib* as an official intermediary between them and the higher authorities of the city. It is an attestation which denies vilifications levelled against the *muḥtasib*. The text is as follows:

Praise be to God! The persons whose names appear below—craftsmen and artisans, itinerant traders and shopkeepers who have been placed under the control of the Inspection of Markets [*ḥisba*]—have on this date declared that the Inspector [*muḥtasib*] Sī 'l-Hāshimī b. al-Jāhid as-Sayyid ʿAbd al-ʿAzīz Fanīsh, since his appointment by our Master (the Sultan), has not ceased to give proof of his good conduct and to recognise the rights of Muslims, nor has he committed wrong towards anyone—except in so far as it was punishment for a theft, fraud, or abuse of confidence.

The above-mentioned inspector is energetic, knows perfectly well the functions imposed on him and respects the right of each person to consult the people of theology and jurisprudence. He has never demanded money. The objects that he has had to procure for his personal needs have been bought and paid for by him, according to the general practice. Any accusation against him is null and abusive.

The names of 162 people, twenty of them Jews (*ahl adh-dhimma*), appeared on the document. They practised seventeen occupations, and included druggists, repairers of shoes, grocers, bakers, sellers of wheat, sellers of oil, butchers, makers of doughnuts, millers, weavers of mats, plasterers, sellers of balms for the dead, barbers, tinsmiths, sellers of gold, estate agents and makers of rope. The signature which appears is that of the assistant to the qadi, ʿAbd Allah Muḥammad al-Hāshimī Aṭūbī.[23]

The guild organisations and the office of the *muḥtasib* could influence economic affairs in a small city which was self-sufficient. Manufacturing and marketing prices were controllable and so, it appears, was the potential venality of the market officials. There were tested procedures for keeping the industrial and commercial life of the city on an even keel. The guilds appear to have been loosely organised but efficient institutions which served the needs of the administration primarily and the needs of their members only secondarily. Their importance diminished, as did that of the *muḥtasib*, when craftsmen ceased to have much influence or wealth, that is, as the nineteenth century unfolded.[24] The guild organisations and their chiefs had acted primarily to control the quality of products and entrance into certain crafts, but this control had lessened by the end of the century. Informants in Salé who were old and had intimate knowledge of various crafts repeatedly indicated that, at least from the 1870s onwards, neither the guilds nor the *muḥtasib* played any role of economic importance in the life of the city.

Available information about the steps of advancement from apprentice to worker to master similarly indicate a lack of internal organisation within the guilds. Every child who began to learn a craft as an apprentice was simply attached to a master artisan whom he helped in exchange for little or no recompense. When he became a valuable helper he began to receive a salary and could thus be classified as a worker. If later on he accumulated enough capital to open a shop of his own he was considered a master artisan of that particular craft. There were no examinations to pass or approval to receive. The title of master (coll. *mʿallem*) was simply a recognition of the *de facto* position that a man had attained in the mastery and economic success of the craft he practised. The title in itself had no institutional basis; a master craftsman had the respect of the townsmen because he was an expert at his work.

Because of the looseness of the guilds' internal organisation the common knowledge and interests shared by the members of the same craft gave them only a vague sense of solidarity. In most cases their shops would be grouped together along certain streets of the town, and this physical proximity brought them into constant contact with one another. Often, as one still sees today, members of the same craft sat in each other's shops to chat, drink tea and smoke tobacco or hashish. When the time of prayer came they prayed together in the mosque closest to their shops. Such occupational groups tended to share habits of dress and speech, of social background and education, and what could be loosely called a common mentality. Thus, although occupation was important for social ties, the 'guilds' did not possess the qualities of corporate groups in the Weberian sense, i.e. social relationships of a kind either closed to outsiders or restricting their admission by regulation.[25] The framework of the guild was extremely loose, one of many such loose frameworks in which the townsmen moved and related to each other.

The guilds gave little social content to people's lives. The Slawi artisan sought to pursue his craft as long as he could make a living from it. If the craft was no longer viable he tried to change his occupation. To do so he did not need to change his social allegiance. The studies of guilds in Morocco in the 1920s focus on the 'social disintegration' that followed the decline of certain crafts: 'the present corporate spirit of Moroccan artisans,' Massignon wrote in 1924, 'will hardly survive. Yet if the guilds break up, if the crisis of apprenticeship worsens, if workers who formerly specialised do not find work, then all the social life of the cities will be threatened with regression. In the place of artisans there will be only day labourers lacking cohesion or family stability—and ripe for all kinds of disorders!' This analysis lacks foundation, for the crisis of those years was not a result of the dwindling corporate spirit of the guilds. They had long lacked, and perhaps never had, any corporateness. The crisis was simply the plight of townsmen who could no longer support themselves or their families by working at the only trade they knew. Poverty in and of itself bred social unrest; there had been no breakdown of economic and social institutions. In the past social harmony had come not from the guilds but from the capacity most men had for earning

Table IV Value attached to various occupations

M Muslims, *J* Jews, *p* patron or master artisan, *s* shop

Occupation	Comments	Numbers
1 Mokhaznis (troops of the Pasha of the city)	Although all of them were known in the city, none was from old Slawi families. Most seem to have come from the tribes of the Shāwīya or the Dukkāla. There were also some fifty government troops stationed in Dār Bin ʿAṭṭar from about 1890 onward	(10)
2 Grain merchants, including sellers of flour	These people were looked down upon. They were not 'noble'; they made their greatest profits when prices rose and were always suspected of hoarding	(21)
3 Measurers of cereals	They were without nobility	
4 Butchers	Although ignoble people, they cannot easily be dismissed; they are of a particular and sometimes dangerous temperament. Some are from old and respected families of the city[a]	(12 M p; 2 J p)
5 Notaries of the oil market	They were from good families, e.g. Mukhṭār at-Ṭrābulsī and ʿAbd ar-Rahmān al-Mrīnī, etc	
6 Keepers of Turkish baths	These came from old and respected families, e.g. Bin Shlīḥ and Bū Shaʿara. They were often among the wealthiest people in the city	(5 M; 1 J)
7 Animal brokers	There were few of them in Salé, and they were not from Slawi families	(2 M; 1 J)
8 Hawkers of wares and second-hand goods		3 M; 2 J (3 M; 20 J)

9	Bread sellers		(6 M s; 1 J s)
10	Bakers and millers		23 s (17 s) (11)
11	Milkmen		31
12	Stock raisers	None of the above (8–12) was from a decent family; on the whole, they were outsiders and their trades added nothing to their stature	56 (12)
13	Weavers of mats	This is a 'neutral' craft; it neither possesses nor lacks nobility. In the past many people of Salé earned their living at this trade. Those who practise it today are both from old respected families and newcomers to the city	35 (49)
14	Sellers of poultry		6 (3)
15	Sellers of eggs		(16)
16	Sellers of coal		2 s (51 M; 2 J)
17	Wholesalers of coal		
18	Weavers of cloth and spinners of flax		20 M; 5 J 9 J
19	Sellers of cooked ground meat	None of the above (14–19) was from Salé; they were poor and outsiders	(1)

[a] Sīdī Maḍlūm, one of the saints of Salé, is said to have been a butcher. The legend associated with his death is as follows. One day a pregnant woman who was very poor asked the saint the price of a certain cut of meat that she wanted. When she found that it was much more than she could afford she began to walk slowly away. The butcher called after her and told her that she could have the meat as a gift. That night she surprised her husband with a fine meal. When he asked her how she had managed to buy such a good cut of meat she told him what had happened with the butcher. Her husband proceeded to kill both the wife and the butcher, who was buried outside Fez Gate and received the name 'the Oppressed' (coll., *maḍlūm*). It is said that when this gate was closed at night the gatekeeper would call into the night to ask if there were any stragglers on the road. A voice would always respond from the tomb, beseeching the gatekeeper not to leave him outside the city.

Table IV (*contd*)

	Occupation	Comments	Numbers
20	Salt makers	They were all from well known families of Salé, and their trade was a respectable one. Most owned marshes near the river, or rented them from the Ḥabous, and had shops in the Sūq ar-Raḥba where they sold salt and pottery goods	(9)
21	Water carriers	They were mostly Filālīs (from the Tafilalt)	72
22	Quarry owners and workers (for the preparation of cement and plaster)	Some were from well known Slawi families, like the Znībars and the l-Ḥanshīs	42
23	Fritters and smelters of butter		12 (13 M; 8 J)
24	Druggists (ʿaṭṭāra)		
	Sugar	They were all from Salé, and it was a remunerative and respectable way to make a living[b]	66 s (87 M s; 7 J s)
	Tobacco		(8 M s; 4 J s)
	Tea		(3)
	Henna		(2)
	Honey		(1)
25	Makers of rope	Most of them were outsiders, although there were some Slawis. Their work was hard and dirty	
26	Porters	Most of them were Slawis.[c] Their trade did not lack nobility but it was a very tiring way to earn a living	39
27	Shoemakers and retailers of shoes	These people practised a very noble trade, and in the past almost all were from the best families in Salé[d]	67 p (47 M; 15 J)
			3
28	Broom makers		4 s
29	Musicians for processions[e]		13
30	Tailors	Many were Slawis, but it was in no way a noble trade[f]	(21 M; 6 J)

31	Sellers of pottery and tar	These people had a clean, good trade and they were from old and respected families of the city	(7)
32	Potters and makers of bricks		(3) (4)
33	Garbage men, cleaners of sewers		9
34	Jewellers and goldsmiths		10 s (3 M; 2 J)
35	Washers and porters of the dead		
36	Barbers	They lacked any nobility or sense of dignity because they let blood and circumcised children without any repugnance or pity	24 s (27)
37	Fruit sellers		32 (40 M; 4 J)
38	Vegetable sellers	Those that sell anything grown on the land have a noble trade, just as do farmers. Most of the sellers of fruit and vegetables were Slawis	25 s
39	Candy sellers		(3)
40	Women's hairdressers		
41	Women musicians	These kinds of occupation are not practised by decent women	
42	Musicians		(6)

[b] According to Massignon's information, this statement by my informant appears to be untrue. Massignon has only thirty-nine or 58 per cent of the druggists listed as Slawis. Of 149 shopkeepers, in 1924, 66 per cent were 'Shlūḥ' and 30 per cent Slawis. Properly speaking, 'Shlūḥ' refers to southern Berbers from the Anti-Atlas mountains and the Sous valley rather than to Berbers as a whole, that is, to speakers of Shilḥa, or Tashelḥit. However, by extension its use had come to include Moroccan Berbers from various areas, and their languages, in general.

[c] Massignon has only twelve, or 30 per cent, Slawis.

[d] In 1924 only twenty-three, or 35 per cent, of the shoemakers were Slawis.

[e] According to Massignon six of them were Slawis.

[f] Again, according to the 1924 survey none of the tailors was a Slawi.

Table IV (*contd*)

	Occupation	Comments	Numbers
43	Well diggers		17
44	Builders	This has been a very noble profession practised by some of the wealthiest and best people of the city. An important builder was known by name and referred to individually rather than as a member of such-and-such a family[g]	23 (73)
45	Quarry workers and stone cutters		27
46	Plasterers and bricklayers	Those who practised this craft were outstanding artisans, and their occupation a noble one. Some came from well known Slawi families, but they made a poor living—less than that of cleaners of sewers, the least noble occupation[h]	42
47	Builders of terraces		4
48	Carpenters	The experts among them were famous for their art, and came from the finest families of the city[i]	44
49	Sawyers and timber merchants		9 (6)
50	Wood turners		(2)
51	Makers of bellows	They were 'sons of the city' (ūlād l-bled), from the finest families, and their trade was a noble one	5 s
52	Smiths and grinders	They were not Slawis. Their work was very hard and lacked nobility	8 (12) (2 J)
53	Workers of ornamental tiles	There was a Ben Slīmān from Salé, but he had to go to Fez to learn his trade. The others were Fāsis	2 (1)
54	Whitewashers	They were poor people who on the whole worked seasonally. People in Salé have the custom of whitewashing their homes, especially the outsides, every year for ʿAnṣara (the festival celebrating the summer solstice)	(10)

55	Decorators of wood and metal		2 p
56	Dyers of silk and wool	They were not very numerous, for many weavers, especially women, did their own dyeing at home. Those who sold dye did well, for example al-Hājj ʿAbd as-Salām az-Zarmūq, who came to Salé as a young man and started out as a porter, bringing sugar from Rabat to Salé. Then he began buying animals and had soon accumulated enough capital to open a store, in which he sold olives, pickled lemons and dyes. His wife, who originated from the Zaʿīr tribe, wove rugs. They prospered and bought up a good deal of property	10 p (3)
57	Carpet weavers	They were almost never from outstanding families, but they sometimes earned a lot of money	(2)
58	Sellers of silk thread and embroiderers of silk	Mostly Jews worked at this trade, plus some Slawis from excellent families, such as Muḥammad Bil-Qādi, ʿAbd al-Laṭīf l-Mrīnī. However, they made a meagre living	3 M (5 J) (1 J)
59	Leather embroiderers	Some were Slawis, including Aḥmad aṣ-Ṣubīḥī	6 p
60	Harness makers	ʿAbd Allah Fenīsh, two of the Tiyāl brothers, a Maʿanīnū—some of the best families—gained their living at this trade	
61	Tinsmiths and silversmiths	This is a poor trade practised only by Jews. The Jews look for the easiest kind of work—that which demands the least amount of physical exertion or movement. For example, as tailors they do little work and make lots of money. But you do not find any builders or farmers among them	(9 J) (1 J)

[g] That is, the builders' renown had nothing to do with their social origins. They were completely self-made men. According to Massignon, fourteen, or 61 per cent, originated from Salé.

[h] Again, according to the 1924 survey none of them was a Slawi.

[i] Massignon lists nineteen, or 40 per cent, as originating from Salé

Table IV (*contd*)

Occupation	Comments	Numbers
62 Basket weavers		(1)
63 Gatherers of dried palm leaves		4
64 Shipbuilders	They were all from well known families and made a fair living	(5)
65 Rowers (for boats that plied the river)	Although they were poor, many were 'sons of the city' from well known families like the Fenīsh and the Ḥusaynī	
66 Veterinarians		
67 Horseshoers	The people who worked with animals were almost all rural folk (*badwu*), although some of the Slawi family of as-Sammār (lit. 'horseshoer') still worked as veterinarians. In any event, it was not a noble trade	(2)
68 Sellers of guns and powder and scrap iron		(5)
69 Saddle makers	They were mostly Jews. There were not many of them before the French came. When traffic to Salé began increasing after 1912 they moved from an area at the end of the Street of the Barbers to Ceuta Gate. Later, when lorries replaced animals as the main means of transport (in the late 1920s), many of these people turned to sewing mattresses, a job initially done in people's homes by either Jews or women.[j]	5 (6)
70 Cobblers	Most were newcomers to the city and of rural origin	30 (3)
71 Retailers of cotton goods	These people took advantage of the chance to make money	(27 J s) 31 M s (57)

72	Old clothes dealers and dealers in rags		(8) (4 J)
73	Fishermen		
74	Fishmongers		26 s (2)
75	Porters and caterers	Some of them were from good families and did well, especially after the coming of the French	39 M (13 J)
76	Cooks	They were mostly women and often slaves. They would get passed around from house to house to help individual families prepare for celebrations	6
77	Keepers of cook shops (for the sale of cooked heads of sheep)		(10)
78	Coppersmiths	They repaired only copper utensils. None was from Salé. The ʿAlawīs among them, judging from their looks, came from Tafilalt	(18)
79	Tanners	They were wealthy people, from good families. They worked hard and did not have any kind of false pretensions about themselves	14 p (16)
80	Workers in vineyards		
81	Innkeepers	Those who owned hostels (*fundūq*, pl. *fanādiq*) or had tenancy from the Ḥabous were among the wealthiest and best people	15 (26)
82	Teachers in Quranic schools		
83	Repairers of watches		4
84	Agricultural workers in irrigated gardens		61

In 1924 all the saddle makers were Berbers.

Table IV (*contd*)

Occupation	Comments	Numbers
85 Ploughmen		
86 Day labourers		
87 Camel drivers		11 (6)
88 Transporters of coal		
89 Café owners, retailers of tea and coffee		33 (25 M; 1 J) (9 M)
90 Heads of quarters		
91 Official public criers		2
92 Auctioneers[k]		34

[k] On the importance of auctioneers in the Moroccan urban marketing process, *cf.* J. Berque and G. H. Bousquet, 'La criée publique à Fès. Étude concrète d'un marché', *Revue d'Économie Politique*, vol. LIV–LV (1940–45), pp. 321–45.

a decent living. As the possibilities of adapting to economic change lessened, social tensions and conflict increased. Under these conditions the values attached to various ways of making a living were bound to change dramatically.

The ranking of occupations

la ḥanna lil-ḥajjāmīn wala ḥayyāka faḍīlīn. Neither have barbers pity, nor are weavers of cloaks noble.

Until the economic success of its merchants in the late years of the nineteenth century the Slawis had denigrated bazaar commerce. This was but one example of how economic changes influenced ideas about the status and value of different occupations. The prestige attached to various occupations reflected both social stereotypes and economic realities. In some cases an occupation gave a man high status regardless of the amount of income he derived from it. In other cases wealth from certain occupations stigmatised a man. A detailed consideration of the ways in which people earned a living shows the variety of occupations that were available and their relative ranking in economic and social terms.

In order to elicit the values attached to occupations I used a list of guilds compiled in 1924 by the *muḥtasib*.[26] The list is given in table IV, along with a summary of the views of my principal informant, a seventy-year-old former itinerant trader who had a vast knowledge of economic life in Salé. In many cases he judged occupations in terms of the presence or lack of 'nobility'. What he meant will become clear in due course. The numbers represent the statistics gathered in the initial inquiry of the *muḥtasib* in 1924 or, where they are in parentheses, a variant count from other sources used in Massignon's study. From this list we learn how working people earned their livelihood in Salé during the 1920s.[27] It probably includes most of the merchants and many of the agricultural workers and artisans. The total number of individuals engaged in these trades was about 1,800, that is, slightly less than half the estimated adult male population. Although we cannot account for the ways in which everyone earned a living on the basis of this information, it does nonetheless provide an insight into the variety and distribution of occupations and the attitudes and values held in regard to them.

The informant's judgement and ranking of occupations faithfully reflects the views of the established urban population of Salé around the turn of the nineteenth century. He ranks the crafts according to several criteria, the most crucial of which seems to be the type of people who practised them. In most cases highly valued occupations were those engaged in by members of families long known and respected in the city. Conversely the activities of outsiders were generally denigrated. The income derived from various crafts might also figure in the rank attributed to them, good income being equated with high rank. Yet some occupations, although well-paid, were looked upon with disfavour because of moral considerations. Finally there were crafts which had intrinsic qualities that determined their rank, regardless of the identity or income of those who practised them. The noble crafts (sng. *ḥirfa shrīfa*) were shoemaking, carpentry, building and commerce. Shoemaking owed its prestige to the fact that many of those engaged in it belonged to respected urban families. In the previous generation shoemakers had been able to earn a good living: the prestige of their occupation had rested on prosperity rather than on the social origins of those engaged in it. After 1900 they fared badly, but still enjoyed a respectability that had carried over from the previous generation. The 'nobility' of a craft usually outlived its economic viability by a generation. Thus in the 1860s weavers were well off and respected; a generation later they had poverty with dignity; by the end of the century their lot was indigence and disdain.

The other 'noble' crafts were those which provided 'good' people with a decent living. The process that had prevailed half a century earlier among the shoemakers was repeated: the old, respected families of the city directed their sons towards the most promising occupations; by the relative prosperity that certain trades gave to these young men, their status in the city was enhanced; at the same time the trade became 'noble' because of those engaged at it. Another example is the change in attitude towards commerce and towards merchants, which I shall take up in the next chapter.

Some trades were considered to have intrinsically negative or ignoble qualities, and it was said that few 'real' Slawis took them up. But the attitudes towards those who specialised in these occupations were ambivalent. Thus, for example, the disdain expressed for barbers placed them outside the pale of normal behaviour. At the same time, and as a consequence, they played important roles in communication; they alone enjoyed almost universal entrée into the homes of prominent people in the city and could provide information on a wide variety of matters, including crucial ones such as potential marriage partners.[28] These ambivalent attitudes were also expressed in the ascription of outstanding spiritual gifts to some of the despised craftsmen, particularly the local saints of the past.[29] An example can be offered from contemporary Salé. An old man and former weaver, called Ḥmed 'l-Bahlūl' ('The Jester'), spends his days visiting craftsmen and shopkeepers and playing chess—at which he is a master—in one of the local cafés. He is reputed for his sensitive intelligence and uncanny ability to read the moods and thoughts of others. Although this old man is poor and usually shabbily dressed, people of all ranks enjoy and seek his company and conversation, and he is often among those invited to the celebrations of the most important families of the city.[30] On the whole, however, the examples of affection and respect towards the poor and humble, the practitioners of ignoble crafts, were few and far between.

To sum up: the ways in which occupations were ranked in Salé underscored social values. The 'noble' crafts were those practised by people who maintained an urban style of life, and those people, in turn, were considered to be the old and established members of the community. This style of life demanded a relative affluence. During the period of steadily worsening economic conditions from the 1860s onwards a diminishing number of trades allowed men to maintain that style. A man's social relationships might allow him to withstand the denigrating effects of impoverishment for a while, but in the long run failure to earn a good living led to a loss of status for the individual and for his occupation. At the same time those engaged in trades which prospered could achieve high status whatever their social origins, provided that they assumed the urban style of life.

Ethnic groups and economic specialisation

In the discussion of the working people I have differentiated groups according to their occupations. A combination of income and socio-cultural considerations influenced the ranking of these occupations and the people who practised them. My informants put special emphasis on the 'Slawiness' of certain craftsmen, a quality which they valued highly. In distinction they denigrated other crafts, often because those engaged in them were Jews or 'outsiders'. The status of individuals who worked at a specific craft depended on their income and style of life. As most crafts declined under the impact of foreign competition the status of those who practised them fell, along with their standard of living. In consequence fewer of the middle-rung working people—the artisans, shopkeepers, petty functionaries and professionals—were referred to as Slawis. The majority came to be considered outsiders. The nineteenth-century growth in foreign trade and the harm caused to indigenous handicrafts had disrupted the social and economic structure of the city. As a result a growing number of people became impoverished and unable to manage the urban style of life. Salé's community had become more complex and differentiated, less integrated. The French protectorate increased this tendency by setting in motion a process of accelerated demographic growth and urbanisation. The population, which had been relatively stable over most of the period under review, increased by almost 40 per cent during the first two decades of the protectorate. Large-scale migration into Salé strengthened the tendency towards socio-economic complexity and differentiation and accelerated the process of stratification that had begun in the nineteenth century. Among the common people the distinction between Slawis and outsiders became exacerbated. Added to this a new element appeared in the occupational distribution of groups, namely the Berbers.

Generically the term used in Salé for these speakers of Berber languages, whether they came from the Rif, Middle Atlas, High Atlas, Anti-Atlas or

Table V Occupations by ethnic category

	Number of workers	*Slawis* *No.*	*%*	*Berbers* *No.*	*%*	*Others* *No.*	*%*
Food							
1 Grocers	149	45	30	98	66	6	4
2 Water carriers	72			69	96	3	4
3 Druggists	66	39	58	1	2	26	40
4 Café owners	33	4	12	10	30	19	58
5 Milkmen	31	14	45	9	30	8	25
6 Fishmongers	26	2	8	3	12	21	80
7 Fruit sellers	32	13	40	4	12	15	48
8 Vegetable sellers	25	2	8	8	34	15	58
9 Oven keepers	23			4	16	19	84
10 Butchers	12			1	8	11	92
11 Fritters	8			3	36	5	64
12 Sellers of eggs	6					6	100
13 Cooks	6			3	50	3	50
14 Bakers	6			2	33	4	67
Clothing							
15 Shoemakers	67	23	35	10	14	44	51
16 Cloth sellers	31	20	65	3	14	8	21
17 Cobblers	30			16	53	14	47
18 Embroiderers	25	6	25			19	75
19 Belt makers	24	4	16	4	16	16	68
20 Tanners	14	14	100				
21 Tailors	13			1	8	12	92
22 Dyers	10	5	50			5	50
23 Makers of purses	7			2	28	5	72
24 Leather embroiderers	6	1	15			5	85
25 Sewers on machines	4	2	50	2	50		
26 Sellers of shoes	3					3	100
27 Jewellers	3			3	100		
Household furniture							
28 Carpenters	44	19	49	1	2	24	49
29 Weavers of mats	35	8	22			27	78
30 Makers of rope	6			1	16	5	84
31 Makers of bellows	5	3	60			2	40
32 Makers of brooms	4					4	100
Construction							
33 Bricklayers and plasterers	42			20		22	
34 Builders	23	14	61	1	4	8	35
35 Innkeepers	15			2	13	13	87
36 Sawyers	9	4	44	2	22	3	34
37 Porters	9			4	44	5	56
38 Bathkeepers	5					5	100
39 Builders of terraces	4	2	50			2	50

Table V (*contd*)

	Number of workers	Slawis No.	Slawis %	Berbers No.	Berbers %	Others No.	Others %
40 Wood turners	2					2	100
41 Workers in tiles	2					2	100
Agriculture							
42 Gardeners	61	22	36	1	1·6	38	62·4
43 Cowherds	56	18	33	1	2	37	61
44 Coal sellers	32			28	87	4	13
45 Well diggers	17			17	100		
46 Gatherers of dried palm leaves	4					4	100
Transport							
47 Shipbuilders	54	18	33	3	6	33	61
48 Porters	39	12	30	8	8	24	62
49 Camel drivers	11					11	100
50 Saddle makers	5			5	100		
Various							
51 Auctioneers	34	10	29	9	18	15	53
52 Smiths	8	1	12	1	12	6	76
53 Musicians	6	6	100				
54 Arms and gunpowder dealers	3					3	100
55 Public criers	2					2	100
Totals	1,279	331	26	355	28	593	46

the valleys of southern Morocco, was Shlūḥ. (Properly speaking, the inhabitants of and immigrants from southern Morocco.) In fact the majority of Berbers in Salé apparently migrated from the Tafilalt, Draʿ and Sūs valleys. The most visible group of Berbers in economic life were the Sūsis. In 1924 they represented most of the 28 per cent of workers categorised as Berbers. The Slawis made up only 26 per cent of these middle-rung occupations, while 'others' accounted for the remaining 46 per cent. The exact breakdown of occupations and statistics was as in table v.[31]

These statistics show that the Berbers had become the largest definable ethnic group working at these occupations in Salé. No single important trade —except the digging of wells—was practised exclusively by Berbers, but a significant number of them worked as grocers, an occupation at which they have specialised throughout the cities of Morocco since the early years of this century. The number of grocers in Salé probably increased more than threefold between 1912 and 1930; the Berbers—and here one should specify the Sūsis—were almost alone responsible for this growth. In 1924, of the 149 grocers, ninety-eight were Sūsis, whereas around the turn of the century there had been fewer than forty grocers in Salé, almost all of whom were

Slawis. On the whole 'Berbers' as well as 'others' worked in all the occupations listed. With the exception of the tanners and musicians, no group was composed exclusively of Slawis. However, Slawis did predominate in highly ranked crafts such as building, carpentry, tailoring and shoemaking.

It is difficult to ascertain the relevance of religion or ethnicity in matters of economic specialisation during most of the period under study. The explicit differentiation or exclusiveness of certain crafts as essentially practised by Jews or Berbers, for example, seems to have been relatively limited and unimportant. The people who dominated most crafts must have enjoyed an income and practised a style of life which stamped them as Slawis. 'Outsiders', whether the urban poor or the newly arrived immigrants, were classified more by the way they lived than by their origins or occupations. The Jews, too, had their 'insiders' and 'outsiders', identified in terms of life style. With conditions of life among the craftsmen relatively stable and demographic growth limited, most migrant working people could integrate into society and adopt the Slawi customs and sense of identity. However, impoverishment and, later on, large-scale immigration led to widening gaps and greater complexity in social and economic differentiation.

The community of Salé at the end of the nineteenth century no longer absorbed most of the people living within its confines. Because of precarious economic conditions fewer of the middle-rung working people earned enough income to live according to the dominant social and cultural values. The urban poor and immigrants grew in number; they were distinguished not only by their way of life but increasingly by criteria of occupation and ethnicity. Those who defined themselves as Slawis had come to exclude many of the common working people, and they tended to identify the community with the new bourgeoisie who lived by commerce, property ownership and government employment.

IX The enrichment of the few

hel slā,	The people of Salé
hel makr u-blā;	Are treacherous and ill-omened;
minkhārhum mn ḥdīd,	Their steely hoses
ye'adiyū n-nās mn b'īd.	Cause injury to men from afar.

In the period before 1870 a small number of men in the city possessed substantial wealth. They were big farmers and tanners—those who held large quantities of land or leather. The majority of the population supported themselves as small farmers, craftsmen, itinerant traders or petty officials. Most people owned some property and many had small plots of land where they grew cotton, or vegetables for their own consumption. It was not unusual, for example, for a man to work as a weaver and to own his house and a small piece of land. The old men of Salé liked to repeat their grandfathers' stories about those 'good old days' when almost everyone farmed—to earn a living, or for security in case of economic crisis, or simply for prestige and pleasure. On the basis of information on land holding and prices this image of a stable community of property owners seems to be borne out. From 1830 until the 1860s the distribution of ownership over property was widespread and its value relatively steady. However, during the series of crises beginning in the 1860s land prices fluctuated dramatically, and the ownership of most of the land and property in Salé came to be gradually monopolised by a small number of people.

With the growing precariousness of economic life, many people lost their homes and land and came to depend totally on the income from their work to house and feed themselves. Where people had previously felt economically secure, they now struggled against the threat of losing everything. At the same time, some men were becoming rich. The self-appointed guardians of public morality in late nineteenth-century Salé describe an unprecedented race after material goods and a lowering of ethical and moral standards. These were times of moral, social and religious crises—as well as of economic upheaval. A new spirit of aggressiveness and entrepreneurial enthusiasm seems to have marked the Slawis' reaction to the penetration of Europe's capitalist economy into Moroccan life. This spirit allowed most people to survive and a few to become wealthy. It expressed itself in the organisation of commerce and the government administration.

The *suwwāqa*, or itinerant traders, perhaps best represent this spirit of enterprise. At the turn of the century about thirty of them worked and travelled through the circuits of the rural markets. They were absent from Salé for almost all the year with the exceptions of the thirty days of the fast month Ramadan, a week for the Great Festival, and about three weeks for the celebration of the birthday of the Prophet. Each of them worked alone, for his own account if he had the necessary cash, for his creditors or backers if he did not. Each trader had two or three mules laden with merchandise and was aided by several part-time workers who came from the tribes. Every week new merchandise was brought from Salé by carriers, who went to the traders' relatives, friends or partners to place their orders. Cloth was bought and the women of the traders' houses sewed day and night to prepare the garments which had been ordered. On the whole these itinerant merchants sold more raw cloth than sewn garments, but the garments brought a profit of 100 per cent, as compared to the 10 per cent profit on cloth.

Among the traders from Salé there was no spirit of co-operation, only constant dissension and disagreement. The only principle that all abided by was that a newcomer should respect the permanent place of each trader's tent in the various markets. Once a man had chosen a spot in a given market, it belonged to him. If he underpriced his goods the others complained long and loudly, hoping that their insults would reach his ears and influence him to raise his prices. But this kind of pressure seldom succeeded; basically it was a free market, and each merchant ran his business as he chose. In most of these rural markets the tents of Jewish traders tended to outnumber those of Muslims; the Jews came from Ouezzan or Ksar el-Kbir, rather than from Salé, and specialised in sugar, although some of them sold the raw cloth peculiar to Ouezzan.[1] Most of the Slawis dealt only in sewn goods, and, in fact, the generic name for cloth merchants throughout the Gharb was 'Slawi'. Some sewn goods were sold in bulk to the Jewish merchants for their own cities, but most sales were piecemeal.

The merchants of Fez looked down on the itinerant traders from Salé, because they moved about the countryside and ate up their day's profit by feeding themselves and their animals. However, the Slawis could not afford to wait for customers to come to them; they did not have the capital or the organisation to control the market and bring it to Salé in the way the Fasis did. But these traders made a virtue of necessity and took great pride in their mobility and endurance. They flattered themselves that they were reputed for their determination and good manners and proclaimed that they combined the best of the resolute if ill bred Berber with the urban if effeminate Fasi.

Until the 1870s ownership of a shop in the bazaar was neither profitable nor prestigious. Ibn ʿAlī, whose father was an itinerant trader, described the character traits of early merchants as cunning, disputatiousness, caginess and persistence, all of which are the opposite of manliness and nobility.[2] By the end of the nineteenth century the situation had changed; many of the wealthiest and most influential and respected people in the town were bazaar merchants. This transformation in Salé's commercial life was accompanied by a change in attitudes towards different kinds of work. Commerce, land holding and government service became equal sources of economic and social influence.

It is important to understand that the new wealth from commerce was exploited by local people and not by outsiders. In the city of Azemmour, which in many way resembled Salé, the situation developed differently. There the cloth merchants became a kind of capitalistic aristocracy, clearly differentiated in their traditions and alliances from the landholders or officials. Most merchants in Azemmour were Jews, or Fasis who maintained their ties with Fez and married into its society. Their activities were of three kinds: (1) wholesalers, who organised the bringing of goods by caravan from Fez, Mazagan and Casablanca; (2) shopkeepers in the bazaar; and (3) itinerant merchants. Often a single family participated in all three branches of commerce. Their activities were essentially based on buyer–seller relationships in which interest was the only conscious tie, whereas other activities brought into play more complex relationships.[3] These conditions and characteristics stand in marked contrast to those which prevailed in Salé. The merchants who rose to prominence in Salé from the 1870s onward did not differ from landowners and officials in their origins or allegiances, with the exception of the Jews, who had played an important role in all branches of commerce in earlier periods. Indeed, one of the rationalisations given for the relative lack of previous activity in the bazaar by the Slawis was their disdain for an activity practised mainly by Jews. Before the rapid growth of international trade in Morocco the activity of the bazaar had been limited. Salé's commerce had been centred in the rural areas, where cotton goods were sold by itinerant traders, both Jews and Muslims. When, however, European imports began to dominate the economy, Slawis of various occupations and social origins moved into wholesale and retail marketing within the city and its countryside, and in Rabat.

Before the large-scale import of European goods, commerce and speculation in land holdings were frowned upon in Salé. The ideal 'average' man was a farmer or craftsman. The old Slawis whom I interviewed idealised earlier generations as easy-going, decent folk who above all sought other men's company. For those generations social life had been predominant, and they did not need or want to engage in industrious, impersonal economic activity openly aimed at amassing money or power. They constantly searched for any excuse to have a picnic in their gardens, to make a show of their comforts and civilities. They abhorred eating alone and tried to find excuses for festive occasions. If someone could not manage to have a visitor at his table he would invite his cronies, or a *sharīf* who could be counted on to be well dressed, urbane, wise and witty, This idealised past ended when profits from trade in imported goods began to become the measure of a man's worth.

The change in attitude towards commerce as a means of livelihood and as an occupation that gave a man high social status derived partly from the important role that many Slawis had come to play in the ports of Morocco as administrators and notaries. The development of international trade in the country had led to a large expansion of the State bureaucracy. Because of their education, means and contacts with government authorities a number of Slawis received official appointments and managed to place themselves at the hub of the new commercial activity of the ports. In these situations they gained expertise in matters of trade and interacted on an everyday basis with European and Jewish merchants. Often they took on commercial interests of their own, or paved the way for their kin or friends in Salé to take advantage of their access to trading opportunities. Most of these men served as customs agents (*amīn*, pl. *umanā*) or notaries (*ʿadl*, pl. *ʿudūl*). Because of his functions in the port an *amīn* was himself tempted to become involved in commerce, and few resisted the temptation. An agent might ostensibly remain detached from commerce because, as informants explained it, his function allowed him to receive economic benefits without demanding them. For example, an agent might fix low customs duties by accepting a declaration on the value of imported goods which was in fact well below their real value. Then he had the option of buying a quantity of the goods at the declared price. In that way he could accumulate various kinds of goods, for his personal use or otherwise. These were rewards for services rendered. At the same time, those appointed to official positions in the ports had debts for favours granted to them by the friends who had aided them in gaining their appointments. These relationships and exchanges were neither hidden nor illicit. The port officials, it was assumed, would take advantage of their circumstances to exploit the economic opportunities created by foreign trade.

These officials were instrumental in the development of trade in European goods in Salé; their access to the profits of commerce allowed them to establish themselves or their relatives and friends as merchants. Trade in imported goods began to increase, and some of the new merchants were accumulating wealth. They alone among the Slawis had ready capital, and with it they invested and speculated in land and property. The success of these new merchants changed the general attitude towards commerce. Itinerant traders, using their expert knowledge and experience of trade in the rural markets, began to move into the bazaar. New attitudes and new groups of people emerged in the wake of commercial expansion. Some former religious teachers and petty clerks in the law courts who received official posts in the ports and became involved in commercial activities achieved wealth, status and influence in a relatively short time. With their relatives and friends they opened large and well stocked wholesale houses in Rabat and Salé. Former itinerant traders bought goods from them and set up retail stores in Salé to supply the markets of the countryside. Salé's teachers, clerks, farmers, artisans and itinerant traders, long known for their shrewdness and hardheadedness, made good merchants. By the turn of the century most of the bazaar merchants, whether Jews or Muslims, were people who had been involved in these occupations. They had not an age-old tradition of commerce, but they were wily and knowledgeable at their trades, and this served them well. With the beginning of the protectorate Slawi merchants expanded into other cities and some of them did extremely well, especially in towns like Kenitra (Port Lyautey), Khemmiset and Oued Zem.

Not all merchants, of course, succeeded in becoming wealthy and, indeed, some of them lost everything they possessed. The instability of market conditions made commerce a risky enterprise. There were a number of cases in which merchants amassed a considerable fortune during the early years of this century, only to lose it because of mismanagement, unwise investments or simply bad luck. The land records document the losses of property by these formerly successful merchants, just as they illustrate the failures of impoverished artisans and small shopkeepers. Commerce depended on complex matters of credit which unfortunately are not documented by our sources. We do learn from the records, however, that merchandise moved from wholesaler to retailer to itinerant trader on credit, using property as collateral. The failure to repay these debts often led to the loss of property. The same practice was followed by the rich wholesalers, but they turned to Jewish moneylenders and, as soon as the protectorate was established, to European banks to borrow capital for their enterprises.

The Jews and the Muslims of Salé maintained close economic relations, and during the expansion of commerce the Jews often acted as creditors for their Muslim compatriots. Moreover they sometimes formed partnerships in commerce or property, especially in the commercial quarters which developed in the New Mellah and Sīdī Turkī during the early years of the protectorate. Although detailed evidence is lacking, Jews and Muslims in Salé had apparently maintained ties of economic interdependence for centuries, and these developed still further with the penetration of European trade.[4]

Commerce, once a despised and unrewarding way of earning a livelihood, had become an important means of achieving upward economic mobility, and of attaining prestige and influence. However, the newly wealthy merchants did not isolate themselves from other economic or social groups. Many of them were men of learning who had served as government officials; most had become property owners by investing their profits in stores, houses, farms, building plots, etc. With the coming of the protectorate the interest of these merchants began to spread from Salé and its surroundings into the Gharb and among the Zemmour, and into the even further removed rural areas and cities.[5]

The formation and consolidation of this new-based wealth stemming from commerce had encouraged the emergence of a relatively small group of men who dominated the socio-economic and political scene in Salé. This phase in the history of the city and its society, which began in the 1860s, culminated in the late 1920s with the world crisis. The population suffered badly and encountered difficulties in getting the most basic necessities for subsistence.[6] The merchants for the most part fared badly too. Many closed their shops and left the city rather than face poverty and disgrace at home. Moreover 1930 ended a period of social and political development. A new and discontented generation among the elite began to challenge the dominance of their elders and the colonial system born of Europe's economic and political expansion into Morocco.

Government service

An appointment by the central government to an official post of some sort had always given its recipient prestige and sometimes made wealth and influence available to him. Whoever was granted an official appointment received a decree (*ẓahīr*) from the sultan.[7] Theoretically Salé's governor, qadi, market inspector, administrator of pious endowments, tax collector, preacher and prayer leaders of the Friday mosques, and even teachers in the mosque were appointed by the sultan. In effect most of the appointments were made on the recommendation, singly or collectively, of individuals trusted by the sultan and his administration. Thus, for example, in 1861 a group of ten notables from Salé, including the adminstrator of pious endowments, the market inspector and three of the leading merchants, visited the vizier of Sultan Muḥammad I. They recommended to him that one of their number, Muḥammad b. Saʿīd, be appointed to replace the ageing governor of the city, who was no longer able to enforce the collection of taxes. The appointment by decree was an investiture of a prescriptive right not only to the office but to the all-embracing favour of the sultan as well. The appointment of ʿAbd Allah b. Saʿīd as governor of Salé in 1894, following the death of his father, who had ruled for thirty-three years, was also ratified by a 'decree of honour and respect' (*ẓahīr at-tawqīr wa-ʾl-iḥtirām*). This decree freed Bin Saʿid from obligations to serve in the army or pay taxes in consideration of the service that he and his forefathers had rendered to the Makhzan, and promised the same privileges to his children, in-laws and paternal cousins.[8] Such appointments gave the individuals concerned a direct and highly valued relationship with the central government.

The officials who served in Salé, though esteemed and sometimes feared by the population, were not an outside governing group imposed on society. Their roots were in the city, and although they represented the religious and secular authority of the sultan they formed part and parcel of the local community. Even when Slawis occupied official positions in other cities they maintained close ties within their native city and eventually returned to the homes and families that they had kept intact.[9] The town's reputation as a centre of learning and urban culture often led the government to search within its community for appointees to the central administration. The city had provided officials for local and central government, including Ministers and ambassadors in earlier centuries. During the nineteenth century educated Slawis were increasingly called upon by various sultans to fill posts in the central government and bureaucracy, especially in the ports that had been opened up to European trade.

Education for their children had long been considered by the Slawis as a profitable investment, because it opened the door to important economic and political opportunities. They encouraged the children to become literate, even if the level of learning did not always satisfy the standards of the scholars. An amusing anecdote in an eighteenth-century commonplace book makes this point. It is said that in the fourteenth century the famous poet and man of state Ibn al-Khaṭīb described a document concerning a defective donkey drawn up by the notaries of Salé; it contained, he claimed, twelve grammatical errors, and this lamentable situation was due to the unorganised education that the Slawis gave to their children. Merchants used their children in their shops throughout the week and then sent them on Fridays to a notary to learn to read and write. These children became the notaries of the next generation, and, of course, they were equally ignorant. The owner of the book added in the margin that the Slawis had not changed: their handwriting was bad, and they did not know how to express themselves correctly in writing. Moreover, he wrote, they were mean and stingey: a Slawi notary would argue a vegetable seller down to an impossibly low price for a bunch of turnips and then engage him in conversation while surreptitiously adding a turnip or two to his purchase.[10] Salé's historian, Ibn ʿAlī, expressly refuted what he called the calumnies of Ibn al-Khaṭīb against his city. He argued that the attainments of Slawis in government services were wholly deserved. The kings had employed them because of their skill and 'their long-established aptitude and reputation as bearers of an old urban culture'. For these reasons, he noted, the highest secretary of Sultan ʿAbd ar-Raḥmān (1822–59) had been a Slawi, and Sultan Ḥasan (1873–94) had filled the ports with notaries and administrators from Salé.[11]

Throughout the nineteenth century the population of Salé and particularly its authorities and scholars enjoyed the confidence and favour of the Makhzan. Thus, for example, Sultan Sulaymān, travelling from Marrakesh to Fez in 1820, stopped at the Great Mosque of Salé to pray and then visited the house of a local notable, al-Hājj Muḥammad Maʿanīnū. There he met the teacher and astronomer of the Great Mosque, Aḥmad az-Zwāwī, and invited him to join his entourage as official astronomer. He also took some of the artillery experts of Salé with him to Fez. These men of talent recruited by the government bound the fate and fortune of the elite of the city closely to the reigning sultan and his administration. The palace had confidence in the Slawis to the extent that it sent children of the royal household to be educated in the city. In 1849 Sultan ʿAbd ar-Raḥmān sent his twelve-year-old son to the home of the qadi for his education, and other sultans did the same.[12] Contacts between the central government and the city were personalised and carried out by men who knew each other well. A government Minister, writing to the governor in 1836 to thank him for furnishing a list of Ḥabous and Makhzan property in the city, ends his letter on a personal note. 'Praise be to God that there are the likes of you in these times, and please give regards to our friends, the legist Muḥammad ʿAwwād, the merchant Hājj alʿArabī Maʿanīnū, and the legist Tuhāmī Marsīlū.'[13]

Officials in Salé used their special relationship with the Makhzan to maintain and strengthen their power locally. They distributed administrative positions and favours within the city and helped their friends to gain appointments in the central government or its agencies in the port cities. In so doing they created around themselves clientèle groups which furthered their political influence and economic interests. Recruitment to the government administration depended on the intervention and recommendation of local officials. Thus, for example, the qadi of Salé wrote to the grand vizier al-ʿArabī al-Jamʿī in 1849 to suggest the appointment of a fellow Slawi as a customs official. The candidate is described as a respectable and dutiful man who has grown up in an atmosphere of learning and steadfast religion and who would succeed because he was astute and familiar with practical matters.[14] Periodically local officials were called upon to recommend to the Makhzan the names of people suited to administrative positions, and every year the Minister of the Treasury made up a list of the merchants and ulama in Tetuan, Salé, Rabat and Fez who could fulfil the functions of customs officials in the port cities. Recommendations to the Minister came from local officials of the four cities, and appointments were made from the lists thus drawn up. During the reign of Ḥasan I (1873–94), the majority of those appointed to these positions came from Tetuan and Salé. Afterwards priority passed to Fez, but Salé remained an important centre of recruitment.

The appointment of Slawis to the ports in large numbers was a regular practice from the beginning of the period under study until the protectorate began in 1912. Although we lack exact statistics, a general idea of their importance emerges from the correspondence of the governor ʿAbd Allah b. Saʿīd. From 1892 to 1905 at least forty-two Slawis received appointments as notaries or customs agents in the various ports. These positions in the ports provided the key to the fortunes of many men in Salé just as they did in Tetuan, Rabat and Fez. The Fasis claim that for every powerful family in the city of Fez today they can identify an ancestor who was an *amīn* and made them that way.[15] In Salé there is more reticence in discussing the origins of personal fortunes, but the sources of wealth were clearly the same.

The *amīns* have been described as the bankers of the Makhzan, those who provided the Treasury with funds when needed.[16] Sultan Sulaymān (1792–1822) organised a financial system based on the administration of customs income by these officials, but neither during his reign nor after it did the central government attain effective control of their activities and the monies they manipulated. The British consul, Drummond Hay, constantly warned Sultan Muḥammad IV (1859–73) that there could be no security of property, or prosperity in agriculture or commerce, as long as Ministers, governors and port authorities received no fixed salaries, that under these prevailing conditions corruption and thieving would continue to flourish. Attempts to institute reforms which would put an end to the despoliation of government revenues in the ports were tried repeatedly, but ultimately failed. The officials took advantage of the administrative disorder to further their interests, to repay their debts and to reward their friends.

Local officialdom

Local officials within the city were less numerous than the Slawis who acted as customs agents in the various ports. They included the governor (*qā'id*), judge (*qāḍī*), market inspector (*muḥtasib*), an agent of indirect taxes (*amīn al-mustafād*), master of probate and administrator of government property (*abū mawārīth*), head of the descendants of the Prophet (*naqīb ash-shurafā'*), the deputies and assistants to the more important of these offices, and some twenty notaries (*'adl*, pl. *'udūl*) of the court. In addition several customs agents and notaries serving in the port of Rabat–Salé were appointed direct by the sultan. All these officials were recruited locally, and all enjoyed some measure of social and economic prominence.

These administrative positions carried with them prestige, influence and considerable scope for personal gain. To be sure, the positions differed in kind, demanding specific qualifications and offering specific kinds of rewards. The governor was first and foremost a man of action and possessed of sound, pragmatic sense. Informants said that he would have to be intelligent (*'āqil*), and not necessarily learned (*'ālim*); the qadi, on the other hand, would be primarily a man of learning. Governors ruled in the name of the sultan, qadis made judgements in the name of Islamic law. These were not secular as opposed to religious offices, but different types of jurisdiction. A man who aspired to any office was expected to have a share of religious learning, as well as a highly developed sense of the practical. The following lists of governors and qadis for the period of this study allow of some general remarks on the types of person who held these offices and reveal some basic aspects of the city's social structure.

Governors of Salé, 1830–1930

1	Ḥājj Aḥmad b. Muḥammad b. al-Hāshimī 'Awwād	1827–1840
2	Abū 'Amar b. al-Ḥājj aṭ-Ṭahir Fanīsh	1840–
3	'Abd al-'Azīz Maḥbūba	—

4	Muḥammad b. ʿAbd al-Hādī Znībar	–1854
5	ʿAbd al-ʿAzīz Maḥbūba (second term)	1854–1861
6	Ḥājj Muḥammad b. Saʿīd	1861–1892
7	ʿAbd Allah b. Muḥammad b. Saʿīd (son of above)	1892–1905
8	Hājj aṭ-Ṭayyib aṣ-Ṣubīḥī	1905–1914
9	Hājj Muḥammad b. aṭ-Ṭayyib aṣ-Ṣubīḥī (son of above)	1914–1958

All the above belonged to old, established families and had received some education.[17] Without exception they possessed important land holdings in Salé and its hinterland. Most had been connected with commerce, and almost all had served as customs officials in one or more ports before becoming governor of the city.[18] Through ties of kinship and clientèle they were allied to other economically and politically powerful individuals in the city. Most of these governors of Salé had the confidence of the Makhzan, which entrusted them with delicate missions both abroad and in the country.

Before the 1860s the governors of Salé had been nominated by a group of local notables among whom they acted as *primus inter pares*. Muḥammad Bin Saʿīd, appointed by the sultan in 1861 at the request of the notables, changed the nature of local authority by gradually centralising power in his own hands and making the notables dependent on him. This situation continued when his son inherited his office and power. The next and last governors of the period, again father and son, similarly dominated political and economic life in the city. With the penetration of Morocco by European influences a new type of local authority had emerged. The governors came to depend much more on the sultan and their friends at court than on their local constituencies, and they imitated the sultan in their political style. They formed personal clientèles around themselves by furthering the careers and fortunes of chosen individuals in order to consolidate and aggrandise their own wealth and power.

Although the governors represented the authority of the sultan and imitated him in their way of ruling, they had none of the sultan's religious jurisdictions or aura of blessedness. The governors of the city were never members of the ʿAlawī family or descendants of the prophet through any other branch of the *shurafāʾ*. They were, however, careful to include both *shurafāʾ* and ulama within their clientèles and entourages. The basis of the power that belonged to the governors lay in their ability to provide security in and around the city. There had been cases of the overthrow of governors before 1830 but these took place when the governor's power was no longer sufficient to insure security. As long as security reigned in the city the power of the governor remained uncontested. The governor had also to fulfil certain duties to the central government; his primary responsibility was the collection and payment of taxes for the city and the surrounding tribes. Two of the qa'ids listed, ʿAwwād and Muḥbūba, were dismissed from their position, the latter because of his inability to collect taxes.

The office of qadi represented a different source of power. Ibn ʿAlī reports that Sultan Sulaymān (1792–1822) had the excellent policy of changing qadis every few years so that they should not have the opportunity to become oppressors. After his death the policy was not enforced, and the qadis took to oppressing the people and withholding from them their rights.[19] The qadis were the religious representatives of the sultan, the arbiters of Islamic and customary law, the conscience of the Muslim community and the symbols of learning and piety. They had an important influence in city affairs which they could use both to fulfil their specific functions and to further their personal interests and those of their allies.

Judges of Salé, 1830–1930

1	Muḥammad b. Aḥmad 'Bil-Fqīh' (Ibn al-Faqīh) al-Jirārī	1807–1824
2	Muḥammad b. al-Hāshimī Aṭūbī	1824–
3	Muḥammad b. Ḥasūn ʿAwwād	–1850
4	Ḥājj Muḥammad as-Sadrātī	1850–
5	Muḥammad al-ʿArabī b. Aḥmad b. Manṣūr	–1868
6	Abū Bakr b. al-Qāḍī Muḥammad ʿAwwād (son of No. 3 above)	1868–
7	Ibrāhīm 'Bil-Fqīh' al-Jirārī (relation to No. 1 not known)	1878–1884
8	Muḥammad b. aṭ-Ṭālib Maʿanīnū	1884–1891
9	Hājj ʿAlī b. al-Qāḍī Muḥammad ʿAwwād	1891–1898
	(son of 3)	–1905
10	Aḥmad b. Abū Bakr ʿAwwād (son of 6)	1905–1909
11	Ḥājj Muḥammad as-Sadrātī (relation to 4 not known)	1909–1914
12	ʿAlī at-Taghrāwī	1914–1922
13	ʿAbd al-Qādir b. Muḥammad at-Tuhāmī	1922–

All the qadis on this list, with the exception of the next to last, were from old, respected families.[20] The only *sharīf*, or descendant of the Prophet, was the last mentioned. One family, the ʿAwwāds, provided four qadis. These qadis, like the governors, formed clientèle groups because of their influence in the city, but they tended to ally themselves more often with men of learning rather than with merchants or land holders. Qadis and other men of learning did, however, sometimes have significant interests in commerce and property.

Moreover merchants and land holders sought to associate themselves with the learned in order to have access to their special knowledge of the law and to enhance their status. If we compare the position of governors and qadis we find that they had separate bases of power and influence, the former more secular, the latter more religious. They and their clientèles often shared common concerns and goals, but they could and at times did come into conflict. Overall there was a much greater potentiality for co-operation between them than for conflict.

The special advantages that Slawis enjoyed in gaining entrance into government depended on the personal relationships between the palace and the leading personalities of the city. Nāṣirī illustrates the closeness of these relations when he describes visits by sultans to Rabat and Salé. Thus, for example, on the last night of the fast month of Ramadan in 1290/1874 Sultan Ḥasan attended in Rabat the customary reading of the collection of Traditions relating to the life of the Prophet. Delegations from all Morocco attended, and the ulama of the Two Banks were there in full force. When the Traditions had been read the sultan offered a festive meal at which poems were recited and money was dispersed. Afterwards the ulama, the reciters of the Qur'an, the muezzins, artillery men and sailors from both Rabat and Salé were honoured with gifts from the sultan. Three years later the sultan visited Salé, its saints' tombs and the Great Mosque, where he attended the noon prayer led by ʿAbd Allah b. al-Khadrā' (whom he was later to appoint head qadi of Fez). Then the qadi, Abū Bakr ʿAwwād, showed the sultan the library of the mosque and asked him to buy some books for it. One hundred *riyāl* were donated for this purpose, and customary gifts were presented to the ulama and soldiers of the city. Nāṣirī adds that on this occasion he recited a poem in honour of the sultan, and that the poet of his time, Muḥammad Ḥarakāt of Salé, then composed a poem using the same rhyme but with a different metre.[21] On these elaborate occasions, with their pomp and circumstance, the bond between the palace and the leaders of Salé was renewed. The sultan and his retinue came to know the leaders individually, and would call on them at a later time to serve in the administration. These occasions reaffirmed and dramatised the alliance between the Makhzan and the city, and they strengthened the individual power of local officials.

Within the city the governor held court as if he were himself a sultan. An early nineteenth-century traveller who met the pasha was highly impressed by the governor's show of status, even though he misunderstood its significance. 'It is more than probable,' he exclaimed, 'that this hereditary pasha looks upon the emperor as an intruder on legitimacy.' He describes being led into the pasha's garden by black eunuchs who beat back a crowd of onlookers with great ferocity, and he is surprised to find that the governor was tall, extremely handsome, elegant, gracious and dignified. He sees the governor as possessing 'all those advantages which nothing but hereditary rank, and consciousness of high birth, can bestow'.[22] In effect Beauclerk had witnessed what was in Salé a rather commonplace demonstration of the governor's authority. Men of power, even in a relatively small city, assumed an air of dignity and self-importance to demonstrate the authority of their position. This no doubt made a great impression on European travellers, and it is not surprising that they ascribed the status of such men to hereditary rank and high birth.[23] The governor of the city, or for that matter any dignitary, conducted public affairs by imitating the courtly manners of the *makhzan*. The entourage of the governor and the ways in which members conducted themselves and exerted their authority were modelled on the central government, and a reduplication of it on a smaller scale. The demonstration of authority, as well as politeness and the art of diplomacy, were central to the style and process of politics in Salé, just as they were at the sultan's court. Most of the city's affairs, even of the most mundane sort, were handled by delicate negotiations rather than by a show of force. This pattern of behaviour was dominant among all groups within the city regardless of social class or cultural level; marriages, arguments, favours, even buying and selling, not to mention business transactions and government appointments, were negotiated. The art of politics expressed itself in formalised codes of appearance and behaviour. The traveller's description of the governor reflects this style of politics on one level, just as Nāṣirī's account of the visit of the sultan reflects it on another.[24]

Access to economic resources that were in the hands of the government depended on political alliances, on the intermediaries that one could call upon. Put in other terms (those of the people of Salé themselves), a man's reputation depended on one of several factors—his origin, wealth or culture; but his influence depended upon his ability to act as an ally and an intermediary. Slawis say that in their society everything counted on connection or contact (coll. *ttiṣāl*) or acquaintance (coll. *mʿarfa*). Sometimes one turned to a relative by blood or marriage when in need of an intermediary, that is, if one had an influential relative willing to act on one's behalf. If not, one approached someone in a position to help who could be persuaded to do so. On the basis of past or future exchanges of services, it was considered correct and natural to seek assistance in this way. In explaining such behaviour the Slawis usually mentioned the famous saying of the Prophet about the mutual dependence of the community of believers: 'Each believer is to another as [the bricks of] a building: they support one another.' This was the idiom most often used to describe individual alliances and the exchange of services. Of course, as we have seen in Part II, personal alliances and *ad hoc* or more permanent clientèle groups depended on a myriad of relationships at once complex and specific.

The French authorities at the beginning of the protectorate period were aware of the bureaucratic talents and ambitions of the Slawis and to a certain extent wanted to satisfy them. By 1930 thirty of the high-ranking judges and secretaries of the central administration came from Salé, including the president of the High Court and the vice-president of the Court of Appeal. In addition some Slawis were employed by the government as interpreters, clerks, teachers and petty functionaries. Yet in the French view there were too many ambitious and presumptuous people in Salé who considered themselves qualified to make judgements about and participate in the government administration. 'What business,' the Contrôleur Civil demanded, 'did these Slawis have in seeking friendship with important personalities, and in following so attentively every bit of information that concerned the city, or for that matter, all Morocco? How was it that the ambition of every Slawi with any aptitude was to become a judge or a bureaucrat?'[25]

In fact there had been an increase in the number of people capable and desirous of fulfilling government positions. By the late 1920s many of the young had received or were in the process of receiving a modern education in either Arabic or French; some had already found government employment and the benefits of a steady income that came with it. As one of the members of that generation put it, 'The attraction of government work was overwhelming. After all, what else could a man of education do? Where else could a man of breeding find the prestige he needed—and deserved?' However, whether government employees or not, the young educated men in the city had frustrated political ambitions. They knew that their talents and opinions were not and would not be taken into account. They felt powerless and humiliated under the thumb of the protectorate and French officials who, despite the fiction of indirect rule, held *de facto* power.

This generation of Slawis were impatient to assume responsibilities in the government administration which would give them opportunities to influence policies and to wield authority. They were, on the whole, parts of those webs of personal alliances which in the past had assured one success in attaining economic goals and had provided access to the resources necessary for the consolidation of power. With the protectorate, however, the locus of political and economic power had shifted from the Moroccans to the French. The old system of alliance could no longer be used to further the ambitions of the young and educated. Real power was in the hands of the Contrôleur Civil, and all officials, beginning with the governor, had lost much of their prestige and influence because of their dependence.

The French, by the very nature of the protectorate, had become the ruling elite of Moroccan society. Not surprisingly, they were unable to solve the dilemma posed by the existence of growing numbers of young, ambitious, educated urban Moroccans. Whether their educational background was traditional or modern, Arabic or French, the Moroccans were not allowed to fill many posts in the administration. At the same time more and more Frenchmen were being absorbed into the expanding colonial State apparatus. Therein lay the conflict. Though an integral part of and tied inextricably to the society in which they lived, the young educated Slawis could not use social ties to find a position in the administration. They came to resent what they saw as a collusion against them: French rule and the helpless passivity of the leaders of the city.

French native policies in Morocco, to be sure, were filled with contradictions. For some Frenchmen the inhabitants of cities such as Salé were *les maures*, a distinct race that had developed the 'commercial' qualities of flexibility, ruse and intrigue. These 'Moors' maintained their pride in being city dwellers by continually augmenting their wealth and conceit, by proclaiming their education and refinement, and by holding government posts. The French saw these officials, the wealthy, and the intellectual elite, as opportunists whose sole aim was to exploit others and the country for their own benefit. Some French observers believed that the urban elite would undoubtedly be the most hostile element in the country to European penetration. According to one of them, the city dwellers by the 'superior ruse of the cultivated' and the 'expedients of traditional politics' had dominated several million Berbers, taking from them what was necessary to feed their hereditary needs of luxury and idleness. They would necessarily see every project of reform and remedy against profitable abuses as a direct menace to their interests—the retention of official positions and the exercise of uncontrolled authority. According to this view, the older generation of Moors had known how to support and use a regime of corruption and exploitation, but the younger generation, 'without energy and abandoned to the excitation of sensual idleness, will soon fold under this weight, falling victim to the fatal thrust of the Berbers'.[26]

An opposite view was held by Marshal Lyautey, the Resident General during most of the first two decades of the protectorate. Lyautey wanted to retain and institutionalise a Moroccan ruling class through which the French could control the country rather than rule it directly. By gradually preparing the sons of the elite in French schools, leaders would emerge who would work together with the French to improve the administration of the country without cutting it off from its laws and customs or from its own personality. In practice, neither of these two conflicting policies—viz. that the city people were to be excluded from government or that the traditional ruling structures were to be left untouched and encouraged—was successfully pursued. Individuals were incorporated into or excluded from the administration, but few could or would identify with French rule. Although some individuals profited directly from the protectorate, real wealth and power passed into the hands of foreigners. This, with the fact that ties of allegiance and solidarity on the local level were stronger and more vital than anything the French could offer, gave most Slawis, particularly the young, a frustrating sense of second-class citizenship.

The ways and means of wealth

ḥajra fi-l-ḥait khair mn yāqūṭa fi-l-khaiṭ. A stone in a wall is preferable to a ruby on a string.

The word that people in Salé use for landed property or assets—*uṣūl*—comes from the same Arabic root used to express the concepts of roots, origins, descent, fundamentals, principles. The semantic field of this root helps us to understand why property ownership was a *sine qua non* for inclusion in the community of the city. Almost without exception every family considered part of the society of Salé owned its own house. Furthermore wealth and the power that went with it tended to be measured in terms of a man's assets in landed property. Such assets might lie in additional houses, shops, gardens (*sāniya*—irrigated; *jnān*—unirrigated), salt marshes, soap factories, mills, ovens, Turkish baths, tanneries, stables or hotel–warehouses. The ownership of property might be outright (*milk*) or indirect. In the latter case the property usually belonged to the Habous (cl. *ḥubs* or *ḥubus*, pl. *aḥbās*), the city's pious endowments, and was rented for a fixed amount. However, much of this latter property had become, in fact, inalienable, the right to rent the property being sold by tenant to tenant, and inherited by one's descendants.

The records of the Conservation Foncière, the office of land registration, provided much information about the history of property ownership in and around Salé. These records are not, nnfortunately, comprehensive; they contain only those properties that were 'matriculated', or legally registered by their owners. When registration took place all the documents bearing on the ownership of the property had to be produced and deposited in the Conservation Foncière. In Salé nearly half of all privately owned property had been registered, and from these records one can form an idea of land holding patterns. Approximately one-fourth of all property had been put into pious endowments. Some information from the Habous records, particularly the inventory drawn up in 1868, has also proved valuable in understanding the pattern of property holdings.

Property had long been the primary source of wealth and influence in the town. An eighteenth-century decree expropriating the property of the powerful family of Abu Qāʿa declared that their houses, shops, lands, irrigated and unirrigated gardens, hotel–warehouses (sng. *funduq*), and soap factories and salt marshes, within and beyond Salé, had been taken over by the administration of pious endownments.[27] The land records show that the property inherited from a wealthy man included the same kinds of assets, to a greater or lesser degree. Thus, for example, Muḥammad ūʿAmmār, when he died in 1845, left three-sixteenths of a house in Talʿa near the Great Mosque, one-fourth of two separate irrigated gardens and other real estate, their total value being 132 *mithqāl*. The estate of Ḥājj Muḥammad al-Ḥarsh, an important merchant who began as a successful itinerant trader and then went into the wholesale cloth and tea business in Rabat, was, at his death in 1914, worth some twenty-four million réals; his property included houses, stables, gardens and various plots of land. One of the wealthiest merchants of Salé, Ḥājj Muḥammad 'Bil-Ḥasan', was the son of an artisan; he amassed within his own lifetime a considerable fortune, and at his death in 1940 he owned—and the list is incomplete—sixteen and a half houses, one and a half tanneries, six and a half shops, a stable, a Moorish bath (in addition to four baths rented from pious endowments), and three and a half gardens, their total value estimated at three-quarters of a million francs.

In whatever way a man earned his livelihood, his wealth was judged by others in terms of the amount of property he owned. As one informant put it, 'only after a man had accumulated property—a house, some cottages, a store and so on—did people begin to take notice of him and say "he's well off!" [*lā bā's ʿalih*]'.[28] Informants in Salé were explicit about the traditional values regarding investment and the priorities: material goods—especially land and buildings—gave one prestige and wealth. Like gold and wool, they were readily convertible into cash, and owning them gave one insurance for one's entire life.

The estates enumerated above show the kinds of property that people in Salé were wont to invest in. The relative value of houses, gardens, salt marshes, soap factories, mills, ovens, shops, Moorish baths, tanneries, stables, *funduqs* and the like changed during the period under study, and these changes influenced the priority of investment. In the land records from 1830 to 1930 one finds a gradual decrease in the number of leading individuals in the city who bought and sold properties. There was a growing monopolisation of property among a relatively small number of people, i.e. the newly wealthy merchants and officials. A good part of the owners of houses and gardens mentioned in documents before 1880 cease to figure in the land records later on. These are, it would seem, the impoverished craftsmen. Some of the family names in the records have completely disappeared from Salé. The last member of the male line was said to have died out, although in a few cases I found descendants of these forgotten people whose parents had become completely impoverished.

The loss of property by so many families was a direct consequence of the process of change that took place between 1830 and 1930. Property ownership was always precarious in Moroccan cities because of the Islamic laws of inheritance. The distribution of a deceased man's estate is strictly controlled by these laws; each legal heir is stipulated by law, as is his or her proportion of the estate. The effect of this, especially in the case where the family is large, is to break property up into small, even minute, parcels. Thus the heirs of a relatively wealthy man may find themselves at his death without any important assets.

In Salé wealth was seldom perpetuated from father to sons on the basis of inheritance. In each generation the rich men had built their personal fortunes by successively gaining access to capital and then investing it in property, which in turn dissolved among their heirs according to the laws of inheritance. Before the economic crises that began in the 1860s the effects of inheritance laws in dividing estates into small parcels of land and parts of houses seem to have been less disruptive of economic and social equilibrium. That is to say, men could earn a living that allowed them to purchase a house and a garden where they had inherited only small shares of property. In many cases property appears not to have been broken up at all, but to have remained in the joint ownership of the descendants of the deceased.

As we have seen, the period from 1830 until the bad crop years in the mid-1860s was one of relative economic stability. The population seems to have adapted to the cessation of piracy and the international trade that accompanied it by finding profitable markets in the hinterland where the products of the town's industries—cotton, woven cloth, clothing of various kinds—could be sold by itinerant traders from the city. Near the middle of the nineteenth century there was a decade of prosperity—low prices, rising real estate values, activity in building, and such traditional crafts as shoemaking and weaving continued to flourish. The land records for this period show few changes in the ownership of property and no evidence of speculation. Even in those cases where a man died and left no male heir his property remained in the joint ownership of his female heirs.

With the economic crises of the late 1860s, and periodically from then until the protectorate, property began to change hands rapidly. Because of high prices and low income many of the farmers and artisans were obliged to sell their lands and houses to survive. And when men died, the shares of their property were soon sold. The few who possessed capital began to corner the best land and property. From the 1880s we find relatively few land holders, and most of them possessed numerous houses and gardens. These men and their sons were usually merchants and officials, and many served as customs agents in various ports of the empire. When they died the property inherited by their sons enhanced the economic assets which they had already begun to accumulate. If there were many heirs the fortune was dispersed into individual portions, but some sons, no doubt, had already established for themselves situations in which they had begun to invest and speculate in their own property. With their inheritance they were on the path to the solidity of wealth that their fathers had known. Not everyone succeeded in this way, but if only one of many sons became wealthy it was sufficient to perpetuate the idea of a 'family' fortune.

The rise of this moneyed group who concentrated land holdings and allied themselves to each other by partnerships in business and alliances in marriage was accompanied by the progressive impoverishment and social decline of most farmers and craftsmen. Poverty forced people to sell their property cheaply or to lose it because of unpaid loans. In this way extensive land holdings were consolidated by a small number of people. Thus was born the notion of the 'great family' so dearly fostered by the authorities of the French protectorate.

The steady expansion of commerce during the nineteenth century had undermined the traditional economic structure and created a new dimension for economic and social mobility within the society of the city. Possibilities for social mobility in the past had been limited to the accumulation of landed property by regrouping one's inheritance and making judicious marriage alliances. These were the traditional ways in which an individual could forge a position of wealth and, perhaps, of influence. The opportunities in the ports and the growth of commerce dramatically changed and enlarged the vistas for advancement. In the process some individuals favoured at birth neither by wealth nor by name were able to rise to the top of the economic and social ladder, to be counted among the notables and noble families of the city.

As the possibilities for mobility increased, the distribution of wealth altered radically; the number of people with significant economic assets lessened, and the differentiation between them and other members of society grew large. On the eve of the French protectorate there were fewer than two hundred men in Salé who were considered well off, that is, about 5 per cent of the total adult male population.[29] Many of them were related, in most cases through marriages rather than by common descent. Some of them were sons of fathers who had also been economically and socially important. Others had begun with nothing and made their way to important positions. Although some status was attached to descent, high birth and wealth were often unrelated. Most Slawis could point with pride to some ancestor who had distinguished himself in one way or another. But the claim to an illustrious forefather only legitimated a man's power and prestige once he had attained it through wealth. The idea held by the French that the leaders of Salé came from an aristocratic class which had long been dominant because of its origins and inherited wealth does not respond to the complex reality of the city's social structure. There was, to be sure, an elite. It was, however, composed of individuals of various backgrounds who could trace their wealth and importance only to their own endeavours or in some cases to those of their fathers.

The idea of the 'great family' seems to have come about in the following way. Successful merchants and officials of the nineteenth century who may have been descendants of the Prophet, saints, famous captains, or officials used their origins to buttress and rationalise their new economic status. This was commonplace in Salé, where people themselves tended to identify others in this way. Thus if someone should say that such-and-such a family had only recently attained a position of influence, he would be reminded that, after all, some ancestor of the family was known for his exploits, his learning or his religiosity. Everyone was likely to have some ancestor whom he could be proud of. As long as the possible paths to economic advancement seemed open, if not to a given individual, at least to his children, this way of justifying social mobility served a purpose. Moreover most Slawis were probably allied in some way to at least one wealthy man, and such an alliance was the source of hope for economic advancement, as well as a form of social and psychological insurance. Thus most of the stories told about the rich depicted them as fine and decent men aware of their responsibilities towards others.

Cousté, who served as one of the early *contrôleurs civils* in Salé, wrote a study of its noble Muslim families. He believed that only some twenty families, because of birth, influence and wealth, merited the attention of the French authorities. He takes the names of the twenty or so leading personalities of the city and imagines that all the people bearing these family names who can trace a common ancestor are members of a ruling class, just as their ancestors had been. These families, he claimed, guided the rest of the population and determined the city's stance *vis-à-vis* the Makhzan and the protectorate.[30]

His model follows the stated policy of the time—support of indirect rule—and it undoubtedly reflected the views of Salé's leaders at that moment. However, such a model does not take into account the continually fluctuating and malleable economic and social reality of the nineteenth century from which the elite—the new elite—arose. Moreover the elite was composed of individual nuclear families tied by marriages and interests.

French policy attempted and in some cases succeeded in promoting the welfare of those whom they defined as the great families. The sons of these families were admitted to the schools set up by the protectorate authorities and called, aptly enough, *les écoles des fils de notables*. The French assumed that they could win these young people over to their culture and their cause, and that by persuasion of the elite they could control a hierarchically organised and stratified society. But Salé was at once more homogeneous and more fluid in its social structure than they imagined, and the sons of their chosen leaders were to be unexpectedly troublesome.

Part IV Reflections of and reactions to change

As for homo religiosus, homo œconomicus, homo politicus, and all that rigamarole of Latinised men . . . there is grave danger of mistaking them for something else than they really are: phantoms which are convenient provided that they do not become nuisances. The man of flesh and bone, reuniting them all simultaneously, is the only real being.

Marc Bloch[1]

In the previous chapters I have described the community of Salé from three vantage points. Part I situated the problem of social change in this particular Muslim town in its historical and geographical context. In Part II I was concerned with the society as a totality—its structure and cultural values. The focus moved in Part III to the socially disruptive consequences of economic change. The city described from these three perspectives seems at once whole and torn apart, the conservatism of its structures and values contradicted by adaptive and innovative behaviour in economic life, its ideals subverted by realities. These contrasts between conservatism and adaptability, between idealism and realism, can also be seen by focusing on events and ideas.

In this final part I want to direct attention to the lives and ideas of individuals and the structure of certain events. By moving from a topical to a narrative approach my aim is to suggest what it felt like to be alive in Salé and to describe a society in motion. The interrelations between structure and change will be discussed in the light of these narratives in the concluding chapter.

X A community in crisis

What good have the French done for the people of Algiers and Tlemsen? Do we not see that their religion has vanished, that corruption has become widespread and commonplace, that their children for the most part have grown up as atheists and infidels?

Nāṣirī[2]

In 1830 the French conquest of Algeria began, and within twenty years France had established control over the whole of the country. A generation passed before Tunisia, in 1882, fell under the domination of the French empire. Among the Maghreb countries only Morocco remained independent during the nineteenth century. But eventually, with the 1912 treaty of Fez, the French gained control there as well. The rivalries between the European powers, and compromises and concessions by Morocco's sultans, had allowed the country to escape political domination during the nineteenth century. Nonetheless the fear of European domination and its corollary, the growing recognition of Morocco's weakness, had had profound effects on Moroccan society. These effects can be seen in local events and in the writings and oral accounts of people who lived during that period.

In this chapter I examine the reactions of people in Salé to critical events or problems and explain how they saw and defined their situation and that of their antagonists, the Europeans. The first instance concerns the bombardment of the city in 1851 by the French. The second reaction comes from the historian Nāṣirī—his views of Europe, its strengths and weaknesses, and what Morocco could or could not do to defend itself. In the next example, covering the period from about 1858 to 1912, another historian, Ibn ʿAlī, expresses utter dejection about his own society and a resigned admiration for what the Europeans have been able to accomplish. In the following chapter, which concerns the first eighteen years of the protectorate period, I shall discuss a series of reactions to the French presence—their taxes, schools and policies. From the first example to the last a kind of pattern emerges; there is a gradual decline in self-confidence among the Slawis, until their fears of colonial domination are realised. When the French actually do take over the country a new self-confidence begins to assert itself in the city, particularly among the young people. These examples offer the possibility of observing social change within the contexts of actual events and the real lives of people involved in them.

The bombardment of Salé

Soon after the French invasion of Algeria the famous Algerian hero, ʿAbd al-Qādir, and his followers had taken up arms and seriously threatened French rule. By 1844 ʿAbd al-Qādir's attempt to mobilise assistance in Morocco had embroiled the Makhzen in a war with France, a war which offered the French a welcome pretext to expand into Morocco. In August of that year French ships bombarded Mogador and Tangier, and troops engaged the army of the sultan at Isly. For the first time in more than two centuries the army of Morocco was defeated by European military forces. The psychological consequences of this defeat were far-reaching, for the strength of French forces and the weakness of the sultan's army had been suddenly and clearly shown. From that moment on Sultan ʿAbd ar-Raḥmān could not successfully resist European demands and pressures—political or economic.[3] The defeat of the Moroccan forces at Isly caused fear and disorder throughout the country, including a revolt at Rabat. In Salé the leader of the *shurafā'* addressed a letter to the sultan complaining that the people of the city lacked sufficient arms and ammunition to defend themselves against the infidel enemy.[4]

The Moroccan government's fear of France declined following the revolution of 1848, and by October 1849 a series of incidents had led to the rupture of relations between the two countries. Soon plans began to be made in France for a military expedition to Morocco; at the same time French representatives continued to try to implement within the country a policy of severity without recourse to arms.[5] During these external difficulties Morocco was plunged into a prolonged agricultural crisis, a crisis that continued from 1845 to 1851. In 1847 a drought came on the heels of two bad crop years, and the price of wheat and barley quadrupled. The next two years of mediocre harvests made it impossible to replace the depleted reserves of grain. Eighteen-fifty was a disastrous year for all of North Africa. In the Moroccan coastal cities grain prices rose to an unprecedented high and transport between regions came to a standstill. In Salé people were dying from famine.[6]

These factors—the agricultural crisis and France's desire to reassert her influence in Morocco—led to the bombardment of Salé in the autumn of 1851. On 1 April of that year a French freighter of some ninety-eight tons, on its way to Rabat from Gibraltar with a load of wheat and merchandise, struck the bar of the Bou Regreg and went aground on the beach outside Salé. By the next day a crowd of about a hundred men had begun to help itself to some of the sacks of wheat and to strip the ship of its merchandise. Shortly afterwards the governor, Muḥammad Znībar, arrived on the scene with several hundred soldiers and temporarily put an end to the thievery. However, that night and the following one the crowd returned and continued its pillage, despite warnings to the governor by the French vice-consul of Rabat. The total damage to the ship and loss of goods was evaluated at 11,391 francs (the equivalent of about £1,000 at the time) and the French vice-consul demanded that sum as an indemnity from Salé's governor.[7]

Negotiations went on for over six months. The governor denied to the sultan and to the French that the people of Salé had been responsible for the pillage. The local historians claimed that the common people (*al-ʿāmma*) had plundered the ship and that the governor had taken measures to control them by forcing them into a particular section of the city.[8] Meanwhile the French *chargé d'affaires par interim* at Tangiers had accused the Slawis of piracy and suggested to his government that several warships be sent 'to teach the Slawis a lesson'. He believed that the population would rebel against the governor—or at least force him to pay the indemnity, or themselves pay it rather than see the city destroyed. In addition to these calculations the French officials saw in the incident 'the possibility of re-establishing the position of France in Morocco and of taking harsh revenge'.[9]

On 24 November 1851 a French squadron entered the mouth of the Bou Regreg; the governor of Salé was given an hour to settle the indemnity; at the same time the governor of Rabat was informed that if his cannons remained silent his city would be safe.[10] The governor requested ten days' leave to consult the sultan. At ten o'clock in the morning on the twenty-sixth the French squadron opened fire on the city. The batteries of Salé responded immediately and continued firing until the French put them out of action at five o'clock in the evening. The French admiral in his report to the Ministry of the Navy stated that Salé's forts had been 'torn like lace', the minaret of its Great Mosque hit by six bombs, houses destroyed and fires set ablaze. Reports estimated that between eighteen and twenty-two Slawis had died, two-thirds of them civilians, and that the French had lost eighteen lives. The French government then wrote to the sultan at Fez, informing him that they had performed a service for the Makhzan by teaching the Slawis a lesson, for they were like the people of the Rif—undisciplined pirates who did not obey their sultan.[11]

The French evaluation of this event appeared in a Paris journal a year later. 'The expedition of Salé will leave salutary memories among the Moors: it will remind them of the force of that power which the conquest of Algeria has given them for a neighbour, and will inspire them for a long time to come, it may be hoped, with respect for justice and French interests.'[12] However, the Slawis disappointed the French and reacted to the bombardment and intimidation without loss of nerve or self-confidence. Despite the overwhelming superiority of forces and the destruction inflicted on the city, its batteries responded energetically. In the evening the French squadron, fearing a change in the weather, had pulled up anchor. The Slawis were astonished by this sudden departure and interpreted it as a blessing from God and a great victory. The grand vizier wrote to the sultan after the bombardment, stating that the French had failed in their aim of inciting the people to revolt. 'God', he wrote, 'had turned things against the Christians, for it was the Muslims who did the killing.' The French had demanded that those accused of murdering Christians be sentenced to death and that 'the hands of the thieves be cut off'. But Salé's governor had acted according to custom and exiled from the city those who had originally caused the trouble.[13]

Several months later the governor described the situation in a letter to the vizier.

> God made the legs of the people of Islam stand firm and made His religion manifest despite the polytheists. No great harm was done to us, thank God! We have seen with our own eyes the benevolence of God and the unimaginable beauty of His creation. . . . When God repulsed the infidels, they could achieve nothing. God gave the victory to the believers and made them secure from the deceit of the enemy.

Nonetheless pressure had begun to build up among the population, for the governor goes on to say that some of those who had fought wanted to meet with the Sultan 'in order to receive his blessing from seeing and speaking with him and to make yet more profound their faith'. He names some of the city's leading artillerymen and captains and informs the sultan that he is holding them off, despite their insistence.[14]

A poem written in a mixture of literary and colloquial Arabic (*malḥūn*) takes the bombardment of 1851 as its theme. This genre of popular poetry suggests the reactions of the common people to these events—their shock, anger, self-confidence and religious faith. The poem begins with a plea to God to make the Prophet and his people inviolable, to defend Islam and defeat the army of the infidel. The battle is described as a victory by Islam against the French and their religion. The warriors of Salé and especially those from the tribe of ʿĀmir are praised for their bravery, and thanks are rendered to the pious saints of Salé, whose 'secret' zealously guarded the city. The saints are addressed personally: 'O Ibn Ḥassūn, cavalier of solicitude, sultan of Salé, and Sīdī b. ʿĀshir, may God forbid that the infidels enter your city!' The people of Salé ('the city of joy'—*salawān*) are said to be rejoicing over the holy war, which has had no parallel in the cities of the East, in Algeria or Egypt. The poet praises Salé for its circles of learning, its teachers and its God-fearing people. All Salé's people, the Arabs and the Berbers, have been rewarded by God because of their obedience to the sultan and their love for their city, those qualities for which the Slawis always have been admired throughout Morocco.[15]

The bombardment of Salé, although it was interpreted as a victory for Islam, had brought home the reality of Isly—the weakness of the Moroccan government in the face of European military force. The Slawis showed neither loss of confidence nor pride, but their guns had defended the city for the last time.

Nāṣirī's attempts to understand and control change

Know too that during these years the power of Europeans has advanced to a shocking degree and that their triumph is without parallel. Their progress and advancement have grown steadily faster—like the [proverbial] doubling of the grains of wheat in the squares of the chess board. Indeed, we are on the brink of a time of [total] corruption. Knowledge of the consequences of these things and their design belongs to God, may He be exalted, Unique in (knowing) the Divine Secret. 'I know well today and the yesterday before it. But as for knowing what tomorrow holds, I am blind.'[16]

It is hard to imagine any period in the history of Salé when life might have been more unbearable because of physical discomfort and moral uneasiness than the period between 1865 and 1900. Earlier chapters have described the continual economic instability and crises of the later years of the nineteenth century and the ways in which they were compounded by recurrent droughts, epidemics and famines. Nāṣirī writes about the symptoms and effects of cholera epidemics and droughts with brutal frankness, beginning with the epidemic of 1854 in which 120 people died within a few weeks, including the governor who had survived the bombardment of 1851, Muḥammad Znībar. Memories of these woeful times were passed on from father to son, and old Slawis still talk about the past suffering and devastation of the population. One man told me that his father had been the sole member of his family to survive an epidemic (most likely that of 1877), in which people died at the rate of about ten a day. The whole of his quarter, Ṣaff, had become deserted because of deaths caused by the epidemic, and the empty houses were squatted in by outsiders who later could not be removed by the descendants of the original owners.

For these sicknesses most people were apparently unable or unwilling to find successful preventions or treatments. A Spanish doctor living in Rabat between 1861 and 1876 cared for some Muslim patients there and in Salé, and during the cholera epidemic of 1878 Christian doctors treated some of the sick, but most people received no care.[17] Nāṣirī knew that Europeans could successfully treat such diseases and that they believed themselves capable of controlling their spread. In his discussion of the quarantine we learn about his concern with the problem and his attitude towards modern notions of medicine. While passing through El-Jadida in 1879, he tells us, he met some judges, and since the plague had recently struck Morocco their conversation turned to the quarantine (*al-karantīna*) practised by the Christians. However, none of those present ventured to give a legal opinion concerning the matter.

Nāṣirī was disturbed by the question. Several months later he read a work by the Egyptian scholar Rifāʿa at-Ṭahṭāwī, who in the course of describing his voyage to Paris had criticised the quarantine.[18] Thereupon Nāṣirī examined the question thoroughly and concluded in a formal and legal opinion that the advantages of the quarantine were doubtful or non-existent, from the point of view both of Islamic law and of practicality. Its disadvantages, he argued, were both temporal and spiritual: it was harmful to the normal trade of merchants, and it would confuse the masses, undermining their beliefs and resigned confidence in God (*tawakkul*) by making them think that such a measure could affect and counteract the divine decree of God (*qaḍā' Allah*). The masses, according to Nāṣirī, were deluded by appearances and prone to fall into heresy, and this harmed their own lives and religion. The quarantine clearly represented for him a danger from an alien and threatening civilisation; to practise it would be an imitation of foreigners—the taking on of the outward appearances of the erring infidels (*al-kafara aḍ-ḍallāl*), the magnifying of them and the ascribing to them of success and wisdom. These are real fears, Nāṣirī assures his readers, for some of the foolish masses have already been led astray. Even if fate should cause the practice of the quarantine to coincide with well-being, he concludes, it would nonetheless pave the way to anarchy (*al-fitna*).[19] Thus Nāṣirī accepts only those precautions against the plague that do not contravene Islamic law, and the quarantine, in his view, is a contravention because it attempts to thwart predestination.

The French domination over Algeria appeared to Moroccans as a prelude to what their country could expect if it did not become strong. The Spanish defeat of the Moroccan army and the occupation of Tetuan in 1860 were ominous signs: Morocco had lost its prestige, and the Europeans could treat it with utter arrogance. They had demanded and received an enormous indemnity and had increased the number of their protégés at will. The only way to maintain independence seemed to lay in creating a powerful modern army.

Nāṣirī supported the creation of such an army, but ominously warned that its soldiers should be instructed in religious ideology, as well as warfare, so that they would zealously protect Islam rather than undermine it.[20] He suggested to the sultan a programme of ideological instruction. His suggestions reflect both an acceptance of change and a fear of its consequences. He insisted that soldiers must be imbued with traditional religious and moral values—the ideals of manliness (*al-murū'a*), decent dress and speech, respect for the noble, pity for the humble, etc. Most important, in his view, was for soldiers to learn that 'the best qualities in the eyes of God and man are zeal for religion and the homeland [*al-ghīra ʿalā ʿd-dīn wa-'l-waṭan*] and love of the sultan and his advice'. This education could best be accomplished by daily meetings in which the soldiers heard readings from the biography of the Prophet, books about his successors' exploits and victories, and classical works by Muslim scholars.[21] After learning these basic qualities of good breeding (*ādāb*), the soldiers could be instructed in the arts of war.

Nāṣirī expresses an incipient nationalist viewpoint—the army has to be made aware of its own cultural identity in order to know what it is fighting for:

For the army of the Muslims has already been tainted by the customs of the foreigners. They want to learn the ways of war to protect religion, but they lose their religion in the process of learning. Sons of Muslims become foreigners within two or three years, adopting their morals and manners, substituting the salute for the greeting legislated by the Qur'an. Their teachers must change their foreign terminology to Arabic and make the foreign idioms into Arabic ones. Although the principles are taken from foreigners, the skilful teacher must endeavour to Arabise them . . . to teach them in the language in which they grew up and were nourished. . . . Thereby they will stop trying to imitate foreigners—a thing forbidden by Islamic law. Taking on the outward appearance of foreigners will never bring good, and it is one of the things that most corrupts the religion that we desire to protect.[22]

Another consequence of the 1860 battle of Tetuan was the increase in the number of Moroccans who enjoyed the advantages of foreign protection. With the Béclard accord of 1863 between France and Morocco, protection became the cornerstone of European penetration and lay at the heart of Morocco's problems.[23] Nāṣirī claimed that Moroccan Jews formed the majority of those who obtained protection after the Tetuan war.[24] According to him, they were not content with protection, for they also wanted the liberty (*al-ḥurriyya*) enjoyed by the Jews of Egypt and other countries. The 1863 mission of Sir Moses Montefiore to the sultan's court at Marrakesh on behalf of Morocco's Jews is described as an expression of this desire for liberty. As a result of the mission the sultan issued a decree in which he reaffirmed the prescriptions and obligations of Islamic law in regard to the protection of Jews, but he did not give them the liberty of Christians.[25]

At the point in his history where Nāṣirī takes up this matter he also digresses to a fascinating discussion of the concept of liberty. His understanding of the term as used among Europeans is confused with its meaning in Islamic philosophy. For him 'liberty' means libertinism, licentiousness and anarchy.[26] It is equivalent to heresy because it abolishes the rights (*ḥuqūq*) of God and parents, and because it negates the essence of man (*insāniyya*). God's rights are such obligations as prayer and fasting, and explicit punishments of Islamic laws like those against wine and adultery. The rights of parents over their children include authority, obedience and respect. Virtue is the essence of man and distinguishes him from animals. The 'liberty' of Europeans, as seen by Nāṣirī, permits them to indulge in what human nature should shun, and to feel that they are independent and unbridled; the only difference between them and uncontrolled beasts is that each individual gives the same right to others and is not permitted to oppress others. Not unexpectedly, Nāṣirī finds the idea of liberty absurd and dangerous. To oppose it he reiterates the theocratic ideal of Islam, namely that God distinguished man from the animals by giving him intellect in order to impose on him the duties of Islamic law, namely recognition of and submissiveness to God.[27]

Nāṣirī's concern with the quarantine, a modern army and its ideology, and the notion of liberty show an acute awareness of the conditions and ideas of his time. Moreover he had an acquaintance with and strong opinions about European views of reality and human nature. Near the end of his compendium history of Morocco he reproduced a *fatwā*, or judicial opinion, that he had sent to Sultan Ḥasan in 1885. The opinion responded to the sultan's request to the ulama for legal advice concerning the persistent demands by Europeans for a reduction in the total customs duty heretofore set on exports and for recission of the prohibition on the export of certain commodities.[28] The long and involved response by Nāṣirī supported concessions, but it also expressed his despondency over Morocco's weakness and defencelessness. Some of the passages in this letter, like the following, eloquently capture his state of mind and the mood of the times:

> Our weapons are but firewood in their [the Europeans'] eyes. The proof of this is that they sell us various kinds of military weapons whose excellence and perfection astonish us. Yet we are told that they sell us only those things for which they have no use, for they have gone beyond them, invented things even more excellent and valuable. . . . They have now reached an unimagined extent of power. One cannot consider opposing them, unless God should will that we be sufficient against them [i.e. by some natural calamity]. . . . It is clear that the Christians today are extremely strong and well prepared, while the Muslims—may God unite their dispersion and mend their fragments!—are extremely weak and disorganised. This being the case, how can it be permissible from the point of view of an individual legal opinion and of State policy—not to speak of Islamic law—that the weak resist the strong and that the unarmed should make war against those armed to the teeth? How can it be allowed by nature itself that one who is paralysed fight another who stands on his legs? Is it rational that a lamb without horns should butt another who has them? As the poet has said, 'I decide on resolute command if I can; but it is impossible to teach a wild ass to jump.'[29]

Nāṣirī then brings examples from the life of the Prophet (the pact with polytheists during the battle of Ḥudaybiyya, the compromises at the battle of al-Aḥzāb) to buttress his argument that war with Europe is unthinkable and that peace is possible and may offer certain commercial advantages. At the same time he feels threatened by the consequences of peace and free trade: 'I swear that their mixing and coming together with us greatly harms us, and the only ones who realise this are the ulama; but it is less in comparison to the harm of war.'[30]

The discussion of the military situation leads Nāṣirī into an analysis of the internal dissensions and weaknesses within Morocco. He dismisses the cries for war among some Moroccans as the machinations of the ignorant masses, who neither feel injury nor gain experience from wars and severe trials, but only search after anarchy for its own sake. The extreme military weakness and lack of preparation of Morocco is not to be confused with numbers or enthusiasm:

Numbers alone are not sufficient in war, neither can many men nor soldiers in themselves be adequate in any way. For along with them it is necessary to have a unity of purpose for whose sake men are of one heart. Moreover it is necessary to have a leader to unite them and a code of laws [*qanūn*] to govern them. Only then will the community [*al-jamāʿa*] be like a single human body that rises and sits together. If there is no leader or code of laws there must be perspicacity in religion, strength of conviction, harmony among Muslims, zeal for the homeland and the household [*al-ghīra ʿalāʾl-waṭan wa-ʾl-ḥarīm*], intellectual excellence and practice in warfare and the intrigues of the polytheists. Generations of peace and tranquillity have succeeded one another. The time of their [the Muslims'] glorious ancestors has long since passed, as well as that of war and its hardships; they can no longer suffer the affliction of enemies and their intrigues. Rather, what concerns them is their food, drink and clothing. That is quite clear—even to the extent that in this respect there remains no difference between them and their women.[31]

The Moroccans are compared to an injured bird trying to fight off the attacks and torments of a healthy one. They will be continually taunted, until immobilised or completely dominated by the Europeans and their warships. If they are united and not attacked from behind by their own rabble plainsmen (*ghawgāʾ al-aʿrāb*) they may be able to defend themselves. Nāṣirī dismisses out of hand the *jihād*, the holy war of Islamic law. 'How can you call for it now?' he asks. 'If you rush into war, ignoring reality, you will simply ignite the fire of anarchy more quickly and offer the enemy an excuse to attack you and take your ports and your women, money and blood as booty.'[32] The explanation of this weakness and lack of solidarity lay in economic factors. Nāṣirī ends his history of Morocco with an anecdote about the devaluation of money that had occurred between the 1840s and the 1870s. In it he illustrates how economic and social life had been undermined through contact with Europe.

The concerns of our generation are altogether different from those of the preceding generation; people's habits are completely contrary [to what they used to be]. The conditions of merchants and those of other occupations have changed in all their dealings—whether it be in matters of currency, prices, or other of their expenses. The costs of subsistence for people have risen; earning an income and a living have become difficult. When we compare the situation of the preceding generation with our own, we find them vastly different. The main reason for all this is the close contact of people with the Western Europeans and other peoples of Europe and the extent of their commingling and spread into the Muslim countries. Their concerns and habits have dominated the habits of this generation and they have a strong influence over it. I shall tell you a story from which you may learn the moral and draw conclusions. One day I spoke with a man of our generation about this matter, and he said to me, 'I have a government salary which I receive every month. It amounts to thirty *ūqiya*. Around 1260 [1844] I used to receive ten *baṣīta*, the rate of the *baṣīta* being then three *ūqiya*. When the currency began to rise after 1260 I began to receive nine *baṣīta* and some change. Then a year or two afterwards I began receiving eight *baṣīta* and some change, then seven *baṣīta* and some change, and so on until today in the 1290s [1873–82], when thirty *ūqiya* which I receive is worth one *baṣīta*, and some change.' Now consider the tremendous disparity that has overtaken this generation within a period of about thirty years. Currency and prices have risen during them, as you see, some ninety per cent! The reason for this is in what we have said; the more the intermingling and contact with Europeans the more the disparity will increase, and as they lessen so will it! The proof of this is in the fact that the people of Morocco have had least contact with them of all of the nations [of Islam], and that is why the prices here are lower and the standard of living higher and the way of dressing and customs still different from those of the Europeans. For these reasons their [the Moroccans'] religion is whole, as everyone knows, in contrast to Egypt, Syria and other lands. Indeed, what we have heard about them deafens the ear!

From these concluding remarks about inflation and the penetration of European ways it is possible to understand the mood of a generation whose livelihood and way of life had been deeply affected by processes of socio-economic change which it could not control. The work of Nāṣirī expresses the malaise, doubts, fears and pessimism of the learned men of Salé, the men of new wealth who were so deeply involved in matters of commerce and government. They had an awareness of change and of the need for reform. At the same time they felt a deep attachment to their world view and way of life, and they were intensely proud and determined to maintain them.

The inevitability of colonial rule

During the period that brought the nineteenth century to an end European economic and political interests in Morocco increased tremendously. The country retained its independence only because of the conflicts of interests between the various powers of Europe. But that independence became increasingly precarious as the various powers enlarged their influence on Moroccan affairs. In Salé there were some striking examples of the tensions and conflicts in men's minds that resulted from the economic, social and political consequences of the imminent conquest.

When Sultan Ḥasan, in a last-ditch effort to modernise his army, wanted to send sons of the notables of Salé to Europe for military training, the Slawis hesitated. They agreed that Morocco needed modern, European-trained troops but they feared the effects of training on their sons and arranged for others to be sent in their stead. Thus four young Slawis from rather undistinguished families went off to Europe to become soldiers. The old men of Salé who remembered these boys said that their stay in Europe had destroyed them. One had died while away in training, while two others returned mentally deranged and incapable of defending their own interests, let alone their country's. Only one of the four amounted to anything; for a while he served as governor of the Zaʿīr tribe and later held various administrative positions. But people said that his mind too had been warped during his stay in Europe. The stories about these men served to illustrate the ignorance and fear that used to dominate the Slawis attitude towards Europe.[33]

There were rumours and astonishing tales afoot in Salé at the end of the nineteenth century which reflected the unrest among the population. Ibn ʿAlī relates the biography of the last of those famous men in Salé who were 'attracted by God' (*majdhūb*). This saintly man died in 1904. He would not allow himself to be put out of the mosque at night by its custodians because 'he was hiding from the Europeans'. He would say to them, 'It's too early. The Christians have come, the Christians have come'! Ibn ʿAlī adds, 'It was true, before they ever came. If he said something it did not fail to happen.'[34]

Ibn ʿAlī had been a student of Nāṣirī.[35] In his history of Salé and Rabat he comments eloquently and movingly upon the signs of corruption that he sees in his generation. Although still a young man during the years before the turn of the century, there is clear continuity between his tone of moral righteousness and the absolute faith and tenacious conviction of the older scholars who had preceded him. But his description of the times is more bleak than that of any of his predecessors:

Conditions [in Morocco] gradually changed for the worse until this period came upon us. It is a time in which the intelligent believer cries out and seeks relief from uproar and his sense of exile. We have seen at the end of the thirteenth century [1883] good people, great men of God and of wondrous splendour. There was a sense of dignity and virtue among men, women and children. There was complete reliance on God, and there was no impudence or deviation from religion. There were no utterances of abominable things and of what is repugnant from the point of view of Islamic law. Our elders have told us what they understood of these things—what is good, righteousness, virtue, religion, decency and integrity. They sought after what was good for Islam and for the Muslims—unity in word and thought and mutual assistance for the sake of God. They guided us towards this and gave us sincere advice for its realisation. During the years since the end of the last century one cries over the immense scarcity of shame, virtue and vigilance in respect to temporal strategems, negligence in religious matters and impudence towards teachers and parents. Thus if one of us loses something temporal he grieves over it and perhaps mourns as if for the dead. But he cares not at all if he loses something of his religion. How true are the words of Abū Ḥātim al-ʿĀmilī when he says, 'We cry over the trivial things of this world when they disappear. Were religion to disappear completely from our midst we would not cry over it.'[36]

This tone of moral indignation and admonishment had been the hallmark of the learned in Salé for centuries. But the way in which Ibn ʿAlī discussed matters that disturbed him, his mode of expression and depth of feeling have a particular relevance to the period in which he lived and to the experiences of his generation. These concerns are clear in the following passage:

[We see] sickness of the heart, feelings of bitterness, the concealment of hostility by some of us towards others, dissension, and yet unanimity of sentiment for that which does not concern God. People are filled with the desire to manage things and to hold rank. Mosques are built full of phantoms and empty of souls. We see the young admonished, yet they do not accept admonishment. . . . There is lack of obedience to God. One sees it in the way that people amuse themselves, play and gamble. Our elders are witnesses to this situation, yet out of hypocrisy and indulgence in things that are better left unmentioned they do not disapprove. There is staring at the intimate parts of the body. One sees a lack of respect for the descendants of the Prophet and the men of learning. Religion is weakened by these calamities, [which come] from people's lack of vigilance. Abū Ḥātim spoke well when he said, 'We do not listen to what our admonisher said; if our singer performs for us, then we listen!' We ask of God protection from the consequences of these initial symptoms. We seek refuge in Him, lest His wrath include us and He bring down upon us His damnation.[37]

Ibn ʿAlī has an even greater sense of pessimism and foreboding than Nāṣirī. He is less confident about the future and more critical of his contemporaries. In comparison Nāṣirī's view seems cautiously positive and self-assured, despite certain fatalistic overtones: if the Moroccans' faith in God remains strong they will overcome the temptation and anarchy in their midst, and by a careful policy of peace and pragmatism the country may successfully protect its independence against the dreaded European enemies. Ibn ʿAlī, writing several decades later, holds out no hope against either external or internal threats. He paints a picture of his generation as one of corruption, malaise, doubt and fear. The domination of Morocco by the Europeans seems inevitable, only a matter of time.

The Moroccan crisis, 1900–12

During the dozen years that preceded the signing of the treaty of Fez and the establishment of a French protectorate the Slawis lost all hope of seeing their country remain independent. Nonetheless they still appeared formidable to the French ethnologist and traveller Edmond Doutté, who described the city in 1903 as intolerant even in its weakness: 'Salé represses its hate of the Christian, and although powerless to do him harm it remains the most fanatical city of Morocco.'[38]

While the French looked at Salé as a bastion of hatred and fanaticism, most of the leaders of the city were doing their best to keep up with and in control of the rapidly changing economic and political conditions of the country. During the diplomatic manœuvrings over Morocco's future among the competing European powers the more prominent Slawi functionaries and merchants sought to ally themselves—if possible as protégés—with the power they expected would become predominant in Morocco.[39] They showed little reluctance to deal with foreigners and to adopt strictly pragmatic means when the immediate circumstances seemed to demand them. Indeed, almost every foreign power, as well as most Moroccan contenders for the control of the dynasty, had some partisans in Salé.

As a consequence of political instability in the country the population of Salé became torn by dissension. An early manifestation of this dissension was a controversy that broke out in 1905 between the governor, ʿAbh Allah b.

Saʿīd, and the qadi, ʿAlī ʿAwwād, which resulted in the dismissal of both men by the sultan. The conflict arose from the hostility of ʿAwwād to ʿIbn Saʿīd's support of the movement and programme of reform of Muḥammad b. ʿAbd al-Kabīr al-Kattānī and to Ibn Saʿīd's contacts with representatives of Germany.[40] By the beginning of 1908 Sultan ʿAbd al-ʿAzīz had been deposed and his brother, ʿAbd al-Hafīẓ, proclaimed as the 'Sultan of the Holy War', initially in Marrakesh and later in Fez. When the news reached Salé the population became agitated in favour of the newly invested sultan. The city had been restless since the French military intervened in Casablanca in July 1907, and only the appearance of two French cruisers just outside the port of Rabat–Salé had pacified the population. The situation had become sufficiently unstable to cause the Jewish community of the city to panic and flee. The French authorities at Rabat had threatened Salé's governor with military intervention if order were not restored, while French troops had already occupied Oujda, Casablanca, the Chaouia, Fedala and Bouznika.[41]

In 1908 Mawlāy ʿAbd al-ʿAzīz, the dethroned sultan, organised an expeditionary column at Rabat and forced the governors of Rabat and Salé to give him their allegiance. Some of the leading personalities of the latter were taken as hostages to assure the continued support of the city's population.[42] Later in the year, after the defeat of ʿAbd al-ʿAzīz, Salé was again restive. The governor, Ṭayyib aṣ-Ṣubīḥī, was forced by popular pressure to go to Fez to pay homage to the new sultan. Although few people expected that he would escape with his life, Ṣubīḥī returned and continued to serve as governor until his death in 1914. He had retained his position thanks to the intervention of his Slawi friends at court. Meanwhile the pressures exerted by the French on the affairs of Salé had gradually increased in intensity. In 1910 the French ambassador had asked for the removal from office of the qadi because of his treatment of a French protégé. But ʿAwwād had remained in office and continued to be a bitter opponent of the French. However, Salé's governor had found it expedient to co-operate with the French authorities.[43]

On the eve of the French protectorate the difficulties in the city increased. Early in 1911, when it was announced that French troops would pass through Salé on their way to quell the tribes of Fez, the population revolted and proclaimed the reinstated qadi, Ḥājj ʿAlī ʿAwwād, as its governor. Ṣubīḥī was besieged in his house for several days by a popular revolt. The Slawis were subdued, it would appear, only by the threat of French intervention. In April 1911 30,000 French troops led by General Moinier passed through on their way to Fez. The French had published a proclamation exhorting the population to be calm. The Slawis sullenly but passively watched the powerful army pass through their city—the first foreign army to enter the walls since the thirteenth century. Within a month a permanent contingent of French soldiers had taken up position at Rabat. Less than a year later came the announcement of the treaty of the protectorate.

Fig. 12 K. al-itḥāf al-wajīz bi-akhbār al-ʿudwatayn li-mawlāy ʿAbd al-Azizʿ: 'The civilisation of Europe in our present generation'.

ألم تكن معارف الإسلام   معروفة لسائر الأقوام
ألم تكن دستور أسلاف الرقي   وسر ما قد حل من بوق المعرق
فقل على الإجمال قول حق   من بعد ما سار بها معالي الشرق
ومن توانى قد أضاع الأجرا   وأهمل النفس فنال الخسرا
كان أبو العلا مفيد الجموع   يعي ما أحوال الوقوع والرجوع
حتى استبان عنده الجميل   في أي وقت كان يانبيغل   محمد الفاسي رحمه الله
وأنه خص لذا الجليل   وهو شيء في الأصل عن دليل
فخص فيها من لهذه الأمانة   وبسط أنوي حميرا في البغية
ومنهم علامة البرناطي   خاتمة الأعلام ذو انتباه
إبراهيم التادلي الشيخ الفضلا   بعصرنا الرا البرناطي وصكا
ما شئت من علم ومن معارف   ومن جلالة خلت عن كلف
ومن ذهوب وعكوف بالعلى   ومن تعاطي وانقطاع كملا
فرحم الدهر به الكمالا   بشغله فلم يجد مثالا
حل بفاس بعد ما قد كملا   من العلوم جلها وسائلا
فلازم الدروس لدى الأعيان   في غيبة عظمى وعلو شان
فلم يدع علما بوقته يعرف   إلا انتحاه داريا يعرف
فنال المعروف والمتروكا   وحقق المكنون والمشكوكا   1800
وجمع العقلي في المنقول   ودام في جد وفي تحصيل
وانفرد الموسيقي بالكمال   وألف الأغاني للكمال   كتاب الأغاني
جمع فيه نوب الصناعة   علما وإتقانا جلا إبداعه
وقد أتى البرناطي في كمله   مولي العلوم زاخرا فلا يهمله

The reaction of Slawis to their new foreign rulers varied among individuals, sometimes in accordance with their particular experiences with the French. In a few cases men who had taken an oath that they would not set eyes on a Christian in their city in fact never again left the confines of their home until the day they died. Slightly more common were the embittered men like the father of one of my informants. In the evening while his son prepared for lessons he would sit, finger his string of beads and endlessly repeat a refrain: 'The infidels have come, Islam has perished.'

Most people, however, were genuinely curious about and slightly amazed by the French. A case in point was the historian Ibn ʿAlī. In the long rhymed prose poem that he dedicated in 1912 to the new sultan, Mawlāy Yūsuf, there appeared a long passage which, he explained in a note in the margin of the manuscript, summarised his views on 'the civilisation of Europe in our present generation'.

Here is a useful piece of advice for you from the author,
Which is neither verbiage nor extraneous.
An insight for whomever wants to see
The state of the non-Muslim among mankind.
For this generation is a generation of knowledge,
Profound in its knowledge of the state of the world.
The nations of the West have performed their work well,
And given people a share in what is small and great.
They possess manifest power,
And have given the world its prosperity.
They have perfected their knowledge of things,
And have made prosperity grow.
They have honoured the customs of most men
In every land without oversight.
They have freed the mind from its bonds,
And opened up thought in every way.
They have taken upon themselves the traits of science
and knowledge,
And of skill in every matter.
They have undeniably taken the lead,
For they have attained the knowledge of prosperity.
They have reached the most distant lands,
And exchange talk by telegraph and wires.
They swim in sea and air alike,
And descend under the surface of water.
They have discovered the wonders of the universe
And invented the most astonishing things possible.
They have grasped the reins of government,
And rule with the authority of one who knows.
If the East had gone the way of the West
It would have attained success in every domain.
But it neglected the knowledge
With which it had been endowed, and it remained idle.
Was not the East wondrous
In its science, power and wealth?

Was not the East the locus of glory
In everything that it attained by its efforts?
Did it not govern the affairs of the world
In the East and the West with the greatest ability?
Was not the learning of Islam
Adored by the other nations?
Was it not a model of the means for advancement
And a sign of dignity that appeared upon the brow?
Now say in summary a word of truth:
Whoever exerts himself, reaches the highest peak.
And whoever flags has forfeited glory,
Neglected himself and thereby overstepped all bounds.[44]

XI Reassertion of an identity

Our mehallas are at the frontiers but the enemy is at the heart of the market place; it is in Fez that we need cannons. Make the ulama submit first, and the submission of the Berbers will be only child's play.[1]

In the countryside the French were forced to resort to arms to defeat the people. In our cities arms had not been necessary, but then we were never defeated.[2]

The first outbreak of serious difficulties in Salé took place in 1921, nine years after the beginning of the protectorate. Some of the leaders of the city, including a member of the municipal council and ʿAbd Allah b. Saʿīd, the former governor, organised opposition to the introduction of direct taxation. A petition was circulated, a delegation sent to the sultan and a strike enforced. The French authorities reacted quickly and vigorously by sarreting the leaders and sending some of them, including Bin Saʿīd, to Oujda, where they were kept under supervision.[3] A report by the Contrôleur Civil explained the opposition by pointing out the approbium of direct taxes to an urban population with limited economic resources, the majority of whom were small merchants and craftsmen of modest means.[4] Moreover taxes levied on the surrounding farmers had indirectly caused rising prices in labour and foodstuffs. The vineyards of Slawis were no longer taxed according to yield but according to the area under cultivation. The population of the city was held responsible for people who did not pay taxes both within and beyond its boundaries. Merchants were harassed, each obliged to have in his possession an up-to-date licence which might be verified at any moment. 'In the city as well as the countryside,' wrote the Contrôleur Civil, 'procedures that necessitated investigations, declarations, payments and anxieties sometimes appeared as clear provocations and seemed insupportable to the shopkeepers and craftsmen—these humble people who live by trafficking in merchandise which, although it lacks value, nonetheless allows them to participate in the realisation of profits.'[5]

Undoubtedly the participation of the bulk of the population in the opposition to the taxes resulted at least in part from their precarious economic situation. However, the leaders of the opposition were motivated by more than economic considerations. The imposition of taxes had led to a crystallisation of animosity towards the French and their intervention in local affairs. The local leaders resented deeply, and now consciously and openly, the consequences of foreign domination and the loss of autonomy as a community. Older townsmen, in particular, took offence at what they saw as an undermining of religious law, and they considered the disquieting behaviour and attitudes of their sons a result of French interference in religious matters. Thus their opposition to taxes was aimed partly at the protectorate authorities and partly at reasserting their control over the younger generation. Within the community the new taxes were seen as a head tax (*jizya*), which according to Islamic law was to be imposed by Muslims on their Christian and Jewish protégés. To pay such taxes to Christians, people said, amounted to a kind of apostasy.

A NEW GENERATION

In chapter IV I discussed the creation of the French 'School for the Sons of Notables' in 1913 and the foundation of Salé's first 'Free School' in 1921. During the first decade of the protectorate only a small number of Slawi youths had studied in the French school. This was largely due to the Residency policy of limiting French education for Muslims to the sons of notables, as seen in the small budgets and enrolments for these schools throughout the country.[6] The opening of free schools in Morocco, that is, the local private schools supported by community leaders in the various cities, had a double purpose: to reinforce and modernise Islamic education in order to instil a sense of Moroccan patriotism among the young, and to expand the number of educated youth who would have access to jobs that demanded literacy. Of the twenty-two free schools founded in Morocco between 1919 and 1925 four were in Salé, and their enrolment probably approached 200.[7] The protectorate authorities, alarmed at the success of the free schools and convinced that anti-French propaganda and politics were being taught in them, harassed the schools' supporters and teachers. At the same time they sought to counteract and undermine the potential threat of an educational system not under their control by enlarging the School for the Sons of Notables and by expanding its curriculum in Arabic and religious studies. Pressure was exerted on parents to transfer their children from the private schools, and teachers were offered better-paid jobs in the government school.[8] By 1925 the government school had increased its enrolment to seventy-seven students and the free schools had temporarily diminished in importance.[9] The overall result of this process was that the Slawis had forced the authorities to open up French schools to them further. At the same time they had laid the foundations of a modern Arabic education. This extension of modern education strongly influenced the experience of those who grew to maturity in the 1920s and who became actively engaged in political nationalism in later years. Most of those who participated in the nationalist movement had attended a French and a free school for at least a few years. Although their education was not overtly political, it did awaken in them a sense of pride in their religion, civilisation, history, language and homeland.[10] The emergence of modern education was an important factor in that process of development from political consciousness to modern nationalism which took place during the 1920s.[11]

In Salé the first dozen years of the protectorate were crucial in shaping the ideas of the younger generation. Those who studied in private and governmental schools took a growing interest in the press, French and Arabic, internal and international. Thus, for example, they closely followed reports of the progress of the Rifian war of 1921–26, applauding the Moroccan forces who, under the leadership of ʿAbd al-Karīm, threatened the combined armies of Spain and France, and suffering keen disappointment at the ultimate defeat of the Rifians. Michaux-Bellaire, writing from Salé in 1928, noted that the defeat of ʿAbd al-Karīm was a cruel disappointment to the hopes of all Moroccans. Although he attributed the popularity of the Rifian cause to the 'latent force of traditional xenophobia', rather than to any nationalist sentiment, young Slawis, and indeed some of the notables as well, saw ʿAbd al-Karīm as a nationalist hero.[12] Moreover there were direct links between individuals in Salé and ʿAbd al-Karīm, such as his former school-mate Idrīs b. Saʿīd, the son of the former governor. And during the war Bin Saʿīd mysteriously died in the Rif while on a mission to arrange negotiations between ʿAbd al-Karīm and the Spanish.[13]

The first protectorate generation in Salé followed politics attentively, on the local, national and world scenes. They felt confident that the future belonged to them, that the struggles of Muslim peoples over the world would be victorious. This new generation of Slawis did not believe that the colonial powers were infallible or intrinsically superior, nor did they accept the European view of Moroccans as inherently weak and inferior. Their self-confidence seems to have reawakened the pride of their elders. The French authorities worried about the intransigence of Salé's population, and made special mention to it in a preparatory course for French administrative officers given in Rabat in 1928. Indeed, the Section Sociologique des Affaires Indigènes had been moved in 1925 from Tangier to Salé at the special request of the Résidence Générale, so that it might be in contact with what was considered a particularly closed segment of the Muslim population. The officers on the course learned that Salé stood out among the urban centres of Morocco as 'a sort of centre of opposition where one best finds the echo of much discontent, well founded or not, even among those who are personages in the *makhzan*'.[14] In effect the French correctly sensed that not only the young but the whole population of Salé was potentially hostile to them.

By the end of the Rifian war in 1926 the young of Salé had come a good way in their political education. In the homes of such young men as ʿAbd al-Laṭīf aṣ-Ṣubḥī. French and Eastern newspapers were read assiduously and discussed endlessly. In 1927 a seventeen-year-old, Muḥammad Ashamaʿū, returned from his studies at the Qarawiyīn and opened a book shop which sold classical Islamic works, a variety of modern books and many of the important eastern Arabic journals and newspapers. Most of the customers were young schoolboys, and though particularly interested in the contemporary press they also bought Arabic translations of French classics, books about history, geography, travel, recent studies of the Crusades, the Arab domination of Spain and Sicily and the Arab conquest of North Africa.[15]

Before the end of 1927 Ashamaʿū and some of his young friends began to issue from time to time a mimeographed newspaper called *al-Widād* (*Friendship*). Their avowed purpose was to form a united front of Moroccans in opposition to French colonialism and the rule of Christian nations over Muslim lands. The newspaper also aimed at healing the breach between the older and younger generations, a breach exacerbated by attacks against religious brotherhoods on the part of those influenced by reformist ideologies. Articles in the newspaper often pleaded that the young respect the older generation in order to close the ranks of all Muslims. The paper regularly reported on major events in the Muslim and Arab world and took a stand opposing the colonial powers in general and supporting causes such as those of the Palestinian Arabs, on whose behalf a collection was organised following the riots of 1929. In 1930 the columns of the newspaper played a role in stirring up resentment against the French in Salé by vociferously criticising the Eucharistic Congress of Tunis and the celebrations of the centenary of the conquest of Algiers.[16]

During the summer of 1927 a group of former students in Salé formed a kind of old boys' association (*qudamāʾ at-talāmīdh—les anciens éleves*).[17] They elected officers, met regularly and discussed contemporary cultural and political issues. By early 1928 the association had transformed itself into 'The Islamic Literary Club' (*an-nādī al-adabī al-islāmī*) and extended its membership to include young Slawis who were still students. It held regular meetings in the School for the Sons of Notables and organised lectures, such as one on the history of Salé given by the Minister Muḥammad an-Nāṣirī (a son of Salé's famous historian) and attended by some two hundred listeners.

In addition the club attracted attention by a brilliant theatrical performance. The modern theatre in Morocco had come alive in 1923 when a mixed Egyptian and Tunisian professional group, joined by several Moroccan amateurs, had toured the principal cities of the country. The group's outstanding performance was a tragedy whose theme was the chivalrous adventures of the medieval Muslim hero Salāḥ ad-Dīn and his defeat of the famous Crusader, Richard the Lionheart. Soon afterwards an association of students in Fez began to perform Egyptian and Lebanese plays, Arabic translations of European works such as Molière's comedies, and even some original works. These were followed by the establishment of theatrical groups in other cities where similar performances were staged. The crowning achievements of this period were Fasi productions of *Romeo and Juliet* (translated by the Egyptian poet Najīb al-Ḥaddād) and an original play entitled *Science and its fruits*, performances in Rabat of *Ṣalāḥ ad-Dīn al-ʿAyyūbī and the Conquest of Andalusia* (by the Egyptian politician and writer Muṣṭafā Kāmil), and the presentation by Salé's group of *Hārūn ar-Rāshīd wa-ʾl-Barāmika* (published in Cairo in the early 1920s).[18]

The young members of Salé's club performed the play—a tragedy in prose and verse about the legendary Baghdad caliph of the eighth century—in the Renaissance Cinema in Rabat in June 1928 and later in Casablanca. The performance won widespread praise and served to breach boundaries between generations and between local communities. The old people of Salé, many of whom had given up hope for the younger generation, delighted in the play because they found in it proof of the attachment of their sons to the glory of Islam and the beauty of the Arabic language. Equally important was the way in which the play brought together in a bond of friendship and admiration the youth groups of Rabat and Salé. Until that moment the relationship between the two had remained like that of their parents, one of guarded suspicion. When the first performance of the play ended, a delegation of young Rabatis presented the Slawi actors with bouquets of flowers, and the two groups publicly embraced and declared their unity. Thereafter the literary clubs of the two cities began to meet in order to exchange ideas, even though they did not form a joint association until 1933.[19]

The young men of Salé who had attained an education and a familiarity with world politics in the 1920s were dynamic and ambitious. Not unnaturally they also wanted to have a voice in the affairs of government in their country. Many had been encouraged by the French authorities to believe that by virtue of their education administrative careers would be open to them. These ambitions and promises remained unrealised, partly at least because the protectorate had since 1925 favoured a policy of excluding Moroccan personnel from even the lower echelons of the administration and of increasing the number of French functionaries. The educated young in Salé felt that the French were less than indifferent to their capacities and hopes, and wanted to block their careers and denigrate and humiliate them. They began to see themselves through French eyes as second-class citizens in both political and economic terms.

The attitude of the protectorate authorities towards the young, both throughout Morocco and in Salé, was more ambiguous than it seemed, but was not noteworthy for its sympathy. The Contrôleur Civil described those who had studied in French schools and benefited from the prestige of knowing the French language as 'the tainted little terrors of Slawi society'; in his view they believed that their esoteric knowledge would enable them to judge and penetrate the mysteries of the Christians and then to collaborate with and eventually replace them. He sarcastically and paternalistically depicted the typical young educated Slawi of those days as one who felt that the time had come for the French protectorate to open to him freely the doors of the various administrative services, to profit from his enlightenment, and to proceed with his aid towards the rejuvenation of Morocco. The young Slawis, he reported, detested the parsimony of the French in giving out administrative posts and saw it as part of a Machiavellian plot. In his opinion they were a decent but discontented group, ready to succumb to any propaganda calling for agitation because circumstances had frustrated their ambitions.[20]

The French authorities were cynical about the young and at the same time recognised in them a potential political threat. The first attempts to control the disquieting political activities of the young was by the exertion of pressure upon their parents. In many cases such pressure simply aggravated already existent tensions between the older and younger generations. Some older men had been anxious about and considered unreasonable the tendencies of the young to speak out against and take exception to the state of affairs in the city and in the country. But because they were either unable or unwilling these fathers did not prevail upon their sons to mend their ways. However, as a result of this tension there did exist a degree of estrangement between the two generations. To some extent the performance of *Hārūn ar-Rashīd* by the young dispelled these feelings. The play's extolment of the past, of Islam and of the Arabic language made the older generation feel proud and respected, and the young found this response on the part of their elders gratifying and reassuring. The authorities had played off the generations against one another and had created tensions and conflicts between them. But the resolution of these generational conflicts, in the theatre or in the mosque, in the long run strengthened opposition to the French.

The summer of 1930

fils mn j-jāwī ybakhkhr slā. A pennyworth of benzoin fills Salé with its fragrance.

Local Slawi proverb

On 16 May 1930 the Residency promulgated a new sharifian decree. This 'Berber Dahir', as it came to be called by its adversaries, set off the first eruption of modern nationalism in Morocco. Young people in Salé were in the forefront of opposition to the Berber Dahir, and they successfully mobilised most of the population of the city in a movement of political resistance.[21] The decree of 1930 marked a further step in a Berber policy which had been favoured from time to time by the French authorities since the early years of the protectorate and before then in Algeria.[22] An earlier decree issued in 1914 had established Berber customary law tribunals and courts of appeal and recognised the competence of French penal courts in Berber territories whatever the status of the defender.[23] The decree of 1930 went further and undermined the integrity of Muslim religious institutions and the spiritual authority of the dynasty. In effect it formally placed the Berbers beyond the jurisdiction of Islamic law and the courts of the qadis and, whatever the *de facto* position of customary law may have been in some Berber areas in the past, Berbers now became juridicially independent by writ. The French authorities claimed that the decree represented an administrative measure designed to rationalise the judicial system. The Moroccans, however, became convinced that its aim was to separate Berbers from Arabs as part of a more basic French policy of proselytism and assimilation.

The campaign against the Berber Dahir began in the mosques of the cities and developed into an important protest movement against France's colonial policies. Where the French authorities, not unexpectedly, interpreted the movement as a manifestation of religious fanaticism, the Moroccans saw it as a demonstration of their identity as a nation. The circumstances of the protest campaign in Salé help to explain the use of religious symbols in the ideological development of Moroccan nationalism. A discussion of the situation in Salé in 1930 helps us to understand the nature of social change in the city and, incidentally, unwraps Moroccan nationalism from some of the rhetoric with which it has clothed itself.[24]

The Berber Dahir first came to the notice of the young because of the activities of ʿAbd al-Laṭīf aṣ-Ṣubīḥī of Salé and Muḥammed al-Yazīdī of Rabat, both of whom worked in the administration as interpreters. By mid-May, when the decree was promulgated, Ṣubīḥī had left his job and was devoting all of his energies to the organised protest. He concentrated his efforts among young students, particularly those whom he had directed in the production of *Hārūn ar-Rashīd*; he would meet them early in the evening, gathering together boys from both the French and Arabic schools. According to people who used to attend those informal gatherings, Ṣubīḥī performed the role of political mobiliser and indoctrinator with consummate skill. He would lecture to the young about the nationalist struggles in Turkey, India and Egypt and alert them to France's desire to destroy the territorial integrity of Morocco by a policy of divide and rule. At first Ṣubīḥī stressed the territorial aspect of Morocco's national identity, not its religion or Islamic law system. This approach may have convinced the young, but it did little to dramatise the issue and to stir up the older people. Then Ṣubīḥī changed his tactics and began to argue that the decree engineered by France 'violated the very essence of Islam'.[25]

When the schools broke up for the summer vacation the campaign against the Dahir grew more intensive. The youth who would gather daily at Salé's beach became increasingly involved in the political issues and receptive to the haranguing of Ṣubīḥī. He had an unusual ability to create a consensus and activate the social control of the group upon its members by exciting, intimidating and ridiculing them in turn. At the end of the day the young would spread themselves throughout the city to alert the inhabitants about 'the great danger that was menacing Islam'.

In early June one of the boys suggested that a recitation of the *laṭīf*, the prayer recited in times of distress, might well dramatise the situation and mobilise the community in the campaign against the Dahir.[26] Accordingly a *fqih* in the city was given a few coins and asked to recite the supplication, supposedly in behalf of the sick grandfather of one of the boys. When the French authorities in Salé learned of these machinations they began to exert pressure on the youth, their parents and the local notability. It was at this point that the campaign became an important public issue for the community.

While the French authorities threatened the boys and their parents, many of whom had positions of influence within the town, the young, under the leadership of Ṣubīḥī, increased their campaign of propaganda. The pressure from the authorities and chastisement from the boys' parents served only to increase their determination and rebelliousness, and, in turn, the turmoil in the city. The people began to believe and to say that the French were trying to make them into Christians; as one informant put it, 'that idea got into the heads of Moroccans; both the simplest and the most cultivated among them became convinced that France wanted to eliminate Islam and its law'.[27]

The young visited the lodge of the Darqāwā religious order, where a reception was being held for those who had just returned from the Pilgrimage. Their visit apparently shocked those who were present, and their modern 'Christian' ways (shaved faces, long hair, tarbushes) seemed to some a desecration of the lodge; others argued that they should enter the lodge—to return to the Islamic way, for they too belonged to God. Ṣubīḥī went to the head of the lodge, a man who also served as khatib of one of the Friday mosques, and accused him of not serving the true interests of religion, of standing idly by while the French undermined Islamic law, and he asked everyone to recite the *laṭīf* in the mosque on the following Friday.

Ṣubīḥī then changed his behaviour entirely. He began to read the Quran publicly and pray, to cry and to shout to those who gathered around him that they must be brave Muslims and reject French attempts to destroy their religion. The French authorities, knowing Ṣubīḥī to be a dandified and secularised young man, found his behaviour particularly ominous and decided to arrest him. By that time the young had become determined to organise a recitation of the *laṭīf* in the mosques following the noon prayer on Friday, and the authorities were equally determined that it should not take place. The prayer leader of the Great Mosque, Ḥājj ʿAli ʿAwwād (the former, pre-protectorate qadi), was contacted by some of the youths and asked to lead the recitation of the *latīf* following the next day's noon prayer. A similar request was made to the prayer leader of Salé's other Friday mosque, the Shahba mosque. Meanwhile the French had instructed the pasha of the city, Hajj Muḥammad aṣ-Ṣubīḥī, to keep the ring-leaders o the youth in his house during the Friday prayer. On Friday 20 June 193 the two mosques were filled. Most of the males in the city had turned up, with the exception of the five boys shut up in the pasha's house. The pasha himself had gone off to Rabat to pray with the sultan, leaving the boys in the care of his brother and deputy.

Most of the youth involved in the campaign against the Dahir were from well known Slawi families, and they had used friends and kinsmen of their parents to gain access to such people as the prayer leaders of the Friday mosques. Those being kept in the pasha's house were part of a network of friends and relatives, and no doubt the French had chosen deliberately to emphasise the 'familial' side of the affair by putting them in the care of a relative. Indeed, one of the boys had ironically asked the pasha (who was his cousin) how he presumed to go and pray and not allow them the same right and duty to know God. The pasha, known to be a modest and learned man, did not like to upset people, particularly not his kith and kin. So he told his brother to allow the boys to pray in Shahbah mosque provided the *laṭīf* prayer was recited in the Great Mosque, for that would prove they were not its instigators.

The khatib of the Great Mosque, Ḥājj ʿAli ʿAwwād, evidently put on a marvellous dramatic performance in leading the recitations of the *laṭīf*. He was then about eighty years old but had not lost his booming voice and formidable appearance. According to people who were present, the recitation of the prayer electrified the whole congregation. The mosque was packed and its roof filled by women who had come specially to follow the invocations. After the recitation of the *laṭīf* everyone there spontaneously recited the opening verse of the Qur'an. The mood created seems to have been one of exultation and determination.

After the recitation of the *laṭīf* in the Great Mosque the youths who had been held in the pasha's house were allowed to go to prayer in the Shahba mosque. According to one informant, the boys sat down directly in front of the prayer leader. When the latter saw them he realised that they expected him to lead a recitation of the *laṭīf*. This he eventually did, after a sermon in which he castigated Salé's youth for their indifference to religion and their indecent behaviour. In his mind the catastrophe that threatened the city would be caused by their behaviour; thus he recited the *laṭīf*, but for his own reasons.

Thereafter during the summer of 1930 the campaign against the Berber Dahir intensified in all the large cities in Morocco. The main tactic became the recitation in the mosques of the *laṭīf*, with its words now changed to convey explicitly its political content: 'Oh God, the Benevolent, we ask of you benevolence in what fate has brought and that you do not separate us from our Berber brothers!'[28] In Salé some of the young leaders of the campaign, such as Ṣubīḥī, Malkī and Ashamaʿū, were exiled, put under house arrest, imprisoned or threatened. Thereafter members of the community of Salé continued to play an active and important role in the nationalist movement, and in the subsequent politics of the independence period, but always of a secondary kind. Looked at retrospectively, the campaign against the Berber Dahir and the discovery of the *laṭīf* as a political weapon became Salé's principal claim to having participated in Morocco's struggle for independence.[29]

Nationalism and social change

To attribute to fanaticism what is simply the result of interests that have been hurt is deliberately to deprive oneself of elements that could on a suitable occasion be used for reconciliation.

de Gobineau

At this point I want to turn from the undeniable importance of the protest movement against the Berber Dahir in the development of Moroccan nationalism and to look at it as an expression of social change within the community of Salé. Three conspicuous features of the situation that arose in 1930 call for sociological explanation: (1) the emergence of political activity and leadership among the young; (2) the choice of particular values and emblems to symbolise and to communicate the meaning of the campaign; (3) the participation in the movement of all or most segments of the community.

The older generation of leaders in Salé had not made a concerted effort to resist the imposition of the French protectorate, and the only manifestations of resistance by them had been sporadic and ineffectual. The general attitude towards Morocco's foreign rulers was a kind of despondent passivity, mixed with a degree of opportunism. The leaders of the city had tied their fate to those parties struggling for control of the dynasty—ʿAbd al-ʿAzīz, the constitutionalists and ʿAbd al-Hafīẓ. The failure of these contenders within the palace to solve Morocco's crisis and to retain its independence had been a failure for the local leaders as well. They recognised the weakness of their country's government and army, accepted the inevitability of French domination and hoped that the stability and indirect rule promised by the French protectorate would allow them to pursue their individual interests without undue interference.

In effect a French Contrôleur Civil was governing Salé behind the façade of the pasha and the local municipal council. Those who displeased the Contrôleur, or opposed such administrative matters as patent taxes, learned that he had at his disposal the means to impose the will of the protectorate authorities. Moreover there were economic and political incentives to co-operate with the French—salaried positions in the administration, favours, a modern education for one's children, and the prospect that they in turn would have positions among the indigenous elite.

During the first decade of the protectorate a handful of these men prospered, but because of the colonial situation their leadership became weakened and lost one of its main functions—the capacity to offer rewards and services to a large following of clients. At the same time the economic situation of most of the city's inhabitants worsened, including those who had been allies and supporters of these traditional leaders. In the past the constant competition for political influence in the city had assured the replacement of weakened leaders by strong ones. Under the French such competition was thwarted, for the colonial authorities had congealed local leadership and made it weak and dependent. Such a situation served both to undermine widespread patron–client coalitions and to eliminate opportunities for political competition. It left most of Salé's population frustrated, bitter and resigned. It also paved the way for a challenge to authority and a quest for leadership by the younger generation.

The School for the Sons of Notables and the *collège* in Rabat established by the French authorities appeared to protect and to further the interests of the protectorate and of the native elite. The free schools founded by people who had been excluded from influence and political power in effect disputed the right of the colonial authorities to determine the composition of the future elite.

This competition over access to positions of influence and power had to do not only with politics and economics but with religion and culture as well. Indeed, concern about the future of the young was almost inevitably and exclusively formulated in the language of religion and culture. The French schools, in the eyes of most Slawis, were preparing the elite of the next generation by carrying out the *mission civilisatrice*, that is, by transforming their students into replicas of Frenchmen. The free schools, on the other hand, were trying to make the Arabic language and the religious and cultural values of Islam the basis of the education of the young generation. The struggle became formulated in terms of a conflict between Islamic and French civilisation.

In the long run the dominance of Islamic civilisation, or, more simply, the vitality of Moroccan culture, appeared more significant than the changes that had taken place in the social system. Yet the situation in Salé shows that the resurgence of religious and cultural values depended upon changing social relationships.[30] The experience of Salé's young generation in modern schools, whether French or Arabic, provided them with new patterns of association. Thus they formed a club and a theatre group, established a bookshop and a newspaper, and spent most of their free time together engaged in the activities particular to those associations. The separateness of these youths from other members of the community expressed itself in speech, dress and mannerisms to a degree unparalleled in earlier generations. This separateness was reinforced by an actual or anticipated absence of economic dependence on their families. Some young men were already earning their own way in the administration or in private business, and the students, though still supported by their parents, expected that their education would soon free them from complete economic dependence upon their families. Such an attitude among a relatively large group of young people was unprecedented in Salé. This group of some thirty young men between the ages of fifteen and twenty-five appears to have been highly self-assured —unrestrained and unabashed by their parents, and unintimidated by the colonial authorities. Their confidence allowed them to believe that the future of Morocco belonged to them, all signs to the contrary notwithstanding.

The objective signs in Morocco, as well as in the rest of North Africa, seemed to indicate the infallibility of French rule. Morocco, it was true, had not yet been totally conquered ('pacified' in the terminology of the protectorate authorities), but the main resistance had failed and the few areas that remained beyond the pale would soon capitulate. France's hold on the country was secure, and the central authority completely in her hands. The sultan initially appointed by the French, Mawlāy Yūsuf, had died in 1927 and been replaced by his eighteen-year-old son, Sīdī Muḥammed. Like most of the local authorities set up by the French, he had no power to abuse.

In 1930 France was preparing for the celebrations of the centenary of the conquest of Algiers and was about to hold a massive Eucharistic Congress at Carthage. It was, as C. Gallagher has written, 'the year of the false apogee of the *pax Gallica*'. In Salé the young people followed the reports of French celebrations and of opposition to them by North African students in Paris with great interest and passion. They were ripe for some kind of manifestation of their frustration and anger when, on 16 May 1930, the French authorities had the palace proclaim the Berber Dahir. The implications of the decree seemed clear to the young Slawis: *divide ut imperes*—a policy that aimed through legislation to divide Berbers and Arabs and to weaken and humiliate the country's inhabitants further. The French have claimed, if not total innocence, at least complete surprise at the reactions to the decree. In effect no policy decision by the protectorate authorities could have been better calculated to bring forth the latent political ambitions of the young and to make manifest the hostility of the urban populations to French rule. The young people in Salé had found the perfect issue on which to mobilise the community and secure for themselves a leading influence within the city. The explanation of the activism and competition for leadership by the young lies in the changing state of social relations within the city. The 'young tarbrushes' (as the French liked to call them) had become a coherent and ambitious group which did not accept or believe in the leadership of its elders and wanted to challenge the self-assured colonial system.

Initially the leaders of the young in Salé, particularly ʿAbd al-Laṭīf aṣ Ṣubīḥī, had begun the campaign against the Dahir with the argument that by it France sought to destroy the territorial integrity of Morocco. Thus for a brief period during the early days of the campaign we find Moroccan nationalist sentiments formulated in terms of territorial patriotism. Propaganda formulated along these lines effectively stirred young people in Salé and gave them a message particular to them alone, but it failed to agitate the spirits of the wider community. Indeed, the older leaders of the city were hostile to the idea of a territorial nationalism, confounding it with the likes of European liberalism and Turkish secularism. They tended to dismiss the young as troublemakers who ignored the meaning of their own religion and culture. In effect, the young were in this way being denied the right which they had appropriated to themselves—the right to take up leadership in the community and to challenge the political system.

At this juncture the group of young people changed their way of talking about the threat posed by the Dahir. They began to use the values and emblems of Islam to communicate to the wider public the meaning of the campaign. They rediscovered the effectiveness of the recitation of the prayer said in times of calamity—the *laṭīf*—and used it to awaken people to the great danger menacing Morocco's *religious* integrity. The strategy succeeded beyond all expectations: the prayer interpreted as a 'gift from God' mobilised the community of Salé and eventually transformed the campaign into a national movement.

The use of religious symbols transformed the campaign against the Dahir into a protest movement against both political and cultural colonialism. Religious and cultured pride, together with the fear of proselytism and assimilation, were deeply rooted in most of Salé's inhabitants. When the young began to play upon these sentiments they succeeded in arousing the community to their cause. Thus the protest movement had its roots in social change. In order to attract a large following it had expressed itself in the cultural emblems that made people respond. These were the symbols and values of Islam. Their invocation responded to the anxieties of young and old—to cultural uprootedness, economic distress, fear for the spiritual and material well-being of the young, disruption of the community's social fabric and, finally, to the humiliation and resentment of being second-class citizens.[31]

The closing of ranks against the French under the cloak of Islam reactivated social ties of family and friendship among different generations, rekindled respect and affection between old and young, and ironically gave both groups the feeling that they were leading the campaign against the French. Both old and young manipulated cultural values and emblems while at the same time responding to them. The meanings of actions received different interpretations by various individuals and groups, but the whole community shared in the euphoria of manifesting opposition and hostility to French policy and culture, particularly from within the safe confines of the mosque.

The conflict between generations that had accompanied social change receded into the background. In effect the younger generation had created and assumed leadership of a nationalist movement without, however, feeling that it had betrayed the elders or the traditions that they represented.

Religion had been used to provide a statement about the ideal relations that pertained in the community—the brotherhood of Muslims, whether Berber or Arab. The reality of social relations was again specifically different from the ideal: a small number of young and educated men in Salé, and in the other cities with an old urban tradition, had moved into the forefront of Moroccan politics.

Conclusions

The difference between the eighteenth and nineteenth centuries is greater than between the first and eighteenth centuries as far as civilised Europe is concerned.

The Economist, London, 1851

After 1830 the old Maghrib was no more than on reprieve; the same can be said for colonisation after 1930.[1]

In this study of the social history of Salé between 1830 and 1930 I have been concerned essentially with two issues: the structure of this particular Moroccan city and the processes of change that took place within it. Parts I and II ('Market and town'; 'The fabric of society') deal primarily with the first issue, while Parts III and IV ('The disruption of economic life'; 'Reflections of and reactions to change') consider mainly the second. In these concluding remarks I want to relate this study to some general discussions about pre-industrial Muslim cities and about urban social change in the Maghrib. Before I take up these discussions it is necessary to sketch the general lines of Morocco's political structure during the pre-colonial period.

City and State

The Fasis have gone too far down the slope of refinement and decadence ever to have recourse to force, but their tongue is quick, their criticisms are acute and their sarcasm mordant.[2]

Aubin's remarks about the inhabitants of Fez at the turn of the nineteenth century would have applied equally to other townsmen, especially to those from the centres of urban civilisation in Morocco, Tetuan, Rabat and Salé. The city people lived by their wits rather than by might, and this was one of the main distinctions between them and the people of the countryside. To be sure, Moroccan cities had always drawn migrants from the countryside, and for their prosperity they depended on rural producers and consumers. But, while townsmen assimilated these immigrants and continually interacted with surrounding peasants, they looked down upon them disdainfully as 'primitives', and referred to them pejoratively as 'Bedouins' or

'Arabs'.[3] The Moroccan city, encapsulated within a larger society and a State system, had particular cultural characteristics and roles, as well as economic and political ones. From some perspectives the totality of nineteenth-century Moroccan society seems like a whole and continuous cloth; from others it looks like patchwork. Historical research so far provides only the simplest classification of component parts. But we have to make do with these in order to try to understand the relations of city and countryside and the ways in which people conceived of these relations.

We may consider the whole of nineteenth-century Morocco in schematic terms according to three basic axes: (1) from the point of view of language, whence a distinction between Arabs and Berbers; (2) from the socio-economic perspective, thus a separation between urban and rural (or tribal); (3) from the political angle, thereby a divergence between *makhzan* and *sība*.[4] This scheme, if carefully elaborated upon, can be useful in understanding the role and situation of a city like Salé. The dichotomy between language groups need not detail us long: most cities were identified with an urban dialect of Arabic; the people living in the plains surrounding cities tended for the most part to speak a rural dialect of Arabic; the inhabitants of the mountains almost always spoke some dialect of Berber. The people of the cities did distinguish between 'Arabs' and 'Berbers' (*shlūḥ*) on the basis of language, but indiscriminantly looked down upon both groups because of their primitive rural way of life. To be sure, these stereotypes did not prevent city dwellers from entering into individual relationships with peasants, Arab or Berber, on the basis of mutual interests.

In regard to the political system of the State, the city had an important and complicated role to play. The central authority of the Moroccan State, that is, its ruling dynasty, military forces, Ministers, officers, governors and palace staff, had taken on a particular organisation and a name—*al-makhzan*—late in the sixteenth century. The structure of the *makhzan*, which despite modifications endured until the French protectorate of 1912, underwent significant changes during the nineteenth century. Aubin traced these changes in detail and vividly described the particular political organisation that existed in the early years of this century.[5] The *guich* tribes of Morocco (from cl. *jaysh*, 'army') had been military tribes exempt from taxation and provided with government land. By 1900 they had lost their exclusive right to provide soldiers to the sultan and most of their privileged positions in the government bureaucracy. The relative decline of this military government and of the predominance of a kind of rural aristocracy had been accompanied by the ascendancy of urban scholars and wealthy merchants who became the majority of secretaries and officials in the palace cabinet and the government bureaucracy. Aubin wrote about a new regime of learning and wealth in which force no longer represented the real basis of the State's authority: 'power is coming into the hands of "intellect", and Morocco is watching the dawn of a Government of scholars'. The majority of these officials and secretaries came from the *ḥaḍariyya* cities—Fez, Rabat, Salé and Tetuan—and because of their 'peaceable tastes' and ability to handle practical affairs they were 'inclined to consider policy a more efficacious instrument than war'.[6]

Makhzan was the term used for the army and administration of the central government, but it also referred to the authority of the sultan and to the seats and realms of his government.[7] Fez, Meknes, Rabat and Marrakesh had the qualifications of *makhzan* or imperial cities. These provided residences for the sultan, had military governors, and contained important storehouses and garrisons for troops. The *makhzan*, accompanied by the whole army, periodically shifted from north to south, from Fez to Marrakesh by way of Meknes and Rabat. Rabat and Marrakesh had military garrisons (qasbahs), separate from the city proper. Fez, in fact, consisted of two cities, the imperial Fās al-Jadīd (New Fez) and the proper *madīna*, Fās al-Bālī (Old Fez). These two cities of Fez illustrate the difference between cities of *makhzan* and those of *ḥaḍāra*. The wealthy and refined merchants and scholars, the people of 'culture', scorned and feared the 'primitive' inhabitants of the *makhzan* city.[8] Nonetheless 'men of the pen' as well as 'men of the sword' participated in the *makhzan*, and during the nineteenth century officials and secretaries from the *ḥaḍāra* cities of Fez, Rabat, Salé and Tetuan had become important, if not dominant, in the administration of the central government.

Some of these officials served at the court but many others held positions of responsibility as governors, qadis, customs officials and clerks in various cities of the empire. In part, at least, the economic and political unity of the country depended upon them. They controlled the collection and payment of duties in the ports, administered justice in the cities and handled correspondence for the central administration. In respect of the rural areas surrounding the four *ḥaḍāra* cities these local officials acted as intermediaries for the government with the tribes. In such places as Casablanca, Safi, Mogador and Marrakesh officials from *ḥaḍāra* cities were responsible for maintaining relations with and collecting taxes from the surrounding rural populations.[9]

The territory firmly controlled and taxed by the government was the *bled l-makhzan*, and that beyond its effective control the *bled s-sība*, that is, respectively, the 'submissive' and the 'unsubmissive' realms of the State.[10] The ebb and flow of the central government's power in the countryside determined the fluctuating frontiers between these realms. The cities, particularly the *ḥaḍāra* ones, were within the heartland of *makhzan* control. Although they might maintain relations with unsubmissive tribes, even negotiate with them on behalf of the sultan, they ultimately depended on the central government for their protection.

What may have appeared to some people in the rural areas as a state of freedom and independence was in the eyes of the city dwellers a form of upheaval that threatened to become anarchy. Ernest Gellner has vividly characterised the Moroccan situation before the twentieth century as a relationship between sheepdogs, sheep and wolves ('a parable on the human condition in general'): an inner circle extracted taxes, a middle circle had taxes extracted from it and an outer circle refused taxation altogether.[11] The people of the cities were the sheep—controlled and defended by the State, and threatened by the potential depredations by the countryside. This image of society, of course, oversimplifies the patterns of interactions and relations among persons and the ways in which these were shaped by particular circumstances or goals. Nonetheless it does resemble the urban self-image: between the two groups of society that depended on brute force, the *makhzan* and the tribes, the townsmen who made up the third group had recourse only to their tongues and wits. The townsmen, moreover, made the relatively peaceful coexistence of these groups possible, because they provided the officials who kept the administration and bureaucracy of the government functioning.

The structure of the pre-colonial Moroccan State seems to fit Max Weber's model of the patrimonial regime: traditional domination by a chief who inherited his personal authority and required officials for the exercise of that authority.[12] Throughout the nineteenth century the needs of a relatively centralised and large-scale administration in Morocco increased. Most of the officials who were recruited into these administrative posts came from the cities, particularly those with a reputation for learning and culture, and they owed their appointments to the sultan or his retainers. The participation of officials from the cities in the administration, and the ascendance of urban merchants whose interests were tied to the government, served to attach these townsmen to the State machinery. As a result the *makhzan* in some ways included two interrelated elites—the sultan and his retinue, and the urban notables composed of officials and merchants. This interdependence was the basis of patrimonialism in Morocco, and along with the relative centralisation of the power of the government it militated against the autonomy of the cities.

Weber argued that Islamic political institutions were basically patrimonial in nature, and as such they precluded the emergence of any autonomous groups or institutions. Thus whereas the European city, unfettered by a patrimonial order, was an autonomous and unified community—with its own associational life, legal and political freedom, and especially its readiness and ability to defend itself—the Islamic city, limited by patrimonialism, could not achieve autonomy. In Weber's view, Asian cities were collections of divided clan and tribal groups which did not join together in common action or exist as urban communities.[13]

The Moroccan cities were controlled by patrimonial rulers and lacked autonomy, and these two factors appear to be interrelated. However, the example of Salé suggests that these cities nevertheless existed and acted as socially unified communities. This variation of Weber's model becomes clearer if we consider the typology of the medieval Muslim city drawn from recent historical studies.

The Muslim city: a type of civilisation and society

Most of the literature on Muslim cities explicitly or implicitly contrasts them with the ancient and medieval cities of Europe. Thus, for example, X. de Planhol, synthesising the works of Marçais, Weullerse, von Grunebaum, Gibb and Bowen and others, notes the absence of municipal life and cohesion, and the lack of any essential unity or organisation in the cities of Islam.[14] G. E. von Grunebaum points out that the Muslim town is not a body politic, an autonomous association of citizens or a closed corporation: it is merely a functionally unified administrative entity with a more or less stable complement of inhabitants. Although the town made it possible for a Muslim to fulfil completely his religious duties and social ideals, he was basically 'a citizen of the *umma Muḥammadiyya* but a mere resident of the town'.[15] These views support the analysis of Weber—that in the East the associational character of the city and the concept of a burgher never developed at all or existed only in rudiments, or of Spengler—that the Eastern city 'has no soul', that it is but a conglomeration of units, not a complex and living organism.[16] Lapidus' study of Aleppo and Damascus during the Mamluk empire (1250–1570) stands as a corrective to these views, for it identifies social relationships in the cities that made order and community possible. These urban communities were loose-knit and basically disaggregative, but tied together by networks of overlapping and criss-crossing relationships.[17] The medieval Eastern Muslim city, as described by Lapidus, did not have characteristics similar to the ancient or medieval European city, but was a functioning and in some ways a total community. This study of nineteenth-century Salé suggests that in the Muslim West the city tended to be an aggregative community, and that its inhabitants had a highly developed sense of urban solidarity and pride.

The Arabic word for city, *madīna*, came from an Aramaic term which meant a place where justice was rendered. It was first used in Islamic times to designate the city of Yathrib, to which the Prophet Muhammad made the Hijra; Medina was an agglomeration with a cultic purpose—to assemble the believers for communal prayer and for the rendering of justice.[18] In the medieval Islamic East the term apparently meant an administrative centre within a State structure rather than a 'city' in the European sense. In the Muslim West, however, the *madīna* was a city (with the sense of the Latin *civitas*), and from that term came the word for civilisation (*tamaddun*). In the west the life of the city was characterised and solidified by Islam, and its inhabitants were characterised by their attachment to the cultural ideals of Islam.

If cities in general are the symbol and carrier of a civilisation (i.e. an advanced state of human society with a high level of art, science, religion and government), then the specificity of the Muslim city derives from the fact that it symbolises and carries the civilisation of Islam.[19] In Morocco some cities were considered beacons of prosperity and civilised culture (*al-ḥaḍāra*), in contrast to what may be termed primitive culture (*al-bādiya*).[20] The inhabitants of Salé were primarily 'people of the city' or the 'people of civilised culture', and as such distinguished themselves from outsiders, peasants or primitives. Their civilisation expressed itself as a total way of life —a complex pattern of behaviour, a mode of dress, a style of cooking, a manner of speech. Individuals were included in or excluded from this civilisation according to the presence or absence of conformity to its rules in their way of life. The city lent its specific quality and texture to the lives of its inhabitants if they followed or adopted its rules of conduct. The outsider, or the 'primitive', could and often did become civilised, integrated, woven into the fabric of the urban society by taking on the traits that were considered the defining criteria of Slawiness. To be or to become a man of the city meant to participate in a kind of diffused solidarity and a characteristic order. It denoted an identification with and an attachment to a particular urban community. In fact these cultural traits were not common to all Slawis and did not differentiate them from all others. But in local theory they were the criteria for defining Slawiness. The identification of the people of the city with a particular culture represented a concept, what Nadel has called a 'spiritual reality', rather than the objective observation of cultural facts. It reflected a theory and an ideology.[21]

Studies of the Muslim city have indicated as its landmarks the mosque, market and palace.[22] The Moroccan cities, as I have shown, also acted as focal points for cultural, economic and political life. The urban quality of Salé was especially bound up with religion and culture, and perhaps, as Lapidus has suggested, the unique qualities of the Muslim city lay in the religious identification of the majority of its inhabitants.[23] Whereas in the Muslim East there were religious minorities, sectarian differences among Muslims and divergences in their affiliations to the four legal schools, in the Muslim West the cities all followed the Sunni creed and the Maliki school of law. There were, to be sure, some differences in beliefs and practices among Muslims within the city, as well as a sizeable Jewish minority, but the dominant overarching religious tenor of the city was classical in style and embedded in literacy, both amongst Muslims and Jews.

The cohesiveness of the Moroccan city and its inherent cultural unity found their clearest expression in the Friday mosques.[24] The centrality of Salé's Great Mosque—at the heart of the residential district of the bourgeoisie and at the highest point in the city—visibly demonstrated and symbolised the dominance of religious and cultural factors in the town. When the Friday prayer was held the gates were locked, the city was enclosed and protected, and almost all adult males were likely to be at prayer.[25]

At moments of individual or communal crisis the people of the city usually went to pray in the mosques. And at times of natural calamities or political exigencies the Great Mosque became the focal point of the city.[26] Thus the mosque served to rally public sentiment amongst an urban community which, in any case, proudly defined itself as a standard-bearer of Islamic civilised culture. The parochial solidarity and local patriotism of the people of the city flowed from two sources—from this definition of a shared culture and from a particular concept of the city's social cohesiveness.

The images by which Slawis conceived of the transmission of their culture from generation to generation resembled the ways in which they envisaged the connections that united individuals in a cohesive social structure. According to their ideas and concepts, they composed one family, they were like the buckets on a watermill wheel that drew from a single source and irrigated a single garden. In theory each individual was related or tied to others by bonds of consanguinity, marriage, friendship, mutual interest or loyalty, and these relationships and ties overlapped and interconnected in such a way as to unite individuals into the fabric of a total, cohesive urban community. For descriptive purposes I have divided people into social groups on the basis of family, residential quarter, occupation, affiliation to religious orders; but none of these categories satisfactorily explains the nexus of human relationships which gave the community its peculiar social structure. The basic social groupings within the town were networks, or coalitions formed around relatively powerful individuals who could and often did act as patrons to clients. These groupings became latent or effective, factionalised, antagonistic and competitive or co-operative and coalescent according to circumstances. Such vertical groupings crossed the social hierarchy and provided the main means of social action in the city. They cut across urban horizontal categories—the elite and the masses—and sometimes extended into the countryside or other cities.

This pattern of social organisation differs somewhat from the analysis suggested by studies of eastern Muslim cities. Lapidus sees the social organisation of the Muslim city as essentially three-tiered: (1) parochial groups (families, neighbourhoods, fraternities), (2) religious communities (schools of law, Shīʿite sects, Sufi brotherhoods), (3) imperial regimes (ethnically alien elites). The interrelationships between individuals and groups on these three levels give each city its particular structure.[27] In Salé parochial groups did not represent fundamental units, religious communities did not exist in any comparable way, and the regime had no similar presence in the city (nor was it ethnically alien). Nonetheless the pattern of social ties among people in Salé bears some resemblance to the eastern Muslim cities in that two levels of urban society, the elite and the masses, interrelate in a particular structure. Networks and coalitions exist within and beyond each of these levels, binding elite and masses together and in some cases bringing them into relation with individuals and groups outside the city proper.

The central figures in networks and coalitions were individuals who had some measure of political, economic or religious influence and a capacity and willingness to use that influence for the benefit of others. In the medieval Muslim cities of the East the ties of the ulama to the rest of society and their crucial political roles as intermediaries between the regime and urban society were crucial for social and political order.[28] In nineteenth-century cities of the Muslim West influential individuals (ulama, officials, merchants, craftsmen) fulfilled similar social and political roles on the basis of their status and wealth, often without any religious expertise or prestige. Thus the main feature of urban social structure did not directly relate to Islamic civilisation except in one respect: the people of the city conceived of their interrelationships with one another in the same way that they conceived of their participation in the civilised culture of Islam. Accordingly Salé was considered a family and a religious community.

In order to explain the similarities and regularities found among pre-industrial in contrast to industrial cities G. Sjoberg argued that priority needed to be given to technology over other significant variables, such as urban–rural relations, cultural values or power structures.[29] In his view a society's ability to produce sizeable surpluses to support large non-agricultural populations was associated with the emergence of the pre-industrial city and its particular system of stratification—a well defined and rigid class structure and a clear-cut division of labour according to age, sex and occupation. In these cities a small, privileged upper class dominated political, religious and educational institutions. This governing elite, freed from food production or other physical labour, extracted surplus products from the countryside to feed the city, administered the labour force, maintained political stability, etc. The majority of the inhabitants of the city consisted of lower-class and outcast groups. The elite received an education and maintained the written culture of the society. Their cohesiveness and dominance were reinforced and justified by their monopolisation of literacy, which allowed them to appear as the spokesmen and model of ideal religious norms. Such people generally had high status ascribed to them by birth, a status strengthened by their access to posts in the governmental administration. The only people who did not easily fit into this pattern of a bifurcated class structure, with its literate elite and its lower class of masses, were the merchants. Commoners who succeeded in commerce and had a talent for manipulation could achieve upward mobility. On the whole, however, the pre-industrial city, according to Sjoberg, was characterised by rigidity in its class structure, by a lack of social mobility and by particularism amongst component groups. In contrast, he argued, class flexibility and fluidity and universalism distinguish the structure of the industrial city. Sjoberg's model of the pre-industrial city does not fit the case of Salé, but it allows for a shift of focus from the social structure of Muslim cities to pre-modern cities in general. Moreover it makes it possible for me to direct attention to social relationships within the city, in regard to both networks and 'classes', on a wider comparative level.

Three different orders of social relationships seem to be characteristic of urban social systems:[30] (1) a structural order, i.e. an interpretation of behaviour according to the positions that people occupy in an ordered set of positions, (2) a categorical order, i.e. an interpretation of behaviour in unstructured situations according to social stereotypes such as class, race or ethnicity, (3) a personal order, i.e. an interpretation of behaviour in either structured or unstructured situations according to the social links among individuals, such as social networks. As Mitchell points out, these are not different types of actual behaviour but different ways of making abstractions to achieve different kinds of understanding and explanation of the same actual behaviour. I have discussed the structural order in treating the *shurafā'*, ulama and various occupations, and the personal order in considering networks and coalitions. I want now to discuss the categorical order, particularly with regard to 'class'.

In nineteenth-century Salé the indigenous model of social structure contained horizontal, hierarchically arranged strata somewhat similar to the classes of the pre-industrial city as analysed by Sjoberg. The inhabitants of the city divided themselves into two categories—the elite and the masses.[31] The masses included both 'people of the city' and 'outsiders' (the civilised and the primitive). The elite wielded social power on the basis of their personal authority, influence, wealth or prestige. The composition and size of the elite, or notables (*a'yān*), although never precisely defined, changed over time. Wealth in and of itself was not usually sufficient for inclusion among the elite, but the absence of a style of life made possible only by wealth served to exclude individuals. When agriculture provided people with opportunities for an affluent way of life some farmers were included among the elite. The same held true later in regard to commerce and merchants. The wealthy tended to achieve high status, provided they took on the cultural characteristics of the elite and linked themselves and their fortunes to others within the same category. No term defined the *nouveaux riches*, but the elite were sometimes referred to as 'the sons of [important] people' or as members of 'noble households', and this implied the denigration if not exclusion of those with new wealth.

Upward and downward mobility into and out of this elite was relatively common during the first half-century of the period under study but less so during the second half, when the category of the elite shrunk in size and became more rigid. The masses remained a residual category and grew in size and rigidity. The dichotomy between elite and masses suggested by Sjoberg's model of the pre-industrial city fits the situation in Salé, but few of the explanations which he offers seem relevant. The elite appear to be a status group, as defined by Weber: not purely economically defined, but determined by a social estimation of honour.[32] However, in the late nineteenth century status groups began to harden into 'classes'.

The social structure of Moroccan cities, at its most complicated in terms of these categories, has been described by Le Tourneau in his study of pre-protectorate Fez.[33] Le Tourneau distinguished (1) the *makhzan*, i.e. the central government, with its palace, army and administrators; (2) the Jewish community (both 1 and 2 resided in New Fez and had their own internal hierarchies); (3) the floating population; (4) heterogeneous colonies, each with a degree of internal cohesion (including groups from specific regions and black slaves); and (5) the 'people of Fez'. The last-named possessed the 'right of citizenship' (*droit de cité*) by virtue of having lived in and been part of the community for generations. These 'real Fasis' were divided according to criteria of wealth and status. The upper category comprised merchants, scholars, holy men (*shurafā'*) and government officials (although the last were invariably merchants or scholars to begin with). These were not, in his view, absolutely coherent 'social classes', because family origins, degree of culture, affinities and traditional animosities divided them into clans and coteries among whom alliances were formed and broken according to circumstances. The lower category included shop-keepers, artisans and petty officials, and acted as a reserve from which the elite of Fez was perpetually reconstituted. The rest of the population, although marginal, became absorbed or digested into the urban society by a slow process. These social strata lived in harmony despite the differences of wealth among them. The capitalism of the city, neither omnipotent nor impersonal, was complemented by a redistribution of resources by way of ceremonies, gifts and favours in which all groups participated. Thus in Fez prior to 1912 economic criteria appear to have influenced the structure of society, but only partially, for differentials in wealth were mitigated by traditional modes of redistribution.

An economic study of incomes and standards of living in Fez in 1934 showed a similar distribution of wealth and patterns of consumption. It defined the people of the city as those who on the whole derived their income from handicrafts or commerce and provided themselves with consumption goods by means of exchange. The social and economic structure included three overlapping classes: (1) the wealthy, who made up about 8 per cent of the total working population (composed of less than 0·001 per cent of high officials, 3 per cent of wealthy merchants and 5 per cent of wealthy proprietors), (2) the middle class, who comprised about 65 per cent of the total working population (50 per cent artisans, 9 per cent shopkeepers, 5 per cent petty officials, 1 per cent liberal professional people), (3) the working class, who represented about 27 per cent of the total employed population (25 per cent workers, 2 per cent domestics).[34] The actual distribution of wealth closely resembled the model of social structure suggested above, but the upper, lower and marginal categories had become upper, middle and working classes. The question arises: how useful is it to extend the analysis of urban social structure in Morocco towards a model of class that implicitly comprehends the concepts of exploitation and consciousness?

Le Tourneau's view of Fez precludes a class analysis. He describes it as a city in which the various social strata, because of their interactions and interrelations and because of at least some measure of wealth redistribution, live in harmony:

> . . . to my knowledge, there was no trace of irremediable opposition, no symptom of class conflict. I do not mean to say that agreement always reigned and that domestic quarrels were unknown: history proves the contrary. But these discords, the fruits of ephemeral and changing oppositions among clans not among classes, were of a political, not a social nature.[35]

In regard to Salé there is little doubt that some redistribution of wealth took place and that economic inequalities and social antagonisms were thereby mitigated. Yet during this period of accelerated economic change there are clear indications of exploitation and conflict among social groups. As the century between 1830 and 1930 wore on, a greater amount of surplus value was extracted from the countryside and from the poor of the city by fewer people, and less wealth was redistributed by the rich to the poor. By the end of the nineteenth century a privileged class of townsmen had cut themselves off from production and begun to be involved exclusively in commerce or the government bureaucracy. This was exploitation through patrimonialism and trade at the expense of the urban craftsmen and the peasant producers. Those who profited from the situation should not be confused with the bourgeoisie, described by Marx and Engels, that 'left remaining no other nexus between man and man than naked self-interest, than callous cash payment'. The urban bourgeoisie in Morocco at the turn of the century had concentrated in its hands new sources of wealth, and by so doing *began*, however imperceptively, to challenge an old political and social system.

The new bourgeoisie of the late nineteenth century, particularly the officials and merchants, were responsible for collecting taxes from the surrounding countryside and from the rest of the urban population; a portion of these taxes were in turn extracted from them by the *makhzan*. Moreover the surplus value of the countryside was drawn to the bourgeoisie by its control of the market and the law. Although detailed information on market processes is lacking, the material from Salé indicates that the prices of agricultural products and locally manufactured, and especially imported, goods were increasingly determined by the urban bourgeoisie and through them by the movements of international trade. The gradual impoverishment of the great bulk of the urban population and the enrichment of a small elite were direct and interconnected effects of these processes whose consequences for the countryside were equally disastrous.[36]

The emergence of this new bourgeoisie was tied to the exploitation of the people in the countryside and of the mass of the urban population, but, as Laslett reminds us in another historical context, 'the rise of a capitalist class interpretation can be misleading as well as informative'.[37] The growth of commerce and the bureaucracy intensified an already existent pattern in the social structure of these cities; it increased the opportunities for social mobility, but with the consequence that fewer people ascended the social hierarchy and more descended. The economic differential between the wealthy and the poor became greater and in time more permanent, even if it did not clearly express itself in class antagonisms.

Yet, despite this growing socio-economic differentiation, older patterns of social relationships maintained themselves. The new bourgeoisie, for all their aggressiveness and monopolisation of wealth, adapted themselves to the ways of the traditional urban elite—its style of life, form of consumption and redistribution of wealth, and pattern of cross-cutting social ties. In adapting to the urban style of life they exaggerated the ostentatious luxury and refinement of earlier generations. They did not save or accumulate capital but spent most of their fortunes on consumption for themselves and others, or on pious endowments. Berque has described the lives of these townsmen as a kind of perpetual cycle between astuteness, piety and usurpation, between the heat of youth and the penitence of age, between rough individualism and municipal service.[38]

In these phases of life merchants, scholars and officials became tied to different individuals and clusters of persons at various levels of the social hierarchy. The networks of social relations that evolved from these ties continued to be fundamental to the structure of society. *Intuitus personal*—knowing and having contacts with people, not only within the different groups of the city but, if possible, in the *makhzan* or the countryside as well—was basic to the art of living and prospering in a city. In some cities the specific linkages among defined sets of persons apparently followed vertical lines of cleavage according to historically rooted patterns. In Salé social networks seemed to have formed on the basis of interest and contingency rather than traditional cleavages. The precise contours of these relationships remain an object for further study, for network analysis, especially from written sources, has only begun to capture the interest of research.

City and State: social history

In our period of industrial civilisation the conquering spirit has become more subtle. Represented by merchants, capitalists and engineers, most of whom frankly have no desire other than profit, it proposes to provide a new country with the modern equipment which it lacks. But for these creations capital is necessary, and a nation in Morocco's situation has none. Usually it can be lent. If the finances of these countries are in disorder it quickly becomes a question of foreign control. The use of borrowed money thus becomes, for the new country in question, a cause of the gradual loss of its independence. Finally political control is necessary to give security. Will not the present circumstances facilitate an evolution of this kind in Morocco?

Bulletin du Comité de l'Afrique Française, 1902[39]

The manifestations of change in nineteenth-century Moroccan society are multi-dimensional and cannot be traced back to a simple inventory of causes. The impact of European expansion, the actions and reactions of governments, the growth and movement of populations, the distribution of resources, the development of ideas, are interrelated and represent at one and the same time combinations of external and internal causes and effects. Economic imperialism, pre-colonial mercantilism, military conquest and finally colonisation by Europe were fundamental influences towards change in Morocco. They strengthened and in turn were reinforced by the weakness or unpreparedness of the *makhzan*, the growing demand for imported goods, the need for foreign capital, the process of urbanisation, the profits of the bourgeoisie (European and Moroccan), the questioning and redefinition of values and ideologies.

Miège has traced in detail the ways in which the *makhzan* was gradually orced to open Morocco to European trade and how the growing commercial interests of Europe eventually undermined the ability and power of the government to maintain its sovereignty. Although the government realised the necessity for reforms, external pressures and internal resistance frustrated its attempts to achieve them. While European military pressure continued more or less unabated, a new army, formed at the cost of a tremendous drain on finances, proved incapable of controlling the country or staving off European intervention. Millions of gold francs wasted on fortifications and armaments, over a billion gold francs paid in indemnities (partly by foreign loans), deficits of dozens of millions of francs in trade balances, all contributed to the growing monetary crisis that left Morocco on the eve of the protectorate a country without financial reserves. The subjugation of the *makhzan* marked the end of a process during which the country had been steadily drawn into the international economy and become subject to foreign financial and political influences. The *makhzan* lost jurisdiction over those of its subjects who became protégés of foreign powers and failed to control part of the countryside. This process of 'peaceful conquest', a well articulated aim of French policy, eventually led to Morocco's loss of independence.

The economy of the country still remained agriculturally based. To the rhythm of natural crises—droughts and famines—were added the phases and rhythm of the world economy, the abrupt crises of supply and demand and monetary fluctuations. The consequences for the countryside and cities of Morocco were far-reaching: the impoverishment of a large part of the rural and urban population, the enrichment of an emergent bourgeoisie in the cities and perhaps of the great chiefs of the countryside as well.[40] These factors influenced movements of population towards the cities, particularly the ports. Where in 1830 there had been only three mediocre port cities—Tetuan, Rabat–Salé and Mogador—by the end of the century there were eight important ports with populations that had more than tripled in size. The growth in population of these ports, although due in part to movement from other cities and the beginnings of European settlements, largely resulted from rural migration. The earliest estimates, those of 1900, showed slightly less than 10 per cent of a total population of about 4·6 million living in the twenty-seven cities of over 2,000 inhabitants. About half the urban population still lived in the six *makhzan* or *ḥaḍāra* cities. Although we cannot reliably estimate the rate of urban growth during the nineteenth century, the tendency towards large-scale urbanisation (which led to an urban population of 19 per cent in 1936 and over 30 per cent in 1960) had already begun in the mid-nineteenth century. The *ḥaḍāra* cities participated less directly in the expansion of trade than did the developing ports, but the commercial acumen and cultural prestige of their inhabitants drew them into trade and into the expanding bureaucracy, and enabled them to take a leading place within the new bourgeoisie.

The expansion of Europe, with its political, economic and cultural effects, is generally adduced as the primary explanation for political change in Morocco. Other external influences or internal processes, whether latent or active, have received little if any attention in the literature. The growing importance of the urban elite, albeit closely tied to the spread of European power, should also be seen within the context of competition for influence and wealth within Morocco. The beginning of 'a regime of learning and wealth' described by Aubin at the turn of this century indicates a tendency towards the predominance of an urban elite over some of the rural and military influences within the *makhzan*. This elite, though disunited and without a coherent ideology, affected the political and administrative system and the destinies of the *makhzan*. The plans and attempts to carry out military and fiscal policies of war and peace and the attitudes towards religious beliefs and practices became increasingly influenced by the views of different members or groups from within the urban elite. In 1907–08 ulama, officials and merchants from Marrakesh, Fez, Rabat, Salé and Tetuan were directly involved in and, in some cases, leaders of the 'Ḥafīẓiyya movement' aimed at the deposition of Sultan ʿAbd Al-ʿAzīz and the proclamation of his brother, ʿAbd al-Ḥafīẓ. They were also the primary participants in the abortive constitutional movement of 1908.[41] An interpretation of modern Moroccan history which stresses that before 1912 the urban elite were moving towards a position of predominance within the *makhzan* has to be advanced with caution and qualifications. The study of Salé suggests such an interpretation, but knowledge of other parts of Moroccan society remains all too fragmentary. More information is needed about the personalities within the *makhzan* about the ties and conflicts among them, and their relations with local political structures, urban and rural.

The establishment of the protectorate in 1912 greatly influenced the direction and momentum of change in Morocco. Interrelations and interactions between *makhzan*, cities and countryside, and the coexistence and conflict that had marked those relations, were placed in a radically different framework. Colonialism, under the guise of a protectorate and in the name of the *makhzan*, caused Morocco to evolve much further along the way to becoming an integrated nation State. Using both persuasion and the force of arms, the French extended their rule over the country and made it an administrative whole. The sultan and his bureaucracy, and the local qa'ids and pashas, became directly and absolutely dependent on the centralised authority of foreign rulers. The result was a bifurcated society in which a colonial administration and a colonial bourgeoisie dominated political and economic life, while the indigenous social categories became compressed if not undifferentiated. Colonialism in Morocco, as elsewhere, was bound to lead to an economic and political confrontation and beyond that to a spiritual one.[42]

Modern nationalism emerged as an important political force in Morocco within a generation after the beginning of the protectorate. The nationalist movement was dominated, particularly in its early years, by men who were young, educated and urban, and who, in the great majority of cases, came from the *ḥaḍāra* cities—Fez, Rabat, Salé and Tetuan.[43] In some ways, of course, the nationalist movement also represented a continuation of processes of political change that had begun in the nineteenth century. Thus it was shaped by Salafiyya fundamentalism and by notions of political sovereignty, ideas that had begun to take root earlier among the urban elite. But the campaign against the Berber Dahir, which marked the beginning of modern nationalism, was a kind of youth crusade, as well as a reaction against the policies of colonialism. At the same time it can be interpreted as an attempt by the urban elite to dominate the countryside and to define the identity of the Moroccan State. The people of the city were making a claim over the countryside in the name of Islam and Islamic law by their opposition to the French attempt to divide both a religious community and a national territory.

Nationalism considered in this light becomes part of an on-going process. Nāṣirī's statement that 'the best qualities in the eyes of God and man are zeal for religion and the homeland and love of the sultan and his advice', the political activities of the urban elite on the eve of the protectorate, and the actions of the young nationalists from the 1920s, represent different attempts by townsmen to define the nature of the Moroccan State.[44] These attempts cannot be explained without reference to the impact of European expansion, nor to the particular circumstances that pertained in each case. Yet in explaining these processes social change should be considered not simply as a reaction or response to external influences and conjunctures but as part of an internal dynamic. Thus nationalism opposes colonialism, but it also becomes a concerted effort by the urban elite to dominate the countryside and the *makhzan*.

Cultural change in urban Morocco is another aspect upon which this study may shed some light. The *ḥaḍāra* cities owed a good deal of their reputation and importance to their monopolisation of learning. Consequently a high proportion of those who profited from the increased opportunities in the bureaucracy and in commerce came from those cities. Not surprisingly, members of the urban elite had the most contact with new ideas, both European and Near Eastern, and a predominant role in shaping Moroccan culture. The stirrings of a cultural renaissance during the decades before the protectorate and the intellectual awakening afterwards were apparently a wholly urban affair and closely tied to the educational facilities of the cities—the traditional madrasahs, French schools and free schools.

In the cities the learned or educated wrestled with the central problem of Islamic political thought—how to preserve the community and make it strong.[45] They played a key role in making sure that Islam remained an actor of political strength and did not become simply a regulative principle of society. The development of ideas and attitudes in Salé may or may not be representative of other Moroccan cities, for only further research will show how Moroccan culture as a whole was affected by change. Until the 1880s the Islamic world view and the Moroccan political system that characterised Salé were questioned, measured against the West and found superior; in the early 1900s an awareness of new ideas and alternatives developed, and views such as those of the constitutionalists found some supporters; in 1912 the Slawis expressed pessimism and nostalgia for the past, mixed with curiosity and admiration for the Europeans; in the 1920s young men thought about religious reform, a renewed Arabic culture and a secular State; and in 1930 religion became the basis of a national identity.

During a brief period in Salé the vision of Morocco as a secularised society and culture and a nation based on the principle of territorial integrity took hold of the imagination of some of the young and educated. This phase quickly passed, and in 1930 religion became the predominant factor in defining the Moroccan society, culture and nation. Some informants explained this change as literally a godsend; others saw it as a tactical way of coping with the Moroccan reality. The brief existence of secular thinking in Salé (and there are other indications of it in Fez, Rabat and Tetuan as well) may be connected to earlier phases of cultural change and ideas about constitutional government, and to the openness of the urban educated to external ideas. But the nationalists soon discovered that religious symbols, not secular ones, most successfully stirred the Moroccan imagination.[46]

Religion played a fundamental role in maintaining the Moroccan social personality in opposition to the cultural confrontation with Europe and as a means of self-purification and political self-assertion.[47] What Europeans called religious fanaticism meant something else to Moroccans. For them opposition to cultural assimilation defined the nature of Moroccan nationalism.[48] It represented an affirmation of an intangible identity (in the form of religious fervour) and the refusal of social exploitation.[49] In Salé nationalism and religion became inseparable for all these reasons, but also because it was the best means of effectively mobilising the community and making the French authorities take notice. When the leader of the campaign against the Dahir began to pray, with tears streaming down his face and people gathered around him 'as in the days of the Prophet', the young were exercising their dramatic skills and applying sound theatrical tactics. At the same time what another informant told me in relating the same events is equally true: 'Whoever fails to understand the depths of our religious feelings as Muslims will inevitably fail to grasp the essence of our existence.' Islam was central to the self-definition of these Moroccans, as well as an arm in their political struggle. The nationalists believed that religious symbols, as they used them and interpreted them, would unite all Moroccans under their leadership. In their minds *ḥaḍāra* no longer stood only for the civilised culture of the city but included the whole of Moroccan culture. As such it implied a programmatic statement about national integration under urban domination.

The spread and conquest of urban culture and the national integration that it aimed at have not been realised to a very great extent in Morocco. A recent book on the contemporary Moroccan political elite suggests that its findings be considered 'a case study of the immobilism inherent in prolonged transition and the seemingly permanent integrative revolution'.[50] The social history of Salé since 1830 and until the present could be characterised in a similar way, with the proviso that the immobilism not be taken as a kind of *plus ça change, plus c'est la même chose* interpretation. For social ties that defined the networks of relationships in Salé have become gradually less locally based and more diffuse. In the nineteenth century the principal ties that held individuals together were within the city; among the nascent bourgeoisie links began to be formed both within the city and with personalities in the *makhzan* and merchants and scholars from other cities. By 1930 the city had increased appreciably in size, and relationships among the Slawis and urban migrants were often tenuous or non-existent. At the same time a number of people from the city were working or studying in Rabat or settled in other parts of the country. Although they maintained ties in Salé, they began to establish significant bonds of friendship and mutual interest among those with whom they came in contact.

In the 1920s the young Slawis felt a need to assert an end to what they considered their in-breeding and isolation. Thus after performing the play in Rabat they symbolically exchanged gifts with and embraced their Rabati cohorts. The youth groups of the two cities, many of whom studied in the same schools, also demonstrated their desire to escape from parochial ties by ceremoniously visiting one another's homes and clubs during the religious holidays. The young nationalists tended to lessen the intensity of their ties within the city, and in time many of them would move out of the *madīna* to its modern suburb of Bettana, or to Rabat or Casablanca. Even marriages became less of an almost wholly local affair, and young men and women began to marry into families from other cities.

Nonetheless most Slawis remained to some extent bound to and by networks of social relationships within the community itself. In 1966–67, when Salé had a population of over 100,000 and had become largely a suburb of Rabat, those in the city who could be called the 'people of Salé' were a small minority, and many who considered themselves *bona fide* Slawis no longer resided there. Yet even at that recent date the social ties amongst the Slawis still counted for much, and so did their proud sense of identity with the city. In the course of my research the Slawis sometimes dismissed talk of parochial identities and solidarities as folklore, or as stereotypes perpetuated by colonialists to divide Moroccans among themselves. A few Slawis honestly believed this, and a great many more regretted what they considered to be the loss of urban cohesiveness. However, most people admitted, whether disapprovingly or proudly, the reality, specificity and importance of their identity as Slawis.

In an attempt to understand the meaning and significance of this specific urban identity, through reading, listening and observing, I was led to the history of the city and to the social, cultural, economic and political ties that have bound together some or all of its people. There is no simple explanation for the fact that most Moroccans, including the people of Salé, have apparently maintained local solidarities and networks of social relationships at the expense of national integration and the pattern of social stratification which it implies. From the purely economic point of view the movement towards the formation of social classes begun over a century ago has continued, without leading, so far, to a class-based social structure. The local patterns of relationships remain strong. The study of Salé's social history between 1830 and 1930 describes the conservatism and adaptiveness of this Moroccan urban community. It seeks, as well, to explain why and how 'people resemble their times more than they do their fathers', for the social relationships and the cultural ideas that supported them, while constraining actions, were also shaped by the Slawis and by the changing conditions of their lives.

Notes and references

INTRODUCTION, pp. 1–11

1 From the editor's introduction to *The Adventures of Thomas Pellow of Penryn, Mariner. Three and Twenty Years in Captivity among the Moors*, second edition (London, 1890). The original edition of Pellow's *Adventures* was edited in 1740.

2 *The Land of the Moors* (New York and London, 1901), p. 165.

3 For a detailed summary of the historical background of Salé *cf.* K. Brown, 'An urban view of Moroccan history: Salé, 1000–1800', *Hespéris-Tamuda*, XII (1971).

4 Ibn ʿAlī, *I.W.*, p. 19.

5 For their biographies *cf.* K. Brown, *op. cit.*

6 *Cf.* A. Adam, *Casablanca. Essai sur la transformation de la société marocaine au contact de l'Occident* (Paris, 1968), I, pp. 14 ff. Many writers have ascribed the reputation of these cities to the influence of emigrants from the cities of al-Andalus (Muslim Spain). In the case of Salé, at least, the importance of this influence has been overestimated.

7 L. Wirth, 'Urbanism as a way of life', *American Journal of Sociology*, XLIV (1938), pp. 1–24. Although Wirth's model has long been shown to be inapplicable to most Third World cities, it provides a useful and stark contrast with Salé's type of urbanism.

8 *Cf.* A. L. Epstein, 'Urbanisation and social change in Africa', in G. Breese (ed.), *The City in Newly Developing Countries* (Englewood Cliffs, N.J., 1969), pp. 255 ff.

9 In the conclusion I discuss the models of Muslim and pre-industrial cities at some length.

10 *Cf.* X. de Planhol, *The World of Islam* (Ithaca, N.Y., 1959), pp. 9 ff. and R. Le Tourneau, *Les Villes musulmanes de l'Afrique du Nord* (Algiers, 1957), pp. 11 ff.

11 This freedom of choice creates the structure of society such that all relationships are dyadic and of a contractual and temporary nature.

12 I. Lapidus, *Muslim Cities in the Later Middle Ages* (Cambridge, Mass., 1967), p. 1.

13. *Ibid.*, pp. 185–8

14 Ibn ʿAlī, *I.W.*, p. 22.

15 *Cf.* 'The cultural role of cities', *Economic Development and Cultural Change*, III (1954), pp. 53–77.

16 *Cf.* G. Ayache, 'Aspects de la crise financierè au Maroc . . .', *Revue Historique*, CCXX, No. 4 (1958), and E. Szymanski, 'La guerre hispano-marocaine (1859–60) debut de l'histoire du Maroc contemporain (essai de periodisation)', *Roeznik Orientalistepzny*, XXIX, No. 2 (1965).

17 J-L. Miège, *Le Maroc et l'Europe, 1830–94*, four vols. (Paris, 1961–63).

18 For a discussion of 'informal empire' *cf.* J. Gallagher and R. Robinson, 'The imperialism of free trade', *Economic History Review*, second series, VI (1953), pp. 1–13.

19 *Cf.* J. H. Hexter, 'A new framework for social history', in his *Reappraisals in History* (London, 1961), p. 14, and M. Rodinson, 'Histoire économique et histoire des classes sociales dans le monde musulman', in M. A. Cook (ed.), *Studies in the Economic History of the Middle East* (London, 1970), p. 154.

PART I

CHAPTER I, pp. 15–26

1 Quoted in *Villes et tribus*, I, 86.

2 J. Dethier, 'Evolution of concepts of housing, urbanism, and country planning in a developing country: Morocco, 1900–72', in L. C. Brown (ed.), *From Madina to Metropolis* (Princeton, N.J., 1973), p. 201.

3 The tribal movements and the existence or lack of security for private or governmental passage during the nineteenth century have still to be sufficiently studied. There is some information on the western expansion of the Zemmour at the expense of the Banū Ḥasan in M. Lesne, *Evolution d'un groupement berbère. Les Zemmour* (Rabat, 1959), p. 41. A letter written in 1890 in the archives of the former governor of Salé, ʿAbd Allah b. Saʿīd, names the Zemmour fractions that had agreed to allow caravans to pass through their territories.

4 Correspondence from the Sultans to the governors of Salé show that they acted for the *makhzan* in regard to the following tribes: Ḥuṣayn, ʿĀmir, Sahūl, Banū Ḥasan, Zemmour, Shlīḥ, Zaʿīr, and ʿArab. (Archives of alʿArabī b. Saʿīd.)

5 One hectare equals 2·471 acres.

6 *Cf. V.T.*, I, 266.

7 Archives of the Alliance Israelite, Paris, dossier Salé

8 E. Gautier, *Les Siècles obscurs du Maghreb* (Paris, 1927), p. 412.

9 *V.T.*, II, p. 57.

10 The term *sība* comes from the classical Arabic word *sā'iba*, a 'freed, untethered camel', from which 'unsubmissive' or 'unrestrained' when applied to people. Mr N. Cigar has called my attention to the sole example, as far as I am aware, of the term in a written source: al-Khayyāt, *Taqāyidtārikhiyya*, MS. 248 P.A., p. 17. It is a description of events following the death of Sultan Ismāʿil in 1727/1139: 'thumma waqaʿa bayna 's-sulṭānayn al-madhkūrayn ḥarb kana aẓ-ẓufr fīha li'lʿabīd. thumma sābat bilādu 'l-maghrib wa-'ahluha wa-ʿajaza mawlay Aḥmad ʿalā tamlīdi 'l-bilād wa-ḥukmi 'l-ʿibād. . . .' 'Then a war took place between the two above-mentioned sultans (Aḥmad adh-Dhahabi and his brother ʿAbd al Mālik), in which victory fell to the ʿAbīd. At that time Morocco and its population were unrestrained; Sultan Ahmad was incapable of controlling the country and governing the subjects. . . .' The division of Morocco into *bled l-makhzan*, the area of government control, and *bled s-sība*, the area of dissidence, by some of the French historians, apparently derives from an oral tradition; this static division distorts a political situation that was one of flux. Examples of this misinterpretation may be found in H. Terrasse, *Histoire du Maghreb* (Casablanca, 1950), II, pp. 357–8, 423, and Michaux-Bellaire (who gives the wrong etymology, viz. *sibā'*) in *E.I.*, art. 'Makhzan', A good analysis of the French view of *makhzan/ sība* is given by E. Burke, 'The image of the Moroccan State in French historical literature', in E. Gellner and C. Micaud (eds.), *Arabs and Berbers. From Tribe to Nation in North Africa* (London, 1973). See the index in the same volume for other discussions of *makhzan* and *sība*.

11 *K.I.*, IV, p. 230.

12 *Cf.* D. Noin, *Le Population rurale du Maroc* (Paris, 1970), I, pp. 238–9.

13 This was reported to me by an old man of the Zemmour who, like his father,

had regularly visited the market of Salé to buy cloth goods to sell in the Zemmour markets.

14 By religious orders I refer to the groups who pursued the sufi mystical way. In Salé these orders were indiscriminately called *ṭarīqa*, pl. *ṭurūq*, or *ṭa'ifa*, pl. *ṭawā'if*. Brunot, in R. S. Harrell, *A Short Reference Grammar of Moroccan Arabic* (Washington, D.C., 1962), p. 243, distinguishes between the former term as referring to respected orders, and the latter as referring to the popular orders that practised 'vulgar' rituals.

15 *Cf.* G. Salmon, 'Notes sur Salé', *A.M.*, III (1905), pp. 320–5.

16 *Cf.* M. Naciri, *op. cit.*, p. 46.

17 Much of the information in this section comes from interviews with old Slawi traders. Further material may be found in Naciri, *op. cit.*; *V.T.* I and III, J. LeCoz, *Le Gharb. Fellahs et colons. Étude de géographie régionale*, I (Rabat, 1964), 257; and Miège, *op. cit.*, II, p. 340, n. 7.

18 D. Urquhart, *The Pillars of Hercules, or a Narrative of Travels in Spain and Morocco in 1848* (London, 1850), I, p. 258.

19 The usually accepted etymology is *raqraqa*: 'water whose flow is gentle' (*Mujma' al-lugha al-'aribīya*, ed. Cairo, 1960).

20 Fishing rights in the river belonged to the Habous, the pious endowment of the Great Mosques of Rabat and Salé, and a percentage of the profits of fishermen from the two cities was set aside for the upkeep of the mosques.

21 L. Brunot, *La Mer dans les traditions et les industries indigénes à Rabat et Salé* (Paris, 1920), p. 89.

22 L. Darmois, *Manuel de l'officier dans l'empire du Maroc ou tableau géographique, statistique, historique, politique et militaire de ce pays*, translated from a Spanish book by Don Serafin E. Calderon (Madrid, 1844). In Archives du Ministère de la guerre, series C, carton I, n. 29-I.

23 Miège, *op. cit.*, II, pp. 175 ff.

24 *V.T.*, I, p. 3.

25 Mouette, *op. cit.*, p. 5; and *cf.* Mercier, 'Rabat, description topographique', *A.M.*, VII (1907), p. 343.

26 'Notice sur la ville de Salé', by Schlumberger, 15 April 1892, in Archives de la Marine (Paris), n. BB 4, 2458, dossier K, ff. 22–4.

27 *Cf.* Miège, *op. cit.*, II, p. 177.

28 The geographical description that follows is based largely on Naciri, *op. cit.*, pp. 55 ff; *cf. V.T.*, III, pp. 3 ff.

29 In the early seventeenth century the Slawis defended those pasturage lands against the Portuguese, who had established themselves at Mehdiya. *Cf. I.W.*, p. 11.

30 J. G. Jackson, *An Account of Timbuctoo and Hausa Territories . . . to which is added Letters Descriptive of Travels through West and South Barbary and across the Mountains of Atlas* (London, 1820), p. 43.

CHAPTER II, pp. 27–49

1 For purposes of description I have relied on a register of Habous property in Salé drawn up in 1868, and on information culled from my oldest informants in the field. The latter recall the spatial organisation of the city for the period around the turn of the century. This method is not completely satisfactory, as a glance at a Habous register of the early eighteenth century shows, for place names and functions undoubtedly changed during the nineteenth century. The description, then, is most reliable for the period 1885–1930. Place names have been rendered, in most cases, according to their local colloquial pronunciation.

2 M. de Périgny, *Au Maroc. Casablanca–Rabat–Meknès* (Paris, 1919), p. 118.

3 Coll. *qallit bn ʿabd l-hādī.*

4 The first qadi to hold court regularly in the Thread Market, ʿAllāl at-Taghrāwī, appointed after the protectorate began, was also the first outsider to hold that position in Salé.

5 *I.W.*, p. 25.

6 *Cf.* Naciri, *op. cit.*, pp. 28 ff; there is an expression which refers to an inhabitant of these quarters: 'he is still an outsider in the city'.

7 He held this office in Salé from 1895 to 1907.

8 The Habous property in the commercial district is listed by market or street, e.g. the *qaysariyya, sūq al-kharrāzīn, sūq ar-raḥba*, etc.

9 Schlumberger, in his report of 1892, *op. cit.*, lists six quarters: Nos. 1, 3, 5, 7, 8, and Zanāta.

10 *V.T.*, I, p. 196.

11 *Op. cit.*, pp. 28 ff.

12 With the exception of Bāb Fard, all these quarters were built-up areas by 1930.

13 *I.W.*, p. 57. The reasons are not given. Was it to defend the city quarter by quarter should Europeans attempt to conquer it, or a means to control the local population should it become afraid and disruptive?

14 Fez's quarters were similarly vague, although they seem to have retained the offices of *muqaddim* from the medieval Muslim town; by 1900, in any case, these chiefs fulfilled relatively unimportant roles. *Cf.* R. Le Tourneau, *Fès avant le protectorat. Étude économique et sociale d'une ville de l'occident musulman* (Casablanca, 1949), pp. 217 ff.

15 *Cf.* Naciri, *op. cit.*, p. 21, who formulates the distinction nicely: 'Ce qui incite à dégager cette classification en quartiers aisés et quartiers pauvres, c'est l'impression d'ensemble, la frequence du type d'habitat bourgeois ou populaire, la proportion de commerçants, de fonctionnaires, d'artisans et d'agriculteurs dans chaque quartier.'

16 M. Lapidus indicates that the Middle Eastern cities of the fourteenth century evinced a solidarity of quarter based on agnatic lines: *Muslim Cities in the Later Middle Ages* (Cambridge, Mass., 1957), pp. 15, 87, 91. Le Tourneau, in describing the quarters of Fez during the last decades of the nineteenth century, distinguishes between the 'administrative quarter', which he calls a 'tenacious and convenient survival', and the 'social quarter', a cell composed of the personal bonds of proximity. But, as he points out, the quarters lack the particularisms of Muslim cities of the East; *op. cit.*, p. 220. The overall distribution of space in Salé resembles many of the North African cities. *Cf.* Le Tourneau, *Les Villes musulmanes de l'Afrique du Nord* (Algiers, 1957), p. 16.

17 The plan and decor of these houses has remained much the same to the present day. Informants did mention, however, that decorating fashions were always fluctuating. Some minor architectural innovations were made by the very rich, especially after the 1880s.

18 *Cf.* Naciri, *op. cit.*, p. 21.

19 *An Introduction to History. The Muqaddima*, translated by F. Rosenthal, abridged and edited by N. J. Dawood (London, 1967), p. 269.

20 G. Colin has shown that this term, which designated Jewish quarters throughout Morocco, originally referred to the former salt marsh in Fez where the Jews first settled. The popular etymology, viz. that Jews were 'salters' of heads of the dead, is fallacious; *cf. E.I.*, art. 'Mellāḥ'.

21 *I.W.*, p. 59.

22 The latter was kept permanently closed until the French arrived in 1912. The Gate of the Mellah opened on to the place of the Gate of Sīdī Bū Ḥājja, along the southern wall.

23 *Cf.* Naciri, *op. cit.*, p. 22. The total area within the walls was approximately ninety hectares.
24 *Cf.* X. de Planhol, *The World of Islam* (New York, 1959), p. 11.
25 K. Brown, 'An urban view . . .', *op. cit.*, pp. 35 ff.
26 *Cf.* the introduction by R. Brown to *The Adventures of Thomas Pellow of Penryn, Mariner. Three and Twenty Years in Captivity Among the Moors* (London, 1890).
27 Documents refer to the wall along the ocean as *jawf*, or north, that along the river as *gharb*, west, and that parallel to the latter as *sharq*, or east. Ibn ʿAli says that after the original eleventh-century Almoravid walls were destroyed the Almohads rebuilt part of them in the twelfth century and the Marinids completed them in the thirteenth century (*I.W.*, pp. 61–2).
28 Bāb al-muʿallaqa, also sometimes called the Gate of Mercy (*bāb ar-riḥma*), for the dead buried in the cemetery. Several legends told in Salé are associated with the various gates.
29 *Cf.* Ibn Zīdān, *Itḥāf ʿalām an-nās bi-jamāl akhbār ḥāḍirat miknās* (Rabat, 1933), III, p. 236, n. 1. The names include many of the old, urban families of Salé.
30 The guards were under the authority of the governor but paid by the merchants for protecting the bazaar. A decree from the sultan in 1880 instructed the qa'id to keep the city clean and well policed (in Archives of al-ʿArabī b. Saʿīd).
31 *Cf.* Naciri, *op. cit.*, pp. 22 ff.
32 I do not mean places of origin in the genealogical sense. I wanted to know where the first member of the family to reach Salé had migrated from. Many families also knew and celebrated their genealogies, but this is a different matter and will be discussed separately.
33 *Cf.* D. Noin, *op. cit.*, I (Paris, 1970), pp. 21 ff, for an excellent and detailed discussion of the problems of demographic research.
34 *Cf.* C. N. Larras, 'La population du Maroc', *La Géographie, Bull. Soc. Géogr.* (Paris, 1906), pp. 337–48, cited in Noin, *op. cit.*, p. 27.
35 *Rapport général sur la situation du protectorat du Maroc au 31 juillet* (Rabat, 1914), in *ibid.*
36 *Cf.* R. Gallisot, *Le Patronat european au Maroc, 1931–42* (Rabat, 1964), pp. 13 ff.
37 Figures given in the tables come from the following sources: for the nineteenth century *cf.* Miège, *op. cit.*, III, pp. 14 ff; the 1900 estimates are from Larras, and the census material for 1931 from Gallisot; for 1971 *cf.* J. F. Troin, 'Les premiers resultats du recensement de la population du Maroc (20 juillet–13 août) 1971), *Revue de Géographie du Maroc*, XX (1971), pp. 139 ff.
38 *Cf.* Miège, *op. cit.*, IV, p. 414, and *Documents d'histoire économique et sociale marocaine au XIXe siècle* (Paris, 1969), p. 273: 'Population des ports marocains.'
39 The most reliable estimate for the early period is Arlett's (1836). See Miège, *op. cit.*, II, p. 177, and E. Renou, *Description géographique de l'empire de Maroc* (Paris, 1846), p. 246. The 1931 figure is from the census; *cf.* R. Hoffherr and R. Morris, *Revenus et niveaux de vie au Maroc* (Paris, 1934), pp. 26, 38, 40. Gallisot, *op. cit.*, gives a slightly higher figure for Europeans.
40 *Cf.* E. Mauret, 'Le développement de l'agglomeration Rabat–Salé', *Bull. Econ. et Soc. du Maroc*, LX–LXI (1954).
41 *I.W.*, p. 25. For the estimate of five persons per household *cf.* Massignon, *op. cit.*, and J. C. Forichon, 'Note sur la démographie et la densité urbaine de Rabat et Salé', *C.H.E.A.M.*, LVI (1947), p. 9.
42 *Cf.* Hoffherr, *op. cit.*, p. 3.
43 Miège, *op. cit.*, II, p. 177; Caillé, *op. cit.*, pp. 813 ff.
44 An attestation by the corporation of Salé (1810) contains approximately one Jewish name for every ten Muslims. The censuses for 1913, 1926 and 1931 also show a Jewish population in the city of about 10 per cent. *Cf.* Fornichon, *op. cit.*

Part II

Chapter III, pp. 52–66

1 The verse is quoted in *I.W.* and attributed to ʿAbd as-Salām al-Yamanī.

2 *Al-Muqaddima*, abridged translation (London, 1967), p. 103.

3 Maʿnīnū, 'The Little Maʿn', is a diminutive form of Romance language origin, and indeed the family came to Salé from Muslim Spain. The Fannīsh were originally renegade converts from the Iberian peninsula. Dr J. R. Latham has kindly pointed out to me the Andalusian origins of a few other family names in Salé, e.g. ad-Dabbāghīn.

4 *I.W.*, pp. 35–6.

5 *amghār* is a Berber term which means 'leader'.

6 Documents made up by notaries of the qadi's court refer to individuals in the most vague honorific manner, while concretely establishing their identity. In some cases 'as-Salawī' may be added to names that refer to a person's place of origin in order to establish place of residence, but in those cases the qualitative *as-sukna* will be added; or the phrase *as-sākin Salā*, 'residing in Salé', will be appended. Material is lacking to detail how the Amghar came to be considered among the leading families of the city. A marriage contract from 1938 shows how a descendant of the family had accumulated urban-type honorific attributes. The contract is between 'ash-sharīf aṭ-ṭālib at-tājir' (the descendant of the prophet, scholar, merchant) Sīdī al-Ḥājj Muḥammad b. BūʿAzza b. Moḥammad b. Ismāʿīl b. al-Walī aṣ-Ṣāliḥ, Mawlāy ʿAbd Allah Amghār (buried among the Dukkāla) and Aḥmed b. al-Faqih Muḥammad b. al-Ḥājj ʿUmar Galzīm (this last from a leading family of Salé, acting for his daughter).

7 These views expressed by old men interviewed in Salé echo the sentiments of Ibn ʿAlī, writing in the 1890s, i.e. a nostalgia for the egalitarianism of some imagined past.

8 Informants were asked to characterise the life styles of these families. The categories that they used were based on what they called the deep-rootedness or extraneousness of the various families.

9 Various terms express the notion of family name: *bayt* and *ḍāṛ*, 'house', *ūlād* (cl. *awlād*) and *banū*, 'sons of', and *qabīla*, literally 'tribe'. All are used in the construct state, that is, followed by the name of the family. Most commonly *ḍaṛ* and *ūlād* are used in the dialect, while the other terms more usually appear in written form. The most common words for family in the dialect are *ʿāʾila*, or the Spanish borrowing, *fāmīliyya*.

10 A document from the 1850s mentions the grandfather as *al-muʿallim*, the 'master craftsman', Muḥammad ash-Shāwī (Muḥammad of Chaouia) at-Tiṭwānī (of Tetuan) *as-sākin* Salā (domiciled in Salé). The story was told to me as a literal answer to my question 'What is a Slawi?' The point of the story was that a Slawi, i.e. someone with a name '*as-Salaw*ī', was a man who has left Salé to settle in a new city.

11 *I.W.*, pp. 31–2.

12 *Ibid.*

13 This kind of self-definition was often expressed to me in the course of field research and is common in the literature written about Salé.

14 *I.W.*, pp. 31–2.

15 Palace archives. A *bayʿa* from Rabat for the same occasion includes the following categories: *maʿshar ahl ar-Ribāṭ*, the total community of Rabat; *sadātunā ash-shurafāʾ* (our lords, descendants of the Prophet); *al-fuqahāʾ* (jurists); *al-ʿulamāʾ* (men of learning); *aṭ-ṭalabā* (students, or chanters of the Qurʾan); *al-mujāhidūn ar-rūʾasāʾ min aṭ-ṭubjīya wa-ʾl-baḥrīya* (holy warrior captains from among artillery-men and sailors); *ahl al-ḥirāf* (craftsmen).

16 *K.I.*, IV, pp. 154–5 and 269 ff; *cf.* Lapidus, *Muslim Cities*, pp. 82 ff, on *ghawgha*—'troublemakers in the city streets' and *al-ʿāmma*—'the trading and working people of the cities'. Brunshvig notes that in Tunis during the fifteenth century the
17 masses were called, interchangeably, *ʿawwām* (pl. of *ʿāmma*) and *ghawghā'*, whose original meaning is 'agitated coal'; *cf. La Berbèrie orientale sous les Hafsids des origines à la fin du XVe siècle* (Paris, 1947), II, p. 168.

David Hart, in a personal communication, mentions that among the Berber-speaking people of the central Atlas *ʿāmma* refers to the 'lay tribesmen', in contrast to the descendants of holy lineages.

18 The connotations of these terms resemble those in the urban societies analysed by Lapidus, but Salé's community is less complex than those of the later Middle Ages, and the sense of the terms less nuanced. *Cf.* Lapidus, *Muslim Cities*, pp. 80 ff and accompanying notes.

19 Non-Sharifian families (i.e. those who were not descendants of the Prophet), including most descendants of saints, did not generally trace their genealogies back to their eponymic ancestor. In most cases a man was able to trace his family genealogy over a period of only three or four generations, including his own. But there was always some specialist in Salé who would obligingly draw up a family tree for the family that wanted one and could afford the price.

20 Early in the twentieth century the Pasha tried to regain some of these properties, claiming that the families were no longer in need of them.

21 A term preferable in the urban context to the 'patrilineages' of tribal society, as David Hart has kindly pointed out to me.

22 The story is historical. *Cf.* K. Brown, 'An urban view of Moroccan history . . .', pp. 65–8.

23 *Cf. E.I.*, second edition, art. 'dhimma'. In the article cited above I misunderstood the meaning of this term.

24 A number of family names in Salé are formed into plurals. Usually, however, the terms *ūlād, banū, dār*, followed by a family name, indicated the totality of a patrilineal group and the notions of continuity and solidarity that might go with it.

25 Cousté, *op. cit.*, p. 11: 'The great families compose the aristocratic and bourgeois elements of the society of the city. They guide the masses and set the tone which determines the intellectual temper of the city, which must be taken into consideration by the *makhzan* and the authorities of the protectorate.'

26 *The Muqaddimah. An Introduction to History*, trans. F. Rosenthal (New York, 1958), I, p. 274.

27 Abbadie, *op. cit.*, p. 18.

28 I do not pretend that the codes of social distance and interpersonal behaviour held no significance. On the contrary, I suspect that had I been able to observe them in the past my analysis would have probed deeper. On the whole, however, I have preferred to let my informants interpret these codes rather than judge on the basis of observations of conduct that I observed in the field in the 1960s.

29 Kinsmen related through their wives or daughters, cl. *nasīb*, pl. *ansibā'*; coll. *nsīb*, pl. *nsāb*. On the colloquial range of meaning for *ṣaḥb* (pl. *ṣḥab*), friend, partisan, patron, etc, *cf.* D. Ferré, *Lexique marocain–français* (Casablanca, n.d.).

30 E. Wolf, 'Kinship, friendship and patron–client relations in complex societies', in M. Banton (ed.), *The Social Anthropology of Complex Societies* (London, 1966), pp. 1–22.

CHAPTER IV, pp. 66–84

1 *I.W.*, p. 33.

2 'Nobles' by virtue of their descent from the Prophet's line through his daughter Faṭīma, her husband, ʿAlī, and their sons Ḥasan and Ḥusayn. *Shurafā'* is used

interchangeably in written Moroccan texts with the more common plural, *ashrāf*. In the dialect the forms are *shrīf*, pl. *shurfa*. On the term and its semantic development *cf.* H. L. Bodman, *Political Factions in Aleppo, 1760–1826,* James Sprunt Studies in History and Political Science, 45 (Chapel Hill, N.C., 1963), pp. 79 ff, and *E.I.*, art. 'Shorfa'.

3 *Les Historiens des chorfa* (Paris, 1922), p. 45; on the three branches of *shurafā'* in Morocco *cf. E.I.*, art. 'Morocco'.

4 The *naqīb* judged all affairs of the ʿAlawi *shurafā'* in the city, for they did not come under the jurisdiction of the qa'id. He also divided among the members of this group the gifts sent to them from the palace.

5 A local anecdote reflects the ambivalence felt towards these personages by the Slawis: an ʿAlawī of Salé went to the sultan every two months to announce the birth of a child. Finally the sultan, noticing the frequency of these visits, greeted his visitor by asking the name of the child whom he had come to announce. The *sharīf*, taken aback and confused, is said to have answered that her name was *kedba* (coll. 'lie'). The sultan was amused and forgave the *sharīf*'s deceit.

6 *ūlād siyyid* is a colloquial term from the classical *awlād sayyid* and in Morocco means 'descendants of a saint'.

7 For the biographies of these saints *cf.* K. Brown, 'An urban view . . .', pp. 35 ff.

8 G. Drague (pseudonym of G. Spillman), *Esquise d'histoire religieuse du Maroc* (Paris, 1951), pp. 87 ff, provides the main source for these questions. C. Geertz discusses this 'makhzan–marabout–zawiya' complex in a general, historical–sociological context in *Islam Observed* (New Haven, Conn., 1969).

9 J. Abun-Nasr, 'The Salafiyya movement in Morocco', *St Anthony's Papers,* No. 16, *Middle Eastern Affairs,* III (London, 1963), attempts to summarise religious developments in the nineteenth century, but this is not his main concern in the article.

10 The expression *ma yidkhl-sh s-sūq* referred in this case to the man's unawareness of the political events surrounding the Berber Dahir of 1930. It also means 'he was not involved in business'; the Sufi expression for someone who has given up the life of meditation is similarly concerned with the market place: *yalḥaq as-sūq*—'let him take up business'; *cf.* S. D. Goitein, 'The rise of the Middle Eastern bourgeoisie in early Islamic times', *Studies in Islamic History and Institutions* (Leiden, 1966), p. 229.

11 *K.I.*, IV, p. 263; *cf. I.A.*, p. 48.

12 Although it has been stressed that the quarter was not a corporate group, there were in a few cases *shurafā'* or *ūlād siyyid* whose role was of special significance in the particular quarters in which they lived. This was the case in regard to al-Qādirī and the Zanāta quarter where his home was.

13 *K.I.*, IV, p. 192; from the root of the Arabic word for knowledge *ʿilm* comes the term *ʿālim* (pl. *ʿulamā'*), a learned man.

14 *Cf.* K. Brown, 'Portrait of a nineteenth-century Moroccan scholar', in N. L. Keddie (ed.), *Sufis, Saints and Scholars* (Berkeley, Cal., 1972).

15 *Ibid.*, and introduction to *K.I.* (Casablanca, 1956) and *A.M.*, XXX (1923), pp. 1–23; *cf.* Lévi-Provençal, *Les Historiens des chorfa*, pp. 350 ff, and Cousté, *op. cit.*, pp. 20 ff.

16 They also claimed what amounts to Prophetic descent as Jaʿfarites through Muḥammad's paternal cousin, ʿAbd Allah b. Jaʿfar, and his granddaughter, Zaynab b. ʿAlī b. Abū Ṭālib.

17 *Cf.* Michaux-Bellaire, 'L'enseignement indigène au Maroc', *R.M.M.*, XV (1911), pp. 422–52; and J. Berque, 'Ville et université: aperçu sur l'histoire de l'école de Fès', *Revue historique de droit français et étranger* (1949), pp. 64–117.

18 Lévi-Provençal, *Les Historiens des chorfa*, p. 352.

19 Berque, 'Ville et université . . .', p. 87.

20 *K.I.* (second edition, Casablanca), I, pp. 11 ff.

21 *Ibid.*
22 *Cf.* Michaux-Bellaire, *R.M.M.*, xv (1911), p. 423.
23 In his words, 'They were not *mizrāgs*'.
24 These public courses or moral sermons (*waʿẓ*), were taught by the leading scholars at various times during the year.
25 *I.W.*, p. 82.
26 *Cf.* Mercier, *A.M.*, VIII (1906), p. 114.
27 *Cf.* Lévi-Provençal, *Les Historiens des chorfa*, pp. 349 ff. The lack of a good scholarly study of the cultural history of Morocco during this period is most unfortunate. Recent important contributions are M. al-Manūnī, *Maẓāhir yaqẓat al-Maghrib al-ḥadīth*, I (Rabat, 1973), E. Burke, 'The political role of the Ulama in Morocco' in Keddie, *op. cit.*, and A. Laroui, *L'Histoire du Maghreb* (Paris, 1970).
28 E.g. a copybook of Ibn ʿAlī (*A.N.R.*, No. 91) which contains mention of books he has read, copies of aphorisms, judicial decisions, letters, biographical information, thoughts, etc. Few of these sources have been studied. References to printed materials are in M. Ben Cheneb and E. Lévi-Provençal, 'Essai de répertoire chronologique des éditions de Fès', *Revue Africaine*, LXII (1921), pp. 158–73, 275–290, and LXIII (1922), pp. 175–85, 333–47, and M. Al-Manūnī, 'al-ṭabaʿat al-ḥajariyyat al-fāsiyya', in *Tiṭwān*, No. 10 (1965), pp. 131–75.
29 The biography is among some papers of Ibn ʿAlī that are in the Kattanī collection of the National Archives, Rabat, No. 1264, ff. 414–15. *Baraka* in this context should be understood as an outward sign of inward qualities of piety, dignity and learning.
30 ʿAbd ar-Raḥmān ʿAwwād, in *al-Īmān*, No. 3 (January 1964), pp. 64–8.
31 Lévi-Provençal, *op. cit.*, although recognising the beginnings of intellectual change in the late nineteenth century (pp. 349 ff), claims quite wrongly that the Moroccan scholar of the 1920s possessed the same corpus of knowledge as his predecessors during the previous 400 years (pp. 10 ff).
32 A Jewish Minister during the reign of Sultan Ismāʿīl.
33 According to some French spokesmen, the goals of French education in the colonies were committed to the *mission civilisatrice* and *assimilation*, 'to educate natives to be Frenchmen' and then absorb them into a 'Greater France', *cf.* Halstead, *op. cit.*, pp. 100 ff. I discuss this in greater detail in chapter XI.
34 *Cf.* J. Damis, 'The Free School movement in Morocco, 1919–70', unpublished Ph.D. thesis, Fletcher School of Law and Diplomacy, 1971. According to the record book of Salé's school (Damis, appendix A, p. 254), it was founded in July 1921 in order to 'renovate Muslim culture'. A group of four men established a committee to administer the school. In the first month 110–20 students from forty-eight families were enrolled. The school was called *al-madrasat al-islamiyyat al-waṭaniyya*, 'the patriotic Islamic school'.
35 Halstead, *op. cit.*, pp. 161 ff, suggests that the schools in Fez founded in 1921 were influenced by Salafiyya reformist ideas. The opening of the school in Salé probably followed the model of Fez's Free Schools, but no mention of Salafiyya ideas was made by my informants. Damis has found that a few notables and teachers involved in Salé's first school may have been influenced by reformist ideas preached by Abū Shuʿayb ad-Dukkālī, then teaching in Rabat.
36 Cousté, *op. cit.*, p. 66.
37 *Cf.* K. Brown, 'The impact of the Dahir Berbère in Salé', in E. Gellner and C. Micaud (eds.), *Arabs and Berbers. From Tribe to Nation in North Africa* (London, 1973).

CHAPTER V, pp. 85–99
1 *The Social Origins of Dictatorship and Democracy* (Boston, Mass., 1966).
2 The metaphor of the *qādūs* was used to represent the community of Salé—people

linked by ties of agnation, affinity, loyalty and friendship—and its commonly shared way of life.

3 For an overview of North African Islam, *cf.* L. Gardet, *La Cité musulmane. Vie sociale et politique* (Paris, 1961); C. Geertz, *Islam Observed* (New Haven, Conn., 1971); E. Westermarck, *Ritual and Belief in Morocco* (London, 1926); and N. Zerdoumi, *Enfants d'hier. Education de l'enfant en milieu traditionnel algerien* (Paris, 1970).

4 The religious tenor of life apparently marked the atmosphere of most or all North African cities. *Cf.* R. Le Tourneau, *Les Villes musulmanes de l'Afrique du Nord* (Algiers, 1957), especially pp. 89 ff. The following interpretative description is essentially based on extensive discussions that I held with old men during my twenty months of field research.

5 The Moroccan tradition forbids a child to express judgements about relatives, or adults in general, by the threat of *sukhṭ* (parental–divine malediction). *Cf.* A. Radi, 'Processus de socialisation de l'enfant marocain', *Études philosophiques et littéraires*, No. 4 (April 1969), Rabat, p. 44.

6 Salé's Great Mosque, it will be remembered, stood in the midst of a residential area, in contrast to most Muslim cities, where it adjoined the bazaar. *Cf.* E. Lévi-Provençal, 'Les villes et les institutions urbaines en Occident musulman au moyen âge, II', in *Conferences sur l'Espagne musulmane* (Cairo, 1951), p. 99.

7 The Muslim year is made up of twelve lunar months. It is eleven or twelve days shorter than the Gregorian solar year, and completes its rounds through the seasons every thirty-three years. For a detailed description of rites and beliefs connected with the Muslim calendar in Morocco see E. Westermarck, *Ritual and Belief in Morocco* (London, 1926), II, especially pp. 58 ff.

8 Ḥusayn's martyrdom at Karbalā' on 10 Muḥarram 61 A.H. (10 October 680) was the crucial event in the formation of the Shīʿa sect of Islam, and has since been a day of mourning by pilgrims to the sacred places of the Shīʿa, marked by the performance of the passion play (*taʿziya*). The first independent Shīʿa principality was founded in Morocco by Idrīs I in 172 A.H./789 A.D. Although there is no evidence of Shīʿa beliefs having taken permanent root in Morocco, celebration of the ʿāshūrā' may represent a remnant of Shīʿa influences. *Cf.* R. Strothmann, 'Shīʿa', in *Shorter Encyclopaedia of Islam* (Ishaca, N.Y.; reprint, n.d.).

9 For a brief summary of the history of this celebration see *E.I.*, art. 'mawlid'.

10 The first *mawlid* for the prophet, celebrated in great pomp as a festival of the people, apparently took place in Arbela, Iraq, early in the thirteenth century. It included a procession of persons bearing wax lights, a public meal for the poor, and religious prayers held in a lodge throughout the night; all these activities are carried out in Salé in honour of its patron saint. For the celebration in Arbela see von Grunebaum, *op. cit.*, pp. 73 ff, and *E.I.*, art. 'mawlid'.

11 *Cf.* V. Loubignac, 'La procession des cièrges à Salé, *Hesp.* XXXIII (1946), pp. 5–30, and note in *Hesp.* XXXV (1948), p. 192.

12 It was said that the corsairs of the seventeenth and eighteenth centuries used to celebrate this procession either before or after their exploits on the seas, and that Sīdī ʿAbd Allah was their particular saint. The procession continues to be held annually in Salé. Part of my description comes from oral tradition, part from observations.

13 People said that 'in principle' seven perambulations were made, just as they are at the Kaʿba.

14 This ritual has been discussed in some detail; *cf.* A. Bel, 'Quelques rites pour obtenir la pluie en temps de sècheresse chez les Musulmans maghrebins', *Recueil de Mémoires et de Textes, XIV Congrès des Orientalistes* (Algiers, 1905), pp. 49–98; Westermarck, *op. cit.*, II, pp. 254 ff, and *Ceremonies and Beliefs connected with*

Agriculture, certain Dates of the Solar Year, and the Weather in Morocco (Helsingfors, 1913), pp. 105 ff; also I. Goldziher, *Muslim Studies*, I (London, 1967), p. 40.

15 Muslims were recommended to fast for three days preceding the prayer and to give alms. The *baraka* of the Jews in bringing rain was thought to be especially effective. A description of the Jewish ritual in Salé is given in *A.A.I.* (M. Ellak, Salé, 13 December 1935). According to this account, the procession of Muslims was led by children, followed by petty merchants, craftsmen, important merchants, landowners, teachers, ulama and *shurafā'*, and finally the pasha and his soldiers, in that hierarchical order. They were followed by the mass of the people, and all were chanting in unison. The Jews also marched together in a separate procession of a similar order.

16 This statement recalls Ibn ʿAlī's account of the visit of some scholars to Sīdī ʿAbd Allah in the late sixteenth century. The saint, seeing the scholars' horror that he should allow the poor to kiss his feet, said to them, 'If it is said that if someone touches your flesh he will not be touched by the fire, how can he not be allowed to approach your flesh . . . ?' (*I.W.*, p. 87.)

17 'The small *laṭīf*' was recited 129 times, to equal the total numerical value of the letters of the word *laṭīf*; 'the grand *laṭif*' 116,487 times (129 × 129 × 7, the days of the week). Other numerical combinations were favoured by various religious orders: the Kattānīs recommended 4,444 recitations, the Darqāwa 70,770, the Tijāniyya 1,000. *Cf.* A. Peretie, 'Les mèdrasas de Fés', *A.M.*, XVIII (1912), p. 326.

18 Informants in Salé said that it was the custom of Muslims to recite the name of God, *al-laṭīf*, during wars, calamities, plagues, drought and flood. Berque mentions that in the sixteenth century, during a war between quarters in Fez, the recitation of a Shadhilī *dhikr* was thought to have given the advantage to one of the warring parties. The greatest scholar of the time had advised this tactic. *Cf.* 'Ville et université', *op. cit.*, p. 85. On the use of the *laṭīf* in the campaign against the Berber Dahir see below, chapter XI.

19 For detailed descriptions of the rites and beliefs connected with the Muslim calendar as practised in various parts of Morocco see E. Westermarck, *Ritual and Belief in Morocco*, chapters XIII–XIV.

20 'Quelques perspectives d'une sociologie de la décolonisation', *Cahiers de Sociologie*, No. 1 (1965), Rabat, pp. 5–12. *Cf.* Zerdoumi, *op. cit.*, pp. 209 ff.

21 *Cf.* J. Plesse, 'Variations de la consommation sous l'influence des coutumes indigènes. L'example d'un ville presque exclusivement musulmane, Salé', *Bull. Econ. du Maroc* (April 1936), p. 158.

22 *Cf.* von Grunebaum, *Medieval Islam*, especially chapter 4, 'The religious foundation: piety'.

23 In gathering material I have been guided by the ethnographic texts in G. Colin, *Chrestomathie marocain* (Paris, 1939), and by C. Le Cœur, 'Les rites de passage d'Azemmour', *Hesp.* XVII (1933), pp. 129–48. Zineb Mikensi tape-recorded for me extensive descriptions by her grandmother of these rites. Zubayr Naciri helped to transcribe, translate and annotate the recorded texts, which I hope to publish separately. The descriptive material has been greatly curtailed in this section, partly because of the excellent and detailed study of Tlemsen by Zerdoumi, *op. cit.*, which appeared subsequently.

24 *Ibid.*, pp. 74 ff.

25 *ez-zwāj u-lmūt hum la yfūt.*

26 *Cf.* the chapter on marriage in R. Le Tourneau, *La Vie quotidienne à Fès en 1900* (Paris, 1965), pp. 195–222, and al-Kattānī, 'al-'usra al-maghribiyya at-taqlīdiyya', *Cahiers de Sociologie*, No. 1 (1965), pp. 13–33.

27 Zerdoumi, *op. cit.*, p. 243, defines *l-qa'ida* as a 'highly elaborate code of *savoir-vivre*'.

28 *katkhurj lhum*, a special term indicating that a married woman shows herself to certain relatives. These terms and other expressions in quotations are from tape-recorded narratives and my translations of them.

29 Zerdoumi, *op. cit.*, pp. 66 ff, emphasises the birth of the first child rather than the establishment of conjugal life as the crucial moment of religious majority. One of the sayings of the prophet, 'When a servant of God marries, verily, he perfects half his religion', is often quoted to emphasise the religious importance of marriage in Islam.

30 *Magic, Science and Religion and other Essays* (Glencoe, Ill., 1948), p. 20.

31 There is a similar practice associated with birth. A. Khatibi evokes this with great force at the beginning of his autobiographical novel: 'I cherish the sacred rite of my birth, a bit of honey placed in my mouth, a drop of lemon juice on my eyes, the first to bring to life my spirit, the second to turn my glance to the world' (*La Mémoire tatouée*, Paris, 1971, p. 9).

32 Some informants mentioned that among certain people these meals had become more elaborate and costly and less modest in tenor since the last decade of the nineteenth century. This would parallel other examples of increased conspicuous consumption at that time.

33 *Cf.* E. Westermarck, *Ritual and Belief in Morocco*, I, pp. 434–560, and Le Tourneau, *La Vie quotidienne à Fès*, pp. 238 ff.

34 *Cf.* I. Goldziher, *Muslim Studies*, I (London, 1967), p. 228, on the incompatibility of wailing, and other manifestations of grief, with resignation to God's will according to the concepts of Islam.

35 Until several decades ago, when musical instruments began to be used to accompany them, the poems were sung simply to the accompaniment of hand clapping.

36 *Cf.* Brunot, *La Mer*, p. 323, for one of the *malḥūns* celebrating a corsair captain of the Two Banks.

37 *Cf.* F. Rahman, *Islam* (Garden City, N.Y., 1966), pp. 117 ff.

38 The definitions and judgements of various types of acts were elaborated at great length by the jurists. *Cf.* J. Schact, *An Introduction to Islamic Law* (Oxford, 1964), pp. 76 ff, 121 ff.

Chapter VI, pp. 100–115

1 E.g. 'Mrs Zubīda Znīber, wife [lit. "sacred possession"] of Mr Ḥājj Muḥammad ash-Shāwī has died [lit. "passed away into God's mercy"]' (*intaqalat ilā raḥmat Allah as-sayyida Ẓubīda Ẓnībar ḥaram as-sayyid H. Muḥammad ash-Shāwī*).

2 Radi, *op. cit.*, p. 41.

3 In the treatment of the condition and roles of women I have drawn from the detailed study of family life in Tlemsen by Zerdoumi, *op. cit.*, that is, to the extent that it corroborated my own admittedly less intimate knowledge of these aspects of Salé.

4 When a child is adopted by someone the same concept is used: *mrbbi*, raised, brought up, educated. *Cf.* 'Education in the family', a text in urban Moroccan Arabic from the notes of L. Brunot in R. S. Harrell, *A Short Reference Grammar of Moroccan Arabic* (Washington, D.C., 1962), p. 252.

5 Zerdoumi, *op. cit.*, p. 159.

6 *Ibid.*, p. 253.

7 *Ibid.*, p. 258.

8 I mean among different social groups, but also—and perhaps more important—between men and women.

9 M. Zeghari, in *Bulletin de l'enseignement public au Maroc*, No. 159 (1938), p. 200, quoted by L. Paye, 'Physionomie de l'enseignement marocain', *Études d'orientalisme dediées à la mémoire de Lévi-Provençal*, II (Paris, 1962), p. 696, n. 5.

10 *Cf.* Radi, *op. cit.*, p. 43.
11 In 1917 there were 700 pupils in *msīds* (*V.T.*, I, 227–8). Age–sex pyramids from the 1960 census place around one-fourth of the Muslim male population between the ages of five and fourteen. If the percentage of boys of that age group was at all similar in 1917—that is, one-fourth of the male population of 9,000—then 700 pupils would have represented almost a third of their number.
12 *I.W.*, p. 22.
13 On the intellectual life of Fez and its university *cf.* R. Le Tourneau, *Fès avant le protectorat* (Casablanca, 1949), pp. 453 ff.
14 *Cf.* p. 34; Massignon, *op. cit.* (1924), p. 142, found that slightly over half of Salé's artisans and merchants admitted affiliation to an order; but, he surmises, the percentage was probably greater, since some of those questioned did not want to indicate their preferences to local authorities. Cousté, *op. cit.* (1925), p. 64, states that almost all important personages followed some order.
15 The term *ṭā'ifa*, which usually means 'faction' or 'sect', was preferred by the Slawis to the more usual *ṭarīqa* (pl. *ṭuruq*), i.e. the 'paths' or orders of Muslim mysticism. For the historial development of mysticism in Islam *cf.* the articles 'ṭarīqa' and 'taṣawwuf' in the *Shorter Encyclopedia of Islam.*
16 The abortive programme and activities of the Kattānīya are discussed by E. Burke, in his 'The Moroccan Ulama, 1860–1912'.
17 *Cf.* Drague (Spillman), *op. cit.*, pp. 87 ff, and Miège, *op. cit.*, III, pp. 139 ff. Lévi-Provençal tends to see this dissension as endemic to the last four centuries of Moroccan history. 'In conclusion, the history of Morocco since the sixteenth century has been no more than a battle by the central power against the religious chiefs.' (*Les Historiens des chorfas*, p. 43.)
18 *K.I.*, I, pp. 63–4. On an-Nāṣirī *cf.* K. Brown, 'Portrait . . .', pp. 227–48.
19 One oral report states that he had violent arguments over the orders with his friend, the qadi Ibn Khaḍrā'. The author's sons mention a manuscript written by their father in 1893 in which he describes in detail the origins, functions and in some cases the 'perverted teachings' of religious orders. Leaders of these orders took offence, wrote to the sultan and slandered the author. However, it is reported that they received no satisfaction because of Nāṣirī's respected position at the court. (*K.I.*, Casablanca, 1954, I, pp. 30–1.)
20 Nāṣirī's ideas bear a striking resemblance to those of the Wahhābī movement.
21 *K.I.*, I, pp. 61–3. In relating the impressions of the doctrine and practices of the Wahhābīs by those who made the pilgrimage to Hijaz in 1812 Nāṣirī gives evidence of his familiarity with and approval of the movement. *Cf. K.I.*, IV, 145–6. For the background of the reformist influences in Morocco *cf.* J. Abun-Nasr, 'The Salafiyya movement in Morocco'.
22 *K.I.*, *loc. cit.*
23 *Cf.* W. C. Smith, *Islam in Modern History* (New York, 1959).
24 E. Gellner, 'Doctor and saint', in Keddie, *op. cit.*, p. 309.

Part III

1 Miège, *op. cit.*, III, p. 75.

Chapter VII, pp. 119–28

2 Commerce with Europeans was forbidden by the sultan, except in those ports, and only Jewish merchants were allowed to travel to Europe. *Cf.* E. Lévé and M. Fournel (eds.), *Les Traités du Maroc*, I (Paris, 1864), p. 505.
3 *I.W.*, pp. 23 ff; Naciri, *op. cit.*, pp. 64 ff. Tobacco was apparently also grown in Salé in the early years of the century. There was a special type called 'Slawi' and

the best of it was exported to Gibraltar. *Cf.* H. Zafrani, *Les Juifs du Maroc* (Paris, 1972).

4 *Cf.* J-L. Miège, 'Coton et cotonnades au Maroc au XIXe siècle', *Hesp.* XLVII (1959), pp. 219–38.

5 On the separation of crafts and trade and the role of public auctions *cf.* Le Tourneau. *Fès avant le protectorat*, pp. 306 ff.

6 *ahl Salā mukaffanūn fī ḥayātihim, I.W.*, pp. 26–7. Ibn ʿAlī uses the term *ṭarrāzāt* (normally *darrāza*) for weavers. These may have included weavers of wool as well. *Cf.* Le Tourneau, *Fès avant le protectorat*, p. 348.

7 *Cf.* Miège, *loc. cit.*, especially pp. 225 ff, and E. Burke, 'Proto-industrialisation and pre-colonialism in the Maghrib in the eighteenth and nineteenth centuries' (forthcoming).

8 *Cf.* A. Laroui, *L'Histoire du Maghreb* (Paris, 1970), p. 297. and J. Abun-Nasr, *A History of the Maghrib* (Cambridge, 1971), p. 284 ff.

9 Miège, *Le Maroc et l'Europe*, II, pp. 540 ff.

10 *I.W.*, p. 73.

11 Miège, *loc. cit.*, II, pp. 261 ff.

12 For the early effects of urbanisation throughout Morocco see Miège, *op. cit.*, III, pp. 23 ff. For Salé's growth see above, chapter II.

13 Miège, *loc. cit.*, II, p. 503; *K.I.*, IV, p. 254.

14 Miège, *op. cit.*, III, pp. 149 ff.

15 *Cf.* Miège, *loc. cit.*, III, pp. 235 ff.

16 *K.I.*, IV, p. 232.

17 Miège, *op. cit.*, III, pp. 382 ff.

18 In the works of Brignon *et al.*, Laroui and Abun-Nasr.

19 *Cf.* E. Michaux-Bellaire, 'Les crises monétaires au Maroc', *R.M.M.*, XXXVIII (1920), pp. 41–57, and G. Ayache, 'Aspects de la crise financière au Maroc'; Miège, *op. cit.*, III, pp. 97 ff; *A.M.*, X (1907), p. 359.

20 I have arrived at these approximate rates of exchange by comparing figures given in the sources cited above with those provided by Le Tourneau, *op. cit.*, p. 282, Nāṣirī, IV, p. 278, and 'Hay à Clarendon, Tangier, 27 Septembre 1869', quoted in Miège, *Documents d'histoire du Maroc* (Paris, 1969), p. 123.

21 Miège, *loc. cit.*, III, p. 464.

22 The material in the Conservation Foncière and information from informants bear out Miège's general conclusions on the consequences of the crisis (*op. cit.*, III, pp. 441 ff). During the years of economic crisis property changed hands often and at low purchase prices. With the crisis of the late 1860s the names of certain Slawis begin to appear on land deeds as proprietors with increasing regularity.

23 *I.W.*, pp. 26, 28.

24 Miège, *op. cit.*, IV, p. 391.

25 Concerning the choice of Rabat, mainly because of strategic considerations, see J. Caillé, *Le Ville de Rabat*, I, pp. 553 ff, and S. Dethier, in L. C. Brown (ed.), *From Madina to Metropolis. Heritage and Change in the Near Eastern City* (Princeton, N.J., 1973).

26 *Cf.* Naciri, *op. cit.*, *p.* 18.

27 Abbadie, *op. cit.*, p. 31.

28 It is difficult to know when the depression began. In all of Morocco, according to the sources, the first symptoms appeared in 1929, when unfavourable climatic conditions in the agricultural areas combined with external market factors; *cf.* J. Jouannet, *L'evolution de la fiscalité marocaine*, III (Paris, 1953), p. 119. Berque, on the other hand, notes the signs of a ten-year depression appearing in 1925 (*Le Maghreb entre les deux guerres*, Paris, 1962, p. 232).

29 Jouannet, *loc. cit.*, p. 47.

30 *Cf.* Jouannet, *op. cit.*, p. 140, and C. F. Stewart, *The Economy of Morocco, 1912–62* (Cambridge, Mass., 1964), pp. 66 ff.

CHAPTER VIII, pp. 129–54

1 The main sources of information for this section are: J. Caillé, 'Les industries de Rabat et Salé au milieu du XIX ciècles', in *La Petite Histoire de Rabat*, pp. 193–6 (based on the 1856 report of the dragoman of the French vice-consul at Rabat) and *La Ville de Rabat jusqu'au protectorat français*, I, p. 439 (notes from the French consul, Beaumier, for 1858); J. L. Miège, 'Documents inédits sur l'artisanat de Rabat et Salé au milieu du XIX siècle', *Bulletin économique et social du Maroc*, XXIII (October 1959), pp. 173–82 (reports of the Spanish vice-consul at Rabat in 1864 and the Wooldridge report of 1872); *V.T.*, II, p. 95; *I.W.*, pp. 28 ff (a catalogue of crafts at which Slawis excelled); *Rapports commerciaux*, pp. 4 ff (for 1912); de Périgny, *op. cit.*, pp. 120–1 (1914): Massignon, *Enquête sur les corporations musulmanes d'artisans et de commerçants au Maroc* (Paris, 1925), pp. 26 ff.

2 *Cf.* A. Hardy, 'Les Babouchiers de Salé', *Bull. Econ. du Maroc*, V (1938), p. 257.

3 It is difficult to believe that the pottery industry died completely. In the 1960s there were several important factories in Oulja, the area of alluvium alongside the Bou Regreg river.

4 de Périgny, *op. cit.*, p. 120.

5 *Cf. Hesp.* V (1925), pp. 119–22, and *A.M.* XV (1911), pp. 131–40. A photo taken several years ago, which is on the wall of one of Salé's most prosperous mat makers, shows him with King Hasan, presenting mats woven in Salé to President Senghor in the Great Mosque of Dakar.

6 Not only buildings were involved. Thus some master carpenters from Salé were experts at building and repairing boats. A letter dated 5 January 1852 to the sultan gives the opinion of master carpenters of Salé on the practicability of repairing some ships in Tangier which they had been sent to look over. (*P.A.*, dossier 'Finances', Affaires étrangères.)

7 The thick carpet (*ar-raqam* or *az-zirbiyya 'r-ribāṭiyya*) was named after Rabat, while the thinner striped rug (*al-ḥanbal as-salāwī*) took its name from Salé. In fact both were primarily products of Salé.

8 *Cf.* Miège, in *Bull. Econ. et Soc. du Maroc*, XXIII (1959), *op. cit.*

9 The number of working days per year may have been much smaller. For workers in Fez Le Tourneau estimates only 200 working days a year (*Fès avant le protectorate*, p. 363). Of course, workers may have had more than one job or source of income.

10 *Cf.* J-P. Busson, 'Frédèric Le Play et l'étude du niveau de vie d'une famille d'artisan marocain il y a un siècle', *Bull. Econ. et Soc. du Maroc*, XVII, No. 59 (1953), pp. 71–83.

11 *Cf. R.M.M.* (1924), *op. cit.*, p. 88.

12 I have not been able to determine the value of '100 Ḥasani' at the turn of the century.

13 R. Brown, introduction to *The Travels of Thomas Pellow*, p. 43.

14 Abbadie, *op. cit.*, p. 10.

15 A. H. Hourani and S. M. Stern (eds.), *The Islamic City. A Colloquium* (Oxford, 1970), pp. 12–14.

16 The case is reported in the responses of Aḥmad al-Wansharīsī (d. 1508), entitled *al-Miʿyār*, translated in *A.M.*, XII (1908), pp. 490 ff.

17 During my field research a policeman in Salé came through the Bazaar one day demanding that the cloth dealers remove their goods from in front of their shops because they were blocking the passage. The merchants as a group—but under the instigation of some of the more 'hot-blooded'—spontaneously closed their

shops and went off to protest to the Pasha of the city. This was cited to me as an example of corporate action by a 'guild'.

18 Massignon, *op. cit.*, p. 126.

19 The *hadiyya* was the only direct tax paid in the city, apart from the religious obligations of *zakāt* and *ʿashūr*. The people of the city also used the term *frīda* (contribution) to designate the amount of money incumbent on each individual towards the *hadiyya*, or any other collection. In the countryside the *frīda* meant an arbitrary imposition levied on the rural population by the government whenever it was short of money, and it had there replaced the regular *zakāt* and *ʿashūr* taxes. *Cf.* Mercier, 'L'administration marocaine à Rabat', *A.M.*, VII (1907), p. 353, and Michaux-Bellaire, 'Les impots marocains', *A.M.*, I (1904), pp. 59–96.

20 Distinguished by the article *l-* from the customs administrator (*amīn*).

21 Massignon, *op. cit.*, p. 218. The surety is dated 1925.

22 *Ibid.*

23 *Ibid.*, pp. 122 ff.

24 Le Tourneau also finds the guilds and the office of *muḥtasib* of little importance in Fez at the turn of the century. His suggestion that their existence, however, maintained equilibrium in the life of the city as a 'force of inertia' would not, it seems to me, hold true for Salé. *Cf. Fès avant le protectorat*, pp. 291 ff, for a detailed description of the organisation of economic life in Fez. For Islamic Spain *cf.* P. Chalmata, *El señor del zoco en España* (Madrid, 1973).

25 M. Weber, *Basic Concepts of Sociology*, second edition (New York, 1963), p. 107.

26 *Cf.* Massignon, *op. cit.*, pp. 27–31, where the Moroccan Arabic terms are given. Informants were asked to evaluate the importance of each craft in relation to other crafts. I interviewed many old craftsmen and merchants, but most of the information used here came from an old itinerant merchant who, because of blindness and enforced idleness, agreed to discuss these matters in great detail.

27 In Fez 164 occupations are listed for the same year. *Cf.* Massignon, *op. cit.*, p. 12.

28 Jewish women who sold clothes, and thus had access to most homes, also served as sources of information about the qualities of young marriageable girls.

29 Sīdī Maḍlūm was a butcher; Sīdī Aḥmad Ḥajjī was a humble weaver according to one biography, a pirate captain and merchant according to another.

30 The barbers, too, are usually present, and prepare and serve tea.

31 Massignon, *op. cit.*, pp. 55 ff. The list includes fifty-five of the previously discussed ninety-three crafts, and accounts for 1,279 of the 1,800 people considered there.

CHAPTER IX, pp. 155–74

1 This was the only competition to the Slawis' monopoly of cloth goods; when the Jews did not come to the markets the Slawis could raise their prices.

2 *I.W.*, p. 10.

3 C. Le Cœur, *Le Rite et l'outil* (Paris, 1941), pp. 135 ff, 150.

4 For information on these interrelationships in the port cities during the nineteenth century *cf.* Miège, II, pp. 560 ff.

5 Naciri, *op. cit.*, p. 26.

6 Abbadie, *op. cit.*, p. 47.

7 A *ẓahīr* (pronounced in Morocco as *ḍahīr* and written in French sources as *dahir*) was a decree emanating from the sultan which accorded some favour or honour to its recipient, such as government property, the revenues of a *zāwiya*, exemption from duties or taxes; it was the equivalent to the Persian *firman*. The favours stipulated by the decree applied only to the beneficiary, unless they were explicitly hereditary. Often, however, at the death of the beneficiary the heirs had the decree renewed. *Cf.* E. Michaux-Bellaire and G. Salmon, in *A.M.*, II (1904), p. 1.

8 The decree is in the 'Sāsī collection', *A.G.R.*, and is reproduced in fig. 14.

9 If a man served for many years in another city he tended to take an additional wife or a concubine from that city. These women and their children would be incorporated into the original family household in Salé when the individual concerned returned home.

10 This passage was called to my attention by ʿAbd as-Salām b. Sūda. *Cf.* 'Kattānī collection', No. 1246, *A.G.R.*

11 *I.W.*, pp. 30–1.

12 *K.I.*, IV, pp. 161–2, and for other examples see pp. 170, 176.

13 In ʿAbd ar-Raḥmān b. Zīdān, *op. cit.*, V, pp. 110–11.

14 'Muḥammad b. Muḥammad ʿAwwād to al-ʿArabī b. al-Mukhṭār al-Jāmʿi (28 Safar 1265 A.H.)', in the palace archives, Rabat.

15 Le Tourneau, *Fès avant le protecorat*, pp. 482 ff, alludes to the new wealth of the nineteenth century. In personal communications with Fasis this point was repeatedly mentioned.

16 *Cf.* Aubin, *Le Maroc d'aujourd'hui* (Paris, 1904), pp. 209, 247 ff; Miège, *op. cit.*, III, pp. 124–5; and M. Lahbabi, *Le Government morocain à l'aube du XXe siècle* (Rabat, 1958), p. 158.

17 The last named studied in the Qarawiyyin University in Fez and taught in Salé, where until his death in 1969 he was reputed to be an excellent teacher of astrology.

18 ʿAwwād had been the chief (*l-amīn*) of Salé's bazaar and was administrator of pious endowments at the same time as his governorship.

19 *I.A.*, p. 101.

20 at-Taghrāwī was from the Banū Ḥasan, in the countryside near Salé. He had studied in the Qarawiyyin in Fez and had long been a respected *muftī* in the city. The French appointed him qadi despite the opposition of the local notables.

21 *K.I.*, IV, pp. 237, 248.

22 G. Beauclerk, *Journey to Morocco* (London, 1828), pp. 89 ff.

23 The Moroccan court was in fact disturbed by the lack of refinement among European officials. The qa'id of Salé, Muḥammad b. Saʿīd, participated in a delegation to Paris (1282 A.H./1865) to press the French into sending representatives to Morocco who would distinguish themselves, in contrast to their predecessors, by moderation, good conduct and reserve. (*K.I.*, IV, p. 229.)

24 *Cf.* Aubin, *op. cit.*, p. 234.

25 Abbadie, *op. cit.*, pp. 35, 128, 134.

26 G. Jeannot, *Étude sociale, politique et économique sur le Maroc* (Dijon, 1907), pp. 120 ff, following A. Chevrillon, *Un Crepuscule d'Islam* (Paris, 1906), pp. 195–6. From these ideas to the 'Berber policy' of the first decades of the protectorate was a natural step; *cf.* J. Halstead, *Rebirth of a Nation. The Origins and Rise of Moroccan Nationalism, 1912–44* (Cambridge, 1967), pp. 68 ff.

27 *I.W.*, p. 57.

28 *la bā's* is one of those evocative Moroccan expressions used often and in various ways. Literally it means 'There is no harm' or 'Nothing is wrong'. Thus it is the typical response to the most common greeting and question, 'What's new?' (*ash-khbārik*), i.e. 'All's well'.

29 The figure is a loose approximation based on lists of men known to have been living in Salé around the turn of the century. A. Nouschi, in an article on the city of Constantine on the eve of the French conquest of Algeria in 1830, guesses that there were some 1,000 Muslim families there of above-average economic situation, out of a total population of some 25,000; some 20 per cent of the population. Their wealth, he writes, came from their administrative function, land or commerce. Privileges of wealth coexisted with those of birth. He believes that a major

part of the population was well off, 'bien nantie'. *Cf.* 'Constantine à le veille de la conquête', *Les Cahiers de Tunisie,* No. 11 (1955), p. 363.

30 Cousté, *op. cit.*, p. 11.

Part IV

1 *The Historian's Crafts* (New York, 1953), p. 151.

Chapter X, pp. 176–92

2 *K.I.*, iv, p. 217.

3 *Cf.* Miège, *op. cit.*, ii, especially pp. 203 ff, and J. Brignon *et al.*, *op. cit.*, pp. 284 ff.

4 The uncatalogued and undated letter is in the Palace archives, Rabat.

5 Miège, *op. cit.*, ii, pp. 214 ff.

6 *Id.*; *K.I.*, iv, 201.

7 Caillé, *op. cit.*, pp. 182–5.

8 *Id.*; *K.I.*, iv, pp. 201 ff; *I.W.*, p. 14.

9 J. Caillé, *Charles Jagerschmidt, Chargé d'Affaires de France au Maroc, 1820–94* (Paris, n.d.), p. 98.

10 The Rabatis did not enter the fray. This was one of the explanations later given for the traditional enmity of the Slawis towards Rabatis.

11 Caillé, *loc. cit.*; see also a *résumé* of a letter from the consul of France to Mawlāy ʿAbd ar-Raḥmān in the Palace archives, Rabat (Affaires étrangères, No. 9, 'Bombardments'), which gives the sultan the opportunity to feign ignorance by accusing his vizier in Tangier of having kept him ignorant of the affair.

12 H. Desprez, 'Maroc. Le bombardement de Salé', *Revue de l'Orient, de l'Algerie et des colonies*, xiii (Paris, 1853), pp. 5–17.

13 Palace archives, *cit.*

14 *Ibid.*

15 For the original poem and a French translation *cf.* C. Sonneck, *Chants arabes du Maghreb* (Paris, 1904), i, p. 145; ii, p. 245.

16 *K.I.*, iv, p. 279. These are the plaintive words with which Nāṣirī ends his history. The verse is from the *muʿallaqa* of Zubayr, a pre-Islamic poet.

17 *Cf.* Miège, *Le Maroc et l'Europe*, ii, p. 470, n. 3, and *K.I.*, iv, p. 255.

18 aṭ-Ṭahṭāwī (d. 1873) was one of the students sent to Paris by Muḥammad ʿAlī in 1826. He remained there five years and immersed himself in French culture. The description of his voyage, *Takhlīṣ al-ibriz ilā talkhīṣ Barīz*, was published shortly after his return to Egypt in 1831. For an evaluation of Ṭahṭāwī's role in the development of modern Arabic thought and his criticism of French positivism in the light of Islamic principles see A. Hourani, *Arabic Thought in the Liberal Age, 1798–1939* (London, 1962), pp. 69 ff, 82.

19 *K.I.*, iii, pp. 93 ff, and *A.M.*, xxxiv (1936), p. 333, n. 1.

20 *K.I.*, iv, p. 217.

21 His reading list includes the *k. al-iktifā'* by a thirteenth-century qadi of Valencia, Abū al-Rabīʿ al-Kulā'ī (*cf. G.A.L.*, i, p. 458), *Faḍā'il al-jihād* by Ibn Naḥḥās, a fifteenth-century jurist (*G.A.L.*, ii, p. 92), and the *Sirāj al-muluk* by aṭ-Ṭurṭūshī (d. 1131) (*G.A.L.*, i, p. 601 and supplement i, p. 829).

22 *K.I.*, iv, p. 222.

23 Miège, *op. cit.*, ii, pp. 401 ff, 549 ff, 560 ff; see also iii, p. 262 ff.

24 They did form the majority of Spanish protégés at that time. According to the unofficial estimates of Sir John Hay, Britain's chargé d'affaires, there were approximately 8,000 protégés in Morocco in the late 1870s. Of these 1,500 were Jews, either naturalised Europeans or protégés. *Cf.* L. Bowie, 'The protégé

system in Morocco, 1880–1904', unpublished Ph.D. dissertation, University of Michigan, 1970, pp. 10–11, 28, 235.

25 *K.I.*, IV, p. 227. A full treatment of Montefiore's mission, its causes and results, may be found in Miège, II, p. 564.

26 His view echoes the position of some of the classical Muslim philosophers; *cf.* F. Rosenthal, *The Muslim Concept of Freedom* (Leiden, 1960), p. 99, regarding Ibn Rushd's commentary on Plato's *Republic*, and *E.I.*, second edition, art. 'Ḥurriyya', by F. Rosenthal and B. Lewis.

27 *K.I.*, IV, pp. 227–8.

28 *Ibid.*, pp. 265–70. It is clear from the sultan's letter that he expected legal reasoning that would support concessions to the Europeans.

29 *Ibid.*, pp. 266–8.

30 *Ibid.*

31 *Ibid.*

32 *Ibid.*, p. 270. Nāṣirī's attention appears to be riveted on the coastal areas and urban populations, without consideration of the possibilities of fighting a defensive war in the interior of the country.

33 Some Slawis who had participated in government delegations to Paris were more sophisticated, but curiosity about or admiration for Europe appear to have been almost totally lacking before the advent of the protectorate. Little research has been done on 'the Moroccan rediscovery of Europe'. Interesting material appears in Muḥammad al-Manūnī, 'Maẓāhir yaqẓat al-Maghrib al-ḥadīth', *al-Baḥth al-ʿilmī*, No. 9 (1966), pp. 1–48.

34 *I.A.*, p. 28.

35 He died in 1946; for his biography see K. Brown in *Hespéris-Tamuda*, pp. 84 ff.

36 *I.W.*, p. 34.

37 *Ibid.*

38 'Les marocains et la société marocaine', *Revue Générale des Sciences*, XIV (1903), p. 377.

39 On this entangled period of diplomatic and internal crisis *cf.* Roberts, *op. cit.*, pp. 549 ff, and Brignon *et al.*, *op. cit.*, pp. 322 ff.

40 On al-Kattānī *cf.* E. Burke, 'The Moroccan ulama, 1860–1912'.

41 *Cf.* René-Leclerc, in *Afrique Française* (1907), pp. 332–3.

42 *Cf. V.T.*, III, pp. 111–14, and Caillé, *La Petite Histoire de Rabat*, p. 206.

43 According to one source the leaders of the opposition in Salé were sympathisers with Germany. They are said to have written to the German consul in Casablanca in 1911, requesting German intervention against the French.

44 *I.A.*, pp. 85–6. A copy of the original text may be found in fig. 12.

CHAPTER XI, pp. 193–206

1 P. Odinot, a French soldier and novelist with long experience in Morocco, in *La Première Communion d'Abd el-Kader* (Paris, 1927), quoted in *Renseignements Coloniaux*, XXXVIII (1928), p. 786.

2 al-Faqīh Muḥammad at-Tiṭwanī, an old and respected Slawi scholar, during an interview in May 1966.

3 According to one informant, ʿAbd Allah had already been expelled earlier, in 1916. On the day he left Salé every shop in the city is said to have closed down. al-Ḥājj ʿAlī ʿAwwād exhorted the people of the city to take up arms against the French. The protectorate authorities threatened to intervene, at which point the pasha succeeded in quietening the population.

4 From a report by the Contrôleur Civil of Salé, Abbadie, *op. cit.*, p. 69.

5 *Ibid.*, pp. 19, 23–4. Abbadie did not mean to justify opposition to the taxes, for he

goes on to say that the population had simply forgotten the former arbitrary taxes and the anarchy that had reigned in the countryside, on the one hand, and that they resented their inability to continue to practise fraud by cheating the government, on the other.

6 In 1920 there were 2,387 Moroccan Muslims out of a school population of about 20,000 in French schools. The 1921 budget set aside less than three million francs for Muslim education and over nine million francs for the education of Europeans. (Damis, *op. cit.*, pp. 30–1.)

7 *Ibid.*, appendix E, pp. 259–60. The first free school in Salé had an enrolment of 110–20; no figures are available for the other schools.

8 *Ibid.*, pp. 82–3.

9 Nonetheless many students in the French school continued to study part-time in the free schools to supplement their education in Arabic and religious subjects.

10 This was emphatically stressed by those whom I interviewed, whether they actively participated in the nationalist cause or not.

11 Damis, *op. cit.*, pp. 272 ff, argues that the 'free schools' provided a cultural dimension for Moroccan nationalism.

12 *Cf.* Michaux-Bellaire, 'Le Wahhabisme au Maroc', *Renseignements coloniaux*, XXXVIII (1928), p. 489, and K. Brown, 'Resistence et nationalisme au Maroc', in *Colloque international d'études historiques et socioloques* (Paris, forthcoming).

13 Idrīs b. Saʿīd is said to have been a man of strong nationalist feelings and to have exerted a decisive influence on ʿAbd al-Karīm's political ideas. He appears to have been murdered by Spanish extremists. *Cf.* D. S. Woolman, *Rebels in the Rif* (Stanford, Cal., 1968), pp. 77, 113.

14 Commandant Tarrit, *La Direction générale des affaires indigènes du Maroc. Cours preparatoire au Service des A.I. Conference faite, le 24 Janvier 1928 à Rabat* (Casablanca, 1928), p. 22. Michaux-Bellaire, the director of the Section Sociologique, lived in Salé *à la marocaine* until his death in 1930. He had written on Moroccan affairs since before the turn of the century. For his biography and an evaluation of his work *cf.* R. Gerofi in *Tinga*, No. 1 (1953), pp. 79–85, and A. Khatibi, *Bilan de la sociologie au Maroc* (Rabat, 1967), pp. 13–14.

15 This information comes from interviews with Ashamaʿū, Aḥmad Maʿanīnū, Abū Bakr aṣ-Subīhī, ʿAbd al-Karīm Ḥajjī and ʿAbd as-Salām ʿAwwād; *cf.* Abbadie, *op. cit.*, p. 34.

16 It should be emphasised that participants in the early phase of political nationalism have personal, sometimes contradictory, versions of events and purposes. The subsequent experiences of some people have given them axes to grind. Unable to locate copies of the early numbers of *al-Widād*, I have had to rely on personal accounts in an attempt to form an idea of their content. The development of the press in Morocco deserves a full study based on the documentation itself. Halstead, also on the basis of interviews, mentions similar journalistic activities in other cities in which reformist and nationalist ideas were predominant. (*Op. cit.*, p. 55.)

17 The association was formed on the model of existing groups in Fez and Rabat.

18 There is no serious study of the Moroccan theatre to compare with A. Roth, *Le Théâtre algérien* (Paris, 1967). The information included comes from interviews and from Abdallah Chakroun, who kindly showed me an unpublished paper written by him in 1963 and entitled 'Origines et aspects du théâtre arabe au Maroc'.

19 Informants stated that the historic enmity between Slawis and Rabatis had created mutual mistrust and misunderstandings that were only slowly overcome. The leaders of the associations of the two cities began their contacts in the late 1920s by formal visits to each others' homes on the occasions of the Muslim holidays. Later they decided to demonstrate their unity by the public display of brotherhood following the performance of the Slawis' play.

20 Abbadie, *op. cit.*, pp. 36–40.

21 For a detailed account of the reaction *cf.* K. Brown, 'The impact of the Dahir Berbère in Salé', *op. cit.*, pp. 201–15.

22 *Cf.* E. Burke, 'The image of the Moroccan State in French ethnological literature: a new look at the origin of Lyautey's Berber policy', pp. 175–200.

23 *Cf.* R. Le Tourneau, *Evolution politique de l'Afrique du Nord musulmane* (Paris, 1962), p. 182, and Halstead, *op. cit.*, pp. 32, 69 ff.

24 A full discussion of the campaign against the Berber Dahir and its importance for Moroccan nationalism may be found in ʿAllāl al-Fāsī, *al-ḥarakāt al-istiqlāliyyat fī 'l-maghrib al ʿarabī* (Cairo, 1948), pp. 161–5; Le Tourreau, *op. cit.*, pp. 185 ff; Halstead, *op. cit.*, pp. 182 ff; Montagne, *Revolution au Maroc* (Paris, 1953), pp. 187 ff; Berque, *Le Maghreb entre les deux guerres*, pp. 230 ff; and C. A. Julien, *L'Afrique du Nord en marche* (Paris, 1952), pp. 176 ff.

25 These are the terms which my informants attributed to aṣ-Ṣubīḥī. Apparently the older people were suspicious of arguments about Morocco's territorial integrity because of associations with Ataturk's Turkish nationalism and its inherent secularism. *Cf.* ʿAbd al-Karīm Ḥajjī, in *al-ʿAlam* (2 April 1967). aṣ-Ṣubīḥī seems to have changed his tactics after a trip to Fez and discussions there.

26 For a discussion of this prayer and Sufi invocations see chapter v and K. Brown, 'The impact of the Dahir Berbère...'.

27 According to the account of Aḥmad Maʿanīnū, in a tape-recorded interview in Salé in June 1966.

28 *Allahumma ya laṭīf nas'aluka 'l-luṭf fīmā jarat bihi 'l-maqādir walā tufarriq bainanā wa-baina ikhwāninā 'l-barābir.*

29 To some extent nationalism effaced local patriotism, and participants from Salé became part of the national elite. Yet there remains in Morocco a clear recognition of the primary position of Fez and Rabat in the nationalist movement and in the political parties. Thus, perhaps as a reaction, the Slawis lay claim to the *laṭīf.* They also vaunted the former pasha, al-Ḥājj Muḥammed aṣ-Ṣubīḥī, one of the four members of the Throne Council that paved the way for the return from exile of King Muḥammed V in 1955. Other Slawis who achieved important influence were Būbkar al-Qādirī who became and remains one of the leaders of the Istiqlāl party, al-Ḥājj Muḥammed Maʿanīnū, who has occupied a similar position in the PSI, and ʿAbd ar-Raḥīm Būʿabīd, who has long played a leading political role, first in the Istiqlāl and then in the UNFP.

30 For a similar argument *cf.* M. Gluckman, *Analysis of a Social Situation in Modern Zululand*, Rhodes–Livingstone Papers, No. 28 (Manchester, 1958), pp. 44 ff.

31 The complexity and ambiguity of these responses are discussed by Berque in *Le Maghreb entre deux guerres*, pp. 77 ff. *Cf.* E. Kedourie, *Nationalism* (New York, 1960), p. 160, and L. Binder, *The Ideological Revolution in the Middle East* (New York, 1964), p. 2.

CONCLUSIONS, pp. 207–24

1 A. Laroui, *L'Histoire du Maghreb. Un essai de synthèse* (Paris, 1970), p. 346.

2 E. Aubin, *Le Maroc d'aujourd'hui* (Paris, 1904). From the English translation, *Morocco of Today* (London, 1906).

3 *ahl-al-bādiyya*, lit. 'people of the plain', or coll. *laʿrubiyya*, 'the countryside', 'the peasants'. Both these terms when used by urbanites imply primitiveness. A similar distinction existed in Ottoman society, where the concept for city dwelling or civilisation was *medeniyet* (from the Arabic *madīna*, 'city'), while by contrast the term 'Turk' was pejorative and meant 'tribal'. *Cf.* S. Mardin, 'Power, civil society and culture in the Ottoman Empire', *Comparative Studies in Society and History*, XI (1969), pp. 270 ff.

4 *Cf.* D. M. Hart, 'The tribe in modern Morocco. Two case studies', in Gellner and Micaud (eds.), *op. cit.*, pp. 26 ff.

5 Aubin, *op. cit.* (English edition), pp. 140 ff.; a good summary of the State organisation is in J. Waterbury *The Commander of the Faithful* (New York, 1970), especially chapter I, 'The Makhzan: a stable system of violence', pp. 15 ff.

6 *Ibid.*, p. 157.

7 The concept of *Makhzan* (cl. *makhzan*, the source of our *magazine*) retained its original meaning of 'storehouse', i.e. a permanent reserve of money, arms, munitions, supplies and provisions. *Cf.* The article in *E.I.* and R. Montaigne, *Les Berbères et le makhzen dans le sud du Maroc* (Paris, 1930), p. 366.

8 Fās al-Jadīd was founded in the thirteenth century, over 500 years after the *madīna*: 'jusqu'à nos jours elle n'a cesse d'être une cité-makhzan, une ville d'étrangers'. (Le Tourneau, *Fès avant le protecorat*, Casablanca, 1949, pp. 93 ff.)

9 The correspondence to Salé's governor from officials serving in other cities shows that they served as intermediaries with the tribes. Networks of ulama from the *ḥaḍāra* cities also served to maintain a cultural unity in the country.

10 I have discussed the term *sība* (cl. *sā'iba*) as 'dissidence' and 'upheaval' in another context in chapter II.

11 *Saints of the Atlas* (Chicago, 1969), pp. 3, 4.

12 *Cf.* M. Weber, *The Theory of Social and Economic Organisation* (Glencoe, Ill., 1964), pp. 62, 347 ff; R. Bendix, *Max Weber. An Intellectual Portrait* (Garden City, N.Y., 1962), pp. 294 ff, 340, 365; B. Turner, *Weber and Islam* (London, 1974), p. 75.

13 M. Weber, *The City*, trans. and ed. D. Martindale and G. Neuwirth (New York, 1962), pp. 80–1, 103, and Turner, *loc. cit.*, pp. 2, 97 ff.

14 *Cf.* chapter I, 'The geographical mark of Islam: the city', in his *The World of Islam* (New York, 1959).

15 *Cf.* chapter VII, 'The structure of the Muslim town', in his *Islam. Essays in the Nature and Growth of a Cultural Tradition* (New York, 1961).

16 *Cf.* M. Weber, *Economy and Society. An outline of Interpretive Sociology*, ed. G. Roth and C. Wittich (New York, 1968), II, p. 1227, and, for Spengler, H. A. R. Gibb and H. Bowen, *Islamic Society and the West*, I, part I (London, 1950), p. 7.

17 *Cf. Muslim Cities in the Later Middle Ages* (Cambridge, Mass., 1967).

18 *Cf.* E. Lévi-Provençal, chapter VI, 'Les villes et les institutions urbaines en Occident musulman', in *Conferences sur l'Espagne musulmane* (Cairo, 1951), pp. 99 ff.

19 A slightly different formulation from saying that Islamic civilisation, like most civilisations, is predominantly urban. *Cf.* S. M. Stern, 'The constitution of the Islamic city', in A. Hourani and S. M. Stern (eds.), *The Islamic City. A Colloquium* (Oxford, 1970), p. 25.

20 These terms as used in Morocco closely resemble the distinctions made by Ibn Khaldun in the fourteenth century. Primitive societies are those in which men concentrate on satisfying limited and necessary needs. *Cf.* M. Mahdi, *Ibn Khaldun's Philosophy of History* (Chicago, 1964), pp. 184, 193. In English there is a remnant of a similar Latin distinction: 'brute' is a synonym of 'uncivilised', i.e. etymologically 'not living in a city'.

21 *Cf.* S. F. Nadel, *A Black Byzantium. The Kingdom of the Nupe in Nigeria* (London, 1942), p. 17.

22 Restated for the Muslim West in R. Le Tourneau, *Les Villes musulmans de l'Afrique du Nord* (Algiers, 1957), p. 11.

23 *Cf.* I. M. Lapidus, 'The evolution of Muslim urban society', *Comparative Studies in Society and History*, XV (1973), p. 47. Lapidus also emphasises the disunity of urban society, and stresses political and social processes more than cultural ones. I discuss these matters presently.

24 There were two Friday mosques in Salé until a third was opened after 1912. The

congregations of these mosques differed, and the differences may have reflected social factors. In other Muslim cities important socio-economic, ethnic or territorial divisions within society were expressed in the attendance of individuals at particular mosques. *Cf.* J. Paden, *Religion and Political Culture in Kano* (Berkeley, Cal., 1973), pp. 48 ff. The crucial importance of the Friday mosque appears in most writings about the Muslim town. *Cf.* W. Marçais, 'L'Islamisme et la vie urbaine', in his *Articles et conferences* (Paris, 1961), p. 66, and his 'La conception des villes dans l'Islam', *Revue d'Alger*, II (1945), pp. 525 ff.

25 Including legendary country folk who regularly walked long distances to reach the city for this purpose.

26 Later examples, after the Berber Dahir, included the tying of a Moroccan flag to the minaret of the Great Mosque in 1944 (following the nationalists' call for Morocco's independence and territorial integrity), and assemblies to protest against Israel's 1967 attack on the Arab countries. The sermon (*khuṭba*) held during the Friday noon prayer acted as an oath of allegiance to the reigning sultan. In 1953 this was dramatically demonstrated when the *khaṭib*, a highly respected member of the ʿAwwād family, gave the sermon in the name of Bin ʿArafa, the puppet sultan enthroned by the protectorate authorities: while leaving the mosque he was attacked and killed.

27 *Cf.* I. M. Lapidus, 'The evolution of Muslim urban society', *op. cit.*, and, for his criticism of earlier studies, the 'Introduction' to *Muslim Cities in the Later Middle Ages.*

28 *Muslim Cities in the Later Middle Ages*, pp. 139–42, 185.

29 *Cf.* G. Sjoberg, *The Pre-industrial City, Past and Present* (New York, 1960), pp. 6–11, 323 ff.

30 *Cf.* J. C. Mitchell, 'The concept and use of social networks', in J. C. Mitchell (ed.), *Social Networks in Urban Situations* (Manchester, 1969), pp. 9–10.

31 I refer to the Muslim community. The Jewish minority (about 10 per cent of the population) formed a separate religious community, but likewise had its own elite and masses.

32 M. Weber, *Economy and Society*, II, p. 932.

33 *Fès avant le protectorat*; *cf.* pp. 190 ff, 481 ff, 491 ff.

34 R. Hoffher and J. Moris, *Revenus et niveaux de vie indigènes au Maroc* (Paris, 1934), pp. 161 ff. I have calculated the percentages from the figures in the book. I do not believe that too much store should be set by these figures, but the research was the first attempt to look at income distribution within a total Moroccan city and offers a general idea of structure on the basis of quantitative methods of analysis.

35 *Fès avant le protectorat*, p. 493. *Cf.* A. Laroui, *L'Idéologie arabe contemporaine*, pp. 131 ff. Laroui's model, which is similar in several respects, attempts to take into consideration all or most of the Arab States.

36 *Cf.* J. Berque, 'Médinas, villeneuves et bidonvilles', in *Les Cahiers de Tunisie*, Nos. 21–2 (1959), p. 18, and S. Schaar in 'Conflict and change in nineteenth-century Morocco', unpublished Ph.D. thesis, Princeton University, 1965, pp. 93–5. Miège (*op. cit.*, IV, pp. 397 ff, 415) discuss urbanisation, particularly in the new port cities, in terms of the expolitation of a cheap labour force.

37 *The World we have Lost* (New York, 1965), p. 158.

38 Berque, 'Médinas . . .', p. 20.

39 In *Bulletin du Comité de l'Afr. Fr.*, No. 10, 1902, p. 346, quoted by Miège, *op. cit.* IV, pp. 421–2, n. 5.

40 The rise of rural qa'ids to positions of great power during this period parallels the ascent of the urban bourgeoisie. It has not, as far as I know, been clearly linked to common economic factors. My research in the Sous suggests that the power of rural qa'ids rested in part on trade links which they controlled with Mogador and

which depended on European commercial expansion. Miège notes that certain qa'ids were tied to the new urban wealth, especially between 1895 and 1912.

41 On the 'Ḥafīẓiyya' *cf.* Burke, *op. cit.*, pp. 119 ff; al-Fāsī and others have argued that the proclamation of ʿAbd al-Ḥafīẓ by the ulama of Fez transformed the system of government from an absolute to a limited, constitutional monarchy. On the draft constitution published in Tangier *cf.* J. Cagne, 'Les origines du mouvement jeune marocain', *Bulletin de la Société d'Histoire du Maroc*, No. 1 (1968), pp. 8–17.

42 *Cf.* C. Geertz, *Islam Observed. Religious Development in Morocco and Indonesia* (New Haven, Conn., 1968), pp. 63 ff, and A. Laroui, *L'Idéologie arabe contemporaine* (Paris, 1967), p. 133.

43 *Cf.* Halstead, *op. cit.*, appendix D: 'The forty-one leading nationalists, 1921–44, and their education', pp. 278–80.

44 The proclamation of a new dynasty by the followers of al-Hayba in 1912 and the Rifian republic declared in 1923 can be interpreted as rural attempts to wrest the power of the State.

45 *Cf.* A. Hourani, *A Vision of History* (Beirut, 1961), p. 154.

46 The Rifian republic is perhaps another example of secular reformism. Laroui discusses the phases of ideological development in *L'Histoire du Maghreb*, pp. 339–340, but fails to see secular development in Morocco.

47 *Cf.* C. Geertz, *Islam Observed*, pp. 64 ff, 73.

48 *Cf.* A. al-Fāsī, *al-ḥarakāt al-istiqlāliyya fī 'l-maghrib al-ʿarabī* (Cairo, 1948), pp. 160–162.

49 A. Laroui, *op. cit.*

50 *Cf.* J. Waterbury, *The Commander of the Faithful*, p. 10.

Fig. 13 'Concerning the distinctive characteristics and tendencies of the people of Salé' (*I.W.*, p. 35)

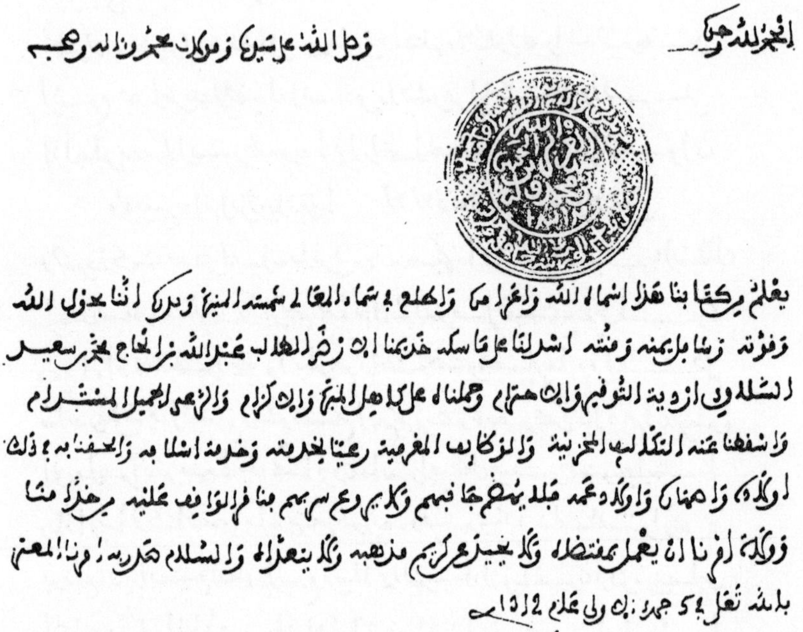

الحمد لله وحده   وصلى الله على سيدنا ومولانا محمد وآله وصحبه

يعلم من كتابنا هذا أسماه الله وأعز أمره وأطلع في سماء المعالي شمسه المنيرة وبدره أننا بحول الله
وقوته وشامل يمنه ومنته أسدلنا على ماسكه خديمنا الأرضى الطالب عبد الله بن الحاج محمد بن سعيد
السلاوي أردية التوقير والاحترام وأحللناه محل أهل المبرة والإكرام والإنعام الجميل المستدام
وأسقطنا عنه التكاليف المخزنية والوظائف المغرمية رعيا لخدمته وخدمة أسلافه وألحقنا به في ذلك
أولاده وإخوانه وأولاد عمه فلا يهتضم جانبهم ولا يروع سربهم بشيء من الوظائف فالواقف عليه من خدامنا
وولاة أمرنا أن يعمل بمقتضاه ولا يحيد عن كريم مذهبه ولا يتعداه والسلام صدر به أمرنا المعتز
بالله تعالى في 5 جمادى الأولى عام 1312

Fig. 14 *Dahir* of honour and respect granted by Sultan ʿAbd al-ʿAziz to ʿAbd Allah b. Saʿid, Governor of Salé (1312 A.H./1894).

Bibliography

1 MANUSCRIPT SOURCES

(a) *Arabic archival material*

1 Archives of the families in Salé

ʿAwwād, ʿAbd as-Salām, *Correspondence and Notes of Muḥammad ʿAwwād*, 1890–1930.

Ibn Saʿīd, al-ʿArabī, *Official Correspondence of Muḥammad and ʿAbd Allah b. Saʿīd*, 1885–1925.

aṣ-Ṣābīhī, ʿAbd Allāh, *The Papers of Muḥammad as-Sāsī.*

2 Archives générales de Rabat

aḍ-Ḍuʿayf, *Taʾrikh aḍ-Ḍuʿayf*, MS No. 666.

Ibn ʿAlī ad-Dukkālī, Muḥammad, *Itḥāf ashrāf al-malā bi-baʿḍ akhbār ar-Ribāṭ wa-Salā*, MS No. D 11; Kattānī collection, No. 466.

—*Kitāb al-Itḥāf al-wajīz bi-akhbār al-ʿudwatayn li-Mawlāy ʿAbd al-ʿAzīz*, MSS Nos. D 1320, D 42; Kattānī collection, No. 2333.

—*Kunnāsh*, Kattānī collection, MS No. 1264.

as-Sāsī, Muḥammad, *Collection of Documents* (uncatalogued, on glass negatives).

3 Archives of the Conservation Foncière de Rabat

Registration of Properties in Salé.

4 Palace archives, Rabat

Affaires Étrangères, No. 9, 'Bombardements'.

5 Palace library, Rabat

Ḥawalāt aḥbās Salā, 1885, MS No. 612.

(b) *European archival material* (*Paris*)

1 Centre de Hautes Études Administratives sur l'Afrique et l'Asie Moderne (CHEAM)

Abbadie, M., *Rôle joué par Salé dans l'évolution de l'opinion marocaine au cours de ces dernières années*, 1937, MS No. 340.

Forichon, J., *Commission du plan d'urbanisme de Rabat et Salé: notes sur la densité urbaine de Rabat et Salé*, MS in vol. LIV, No. 1401, *c.* 1947.

2 Archives de l'Alliance Israélite Universelle

Correspondence relating to Salé, dossier No. IV.B (Salé).

3 Archives de la Marine

Maroc, 1881–93, Schlumberger, 'Notice sur la ville de Salé', No. BB 4, 2458, dossier K, pp. 22–4.

4 Archives du Ministère de la Guerre

Maroc, Série C, carton I.

5 Archives Nationales
Maroc, Série Marine, BB 4, 1026, M-20.
Calderon, S., *Manuel de l'officier dans l'empire du Maroc, ou tableau géographique, statistique, historique, politique de ce pays*, MS translation from the Spanish edition of 1844 by L. Darmois, May 1844.

2 Published sources

(a) *Works in Arabic*

Anon., *Kitāb al-istibṣār fī ʿajāʾib al-amṣār*, ed. S. ʿAbd al-Ḥamīd, Alexandria, 1958. Partly translated by E. Fagnan in *Description extraite de l'Afrique septentrionale au XIIe siècle de notre ère*, Constantine, 1900.
— *Chronique anonyme de la dynastie saʿdienne*, ed. G. Colin, Rabat, 1934.
al-ʿAbbādī, A., *Mushāhadāt Lisān ad-Dīn b. al-Khāṭīb fī bilād al-Maghrib wa-'l-Andalus*, Alexandria, 1958.
ʿAwwād, ʿAbd ar-Rahmān, in *al-Imām*, No. 3, January 1964, pp. 64–8.
al-Bakrī, Abū ʿUbayd, *Description de L'Afrique septentrionale*, ed. W. de Slane, Algiers, 1911–13.
al-Fāsī, A., *al-ḥarakāt al-istiqlāliyyāt fī ʿl-maghrib al-ʿarabi*, Cairo, 1948.
Ibn Abī Zarʿ, *Rawḍ al-qirṭās*, Upsala, 1843–46. Trans. A. Beaumier, *Histoire des souverains du Maghreb et annales de la ville de Fès*, Paris, 1860.
Ibn ʿAdhārī, *al-Bayān al-mughrib*, Tetouan, 1963. Trans. E. Fagnan, *Histoire de l'Afrique et de l'Espagne*, Algiers, 1901–04.
Ibn Ḥawqal, *Kitāb ṣūrat al-arḍ*, Beirut, 1963. Trans. J. H. Kramers and G. Wiet, *Configuration de la terre*, Paris, 1964.
Ibn Khaldūn, ʿAbd ar-Raḥmān, *al-Muqaddimah*, Beirut, 1961. Trans. F. Rosenthal, *The Muqaddimah. An Introduction to History*, three vols., New York, 1958 (translation abridged and edited by N. J. Dawood, London, 1967).
— *Kitāb al-ʿibar*, ed. W. de Slane, Algiers, 1847–51. Trans. W. de Slane, *Histoire des Berbères*, four vols., Algiers, 1854–56.
Ibn Sharīfa, M., Usrat Banī ʿAshara', *Tiṭwān*, No. 10, 1965.
Ibn Sūda, ʿAbd as-Salām, *Dalīl muʾarrikh al-Maghrib al-Aqṣā*, second edition, two vols., Casablanca, 1960.
Ibn Zaydān, Mawlāy ʿAbd ar-Raḥmān, *Itḥāf aʿlām an-nās bi-jamāl akhbār ḥāḍirat Miknās*, five vols., Rabat, 1929.
Ḥajjī, M., *az-Ẓāwiya ad-Dilāʾiyya*, Rabat, 1964.
al-Kattānī, I., 'al-Usrat al-maghribiya at-taqlidiyya', *Les Cahiers de Sociologie*, No. 1, 1965, pp. 13–33.
al-Manūnī, M., *Maẓāhir yaqẓat al-Maghrib al-ḥadīth*, I, Rabat, 1973.
— 'al-Ṭabaʿāt al-ḥajariyyāt āl-Fāsiyya', *Tiṭwān*, No. 10, 1965, pp. 131–75.
— 'Maẓāhir yaqẓat al-Maghrib al-hadīth', *al-Baḥth al-ʿilmi*, No. 9, 1966, pp. 1–48.
an-Nāṣirī (as-Salāwī), Aḥmad b. Khalīd, *Kitāb al-istiqṣāʾ fī akhbār al-Maghrib al-Aqṣā*, four vols., Cairo, 1894; second edition, nine vols., Casablanca, 1954–56. Trans. in *Archives Marocaines*, IX, 1906; X, 1907; XXX, 1923; XXXI, 1925; XXXII, 1927; XXXIII, 1934; XXXIV, 1936.
al-Qādirī, Muhammad, *an-Nashr al-mathānī*, two vols., Fez, 1892. Trans. A. Graulle in *Archives Marocaines*, XXI, 1921.
at-Tadhīlī, Y., *at-Tashawwuf ilā rijāl at-taṣawwuf*, ed. A. Fauré, Rabat, 1958.

(b) *Works in other languages*

Abbou, I., *Musulmans, Andalous et Judéo-Espagnols*, Casablanca, 1953.
Abun-Naṣr, J., 'The Salafiyya movement in Morocco', St. Antony's Papers, No. 16, *Middle Eastern Affairs*, No. 3, London, 1963.

— *A History of the Maghrib*, Cambridge, 1971.

Adam, A., *Casablanca. Essai sur la transformation de la société marocaine au contact de L'Occident*, two vols., Paris, 1968.

Anon., 'Notions de pédagogie musulmane', trans. M. Ben Cheneb, *Revue Africaine*, XLI, 1897.

Aubin, E., *Le Maroc d'aujourd'hui*, Paris, 1904. English edition, *Morocco of Today*, London, 1906.

Ayache, G., 'La question des archives historiques marocaines', *Hespéris-Tamuda*, II 1961.

— 'L'utilisation et l'apport des archives historiques marocaines', *Hespéris-Tamuda*, VII, 1966.

— 'Aspects de la crise financière au Maroc après l'expédition espagnole de 1860', *Revue Historique*, CCXX, 1958.

Balthorpe, J., 'The Streights voyage', *Hespéris*, IV, 1929.

Baretta, B., 'La toma de Salé en tiempos de Alphonso El Sabio', *Al-Andalus*, VIII, 1943.

Beauclerk, G., *Journey to Morocco*, London, 1828.

Bel, A., *La Religion musulmane en Berbérie. Esquisse d'histoire et de sociologie religieuses*, I, Paris, 1938.

— 'Quelques rites pour obtenir la pluie en temps de sécheresse chez les musulmans maghrébins', *Recueil de Mémoires et de textes, XIV Congrès des Orientalistes*, Algiers, 1905.

Ben Cheneb, M., and Lévi-Provençal, E., 'Essai de répertoire chronologiques des éditions de Fès', *Revue Africaine*, LXII, 1921, pp. 158–73, 270–90, and LXIII, 1922, pp. 175–85, 333–47.

Bendix, R., *Max Weber. An Intellectual Portrait*, Garden City, N.Y., 1962.

Berque, J., *Le Maghreb entre les deux guerres*, Paris, 1962. English edition, *The Maghreb between the Two Wars*, London, 1967.

— 'Médinas, villeneuves et bidonvilles', *Les Cahiers de Tunisie*, Nos. 21–22, 1959.

— 'Quelques perspectives d'une sociologie de la décolonisation', *Les Cahiers de Sociologie*, No. 1, 1965.

— 'Les débuts du réformisme religieux au Maroc', in *Études d'Orientalisme dédiées à la mémoire de Lévi-Provençal*, II, Paris, 1962.

— 'Problèmes initiaux de la sociologie juridique en Afrique du Nord', *Studia Islamica*, I, 1953.

— and Bousquet, G. H. 'La criée publique à Fès. Étude concrète d'un marché', *Revue d'Économie Politique*, LIV-LV, 1940–45.

— 'Ville et université. Aperçu sur l'histoire de l'école de Fès', *Revue historique de droit français et étranger*, 1949.

Bloch, M., *The Historian's Craft*, New York, 1953.

Bodman, H. L., 'Political factions in Aleppo, 1760–1826', *James Sprunt Studies in History and Political Science*, XLV, Chapel Hill, N.C., 1963.

Boube, J., 'Fouilles archéologiques à Sala', *Hespéris-Tamuda*, VII, 1966.

Bousquet, G. H., *L'Islam maghrebin*, Algiers, 1944.

Bowie, L., 'The protégé system in Morocco, 1880–1904', unpublished Ph.D. dissertation, University of Michigan, 1970.

Braudel, F., *La Méditerranée et le monde méditerranéen a l'époque de Philippe II*, Paris, 1948.

Brett, M., 'Problems of interpretation of the history of the Maghrib', *Journal of African History*, XIII, 1972.

Brignon, J., *et al.*, *Histoire du Maroc*, Casablanca, 1967.

Brown, K. L., 'An urban view of Moroccan history: Salé, 1000–1800', *Hespéris-Tamuda* XII, 1971.

Brown, K. L., 'The impact of the *Dahir Berbère* in Salé', in E. Gellner and C. Micaud (eds.), *Arabs and Berbers*, London, 1973.
— 'Profile of a nineteenth-century scholar', in N. Keddie (ed.), *Scholars, Saints and Sufis*, Berkeley, Cal., 1972.
— 'Resistance et nationalisme au Maroc', *Colloque international d'études historiques et sociologiques*, Paris, forthcoming.
Brown, L. C. (ed)., *From Medina to Metropolis. Heritage and Change in the Near Eastern City*, Princeton, N.J., 1973.
Brunot, L. C., *La Mer dans les traditions et les industries indigènes à Rabat et Salé*, Paris, 1920.
— *Textes arabes de Rabat*, I, Paris, 1931; II, *Glossaire*, Paris, 1952.
Brunschvig, R., *La Berbérie Orientale sous les Ḥafṣides, des origines à la fin du XVe siècle*, two vols., Paris, 1940, 1947.
Bulletin du Comité de *l'Afrique Française*, 'La population du Maroc', Paris, 1913.
Burke, E., 'The image of the Moroccan State in French historical literature', in E. Gellner and C. Micand (eds.), *Arabs and Berbers*, London, 1973.
— 'The political role of the Ulama in Morocco', in N. Keddie (ed.), *Scholars, Saints and Sufis*, Berkeley, Cal., 1972.
Busson, J. P., 'Frédéric le Play et l'étude du niveau de vie d'une famille d'artisans marocains il y a un siècle' in *Bulletin Économique et Social du Maroc*, XVII, 1953.
Cagne, J., 'Les origines du mouvement jeune marocain', *Bulletin de la Société d'Histoire du Maroc*, No. 1, 1968.
Caillé, J., *Charles Jagerschmidt, chargé d'affaires de France au Maroc, 1820–94*, Paris, n.d.
— *La ville de Rabat jusqu'au protectorat français*, two vols., Paris, 1929.
— *La Petite Histoire de Rabat*, Casablanca, n.d.
— 'Ambassades et missions marocaines en France', *Hespéris*, XLII, 1960.
— and Hainut, J., 'La qasba des gnaoua', *Hespéris*, XLII, 1955.
Carcopino, J., *Le Maroc antique*, Paris, 1944.
Caro-Baroja, J., 'The city and the country. Reflections on some ancient commonplaces, *Mediterranean Countrymen*, ed. J. A. Pitt-Rivers, Paris, 1963.
Castellanos, M., *Historia de Marruecos*, third edition, Tangiers, 1898.
Castries, H. de, 'Le Maroc d'autrefois. Les corsaires de Salé', *Revue des Deux Mondes*, 1903. MS copy AGR, No. A 4 3378.
— 'Les trois républiques du Bou Regreg: Salé–La Kasba–Rabat', *Sources inédites de l'histoire du Maroc de 1530 à 1845*, ed. H. de Castries.
— 'Les moriscos à Salé et Sidi El-Ayachi. Introduction critique', *Sources inédites*, first series, *France*, III, 1911, pp. 187–98.
Chenier, A., *Recherches historiques sur les maures et histoire de l'empire de Maroc*, three vols., Paris, 1787.
Chevrillon, A., *Un Crépuscule d'Islam*, Paris, 1906.
Coindreau R., *Les Corsaires de Salé*, Paris, 1948.
Colin, G., *Chrestomathie marocaine*, Paris, 1939.
— 'Mellah', in *The Encyclopaedia of Islām.*
Cotte, N., *Le Maroc contemporain*, Paris, 1860.
Cousté, J., *Les Grandes Familles indigènes de Salé*, Rabat, 1931.
Damis, J., 'The free-school movement in Morocco, 1919–70', unpublished Ph.D. thesis, Fletcher School of Law and Diplomacy, 1971.
Dan, le R. P. F.-P. P., *Histoire de Barbarie et de ses corsaires*, second edition, Paris, 1649.
Dapper, D. O., *Description de l'Afrique*, Amsterdam, 1686.
Delphy, A., 'Notes sur quelques vestiges de céramique recueillis à Salé', *Hespéris*, XVII, 1955.
Demeersman, A., 'Catégories sociales en Tunisie au XIXe siècle d'après la chronique de A. Ibn Abī ḏ-Ḍiyāf', *Bulletin de I.B.L.A.*, No. 117, 1967.

Desprez, —, 'Le bombardement de Salé', *Revue de l'Orient, de l'Algérie et des Colonies*, XIII, 1853.
Dethier, J., 'Evolution of concepts of housing, urbanism and country planning in a developing country: Morocco, 1900–72', in L. C. Brown (ed.), *From Medina to Metropolis*, Princeton, N.J., 1973.
Doutté, C., 'Les marocaines et la société marocaine', *Revue Générale des Sciences*, XIV, 1903.
Dunton, J., *A True Journall of the Sally Fleet, with the Proceedings of the Voyage*, London, 1637.
Dye, F. A.-H., 'Les ports du Maroc: leur commerce avec la France', *Bulletin de la Société de Géographie Commerciale de Paris*, 1908.
Emerit, M., 'À propos de la caravane de Salé', *Les Cahiers de Tunisie*, No. 11, 1955.
Encylopédie d'Outre-mer, II, 'Maroc. Les villes'.
Epstein, A. L., 'Urbanisation and social change in Africa', in G. Breese (ed.), *The City in Newly Developing Countries*, Englewood Cliffs, N.J., 1969.
Fagnan, E., *Extraits inédits relatifs au Maghreb*, Algiers, 1924.
Ferré, D., *Lexique marocain-français*, Casablanca, n.d.
Fournel, P., and Levé, E. (eds.), *Les Traités du Maroc*, I, Paris, 1864.
Gallagher, C., *The United States and North Africa. Morocco, Algeria, and Tunisia*, Cambridge, Mass., 1963.
— 'A note on the Maghrib', in *American Universities Field Staff, North African Series*, XIII, No. 6, 1967.
Gallagher, J., and Robinson, R., 'The imperialism of free trade', *Economic History Review*, second series, VI, 1953.
Gallisot, R., *Le Patronat européen au Maroc, 1931–42*, Rabat, 1964.
Gardet, L., *La Cité musulmane. Vie sociale et politique*, Paris, 1961.
Gautier, E., *Les Siècles obscurs du Maghreb*, Paris, 1927.
Geertz, C., 'Ritual and social change: a Javanese example', *American Anthropologist*, LIX, 1957.
— *Islam Observed. Religious Development in Morocco and Indonesia*, New Haven, Conn., 1969.
Gellner, E., *Saints of the Atlas*, Chicago, 1969.
— 'Doctor and saint', in N. Keddie (ed.), *Scholars, Saints and Sufis*, Berkeley, Cal., 1972.
Gluckman, M., *Analvsis of a Social Situation in Modern Zululand*, Rhodes-Livingstone Paper No. 28, Manchester, 1938.
Goldziher, I., *Muslim Studies*, ed. and trans. S. M. Stern, I, London, 1967.
Goulven, J., 'Notes sur les origines anciennes des israélites du Maroc', *Hespéris*, I, 1921.
— *Les Mellahs de Rabat–Salé*, Paris, 1927.
Guay, L., 'Forme féminine berbère à Salé', *Archives Berbères*, III, 1918.
Guides Bleus, *Maroc*, Paris, 1966.
Guillen, P., 'Les sources européennes sur le Maroc. Fin XIXe-debut XXe siècle', *Hespéris-Tamuda*, I, 1966.
Halstead, J., *Rebirth of a Nation. The Origins and Rise of Moroccan Nationalism, 1912–44*, Cambridge, Mass.
Hardy, A., 'Les babouchiers de Salé', *Bulletin Économique et Social du Maroc*, V, 1938.
Harrell, R. S., *A Short Reference Grammar of Moroccan Arabic*, Washington, D.C., 1962.
Hart, D., 'The tribe in modern Morocco. Two case studies', in E. Gellner and C. Micaud (eds.), *Arabs and Berbers*, London, 1973.
Hecht, J. J., 'Social history', in *Encyclopedia of the Social Sciences*, second edition, London, 1968.
Hexter, J. H., *Reappraisals in History*, London, 1961.

Hirschberg, H. Z., *A History of the Jews in North Africa* (in Hebrew), two vols., Jerusalem, 1965.
Hoffher, R., and Morris, R., *Revenus et niveaux de vie indigènes au Maroc*, Paris, 1934.
Hourani, A., *Arabic Thought in the Liberal Age, 1798–1939*, London, 1962.
— *A Vision of History*, Beirut, 1961.
— and Stern, S. (eds.), *The Islamic City*, Oxford, 1970.
Jackson, J. G., *An Account of Timbuctoo and Hausa Territories in the Interior of Africa by El Haje Abd Salam Shabeeny, with Notes Critical and Explanatorv, to which is added Letters Descriptive of Travels through West and South Barbary and across the Mountains of Atlas*, London, 1820.
Jean-Léon l'Africain, *Description de L'Afrique*, trans. A. Epaulard, Paris, 1956.
Jeannot, G., *Étude sociale, politique, et économique sur le Maroc*, Dijon, 1904.
Jouannet, J., *L'Évolution de la fiscalité marocaine*, three vols., Paris, 1953.
Julien, C.-A., *L'Afrique de Nord en marche. Nationalismes musulmans et souveraineté française*, Paris, 1952.
— *Histoire de l'Afrique du Nord*, two vols., second edition, Paris, 1961.
Keatinge, M., *Travels through France and Spain to Morocco*, London, 1817.
Khatibi, A., *La Mémoire tatouée*, Paris, 1971.
— *Bilan de la sociologie au Maroc*, Rabat, 1967.
Lahbabi, M., *Le Gouvernement marocain à l'aube du XXe siècle*, Rabat, 1958.
Landau, R., *Moroccan Drama, 1900–55*, San Francisco, 1956.
Lapidus, I., *Muslim Cities in the Later Middle Ages*, Cambridge, Mass., 1967.
— 'The evolution of Muslim urban society', *Comparative Studies in Society and History*, xv, 1973.
La Pirmaudaie, E. de, 'Villes maritimes du Maroc', *Revue Africaine*, 1873.
Laraoui, A., *L'Idéologie arabe contemporaine*, Paris, 1967.
— *L'Histoire du maghreb. Un essai de synthèse*, Paris, 1970.
Laslett, P., *The World we have Lost*, New York, 1965.
Latham, J. D., 'Towns and cities of Barbary. The Andalusian influence', *Islamic Quarterly*, xvi, 1972.
Le Cœur, C., 'Métiers et classes sociales d'Azemmour', *Bulletin Économique et Social du Maroc*, iv, 1937.
— *Le Rite et l'outil*, Paris, 1939.
— 'Métiers et classes sociales d'Azemmour', *Bulletin Économique et Social du Maroc*, iv, 1937.
— 'Les rites de passage d'Azemmour', *Hespéris*, xvii, 1933, pp. 129–48.
Le Coz, J., *Le Gharb: fellahs et colons. Étude de géographie régionale*, two vols., Rabat, 1934.
Légey, Doctoresse, *Essai de folklore*, Paris, 1926.
Lemprière, W., *A Tour from Gibraltar to Tangier, Sallee, Mogador, Santa Cruz, Tarudant, and thence over Mount Atlas to Morocco*, London, 1791.
Lesne, M., *Évolution d'un groupement berbère: les Zemmour*, Rabat, 1959.
Le Tourneau, R., *Évolution politique de l'Afrique du Nord musulmane, 1920–61*, Paris, 1962.
— *Fès avant le protectorat*, Casablanca, 1947.
— *Les Villes musulmanes de l'Afrique du Nord*, Algiers, 1957.
— *La Vie quotidienne è Fès en 1900*, Paris, 1965.
Lévé, E., and Fournel, P. (eds.), *Les Traités du Maroc*, i, Paris, 1864.
Lévi-Provençal, E., *Documents inédits d'histoire almohade*, Paris, 1928.
— *Les Historiens des chorfa. Essai sur la littérature historique et biographique au Maroc XVIe siècle*, Paris, 1922.
— 'Morocco' and 'Rabat', in *Encyclopedia of Islam*, first edition.
— and Basset, H., 'Chella: une nécropole mérinide', *Hespéris*, ii, 1922.

— 'Les villes et les institutions urbaines en Occident musulman au Moyen-âge, II', in *Conférences sur l'Espagne musulmane*, Cairo, 1951.
Loubignac, V., 'La procession des Cièrges à Salé', *Hespéris*, XXXV, 1948.
Mahdi, M., *Ibn Khaldun's Philosophy of History*, Chicago, 1964.
Malinowski, B., *Magic, Science and Religion, and other Essays*, Glencoe, Ill., 1948.
Marçais, W., 'L'Islamisme et la vie urbaine', in his *Articles et Conferences*, Paris, 1961.
— 'La conception des villes dans l'Islam', *Revue d'Alger*, II, 1945.
Mardin, S., 'Power, civil society and culture in the Ottoman empire', *Comparative Studies in Society and History*, II, 1969.
Marty, P., 'La zaouia de Sidi Ben ʿAchir à Salé', *Revue des Études Islamiques*, VII, 1933.
Massignon, L., 'Enquête sur les corporations musulmanes', *Revue du Monde Musulman*, LV, 1924.
Mauny, R., *Tableau géographique de l'Ouest africain au moyen-âge d'après les sources écrites, la tradition et l'archéologie*, Dakar, 1961.
Mauran, Dr, *Le Maroc d'aujourd'hui et de demain*, Rabat, 1909.
Mauriet, E., 'Le développement de l'agglomération Rabat–Salé', *Bulletin Economique et Social du Maroc*, Nos. 60–61, 1954.
Meakin, B., *The Moorish Empire. A Historical Epitome*, London, 1899.
— *The Land of the Moors*, New York and London, 1901.
Mercier, L., 'L'administration marocaine à Rabat', *Archives Marocaines*, VII, 1906.
— 'Les mosquées et la vie religieuse à Rabat', *Archives Marocaines*, VIII, 1906.
— 'Note sur la mentalité religieuse dans la région de Rabat et de Salé, *Archives Marocaines*, VI, 1906.
— 'Rabat; description topographique', *Archives Marocaines*, VII, 1907.
Meunié, J., 'La Zaouiat en Noussak: une fondation mérinite aux abords de Salé', in *Mélange d'histoire et d'archéologie de l'Occident musulman*, II, *Hommage à G. Marçais*, Algiers, 1957.
Michaux-Bellaire, E., 'Les crises monétaires au Maroc', *Revue du Monde Musulman*, XXXVIII, 1920.
— 'L'enseignement indigène au Maroc', *Revue du Monde Musulman*, XV, 1911.
— 'Le wahhabisme au Maroc', *Renseignements coloniaux*, XXXVIII, 1928.
— 'Les impôts marocains', *Archives Marocaines*, I, 1904.
— 'Makhzan', in *Encyclopedia of Islam*.
Miège, J.-L., 'Documents inédits sur l'artisanat de Rabat et Salé au milieu de XIXe siècle', *Bulletin Économique et Social du Maroc*, XXIII, 1952.
— 'Coton et cotonnades au Maroc au XIXe siècle', *Hespéris*, XLVII, 1959, pp. 219–38.
— *Le Maroc et l'Europe, 1830–94*, four vols., Paris, 1961–63.
— *Documents d'histoire économique et sociale marocaine au XIXe siècle*, Paris, 1969.
— and Hainut, E., *Les Européens à Casablanca au XIXe siècle, 1856–1906*, Paris, 19??.
Mission Scientifique du Maroc, *Villes et Tribus au Maroc*, III, *Rabat et sa région*, four vols., Paris, 1918.
Mitchell, C. (ed.), *Social Networks in Urban Situations*, Manchester, 1969.
Monlau, J., *Les États barbaresques*, Paris, 1964.
Montagne, R., *Révolution au Maroc*, Paris, 1953.
— *Les Berbères et le makhzen dans le sud du Morac*, Paris, 1930.
Moore, B., *The Social Origins of Dictatorship and Democracy*, Boston, Mass., 1966.
Mouette, G., *The Travels of the Sieur Mouette in Fez and Morocco, during his Eleven Years' Captivity in those Parts*, London, 1710. Trans. from the French *Relation de captivité*, Paris, 1683.
Moussard, P. 'Arabophones et Berbèrophones au Maroc', *Annales de Géographie*, XXXIII, 1924.
Naciri, M., 'Salé: étude de géographie urbaine', *Revue de Géographie du Maroc*, Nos. 3–4, 1963.

Nadel, S. F., *A Black Byzantium. The Kingdom of the Nupe in Nigeria*, London. 1942.
Nehlil, M., *Lettres chérifiennes*, I, *Textes*, Paris, 1915.
Noin, D., *Le Population rurale du Maroc*, two vols., Paris, 1970.
Nouschi, A., 'Constantine à la veille de la conquête', *Les Cahiers de Tunisie*, No. 11, 1955.
Noy, D., *Seventy and one stories from the Jews of Morocco* (in Hebrew), Jerusalem, 1964.
Nwyia, P., *Ibn ʿAbbād de Ronda, 1332–90*, Beirut, 1961.
Odinot, P., *La Première Communion d'Abd ed-Kader*, Paris, 1927.
Paden, J., *Religion and Political Culture in Kano*, Berkeley, Cal., 1973.
Paye, L., 'Physionomie de l'enseignement marocain', *Études d'Orientalisme dédiées à la mémoire de Lévi-Provençal*, II, Paris, 1962.
Pellow, T., *The Adventures of Thomas Pellow of Penryn, Mariner, Three and Twenty Years in Captivity among the Moors. Written by Himself and Edited with an Introduction and Notes by Dr. Robert Brown*, London, 1890 (first edition 1740).
Penz, C., *Journal du consulat général de France au Maroc, 1767–85*, Casablanca, 1943.
Pèretie, A., 'Les médrasas de Fès', *Archives Marocaines*, XVIII, 1912.
Périgny, C. M. de, *Au Maroc. Casablanca–Rabat–Meknès*, Paris, 1920.
Pitt-Rivers, J., 'Introduction', in *Mediterranean Countrymen*, Paris, 1963.
Planhol, X. de, *The World of Islam*, Ithaca, N.Y., 1959.
Plesse, J., 'Variations de la consommation sous l'influence des coutumes indigènes: l'exemple d'une ville presque exclusivement musulmane: Salé', *Bulletin Économique et Social du Maroc*, 1936.
Rabbe, P. F., *Au Maroc. Sur les rives du Bou Regret–Chella–Salé–Rabat*, second edition, Paris, 1924.
Radi, A., 'Processus de socialisation de l'enfant marocain', *Études Philosophiques et Littéraires*, No. 4, April 1969 (Rabat).
Rahman, F., *Islam*, Garden City, N.Y., 1966.
Rapports commerciaux des Agents diplomatiques et consulaires de France, *Maroc, situation économique actuelle de Rabat et Salé*, I, No. 1036, 1913.
Redfield, R., and Singet, M., 'The cultural role of cities', *Economic Development and Cultural Change*, III, 1954, pp. 53–77.
Renou, E., *Description géographique de l'empire du Maroc*, Paris, 1846.
Ricard, P., *Essai de Rabat–Salé et sa région*, Rabat, 1931.
Ricard, R., 'La côte atlantique au début du XVe siècle d'après des instructions nautiques portugaises', *Hespéris*, VIII, 1937.
Roberts, S. H., *History of French Colonial Policy, 1870–1925*, London, 1929.
Rodinson, M., 'Histoire économique et histoire des classes sociales dans le monde musulman', in M. A. Cook (ed.), *Studies in the Economic History of the Middle East*, London, 1970.
Rohart, S. and N., *Concise Encyclopedia of Arabic Civilization. The Arab West*, Amsterdam, 1966.
Rosenthal, F., *The Muslim Concept of Freedom*, Leiden, 1960.
— and Lewis, B., 'Ḥurriyya' in *Encyclopedia of Islam*, second edition.
Salmon, G., 'Notes sur Salé', *Archives Marocains*, III, 1905.
Sasportas, Y., *Sefer Tzaitzat Novel Tzvi*, ed. Z. Shwartz, Jerusalem, 1954.
Sbihi, A., *Roses marocaine. Choix de poèmes de Si Ahmed Sbihi*, trans. Abdel Kader Benchehida, Casablanca, 1937.
Schact, J., *An Introduction to Islamic Law*, Oxford, 1964.
Schoen, Lt., 'Les institutions administratives, politiques, sociales et juridiques dans le groupe Imaziren', *Bulletin du Comité de l'Afrique française. Renseignements coloniaux*, XXXVIII, 1928.
Semach, Y. D., 'Une chronique juive de Fès: le *Yahas Fès* de Ribbi Abner Hassarfaty', *Hespéris*, XIX, 1934.

Sjoberg, G., *The Pre-industrial City, Past and Present*, New York, 1966.
Smith, W. C., *Islam in Modern History*, New York, 1959.
Sonneck, C., *Chants arabes du Maghreb*, two vols., Paris, 1904.
Spillmann, G., *Du Protectorat à l'indépendance. Maroc, 1912–55*, Paris, 1967.
— (pseud. Dragne, G.), *Esquisse d' histoire religieuse du Maroc*, Cahiers de l'Afrique et l'Asie, II, Paris, 1951.
Stewart, C. F., *The Economy of Morocco, 1912–62*, Cambridge, Mass., 1964.
Szymański, E., 'La guerre hispano-marocaine, 1859–60: début de l'histoire du Maroc contemporain. Essai de periodisation', *Roczenik orientalistyczny*, XXIX, 1965.
Terrasse, C., *Médersas du Maroc*, Paris, 1927.
Terrasse, H., *Histoire du Maroc*, two vols., Casablanca, 1949.
Thouvenot, R., 'Les vestiges de la route romaine de Salé à l'O. Beth', *Hespéris*, XLIV, 1957.
Tissot, M., 'Recherches sur la géographie comparée de la Maurétanie Tingitane', in *Mémoires présentés par divers savants à l'Académie des inscriptions et belles-lettres*, first series, No. 1, 1878.
Toledano, Y., *The Light of the Maghreb. The History of Israel in Morocco* (in Hebrew), Jerusalem, 1904.
Troin, J. F., 'Les premiers résultats du recensement de la population du Maroc, 20 juillet–31 août 1971', *Revue de Géographie du Maroc*, XX, 1971.
Turner, B., *Weber and Islam*, London, 1974.
Urquhart, D., *The Pillars of Hercules, or, A Narrative of Spain and Morocco in 1848*, two vols., London, 1850.
Voinot, L., *Pèlerinages judéo-musulmans du Maroc*, Paris, 1948.
von Grunebaum, G. E., *Islam. Essays in the Nature and Growth of a Cultural Tradition*, New York, 1961.
— *Medieval Islam. A Study in Cultural Orientation*, Chicago, 1946.
— *Muhammadan Festivals*, New York, 1951.
Waterbury, J., *The Commander of the Faithful*, New York, 1970.
Weber, M., *Basic Concepts of Sociology*, New York, 1963.
— *The Theory of Social and Economic Organisation*, Glencoe, Ill., 1964.
— *The City*, New York, 1962.
— *Economy and Society. An Outline of Interpretive Sociology*, two vols., New York, 1968.
Westermarck, E., *Ceremonies and Beliefs Connected with Agriculture, Certain Dates of the Solar Year and the Weather in Morocco*, Helsingfors, 1913.
— *Ritual and Belief in Morocco*, two vols., London, 1926.
Wiche, K., 'Marokkanisch Stadttypen', in *Festschrift zur Hundertjahrfeier Geographischen Gesellschaft in Wien, 1856–1956*, Vienna, 1957.
Wirth, L., 'Urbanism as a way of life', *American Journal of Sociology*, XLIV, 1938, pp. 1–24.
Wolf, E., 'Kinship, friendship and patron–client relations in complex societies', in M. Banton (ed.), *The Social Anthropology of Complex Societies*, London, 1966.
Woolman, S., *Rebels in the Rif*, Stanford, Cal., 1968.
Zafrani, H., *Les Juifs du Maroc. Vie sociale, économique et religieuse*, Paris, 1972.
Zerdoumi, N., *Enfants d'hier. Éducation de l'enfant en milieu traditionnel algérien*, Paris, 1970.

Index

Arabic names are alphabetised according to family names. In alphabetising the Arabic *al* is ignored.

ʿAbd al-ʿAziz, sultan, 21, 20, 188
ʿAbd al-Karīm, Muḥammad b., 195
ʿAbd ar-Raḥmān, sultan, 19, 57, 120, 177
Adam, A., 5
ahl l-bled people of the city, 59; *see also* Community of Salé
ʿAisāwa, 21, 110
ʿAlawiyyin, 21, 66–7
Alliance Israélite, 81
amīn, see *umanāʾ*
ʿĀmir tribe, 17, 19, 21, 35, 67, 179
ʿāmma pl. *ʿawwām*, *see* Masses
ʿAnṣara, 37
Arabic language, 83, 194, 197, 203, 208
Arabs, 57, 179, 199, 204, 208
ʿarīqīn (coll.) deep-rooted, respectable families, 54
Ashamaʿū, M., 196, 201
awliyāʾ saints, 43, 69
ʿAwwād, Abū Bakr, qadi, 76, 166; ʿAlī, qadi, 20, 35, 188, 200–1, 243 n 3; Ṭayyib, 79; family (ʿAwwāda), 60, 165
aʿyan, *see* Notables
Azemmour, 157

bādiya rural way of life, 57, 212
Banū Ḥasan, 17, 21–2, 67
baraka blessing, sign, 79, 102, 106, 233 n 29
barrāḥ town crier, 62
barrānī outsider, newcomer, 35, 54, 98, 101, 110, 112, 114, 149, 151, 154
bayʿa investiture, 75, 230 n 15
bazaar, 33, 127, 156–7
Berbers, 151, 154, 169, 179, 199, 204, 206, 208
Berque, J., 218
bombardment of Salé (1851), 29, 37, 44, 176–9
Bou Regreg, 15, 23, 25, 42, 44
Bū ʿAzzāwiyya, 21

calendar of Muslim year, 89, 234 n 7
caravansaries, 41, 44; *see also funduq*
cemeteries, 43–5
characteristics of Salé, 2–5, 53, 57, 70, 212, 249
cholera, 19, 49
Christianity, 86, 200, 205
classes (socio-economic), 8–9, 11, 64, 135, 173, 214–18, 224
climate, 26
coalitions, 64, 213–15; *see also* Patrons and clients
colonialism, 7, 8, 11, 221; *see also* Protectorate
community, 86–7, 99, 112; of Salé, 3–5, 8, 11, 54, 56, 83, 88, 94, 97, 106, 108, 151, 154, 169, 175, 197, 199, 201, 204–5, 210, 212–14, 223
conflict within Salé, 56, 61, 139, 187, 217; between families, 59; between generations, 198; between religious orders, 113
contrôleur civil, 30, 83, 168, 193, 197, 202
cotton, 9, 25–6, 117, 119–20, 174, 129
countryside, Salé's relations with, 4, 13, 17–20, 22, 55, 221, 226, n 4
craftsmen, 9, 77, 117, 121, 124, 127, 130, 132–9; barbers, 150; salaries of, 132, 134; shoemakers, 129–31

Dahir (*ẓahīr*) decree, 59, 62, 69, 160, 240 n 7, 249; D. Berbère, 11, 92, 198–200, 204, 221, 223, 245 n 24

ḍāṛ pl. *ḍyūṛ* (coll.) house, family, 39, 56, 100–1, 230 n 9
Darqāwa, 41, 110, 111, 115, 200
derb pl. *drūba* (coll.) street, 37
descent, patrilineal, 52, 58–60, 62, 74, 84, 101, 173; *see also* Families
-Dukkālī, M. b. ʿAlī, *see* Ibn ʿAlī

economic crises, 8, 9, 117, 122–3, 125, 128, 139, 171–2, 177, 220, 238 n 22
education, 83, 84; modern, 81, 82, 168, 194–5, 198, 222; moral, 105–6; military, 181; traditional, 76–8, 107–8, 111, 158, 161, 214, 222, 232 n 17; *see also* Alliance Israélite, Free schools, School for the Sons of Notables
elite, *al-khāṣṣa*, 9–10, 49, 56, 58, 60, 68, 73, 84, 112–14, 161–2, 169, 173, 210, 213–15, 220
Essaouira (Mogador), 24, 47, 119, 125
ethnic groups, 151–2
European settlers, 129, 168

families, 49, 52–3, 55, 58–61, 81, 149, 230 n 9, 231 n 24; French notion of *les grandes familles*, 173–4, 231 n 25
family life, 100, 102
famine, 19, 122–3, 177
fanaticism, 187, 199, 222
Fannīsh, ʿAbd al-Ḥaqq, governor, 59
farmers, 77, 124, 155
fatalism, 87, 181
festivals, 89, 92, 93
Fez, 4, 15, 25, 31, 47, 57, 75, 76, 78, 81, 103, 108, 126, 156–7, 162, 207, 216–217
fitna anarchy, 181
free schools, 73, 82, 83, 194, 203, 222, 233 n 34
French policies in Morocco, 168, 174, 198–9, 219; *mission civilisatrice*, 203, 233 n 33; *see also* Dahir Berbère
funduq pl. *fanādiq* caravansary, 27, 33

Gaddārī, M., 21
gardens of Salé, 25, 33, 34, 45
Geertz, C., 232 n 8
Gellner, E., 114, 209
generations in Salé, 128, 160; young, 83, 167–8, 194–205, 221, 223
governors (*qā'id* pl. *quyyād*; *bāshā* pl. *bāshawāt*) of Salé, 16, 163–4, 166
Great mosque of Salé, 30, 31, 35, 62, 88, 166, 178, 200–1, 212–13, 234 n 6, 247 n 24
growth of Salé's commercial district, 33, 43, 126
von Grunebaum, G., 211
guilds (coll. *ḥanṭa* pl. *ḥnāṭī*), 135–8, 149, 240 n 24

Habous (*ḥubus* pl. *aḥbās*), pious endowments, 31, 35, 37, 170, 227, n 20, n 1, 228 n 8
ḥaḍāra civilised, urban culture, 2, 57, 209, 212, 220–3
ḥaḍra presence of God, séance of religious orders, 112–13
Ḥafīẓiyya, movement to proclaim ʿAbd al-Ḥafīz sultan (1907–8), 220, 248 n 41
Ḥajjī, Sīdī Aḥmad (d. 1780), 20, 41, 69; Friday mosque, 22; family, 69, 110
Ḥamādsha, 21
ḥammām public bath, 41
ḥanbal pl. *ḥnābil* striped woollen rugs, 25
ḥaram acts considered illicit, forbidden, 103
Ḥasan I, sultan, 71, 72, 78, 161–2, 166, 183
ḥashūma morally reprehensible, 103–4
Ḥassūniyyin, 110
Hay, D., British consul, 163
ḥayā' (coll. *lə-ḥya*) modesty, decency, 56
heterogeneity of Salé, 6
history of Salé, 1–3, 225 n 3
Hourani, A., 135
household, composition of, 100; distribution of living space, 101
ḥūma (coll.) pl. *ḥwām*, *see* Quarters
human nature, ideas about, 105–6
ḥurma inviolable sanctuary, 21
ḥurriyya liberty, 182
Ḥusayn tribe, 17, 21, 35

Ibn ʿAbd an-Nabī, Aḥmad, 108–9
Ibn ʿAbūd, al-Faqīh, 115
Ibn ʿAli, M. ad-Dukkālī, 37, 42, 49, 52, 53, 56–8, 66, 70, 71, 78–9, 108, 119, 121, 124, 156, 176, 186
Ibn ʿĀshir, Sīdī Aḥmad (d. 1362), 43, 45, 61, 69, 106, 179
Ibn Ḥassūn, Sīdī ʿAbd Allah (d. 1604), 43, 62, 68, 69, 89–90, 179, 234 n 12

Ibn Khaḍrā', 'Abd Allah, qadi, 31, 106, 108, 166
Ibn Khaldūn, 41, 52, 60
Ibn Mansūr, al-'Arabī, qadi, 76, 78
Ibn Sa'īd, 'Abd Allah, governor, 35, 63, 83, 160, 162, 187, 193, 243 n 3; al-'Arabi, 79; Idrīs, 195, 244 n 13; Muḥammad, governor, 35, 73, 164, 241 n 23
Ibn as-Sā'iḥ, al-'Arabi, 80
Ibn Shlīḥ, al-Ṭayyīb, 22
immigration, 46, 49, 122, 127
imported goods, 117, 124, 129; *see also* Trade
impoverishment, 122, 124, 129, 151, 171, 217
inflation, 118, 121, 123–4, 128, 184–5
inheritance, 170–1
Islamic culture, 83
Islamic law, 75, 77, 95, 97, 99, 165, 183, 200, 221, 236 n 38
Isly, Battle of, 177

-Jarīrī, Aḥmad Bil-Fqīh, 80–1
jihād holy war, 62, 184
Jews, 17, 18, 24, 31, 33, 42, 48–9, 55, 81, 91, 121, 138, 151, 154, 156–7, 159, 212, 182, 229 n 44, 235 n 15, 240 n 28, 247 n 31

Kattāniyya, 21, 110, 111, 237 n 16

Lapidus, I. M., 6, 211–13, 228 n 16
laṭīf, 91–2, 200–1, 205, 235 n 17
Le Tourneau, R., 5, 216–17, 228 n 16
Lévi-Provençal, E., 66, 233 n 31
literary club in Salé, 83 196
Lyautey, Marshal, 15, 169

madīna, 27, 44, 211
Makhzan/*makhzan* central administration of Moroccan sultanate, 4, 7, 54, 55, 120, 125, 162, 207–10, 216–17, 219, 226 n 10, 246 n 7; relations with Salé, 59, 71, 77, 160–1, 164, 166, 173, 218, 221, 223
malḥūn popular poetry, 98, 179
maritime port, Rabat–Salé, 23–4
marriage, 86, 95; alliances through affinity, 22, 63, 108, 173, 224
masses, 9–10, 56–8, 113–14, 154, 181, 183, 213, 215, 231 n 16
Massighon, L., 135
Mellah/*mallāḥ* Jewish quarter, 13, 39, 42
menzeh (coll.) picnic site, 26, 40
merchants, 28, 77, 117, 121, 124, 127, 136, 149, 157, 159–60, 162, 172, 210, 214–15, 218, 223
Michaux-Bellaine, E., 195
Miège, J-L., 219
Mitchell, C., 215
mizrag guarantee of safe passage, 18, 233 n 23
Mogador, *see* Essaouira
morality, 78, 104, 107
Moroccan Crisis (1900–1912), 187
muḥtasib market provost, 29, 137
mūlūd (cl. *mawlid* or *mawlūd*) birthday of the Prophet, 89, 234 n 10
muqaddim quarter chief, 37
muṣallā prayer niche in cemetery, 44
mūsim (cl. *mawsim*) pilgrimage-fair, 21, 89
Muslim cities, 4–7, 135, 211–14

Naciri, M., x, 5, 37, 227 n 17, n 28, 228 n 15
Nadel, S. F., 212
-Nāṣirī, Aḥmad, x, 57, 72, 75–6, 79, 81, 106, 108, 113–14, 123, 165–7, 176, 180–2, 221, 237 n 19; Ibn al-Kabīr, 21; Khālid, 75; Muḥammad, 196; family (Nuwāṣra), 21, 70, 75; aṭ-Ṭayyib, 80
Nāṣiriyya, 75
nationalism, 2, 8, 11, 83–4, 182, 194, 198–205, 221, 223, 254 n 29
newspapers in Salé, 196, 203, 224 n 16
new wealth, 34, 121–6, 154–5, 157–60, 171, 185, 215, 217–18
notables, 55–8, 172, 185, 215; *see also* Elite
nsīb pl. (coll.) affines, 64, 231 n 29; *see also* Marriage

occupations, values attached to, 138–51, 215; ethnic groups, 152–3, 240 n 26
officials, 55, 76, 84, 121, 126, 158, 160–167, 172, 208–10, 214, 218

paternal authority, 87, 101, 104, 109, 182, 203
patrimonialism, 210, 217
patrons and clients, 76, 164–7, 203, 213
periodisation, 7–8

pilgrimages, 43
piracy, 23, 119, 178
population growth, 13, 46–9, 151, 220
prayer, 88, 91
pre-industrial cities, 4, 214–15
prices, 134
Procession of Candles (*dawr ash-shama'a*), 89–90
property, 40, 155, 159, 169–72
protectorate, French, 10, 11, 20, 42, 49, 71, 81, 118, 197, 221; effects on Salé, 126–7, 169, 176, 188, 193–5, 202, 204
protégés, 182, 187–8, 219, 242 n 24

-Qādirī, Aḥmad, 73–4; family, 68
Qādiriyya, 21, 68
qadi (*qāḍī* pl. *quḍāt*) judges of Salé, 165
qādūs waterwheel bucket, 4, 63, 85, 97, 213, 233 n 2
qā'ida consecrated tradition, 95, 103, 235 n 27
qaiṣariya, *see* Bazaar
qibla direction of prayer, east, 44
quarantine, Nāṣirī's discussion of, 180–1
quarters, 13, 29, 34–5, 37, 39, 41, 232 n 12

Rabat, 4, 10, 13, 15, 19, 23–5, 42, 44, 47–49, 55, 57, 78, 80, 81, 83, 103, 111, 121, 126, 162, 207, 223, 238 n 25
Ramadan, 93
Redfield, R., 7
reformism (Salafiyya), 79, 114, 232 n 9, 233 n 35
religion, 2–3, 43, 70–1, 78, 82–99, 104, 186, 199, 205–6, 212, 234 n 4, 236 n 29; nationalism, 222–3
religious orders (*ṭā'ifa* pl. *ṭawā'if*), 20, 37, 41, 68–9, 71, 89–90, 92, 106, 109–115, 196, 227 n 14, 237 n 14, n 19
renaissance of Moroccan literature, 78–79, 109, 222
Rifian Republic, 195, 248 n 44, n 46
rites of passage, 94, 97, 235 n 23, 236 n 31

-Ṣabūnjī, Aḥmad, 83
ṣaḥb (coll.) friend, 63
Sahūl tribe, 17–18, 20–1, 35
saints, 2–3, 41, 106–7, 112, 114, 237 n 7; *see also awliyā'*
Salafiyya, *see* Reformism
ṣalat al-istisqā prayer for rain, 91
salt marshes of Salé, 23, 29
saniya pl. *swānī* (coll.) irrigated garden, 25
School for Sons of Notables (*madrasat abnā' al-a'yān*), 81–3, 194, 203
shahāda declaration of faith, 86, 94, 96
Shlūḥ, 153; *see also* Berbers
shurafā' sng. *sharīf* descendants of the prophet, 53, 57, 63, 66–8, 74, 84, 158, 215, 231–2 n 2, n 4; of Salé, 69, 164, 177; decline in prestige, 71, 187
sība upheaval, 19, 208–9, 226 n 10
siqqāya public wells, 41
Sjoberg, G., 214–15
social groups, 6, 11, 37, 55–6, 60, 62, 63, 98, 111–12, 167, 203–4, 212, 218
social mobility, 64, 159, 172, 214–15, 218
social status, 62, 69
socialisation, 100–3
-Ṣubīḥī, 'Abd al-Latīf, 195, 199–201, 204; Muḥammad, governor, 82, 108, 200, 245 n 29; aṭ-Ṭayyib, governor, 188
Sufi lodges (*zāwiya* pl. *zawāyā*), 21, 41, 70, 77, 110
sukhṭ malediction, 87, 102, 234 n 5
sūq al-ghazl Thread Market, 31
sūq al-kabīr Great Market-place, 20, 27
sūq al-khamīs Thursday market, 19, 27
Sūsī pl. Swāsa, someone from the Sous region, 35; *see also* Berbers, Shlūḥ
suwwāqa itinerant traders, 17–18, 77, 124, 156; *see also* Trade, internal

-Taghrāwī, 'Allāl, qadi, 22
-Ṭālbi, Aḥmad, assistant governor, 71–73; Sīdī 'l-Hāshīmī, 83
tarbiya infancy, education, good manners, 102
taxes, 29, 45, 137, 164, 193, 210, 217, 240 n 19
Tetuan, 4, 24, 47, 207; Battle of, 181–2
theatre troupe of Salé 83, 196, 203
Tijāniyya, 21, 41, 80, 110, 111
topography of Salé 27, 29, 30
trade, 9; international, 47, 119–21, 123, 158, 183, 217; internal, 24–5, 27, 31, 33, 55, 119, 121, 127; *see also suwwāqa*
tubjiyya artillerymen, 44

Tuhāmiyya, 21

ʿudūl sng. *ʿadl* notaries, 158
ūlād siyyid (coll.) marabouts, 69–70, 74–75, 232 n 6
ūlād n-nās (coll.) the well born 58–9
ulama (*ʿulamāʾ*) learned men, scholars, 57–8, 63–4, 75–6, 78–80, 84, 108, 161–2, 164, 166, 183, 193, 214–15, 218, 223, 232 n 13, 246 n 9
umanāʾ sng. *amīn* customs agents, 24, 158, 162
urbanisation, 22, 46, 151, 220
ʿurf customary law, 136
uṣūl sng. *aṣl* roots, 169

vineyards of Salé, 25–6

Wazzāniyya, 68
Weber, M., 210–11, 215
Wirth, L., 5, 225 n 7
Wolf, E., 64
women of Salé, 31, 37, 61, 88, 94–5, 101–102, 106–7, 112, 119, 132, 156, 236 n 3
world depression of 1930, effects in Salé, 11, 238 n 28

Zaʿir, tribe 17
Zemmour, 17, 18, 20, 21, 35, 69, 159, 226 n 3, n 13
Zerdoumi, N., 104, 236 n 3
Znībar, M. b. ʿAbd al-Hādī, governor, 29, 73–4, 177–80; family (Znābra), 59, 106